The Working Poor in Europe

The Working Poor in Europe

Employment, Poverty and Globalization

Edited by

Hans-Jürgen Andreß

Professor of Empirical Social and Economic Research, University of Cologne, Germany

Henning Lohmann

Research Associate, German Socio-Economic Panel Study, German Institute for Economic Research (DIW Berlin), Germany

Edward Elgar

Cheltenham, UK • Northampton, MA, USA

Published by
Edward Elgar Publishing Limited
The Lypiatts
15 Lansdown Road
Cheltenham
Glos GL50 2JA
UK

Edward Elgar Publishing, Inc.
William Pratt House
9 Dewey Court
Northampton
Massachusetts 01060
USA

A catalogue record for this book
is available from the British Library

Library of Congress Control Number: 2008932907

ISBN 978 1 84720 798 2

Printed and bound in Great Britain by MPG Books Ltd, Bodmin, Cornwall

Contents

Contributors

Ilpo Airio received his PhD in social policy in 2008. He is a senior assistant in the Department of Social Policy at the University of Turku, Finland. His research interests are labour market poverty and social mobility.

Hans-Jürgen Andreß studied social sciences and research methods at the universities of Frankfurt/Main, Germany and Ann Arbor, USA. He gained his PhD at the University of Frankfurt/Main in 1983 and is at present Professor of Empirical Social and Economic Research at the University of Cologne, Germany. He has published in the field of labour markets, poverty research, social policy, and multivariate statistical methods.

Ferruccio Biolcati-Rinaldi studied sociology and research methods at the universities of Trento, Rome 'La Sapienza' and Naples 'Federico II' and at present he is a lecturer in methodology of social sciences at the University of Milan, Italy. He has published in the field of social policy evaluation, poverty research, and cultural consumption.

Jan de Boom studied sociology at the Erasmus University Rotterdam, the Netherlands. He is currently a researcher at Rotterdam Institute for Social Policy Research (RISBO). His research interests are immigration, immigrant integration, illegality and crime.

Sara Connolly studied economics and maths at Liverpool University, UK. She then moved to Oxford University where she gained her MPhil and DPhil in economics. Sara is currently a senior lecturer in economics at the University of East Anglia, UK. She has published in the fields of applied labour economics and the economics of public policy.

Godfried Engbersen is Professor of Sociology at the Erasmus University of Rotterdam, the Netherlands. He worked at the universities of Leiden, Amsterdam and Utrecht and was a visiting Professor at the Centre for Western European Studies at the University of California, Berkeley, USA. He has written extensively on new forms of social inequality and urban marginality in advanced welfare states.

Marco Gießelmann studied sociology and research methods at the universities of Bielefeld, Germany and Essex, UK. Currently he is a researcher at the University of Cologne (Chair for Empirical Social and Economic

Research) and is preparing a PhD thesis on the working poor phenomenon in Germany.

Björn Halleröd is Professor of Sociology, Umeå University, Sweden. Since the mid-1980s he has worked extensively on issues related to income distribution, poverty and living conditions. He is currently looking at the relationship between different welfare problems and longitudinal research on individual changes in living conditions.

Susan Kuivalainen gained her PhD at the University of Turku, Finland in 2004 and is currently a Professor of Social Policy at the same university. She has published work in the field of social assistance and poverty research.

Daniel Larsson received his PhD in sociology 2006. He is a lecturer at the Department of Sociology in Umeå University, Sweden, and his research interests are poverty, criminology, social policy and the labour market.

Henning Lohmann is a research associate at the German Socio-Economic Panel Study at the German Institute for Economic Research (DIW Berlin), Germany. He is a sociologist, with a Master's degree from the University of Bielefeld and a doctorate from the University of Cologne. He has published on poverty, economic consequences of divorce and self-employment in comparative perspective.

Ive Marx is a senior researcher at the Centre for Social Policy, University of Antwerp, Belgium. He holds MSc degrees in economics and sociology and a PhD in political and social sciences. He has published extensively on the poverty and social policy consequences of labour market change in advanced economies.

Mikko Niemelä, PhD, is a senior researcher at the Social Insurance Institution of Finland. He has also been a visiting scholar at the Social Policy Research Centre at the University of New South Wales, Australia. His main areas of interest are the measurement of poverty and the intergenerational transmission of poverty. His recent publications include 'Perceptions of the causes of poverty in Finland' (*Acta Sociologica*, 2008) and (with Ilpo Airio and Pasi Moisio) 'The intergenerational transmission of poverty in Finland in the 1990s' (*European Journal of Social Security*, 2005).

Brian Nolan is Professor of Public Policy in the School of Applied Social Science, University College Dublin, Ireland. He worked for many years at the Economic and Social Research Institute, Dublin. He is an economist, with a PhD from the London School of Economics. He has published widely on income inequality, poverty, public economics, social policy, and health economics.

Federico Podestà studied sociology and economic sociology at the universities of Trento and Brescia, and at present he is a researcher at the Observatory on social and economic local systems of the University of Trento, Italy. He has published in the field of quantitative methods for comparative research, poverty and social exclusion, and political economy.

Erik Snel is affiliated to the Department of Sociology of the Erasmus University Rotterdam, the Netherlands. He has a PhD in sociology. His main fields of teaching are urban studies and urban policy. His research interests are urban developments and urban policy-making, immigration and immigrant integration, poverty and social exclusion.

Gerlinde Verbist is a senior researcher at the Centre for Social Policy, University of Antwerp, Belgium. She has a PhD in applied economics. Her main research interests include microsimulation modelling and applications, measurement of income inequality and redistribution, taxation, and the interaction between migration and the welfare state. She is a member of the LoWER and Equalsoc research networks.

Acknowledgements

We acknowledge funding of our research and for the establishment of the research network from the Deutsche Forschungsgemeinschaft (project: 'Working Poor in Europa: Armut trotz Erwerbstätigkeit').

Introduction: the working poor in Europe

Hans-Jürgen Andreß and Henning Lohmann

This book is about Europeans who work and are poor. Many people think that the term 'working poor' should be an oxymoron, because nobody who works hard should be poor. Many people also think it is a phenomenon typical for the period of industrialization, as described in Friedrich Engels's seminal work on the 'working class in England' (Engels, 1999) or Benjamin Seebohm Rowntree's study on the 'wage-earning classes in provincial towns' (Rowntree, 2003). Others see it mainly as a problem in the USA, where the situation of the working poor has been a political issue for decades. Just recently, popular books by US journalists like Barbara Ehrenreich (2001) or David K. Shipler (2005) have provided a vivid picture of life at the 'bottom of the working world' in the US economy. In the European context, in-work poverty gained interest only in the late 1990s. The European Councils of Lisbon, Nice and Stockholm highlighted the importance of promoting participation in employment as a means of preventing and alleviating poverty and social exclusion. But recent reports from the European Statistical Office (Eurostat) showed that 7 per cent of the employed population in the EU-15 had an income below the national poverty line (Bardone and Guio, 2005). As a consequence, the European Council stresses in its recent European employment guidelines (EC, 2005) the need to reduce the number of working poor.

But why is in-work poverty back on the European political agenda? Much of the present concern about the working poor has to do with recent changes in labour market policies. High and persistent unemployment in many European countries have led many economists and politicians to believe that creating low-paid and low-skilled jobs will provide the missing job opportunities (European Commission, 2004; OECD, 1994; 2003). In addition, long-term structural changes in the capitalist economy will modify the number and quality of jobs. The change from Fordist to post-Fordist modes of production is increasing the demand for service sector jobs and flexible labour relations. As a consequence, many scholars expect increasing inequalities within the labour market, with high wages and stable work careers on the one side and unfavourable working conditions, low wages, and job instability on the other (Morris and Western, 1999). These structural changes within national economies are enforced by growing economic interdependencies worldwide. In a globalized economy, low-skilled labour in industrialized countries competes with low-skilled labour from less developed countries, which produces similar goods and services at a fraction of the cost (Wood, 1994). This creates a downward pressure on wages for low-skilled labour. Employers, on the other hand, may invest their capital worldwide, and will do so if foreign investments are more profitable. In other words, globalization increases employers' alternatives and thus, their bargaining power. If offshoring is a threat in certain parts of the economy, then employees in these exposed sectors will have to reduce their wage claims (Alderson and Nielsen, 2002; Harrison and Bluestone, 1988).

However, it would be false to blame only the economy for the increase in low-paid jobs. As we already indicated, public policies for the unemployed and the poor have changed as well – partly because former policies have been criticized for not reducing mass unemployment, and partly because of the financial crisis of the welfare state. Benefits have been reduced, and welfare-to-work policies have been implemented in many industrialized countries. Owing to these changes in government policies, work incentives have increased for parts of the inactive population, leading to an increase in the number of workers among those formerly living on welfare or unemployment benefits. Because most of these individuals have no or only lower qualifications, most of them (re)entered the labour market in low-skilled jobs that pay only meagre wages. Furthermore, negative income tax systems or other types of wage subsidies have been introduced which are supposed to make work pay, especially for those already working at the lower end of the wage distribution. In other words, changes in the political system – from welfare to enabling or workfare states (Gilbert, 2002; Jessop, 1993) – have contributed equally well to the increase in low-wage employment.

Finally, it should be noted that the supply of low-paid jobs has also met a certain demand for these kinds of jobs. For example, discriminatory practices in the labour market may leave no other job opportunities available for immigrants. Or flexible working times in the service sector – which are often connected with low-paid jobs – may well be in line with the employment interests of mothers. This does not mean that women or immigrants prefer low pay, but it shows that the increase in low-wage employment cannot be understood without recognizing recent demographic changes (rising female employment, immigration).

But this book is not primarily a book about low pay. Instead, we ask whether gainful employment is sufficient to earn a living – both for oneself

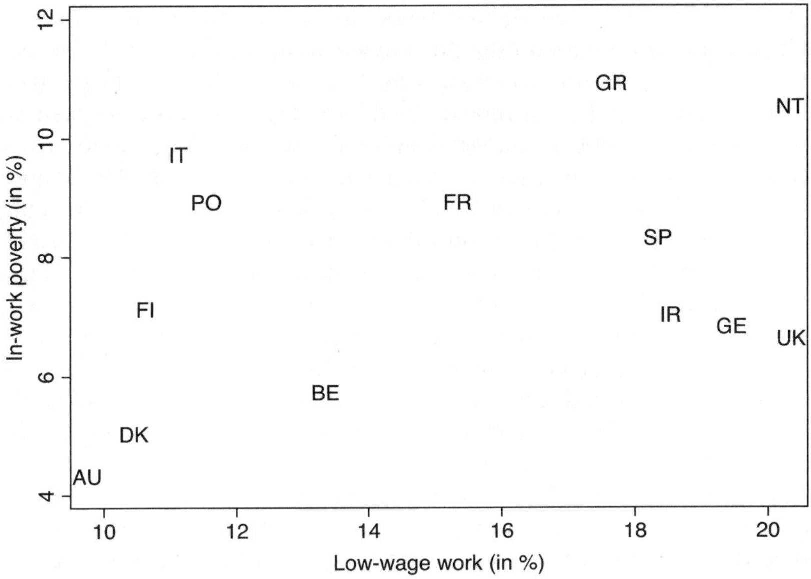

Source: European Community Household Panel 2001, data taken from Chapter 1 by Lohmann and Marx, own computations.

Figure I.1 Low-wage and in-work poverty in selected European countries (2001)

and for one's family members. In answer to that question, low pay is only one among many other explanations. In Figure I.1, we see large variation in in-work poverty as well as in low pay in Europe. However, as the figure shows, low pay and in-work poverty are only modestly correlated. For example, in 2001, we observe countries like Italy with rather high overall poverty rates (in Italy around 11 per cent) that at the same time show a comparatively low percentage of low-wage work (10 per cent in Italy). Similarly, we can find countries with comparatively low overall poverty rates – for example the UK with 7 per cent – in which the incidence of low-wage work is extremely high (20 per cent in the UK).

Many factors contribute to this mismatch, but the main explanation is that low pay is an individual characteristic, while poverty refers to the household. A worker may have a low-paid job, but because he – or more often she – is living with an employed partner, both incomes may lift the household above the poverty line. The same situation applies if labour income is augmented by wage subsidies, family benefits or other sources of non-labour income. In any of these cases, total household income is larger than income from work and thus may well be above the poverty line.

But, of course, the opposite may happen as well. Consider, for example, a single mother who is working. Depending on the kind of job she holds, her wage may be sufficient for herself, but chances are high that it is inadequate for herself and her children. And we should not forget the workers who have to support a large number of dependent family members. If a second earner is missing, or if the state does not provide cash transfers, the breadwinner together with his or her family members may be poor even if the working person's wage is sufficient for an individual. This is the situation described by Benjamin Seebohm Rowntree at the turn of the twentieth century. He found that wage earners live in poverty during certain phases of their lives – namely, when they are the breadwinners for their families and when they retire from their active working careers (Rowntree, 2003: 137). Although family size has decreased considerably during the past century, large family households still exist – especially in the Southern European countries, where young adults tend to stay with their parents because of high youth unemployment.

Low-wage work (based on personal incomes) and in-work poverty (based on household incomes) do not only differ with respect to the size of both groups but also with respect to their socio-demographic profiles. The most obvious difference is the number of women belonging to each risk group. The high share of women in low-wage work (Asplund and Persson, 2000; Keese et al., 1998) reflects the disadvantageous position of women in the labour market. In-work poverty risks, on the other hand, are quite similar with respect to gender because the risk of poverty is moderated within the household context as we have discussed above. In the following, our main interest is not to regard differences between low-wage workers and working poor, but to explain why the socio-demographic profiles of the working poor differ by country. To answer this question it is necessary to regard the distribution of labour market incomes as well as factors which influence how different sources of income (mainly earnings, partner's income and transfers) are combined within the household.

EXPLAINING IN-WORK POVERTY

In recent years, several reports have been published on the working poor problem – many at the national level, but few comparative studies (Bardone and Guio, 2005; Marx and Verbist, 1998; Peña-Casas and Latta, 2004; Strengmann-Kuhn, 2003). Most of them are descriptive surveys presenting quantitative information about the incidence and socio-demographic profile of in-work poverty. This book tries to go several steps further. First, it is comparative from the very beginning by providing country reports and cross-country analyses that follow a similar methodological design (see the next section in this chapter). Second, it is descriptive, but it tries to augment the quantitative information with the qualitative background information necessary to understand and put into context each country's national experience with the working poor problem. Finally, we try to provide explanations for why in-work poverty is high in certain countries while low in others.

In thinking about possible explanations, many results from traditional poverty research can be used to interpret different poverty risks within the working population. For instance, it is well known that poverty risks differ with respect to their individual characteristics. One of these is income capacity. Having a university degree or a high school diploma is connected with higher incomes and less poverty. Other risk factors have to do with household characteristics. For example, one labour income will easily feed one single person, while the same labour income may be insufficient for a family with children. Depending on the household situation, some workers will also have to deal with time constraints that restrict their labour supply. For example, if childcare institutions are missing, single mothers will not be able to work full-time, whereas childless, but otherwise identical women are free in their choice of working time. Obviously, the amount of income – and, thus, poverty status – depends to a large extent on working time.

Generally speaking, individual and household-related risk factors influence the 'needs' and 'resources' of workers and their family members. These individuals will find themselves in poverty if available resources do not satisfy their needs (see the next section for our operational definition of poverty). But even if one controls for all these risk factors, poverty among the working population is still much higher in some countries than in others. Take, as an example, the analysis on levels of deprivation in Europe by Layte et al. (2001). Although controlling for gender, age, household type, marital status, education, employment status and social class position explains a relevant share of the variation between countries, more than half of the variation remains unexplained. Apparently, the national context is another source of variation. Why is this so? And what are the driving forces behind these country differences? These are the major research questions of this book.

The answers are indicated in the preceding examples. For example, a single mother will more likely search for a full-time job if she can be sure that her children are taken care of in a kindergarten or a full-time day school. Hence, public infrastructure for families supports female employment; this is not only a resource for solo mothers, but also for large families, who are now able to increase their labour supply. Family benefits have already been mentioned. They have been implemented, among other reasons, to ease the lives of single-breadwinner families. Or consider the increase in low-wage jobs in some European countries. As discussed earlier, this is in part a result of new labour market policies (deregulation, flexibilization). Similarly, the structure of labour relations has an impact on earnings distribution. Many scholars assume that strong labour unions and centralized wage-bargaining systems decrease the incidence of low pay (for an overview see Flanagan, 1999; Lucifora et al., 2005). The same is assumed for minimum wage legislation and other types of state-enforced wage bargaining. Finally, the amount of public transfers available (welfare payments, unemployment benefits and the like) reduces citizens' reliance on gainful employment (decommodification). Fewer people are forced to work in low-paid jobs. Furthermore, non-working household members are more likely to receive benefits and, hence, to contribute to household income. All these examples demonstrate that the national context – or more specifically, labour market institutions and welfare state provisions – is an additional resource for people of working age. It regulates working conditions, increases bargaining power, supports gainful employment or provides alternative modes of income maintenance. We believe, therefore, that the incidence and socio-demographic profile of the working poor cannot be understood without a thorough understanding of each country's institutional context.

For the moment, we will leave it at these examples. Nevertheless, the institutional explanation could be called the main research hypothesis of this book. Obviously, such a hypothesis cannot be answered without varying the institutional context. Investigating in-work poverty in only one country would not provide the necessary information, because the institutional context within a country is rather constant, at least from a short- or medium-term perspective. Therefore, our research project had to be comparative from the beginning. The next section explains our methodological approach.

METHODOLOGICAL APPROACH

Our research combines the case study method with micro–macro analyses. Correspondingly, the following chapters consist of a series of in-depth case studies focusing on single countries combined with comparative analyses of several European countries based on cross-nationally equivalent survey data. The term 'micro–macro analyses' refers to the fact that the later chapters combine micro data on individuals with macro data describing the institutional context.

Comparative Research Design

But how did we select the countries for our case studies? First, this has been a question of availability. We needed scholars who were both experts on the national contexts in question as well as on research in poverty and low pay. Starting from our own research contacts and from our knowledge of the literature, we were able to build a network of interested sociologists, economists and political scientists from nine different European countries. The group met at several workshops, and this book presents the output of our collaborative work.

Furthermore, when building up the research network, we tried to represent different national institutional settings in order to test the validity of our institutional hypothesis. Current research on welfare states usually assumes that there are more or less coherent clusters of institutional arrangements that embody distinct values and rationales. This assumption has been operationalized in the concept of welfare regimes (Arts and Gelissen, 2002; Esping-Andersen, 1990; 1999), and it has been tempting to use one of the existing welfare state typologies to guide our country selection. But many scholars argue that such a typology should be domain-specific (for example, Gallie and Paugam, 2000). Furthermore, very often the internal heterogeneity of these clusters is remarkable – which is why many authors regard them only as 'ideal types' (Weber) of the real world. In any case, it is important to specify the institutional arrangements that characterize each cluster and why they influence the phenomenon of interest (in-work poverty in our case). If that work needs to be done anyway, then it is natural to test each characteristic individually.

Although we do not deny the importance of regime typologies as a theoretical tool, we have a preference for the latter approach. This implies a definition of the basic components of the institutional context. What are relevant welfare state regulations and labour market institutions? How can we describe them in general terms? And, finally, how can we measure them empirically? Lohmann and Marx (in this volume) discuss potential relevant institutional factors and how these can be measured. As far as our country selection is concerned, we simply tried to include samples from every region of Western Europe in order to represent the variation in in-work poverty between European countries. We tried to select representatives of each region: Finland and Sweden for the Northern European countries; Ireland and the UK for the Anglo-Saxon countries; Belgium, Germany and the Netherlands for the Central European countries; and Italy for the Southern European countries. Each country chapter provides a descriptive overview of the incidence and socio-demographic profile of the working poor, together with an account of national labour market institutions and welfare state regulations. In doing so, each chapter tries to present a comprehensive picture of in-work poverty in each respective country. Is there a working poor problem? Did it increase over time? What characteristics are specific to a given country? And what is a common experience that can also be observed in many other countries?

The single case studies are complemented by two comparative studies including several countries. One of the latter investigates the effect of quantitative measures of the institutional context on poverty status in a sample of workers from 15 European countries. The other evaluates the effect of policies to combat in-work poverty in different European countries. Finally, in a sort of meta-analysis of all the empirical analyses, we try to present some general conclusions concerning the relevance of the working poor problem and the validity of the institutional explanation.

Target Population and Poverty Measures

Every comparative project is confronted with the question of how to define its central concepts and the population under observation. In our case, the main questions were 'What is poverty?' and 'Who are the workers?' In the case of the first question, we decided to use a concept which – being one of the Laeken indicators – has become a de facto standard at European Union (EU) level. Although poverty is regarded as a multidimensional phenomenon, we only use measures of income as indicators of poverty. Since welfare is determined at the level of households, (net) household income is an appropriate indicator. We use an equivalence scale (modified OECD) to take into account the fact that households differ according to size and composition. In sum, equivalized net household income is the main poverty indicator used in the following analyses. Following on the idea that poverty is a relative concept, we define the poverty line as a fraction of the average income in a given country. Again, we take the respective Laeken indicator as a reference and define the poverty threshold at 60 per cent of the median of national equivalized net household income. This definition is the standard which is used in all chapters. In addition, some of the chapters include other poverty measures – either other indicators (for example, consensual deprivation) or other thresholds (for example, 40 per cent or 50 per cent of the median).

With respect to the second question, we tried to follow the criteria of the International Labour Organization (ILO) wherever possible. Hence, people who work at least one hour per week are regarded as workers. People looking for work are regarded as unemployed, given that they are in a position to take up employment within two weeks. All other people are defined as inactive. Unpaid family members are regarded as self-employed workers. Since we do not want to consider people who are younger or older than what is usually considered a 'working age', we tried to restrict the analyses to the age group between 15 and 64 years. Given that the data used in the following analyses do not come from a single source, we had to relax the criteria in some cases. Sometimes the data only includes persons from 17 or 20 years of age onwards. Sometimes no exact information on working hours is included. And sometimes the observation period is not the current week of the interview but the year before data collection, which makes it impossible to categorize workers on the basis of hours worked per week. In that case, employment status is defined on the basis of the number of months a person worked in the past year. Here, persons who worked for at least seven months are regarded as workers.

Combining the definition of poverty and worker we arrive at our definition of the working poor. A working poor individual is a working person who lives in a poor household – that is, a household with an income below the threshold we defined above. Given the variety of the data used in this book, however, it is impossible to give an exact overall description of all the country-specific operationalizations. Discrepancies from our basic definitions will be noted in each chapter.

ORIENTATION OF THE CHAPTERS

The structure of the volume reflects the basic idea of drawing a broad yet detailed picture of in-work poverty in Europe. The two chapters of Part I provide a basic orientation about the incidence, structure and causes of in-work poverty in Western Europe. The main question addressed in this part is this: is there variation by country, and which institutional and economic factors can be assumed to play a vital role in explaining such variation? Part II is a collection of in-depth country studies. The main question of these chapters is: what characteristics are specific to a given country? Therefore, the empirical analysis of in-work poverty is embedded in a discussion of the institutional and economic framework of each country. Part III combines the comparative and national perspectives and discusses policy options to increase overall employment while minimizing poverty risks of the working population.

Chapter 1, by Henning Lohmann and Ive Marx, examines in-work poverty from a perspective of welfare regimes. The purpose of this paper is to highlight the fact that 'poverty in work' comes in many different guises across advanced welfare states. The claim of the chapter is that the incidence as well as the composition of the working poor differs substantially between welfare regimes. The chapter starts with a broad overview of the differing social, economic and political conditions for in-work poverty, providing information on indicators such as replacement rates, social expenditure, childcare coverage, minimum wage levels, bargaining centralization, employment rates and employment shares by sector. Lohmann and Marx discuss how in-work poverty is shaped by the institutional particularities of each welfare cluster and they provide a basic empirical analysis of such differences, which shows that the differences between welfare regimes are less pronounced than expected.

Chapter 2 is aimed at explaining such differences from a micro–macro perspective. Using a multilevel framework, Henning Lohmann analyses the influence of individual or household-related factors and institutional factors on in-work poverty as well as the interaction between the two. The chapter hypothesizes that not only the design of labour market institutions or in-work benefit schemes alters a worker's risk of being poor, but that the general degree of decommodification and defamilization also plays an important role. Transfers paid to non-working household members and services aimed at dual earnership are expected to increase household incomes, and therefore to lower the risk of in-work poverty.

The order of the country studies in Part II is loosely structured by region which – as in many other studies – mirrors quite well the affiliation of each country to an Esping-Andersen-style welfare regime typology. We look at three continental European countries (Belgium, Germany and the Netherlands), two Northern countries (Sweden and Finland), two Anglo-Saxon countries (the UK and Ireland) and Italy as a Southern European representative. Each of the chapters analyses the situation of in-work poverty in the given country in a broader context. Taken together, the selection of cases provides a picture of in-work poverty in times of welfare state reform and changing economic conditions.

Chapter 3 examines the Belgian case. Ive Marx and Gerlinde Verbist argue that on the surface, Belgium appears to epitomize the archetypal continental European welfare state caught in a 'welfare without work' conundrum. At the same time, however, childcare provisions for working parents are extensive, making Belgium a case in point of what has been called 'optional familialism' (Leitner, 2003), where families caring for children at home are supported, but at the same time families are also given the option of being unburdened from care responsibilities. In addition, over the past decades, Belgium has deployed a wide range of measures to improve the disposable income situation of single-earner households with low incomes as well as to boost multi-earnership. In their empirical analysis, the authors show that in-work poverty in Belgium – as elsewhere on the Continent – is principally a problem of single-parent households and single-earner couples with children. This may come as something of a surprise given the extent to which the breadwinner model is institutionally supported and protected in Belgium, especially if there are children.

Chapter 4 starts off by presenting an almost classical paradox in the analysis of in-work poverty, namely, that high levels of low-paid employment do not necessarily result in high levels of in-work poverty. Marco Gießelmann and Henning Lohmann show that exactly this is the case in Germany – at least in West Germany. The authors describe the region as an example of the modified male-breadwinner model where a majority of (female) low-paid workers live together with (male) main earners. In East Germany, however, owing to its differing heritage of a dual-breadwinner model and more difficult economic conditions, the link between low-paid work and in-work poverty is much closer. Furthermore, the chapter discusses how recent German welfare state reforms are likely to alter the dominant earner model and the relationship of low-paid work and in-work poverty throughout Germany.

The question of the consequences of welfare state reform on in-work poverty is also the focus of the analysis of the Netherlands (Chapter 5). Erik Snel, Jan de Boom and Godfried Engbersen see the Netherlands as a continental forerunner of an 'enabling state' (Gilbert, 2002), which puts more emphasis on integration via employment than via social rights. Based on this discussion, they ask whether the 'Dutch miracle' of employment growth has been accompanied by an increase of in-work poverty. In addition to institutional change, the analysis looks at economic and demographic factors as potential causes for the growth of in-work poverty.

In Chapter 6, Björn Halleröd and Daniel Larsson analyse changes in in-work poverty in Sweden since the late 1980s. The fact that economic and labour market conditions have changed severely during this period – a shift from demand to supply-side policies and a harsh recession in the early 1990s followed by economic growth – makes Sweden a suitable candidate for analysing the influence of economic factors on in-work poverty. The authors' empirical focus is on the increase of insecure employment and how this is related to in-work poverty. They show that Sweden is still characterized by low levels of in-work poverty (as one would expect in the prime example of a Northern welfare state), but that the rise in the level of unemployment compared to the 1980s also has consequences for those who are working.

Chapter 7 provides analyses of poverty among working people in Finland from the mid-1990s until 2005. Ilpo Airio, Susan Kuivalainen and Mikko Niemelä describe the main features of the Finnish welfare state and its labour market institutions. Regarding the changes during the past ten years, it appears that changes in the labour market and in welfare state provisions during the end of the 1990s and early 2000s do not give us reason to expect a dramatic increase in in-work poverty, since there are no signs of radical welfare state retrenchment or labour market decentralization. In fact, the development of income poverty among working people has been rather constant. In addition, the authors apply an alternative method of measuring poverty. Using this measure, the situation is even more positive – consensual deprivation decreased during the research period. Thus, the overall picture is such that in-work poverty is relatively low in Finland.

Chapter 8, by Ferruccio Biolcati-Rinaldi and Federico Podestà, deals with the Italian case, which is interesting not only as classical example of Southern European welfare regimes, but also because of the high level of internal heterogeneity. Southern Italy, the Mezzogiorno, experiences poverty and in-work poverty incidences much higher than those in the Northern and Central regions. This situation provides the chance to conduct comparative analyses controlling for different economic conditions, family models and welfare supply at the local level. The general hypothesis of this chapter is that the traditional male breadwinner model that sustained Italian economic development from the end of the Second World War to the beginning of the 1970s has become dysfunctional since it produces, among other things, high levels of in-work poverty. Such a crisis calls for new assets which, at the moment, are being provided more successfully in North-Central Italy than in the Mezzogiorno.

Chapter 9, by Sara Connolly, focuses on the question of whether policies such as earned income tax credits and minimum wages, which have been introduced or extended in the UK during the years of the Labour government, have resulted in a reduction in in-work poverty. The results of the empirical analysis do not support such a conclusion. While the situation of families has, in fact, improved, other groups such as singles face an increased risk of in-work poverty.

Ireland is a case which combines the fact of an unprecedented economic boom and growth in employment with an increasing number of working poor – at least if one focuses on standard income poverty measures. In Chapter 10, Brian Nolan argues that one reason why economic development does not translate into decreasing in-work poverty rates is that the rapid growth in living standards is only poorly reflected in conventional poverty measures. What is – irrespective of the measure used – most distinctive about the households of the working poor is how few of their working-age adult members are actually working. Hence, the chapter concludes that in order to be effective in addressing in-work poverty, policy should focus not only on raising the take-home pay of the low paid, but also on the position of households where more of the adults could be in work.

Part III combines the comparative and national perspectives of Part I and II. Chapter 11, by Ive Marx and Gerlinde Verbist, discusses policy options for fighting in-work poverty. Since they see in-work poverty in

Europe, especially in continental Europe, to a large extent as a problem of underemployment within households, they focus on policies that will boost labour participation rates and thus multi-earnership. They discuss demand-side as well as supply-side measures, including those two policy instruments – minimum wages and in-work benefits – that dominate the current public and policy discourse.

In the final Chapter 12 we will summarize the findings of the eight country and the two comparative analyses. Starting with a recapitulation of the main institutional features of the countries represented in this volume, we attempt to draw some general conclusions on the level and structure of in-work poverty as it is typical under different institutional settings. We conclude with a discussion of the development of in-work poverty over time and whether there is a trade-off between low in-work poverty and employment growth.

REFERENCES

Alderson, A.S. and F. Nielsen (2002), 'Globalization and the great u-turn: income inequality trends in 16 OECD countries', *American Journal of Sociology*, **107** (5), 1244–99.

Arts, W. and J. Gelissen (2002), 'Three worlds of welfare capitalism or more? A state-of-the-art report', *Journal of European Social Policy*, **12** (2), 137–58.

Asplund, R. and I. Persson (2000), 'Low pay – a special affliction of women', in M. Gregory, S. Wiemer and S. Bazen (eds), *Labour Market Inequalities: Problems and Policies of Low-Wage Employment in International Perspective*, Oxford: Oxford University Press, pp. 53–81.

Bardone, L. and A.-C. Guio (2005), 'In-work poverty. New commonly agreed indicators at the EU level', *Statistics in Focus*, **5/2005**.

Ehrenreich, B. (2001), *Nickel and Dimed: On (Not) Getting By in America*, New York: Henry Holt.

Engels, F. (1999), *The Condition of the Working-Class in England in 1844*, Oxford: Oxford University Press.

Esping-Andersen, G. (1990), *The Three Worlds of Welfare Capitalism*, Cambridge: Polity Press.

Esping-Andersen, G. (1999), *Social Foundations of Postindustrial Economies*, Oxford: Oxford University Press.

European Commission (2004), *Employment in Europe 2004. Recent Trends and Prospects*, Luxembourg: Office for Official Publications of the EC.

European Council (EC) (2005), 'Council decision of 12 July 2005 on guidelines for the employment policies of the member states', *Official Journal of the European Union*, **L 205/21**.

Flanagan, R.J. (1999), 'Macroeconomic performance and collective bargaining: an international perspective', *Journal of Economic Literature*, **37**, 1150–75.

Gallie, D. and S. Paugam (2000), 'The experience of unemployment in Europe: the debate', in D. Gallie and S. Paugam (ed.), *Welfare Regimes and the Experience of Unemployment in Europe*, Oxford: Oxford University Press, pp. 1–22.

Gilbert, N. (2002), *Transformation of the Welfare State. The Silent Surrender of Public Responsibility*, Oxford: Oxford University Press.
Harrison, B. and B. Bluestone (1988), *The Great U-Turn*, New York: Basic Books.
Jessop, B. (1993), 'Towards a Schumpetrian workfare state? Preliminary remarks on post-Fordist political economy', *Studies in Political Economy*, **40**, 7–39.
Keese, M., A. Puymoyen and P. Swaim (1998), 'The incidence and dynamics of low-paid employment in OECD countries', in R. Asplund, P.J. Sloane and I. Theodossiou (eds), *Low Pay and Earnings Mobility in Europe*, Cheltenham: Edward Elgar, pp. 223–65.
Layte, R., C.T. Whelan, B. Maître and B. Nolan (2001), 'Explaining levels of deprivation in the European Union', *Acta Sociologica*, **44** (2), 105–22.
Leitner, S. (2003), 'Varieties of familialism. The caring function of the family in comparative perspective', *European Societies*, **5** (4), 353–75.
Lucifora, C., A. McKnight and W. Salverda (2005), 'Low-wage employment in Europe: a review of the evidence', *Socio-Economic Review*, **3**, 259–92.
Marx, I. and G. Verbist (1998), 'Low-paid work and poverty: a cross-country perspective', in S. Bazen, M. Gregory and W. Salverda (eds), *Low-Wage Employment in Europe*, Cheltenham: Edward Elgar, pp. 63–86.
Morris, M. and B. Western (1999), 'Inequality in earnings at the close of the twentieth century', *Annual Review of Sociology*, **25**, 623–57.
Organisation for Economic Co-operation and Development (OECD) (1994), *The OECD Jobs Study. Evidence and Explanations (Part I – Labour Market Trends and Underlying Forces of Change)*, Paris: OECD.
Organisation for Economic Co-operation and Development (OECD) (2003), *Employment Outlook*, Paris: OECD.
Peña-Casas, R. and M. Latta (2004), *Working Poor in the European Union*, Luxembourg: European Foundation for the Improvement of Living and Working Conditions.
Rowntree, B.S. (2003), *Poverty – A Study of Town Life*, Basingstoke: Palgrave Macmillan.
Shipler, D.K. (2005), *The Working Poor: Invisible in America*, New York: Vintage Books.
Strengmann-Kuhn, W. (2003), *Armut trotz Erwerbstätigkeit. Analysen und sozialpolitische Konsequenzen*, Frankfurt and New York: Campus.
Wood, A. (1994), *North–South Trade, Employment and Inequality: Changing Fortunes in a Skill-Driven World*, Oxford: Oxford University Press.

PART I

Comparative Issues

1. The different faces of in-work poverty across welfare state regimes

Henning Lohmann and Ive Marx

INTRODUCTION

The notion of in-work poverty often conjures up stereotypical images of poorly paid service sector workers toiling away in fast-food chains (see, for example, Shipler, 2005). This perception is not altogether wrong. But it is a reductive and, in fact, rather Anglo-Saxon one. Moreover, the overlap between low-paid employment (in services or elsewhere) and financial poverty tends to be very weak, even in the Anglo-Saxon countries (see, for example, Gardiner and Millar, 2006; Nolan, 1994; Nolan and Marx, 2000). But more importantly, it does not capture the whole nature of the phenomenon – certainly not in Northern, Continental and Southern Europe.

The purpose of this chapter is to highlight the fact that 'poverty in work' comes in many different guises across advanced welfare states. A starting point for this task is the notion that in-work poverty cannot be explained solely from a perspective which focuses on low wages or earnings inequalities. This perspective is most useful when the wage of a single earner is the sole income source for a household. The more other sources contribute to the household income, the less one would expect to see a direct link between low-wage work and the working poor. We argue that this is the case – to a differing degree – in European welfare states. Therefore, we will discuss how differences in welfare state regimes – understood as 'the combined, interdependent way in which welfare is produced and allocated between state, market, and family' (Esping-Andersen, 1999: 34f) – can be expected to explain differences in the extent and structure of in-work poverty. This perspective enables us to focus on different causes of in-work poverty such as earnings inequalities, welfare state policies and the role of the family. Our claim is that the incidence as well as the composition of the working poor differs substantially from welfare cluster to welfare cluster. In fact, we argue that in-work poverty can be construed as emanating from quite distinct dysfunctions occurring within each of the dominant welfare clusters in Europe.

The chapter is organized as follows: in the next section we discuss why in-work poverty can be expected to differ from one welfare state regime to another. But instead of simply regarding differences between clusters of countries, we first discuss the expected influences of single factors such as the degree of decommodification, defamilization, mechanisms of wage-setting and how these factors can be expected to affect employment and in-work poverty. The third section hypothesizes about how the considerations made in the second section might translate into in-work poverty patterns across various welfare state regimes. We first show that variation in relevant institutional factors is, in fact, larger between welfare regimes than within any given welfare regime. We then formulate specific hypotheses as to how the extent and structure of in-work poverty can be expected to differ by welfare state regime. In the fourth section, we present empirical evidence on differences in labour market and household structures across various welfare states – particularly as these are likely to pertain to differences in in-work poverty. Then, in the fifth section we present empirical evidence on differences in in-work poverty between welfare regimes and discuss discrepancies between expected and observed outcomes. In the final section, we draw our conclusions.

UNDERLYING DIMENSIONS OF WELFARE STATE REGIMES AND IN-WORK POVERTY

We can look at the working poor from two different perspectives: from a perspective of (financial) poverty and from a perspective of employment. This is not to say that these aspects are not interwoven, quite the contrary. But if we look at poverty, we are stressing the fact that earnings (and income from potential other sources) are too low to lift the household a worker lives in above a – however defined – poverty threshold. Hence, if we try to explain country-specific differences in in-work poverty we need to look at institutions which affect the level of earnings as well as the level and availability of other sources of income, particularly transfers.

Level of Wages and Transfers

We first consider the impact of institutions on wage inequality and the incidence of low-paid employment. In a seminal and influential paper, Blau and Kahn (1996) asked why wage inequality is so much higher in the USA than in most other Organisation for Economic Co-operation and

Development (OECD) countries. Their study analysed male wage inequality in the USA and in nine other OECD countries (Germany, Britain, Austria, Switzerland, Sweden, Norway, Australia, Hungary, Italy and Norway). They argued and demonstrated that labour market institutions – principally the comparatively decentralized wage-setting mechanisms in the USA – provide the most persuasive explanation for these patterns. Many other studies have tried to demonstrate that wage-setting institutions are associated with pay inequality, particularly changes in the distribution of pay (see, for example, Kahn, 2000; Lucifora, 2000).

In addition to earnings, transfers represent a relevant part of the income package in working households. In France, for instance, more than one-third of the income of working poor households consists of transfers (Lagarenne and Legendre, 2000). Furthermore, a number of studies have shown that there are large differences between welfare states in the degree of poverty reduction which is achieved via transfers (see, for example, Atkinson et al., 1995; Moller et al., 2003). There is not as much specific evidence showing to what degree in-work poverty is reduced by transfers, although there is a broad discussion of so-called in-work benefits (see OECD, 2005). However, there is evidence that in-work poverty is not only affected by in-work benefit programmes which are meant to supplement low earned incomes. Even in the UK – which has a long history of paying in-work benefits – other types of transfers are a more important factor for the reduction of poverty among workers with low incomes (Gardiner and Millar, 2006). Poverty reduction in working households can also be achieved through transfers paid to non-working household members, such as unemployment benefits. These contribute to the total household income, in particular when these transfers are not subject to a means test. From this perspective, factors which influence poverty at large are also likely to affect in-work poverty. A higher level of decommodification – which is measured by the level and availability of transfers (for a revised version of a decommodification index see Scruggs and Allan, 2006) – is likely to lower the in-work poverty risk. Furthermore, there are non-contributory benefits like family allowances which also contribute to household income. In Germany, for instance, child allowances represent one of the most relevant types of transfers which reduce in-work poverty (see Strengmann-Kuhn, 2003).

Employment Chances

Although a high degree of decommodification has the side effect of poverty reduction via transfers in working households, its central aspect concerns the ability to 'opt out' of the labour market (see Esping-Andersen, 1990).

If we look at the working poor, the possibility of 'opting out' will prevent workers from accepting work which does not pay them a living. Hence, the degree of decommodification will affect the level of wages and/or the structure of the working population, both of which should lower the risk of belonging to the working poor. While the concept of decommodification stresses protection against the market, the recent discussion on welfare state reform is often based on the notion of low work incentives. A high level of transfers is seen as a cause of poverty via the creation of unemployment and inactivity traps (see OECD, 2005). Empirical evidence on the relationship between transfer payments and individual labour supply seems to support this view (for an overview see Moffitt, 2002).

Another strand of research addresses the question of how labour market institutions – especially employment protection regulation – influence employment, particularly the employment chances of the less skilled. The results of these studies are, generally speaking, ambiguous and not very robust (Marx, 2007). Although there is not a lot of evidence that employment protection regulations have much of an impact on overall unemployment rates, there is stronger and more robust evidence that these regulations affect the employment chances of particular groups. A number of studies suggest that strict employment protection regulations have a negative effect on the employment chances of young people and prime-age women, while positively affecting the employment chances of other segments, such as prime-age men.

More important, perhaps, is the question of the indirect effects of institutions on employment chances via the route of their impact on wage inequality – given the fact that the link between wage-setting institutions and wage inequality is fairly well established. A number of studies have looked in detail at the relationship between earnings dispersion and employment performance. The OECD (1996), for example, concluded 'that unemployment rates for the most vulnerable groups in the labour market – women, youngsters and the low-skilled – do not tend to be consistently higher in countries where low-wage work is more prevalent'. Other cross-country comparative studies have come to similar conclusions (Card et al., 1999; Nickell and Bell, 1995), while still other studies offer some support for the conventional view that institutionally imposed wage compression is harmful to employment (see, for example, Bertola et al., 2002). While no consensus has emerged, there now seems to be an agreement that the link is not necessarily strong or straightforward. More detailed cross-country comparative studies appear to confirm this viewpoint (see, for example, Freeman and Schettkat, 2000a; 2000b).

Family Structures and Employment Patterns

The concept of defamilization (Lister, 1994; McLaughlin and Glendinning, 1994) has become quite prominent in recent welfare state research. It stresses the fact that welfare states not only influence the degree of an individual's dependence on markets, but also a person's dependence on his or her own family. This concept is concerned with women's dependence on the family owing to care obligations and a male main earner. A second dimension focuses on the dependent status of young adults owing to restricted labour market access and no access to transfers in their own right, and on the dependence of the elderly owing to a lack of care options outside the family (and, perhaps, to insufficient income). The latter is often discussed with a focus on Southern welfare states (see Ferrera, 1996; Flaquer, 2000; Leibfried, 1992). If welfare states differ in their degree of defamilization, this means that they differ in their ability to increase female autonomy and to reduce intergenerational dependencies. Thus, while decomodification describes to what extent a person's well-being is dependent on the market, defamilization is about an individual's dependence on his or her family.

Although the concept of defamilization is much broader in scope, we can name at least two ways in which defamilization is related to in-work poverty. First, single-earner households face a much higher risk of poverty. Welfare state measures which lower the restrictions for female employment ('dual-earner policies', see, for example, Gornick et al., 1997; Korpi, 2000) are therefore expected to reduce in-work poverty – although the aim of these policies is not primarily to reduce poverty, but rather to facilitate gender equality and to offer opportunities for combining work and family. Second, intergenerational dependency causes a shift of burdens within the family. The prime example of this is young unemployed people in Southern European countries who fall back on their parents owing to the lack of any other safety net for those with no solid work histories (see Paugam and Russell, 2000). We can make a similar assertion in the case of young low-wage workers. While living with their parents will lower their risk of being poor, the poverty risk for the (working) parents will rise. Thus, this type of family solidarity has an ambiguous effect. On the one hand, the pooling of resources protects family members from being poor. On the other hand, family members earning regular incomes face additional burdens. It is hard to predict whether, in sum, the influence of the protection or of the burdens is stronger. We can, however, expect the degree of intergenerational dependency to have a clear influence on the structure of the working poor. The risk of being poor is partly shifted from the – often younger – low-wage workers to the male, middle-aged workers at the core of the labour market.

Hence, defamilizing policies which affect the degree of intergenerational dependency are likely to affect the composition of the working poor as well (and – depending on the sum of protection and burdens – the level of in-work poverty).

How do we expect all this to translate into patterns of in-work poverty? We know from previous research that what matters increasingly in advanced economies is the *combined* labour market position of household members. Single earnership has become a poverty risk in an era in which the average living standard – and hence the relative poverty threshold – is increasingly determined by the living standard of double-earner households. Two working adults are the best protection against poverty that a household can have in present-day society. Marx and Verbist (1998) found the USA to be just about the only advanced economy where a significant proportion of double-earner couples were living in poverty around the early to mid-1990s, and where such couples made up a substantial proportion of poor working-age households. But in most countries, it did not matter much whether one or both partners in a two-adult household had a low-wage or part-time job. It would therefore appear that the impact of institutions on the employment chances of working-age adults matters more than their impact on the distribution of wages and the incidence of low-paid employment.

It appears that many European households would do better with a second household income. This is certainly the case in the South, where female participation rates remain low. In Italy and Spain, well over half of all working-age couples still live on a single-breadwinner wage. It has been suggested that non-employment rates for less educated women are bound to remain high unless more flexible, relatively low-paid jobs are 'allowed' to emerge in the domestic services sector. Such jobs could then provide many single-earner households with the additional income they need to escape poverty. But as we have just argued, the empirical link between wage flexibility and the employment chances of the less skilled and others is far less straightforward than is often assumed.

While more wage flexibility (for example, lower minimum effective wages) could help boost multi-earnership and reduce single-earner poverty, the larger effect might well be increased poverty among households, which would see their earnings deteriorate but fail to acquire a second household income – either because there is no second adult or because the second adult fails to obtain a job even in a labour market where more (low-paid) jobs are available. In short, the potential poverty-enhancing effects of more wage dispersion (more poverty among low-earnings households) may well outweigh the poverty reduction effects (more multi-earner households). The question of how labour market institutions affect in-work poverty via the route of their impact on employment chances and wages is and remains, therefore, very much an empirical one.

EXPECTED VARIATION BY WELFARE-STATE REGIMES

So far, we have discussed the institutional dimensions which can be expected to influence the incidence and structure of in-work poverty. In doing so, we have deliberately ignored the fact that welfare states do not represent a random collection of disjointed policies, but rather that there are more or less coherent clusters of institutional arrangements which embody distinct values and rationales, as has been stressed in the concept of welfare regimes (Arts and Gelissen, 2002; Esping-Andersen, 1990; 1999). Starting from this perspective, we now show the interconnections between distinct policies and the ways in which they jointly structure the patterns of in-work poverty. Taking into account part of the criticism of Esping-Andersen's 'Three worlds of welfare capitalism' (see, for example, Bonoli, 1997; Ferrera, 1996; Leibfried, 1992), we have specified four different types of welfare state regimes. Along with a discussion of the general characteristics of the different welfare regimes, we present empirical information on institutional differences in order to stress the variation between the clusters despite gradual variation within them (Tables 1.1 and 1.2). The data we have used in this section come from various sources (see remarks in tables). The analyses in the following sections are based on the last wave (2001) of the European Community Household Panel (ECHP), which contains information on individuals and households in the 15 countries that were members of the European Union (EU) prior to Eastern enlargement.[1]

Social-Democratic/Nordic Cluster

These welfare states have been shaped by strongly egalitarian aspirations. They are characterized by high degrees of both decommodification and defamilization. While the first is mirrored in a high Esping-Andersen-style decommodification index and high replacement rates, the latter is indicated by the highest level of childcare provisions and respective expenditure as well as high values in an index of family welfare policy which also considers paid parental leave schemes (Table 1.1). Income protection provisions are – since they are based on citizen rights – universal and explicitly aimed at providing a high degree of adequacy. For decades, both macroeconomic and microeconomic policies have been geared towards stimulating maximum employment participation on a basis of (gender) equality.

Table 1.1 Characteristics of welfare states and labour market institutions

Country	Benefit generosity			Family benefits and services				Labour market institutions			
	Decommodification (index)	Unempl. replacement rate (% of APW)	Spending on ALMP (% of GDP)	% children in official childcare (0–2 y.)	Spending on family cash benefits (% of GDP)	Spending on family services (% of GDP)	Index on welfare family policy	Union density (%)	Minimum wage (% of APW)	Bargaining centralization	Overall strictness of regulation (index)
Denmark	35	78.3	1.5	64	1.54	2.23	93	74	*	0.54	1.4
Finland	30	76.3	0.9	25	1.92	1.44	57	78	*	0.57	1.9
Sweden	33	79.3	1.4	65	1.63	1.68	100	78	*	0.56	1.6
Ø	33	78.0	1.3	51	1.70	1.78	83	77		0.56	1.6
Ireland	27	60.2	0.7	12	1.58	0.16	–	36	56	0.64	0.3
UK	25	57.8	0.3	26	1.73	0.49	27	31	42	0.13	0.3
Ø	26	59.0	0.5	19	1.65	0.32	27	33		0.39	0.3
Austria	29	69.3	0.5	13	1.92	1.11	–	36	*	0.71	1.5
Belgium	31	66.2	1.3	30	2.06	0.16	51	56	49	0.61	2.6
France	27	72.8	1.3	30	1.46	1.23	50	10	61	0.17	3.6
Germany	31	73.5	1.1	9	1.93	0.80	20	24	*	0.47	2.3
Luxembourg	–	81.6	0.1	–	2.40	0.41	31	33	49	0.33	–
Netherlands	34	77.5	1.5	17	0.81	0.40	27	23	47	0.58	1.2
Ø	30	73.5	1.0	20	1.76	0.68	36	30		0.48	2.2

Greece	–	29.7	0.2	3	1.18	0.73	–	25	51	0.39	4.8
Italy	27	27.6	0.5	6	0.58	0.30	41	35	*	0.34	3.6
Portugal	–	65.6	0.6	22	0.65	0.33	–	23	38	0.30	3.0
Spain	–	58.1	0.8	5	0.29	0.11	44	14	32	0.38	3.3
Ø	27	45.2	0.5	9	0.68	0.37	43	24		0.35	3.7
R^2 (Regime)	0.60	0.67	0.39	0.65	0.61	0.73	0.73	0.80	0.35	0.19	0.75

Note: Year of measurement (by column): 2001 (1, 2, 3, 8), 2000 (9), ~2000 (4, 7), 2003 (10), late 1990s (11). * No legal minimum wage.

Source (by column): Scruggs, 2005 (1), OECD, 2004a (2), OECD Social Expenditure Database (3, 5, 6), Immervoll and Barber, 2005 (4), Mandel and Semyonov, 2003 (7), OECD Labour Force Surveys (8, 9), Visser, 2004 (10), OECD, 2004b (11).

The main institutional features include co-ordinated wage-setting mechanisms and institutions ensuring comparatively compressed wage structures and high minimum wage protection. The high unionization rates testify to the degree of corporatism in the Nordic labour markets. Compensating for the possibly negative effects of this on employment are extensive public or subsidized employment opportunities, as well as active labour market programmes. Extensive childcare and career interruption provisions facilitate high levels of labour market participation across the board. Minimum income protection levels are high and citizenship based.

Taking all of these factors into account, we can expect to find a comparatively low incidence of in-work poverty in these countries. To the extent that it exists, it will mostly affect single-earner households in the context of almost generalized double earnership and no preferential tax/benefit treatment for single-earner households. One would also expect more significant poverty in work among single young adults, since they tend to become economically self-reliant at a relatively early age and are culturally expected to do so.

Liberal/Anglo-Saxon Cluster

In many ways the mirror image of the Social Democratic regime, this is the type of regime with the least egalitarian or decommodifying ambitions. Here, a non-interventionist approach is taken to the labour market and the economy as a whole, and the emphasis is on economic self-reliance – including through private social insurance in case of work incapacity. Gender equality is ensured through legislation, but the state takes no role in facilitating equal participation through providing childcare and so on. Social protection is citizen based but means tested and aimed at minimum income protection only. The indicators on decommodification and replacement rates certainly support this view (Table 1.1), although the differences within Europe are not that pronounced as in comparisons which include the USA.

The main institutional features of this regime type include highly decentralized wage-bargaining systems and comparatively low minimum wages. However, given the degree of bargaining centralization in Ireland – which has increased significantly in recent years – this is now true only for the UK. Nevertheless, indices of labour market regulation consistently suggest that the Anglo-Saxon labour markets are among the least regulated. Indices of family policy as well as spending figures suggest that the state plays a minimal role. Spending on active labour market policies is also comparatively low. Minimum income protection systems are residual and build heavily on means-tested benefits aimed at helping the poorest. At the same

Table 1.2 In-work benefit schemes

Country	Benefit scheme	Type	Maximum benefit (as % of APW)
Finland	Income tax allowance	Income tax allowance	1.6% (tax savings)
Netherlands	Combination tax credit	Tax credit	0.62%
Ireland	Family income supplement	Benefit	32.47% (19 hours at minimum wage)
UK	Working families tax credit	Non-wastable tax credit	29.69–35.09% (depending on working time)
Belgium	[Crédit d'impôt, 2002–2005]		
France	Prime pour l'emploi	Non-wastable tax credit	2.16–2.82% (depending on household-type)

Source: OECD, 2005: 141ff.

time, the Anglo-Saxon countries have gone the furthest in implementing in-work benefits (tax credits in particular) aimed at households with low earnings – specifically single-parent households. As Table 1.2 makes clear, this is in fact a distinctive feature of the UK and Ireland. Although in-work benefits are broadly discussed as a means of combating poverty in other countries too, most of these measures have not gone past the experimental stage in those countries, or are at rather a small-scale level.

The Anglo-Saxon countries are widely thought to have the highest overall in-work poverty rates simply because low-wage work is more prevalent there and benefit dependency is generally a less attractive option. The idea here is that because income protection levels are low, people who might otherwise choose to remain dependent on income replacement benefits are pushed into the labour market and into low-paid jobs. However, it is difficult to hypothesize a priori about what the actual impact of the institutional setting is on levels of in-work poverty. This is especially true because of the potentially conflicting impact on multi-earnership – which tends to mitigate the impact of low wages on in-work poverty. On the one hand, since the product and labour markets are not heavily regulated, and minimum wages and non-wage costs are low, we can expect a stronger demand for less-skilled labour and hence more employment opportunities for the less skilled, particularly for less-skilled women. On the other hand, the fact that the state does not play an active role in ensuring that workers are able to combine work and care responsibilities may prevent people – particularly women – from taking full advantage of the opportunities available on the labour market and hence realizing their full earnings capacity. In addition, since benefits are means tested, work disincentive effects tend to be more severe for households where both partners have a low earnings capacity.

Conservative/Northern Continental Cluster

This is arguably the most hybrid cluster. Generally speaking, Continental European welfare states exhibit both considerable levels of decommodification and – although less so – defamilization. But there tends to be considerable internal variation. Income maintenance is comparatively generous, but it is strongly tied to labour market status and even occupational category. Income protection systems are not ungenerous, but they tend to be fragmented. Defamilization is more limited than in Scandinavia, with a continuing but weakening division between breadwinner and caretaker roles. Some countries can be said to be pluralist in nature in that a clear breadwinner bias in taxation and social security is accompanied by extensive spending on family policies and childcare provisions (this is particularly true for France and Belgium, see Table 1.1).

The main institutional features are regulated labour markets (especially for full-time core workers), although there are less regulated labour market segments mainly occupied by young people, part-time workers, migrants, and so on. Collective wage bargaining takes place in a multi-tiered system where the industry level tends to be the most important one. This results in a fairly high degree of wage compression and a comparatively low incidence of low-paid work – although this does exist, mainly in less regulated, that is, peripheral, labour market segments. Social security rights are earnings/contributions related and hence, benefits are generous for those who occupy a strong labour market position. There is universally accessible but generally meagre social assistance, which acts as a safety net of final resort. Social security systems generally contain important derived rights for non-employed spouses, and taxation systems in some countries award a breadwinner premium (Dingeldey, 2001). At the same time, a number of the Continental countries devote considerable resources to family care provisions and active labour market measures.

What can we expect here in terms of the incidence and structure of in-work poverty? A classic argument by Esping-Andersen (1996) is that, in response to the economic crisis of the early 1970s, the post-industrial transition and the secular rise in female labour participation, the Continental European countries have, by and large, mistakenly opted first and foremost to preserve the privileged position of the male breadwinner in the labour market/social security nexus – that is, the breadwinner model. This was achieved in major part through a massive expansion of early retirement in order to absorb the excess labour supply created by the economic crisis and the post-industrial transition. The aim was to avoid mass breadwinner unemployment and hence to safeguard the breadwinner model – that is, high (minimum) wages, strong employment protection and labour market regulation (for example, limits on temporary and part-time employment) and extensive social security rights, primary as well as derived.

This route, Esping-Andersen argues, has been to the detriment of the employment and hence of the (relative) living standard of less-skilled women and the households in which they live. This group – unlike their more skilled counterparts – has been most negatively affected by the preservation of high minimum wages, job protection rules and so on. Moreover, the high cost of mass early retirement has led to the cost of labour having become excessively high, hampering job creation in services.

Hence, we can predict significant in-work poverty levels, especially among households that have to make ends meet on one wage in an era in which the average living standard – and hence the relative poverty threshold – is set by the double-earner household. The latter disproportionately consist of couples where the partners have a relatively high level of educational attainment and hence of earnings. Add to this the reverse effect of educational homogamy as far as the less-skilled are concerned – that is, the accumulated disadvantage of having a higher risk of non-employment as well as a low-earning partner. Because of the insider–outsider characteristics of Continental European countries, we can also expect significant in-work poverty among young people and other non-core workers.

Familialist/Southern Continental Cluster

The Southern cluster is often seen as a variant of the continental regime, although various authors have rather convincingly argued that this is not the case (Bonoli, 1997; Ferrera, 1996; Flaquer, 2000; Leibfried, 1992; Trifiletti, 1999). First, whereas many of the Northern Continental countries exhibit at least mildly egalitarian/decommodifying tendencies, the Southern countries are characterized by the almost complete absence of such aspirations. On the contrary, many institutional features seem to have been put into place in order to maintain certain inequalities – such as those that prevail between core, permanent (male) employees and others, such as temporary or part-time workers. Most importantly, whereas all the other 'conservative' European welfare states are committed to providing at least some form of universally accessible minimum protection, this is not the case in the Southern countries.

Second, as is said to be the case for the conservative countries in the North, women are treated principally as mothers and caretakers, but the ambiguity/pluralism that we find nowadays in the Northern countries (breadwinner bias in social security/taxation coexisting with publicly financed care provisions, career interruption schemes, and so on) does not seem to exist in the Southern countries. Whereas, in the Northern countries, it is recognized that the state has at least some substantial role to play in the conflict women face in combining care and work, this seems not to be the case in the Southern European countries. Family and intergenerational solidarity continue to play a far stronger role, not only in accommodating work–care conflicts but also in providing protection against social risks. The sustained role of family solidarity – which appears to be at a markedly different level than elsewhere on the Continent – is implicitly evident from the underdevelopment of state provisions, and more explicitly so from the family solidarity obligations laid down in civil law (Millar and Warman, 1996).

Much of this is clearly evident from the indicators presented here (Table 1.1). Parts of the labour market are strongly regulated (this can clearly be seen from indicators on dismissal protection in particular), but at the same time, there is a lack of minimum protection provisions that benefit all workers. Income protection is equally fragmented, catering well for particular segments, while not providing at all for others. State-funded childcare facilities are underdeveloped, and spending on active labour market policies is comparatively low.

We expect a comparatively high incidence of in-work poverty, especially related to single earnership, owing to the evident difficulties women face in (first) gaining access to the male-biased labour market, and (second) combining work and care. On the other hand, family solidarity mechanisms may provide more of a buffer than they would elsewhere. Also, because benefits are not means tested and are often strictly categorical (that is, independent of the labour market status of other family members), families are sometimes able to achieve what Trifiletti (1999: 52) calls a 'synthesis of breadcrumbs'. In other words, we can expect quite significant poverty in work, but perhaps not as significant as the levels of female and youth non-employment might lead us to imagine.

DIFFERENCES IN LABOUR MARKETS AND HOUSEHOLD STRUCTURES

In the above section, we hypothesized differences between welfare regimes in the incidence and structure of in-work-poverty. These considerations were based on expectations about the influence of wage-setting mechanisms and decommodification on the distribution of income, the extent of low-wage work and employment chances – in particular, the employment chances of low-skilled workers. Furthermore, we expected the degree of defamilization to have an influence on the styles of family living and patterns of female employment. In this section we show that there are, in fact, respective differences in the structures of the working population and the households they live in. In addition, we will present information on some of the usual suspects in poverty research: economic development and unemployment.

Table 1.3 shows that these considerations about the influence of institutional factors translate quite well into observed differences between countries. We find strong variation by welfare regime type in terms of average household sizes and patterns of female employment. Households tend to be small in Social Democratic and large in Southern European countries (see also Iacovou, 2004).[2] Ireland fits better into the Southern cluster. It is worth noting, however, that large household sizes in Ireland are partly due to a larger number of children, while household sizes in Southern Europe are mainly driven by a larger number of adults. The argument about the pooling of incomes will therefore apply more to the Southern countries, while household size in Ireland is more an issue of greater needs.

Differences in female employment have been the subject of many comparative studies (see, for example, Bettio et al., 2000). Our results are mostly in line with previous research. Female employment rates differ significantly between Nordic and Southern countries. As expected, dual earnership is more widespread in the Nordic countries than elsewhere: 76 per cent of all working-age persons in couple households have working partners. In the South, the share of dual earners is less than 48 per cent; the Anglo-Saxon cluster and Continental Europe lie in between. Remarkably, dual earnership is no more widespread in the Anglo-Saxon cluster than on the Continent. However, this result becomes less clear-cut when we take into account the variations within the Conservative cluster. Furthermore, Ireland clearly differs from the UK and is often discussed as a hybrid case which shares characteristics of the Southern cluster (see, for example, Berthoud and Iacovou, 2004). However, the South stands out significantly in terms of the enduring dominance of single earnership.

In short, the cluster hypotheses are only partially confirmed, in the sense that female employment and dual earnership are clearly most widespread in the North and least prominent in the South. With respect to the Anglo-Saxon cluster, we hypothesized that while the more deregulated nature of the Anglo-Saxon labour market may entail more job opportunities for less-skilled women there, the relative absence of state involvement in childcare

Table 1.3 Household characteristics, employment and macroeconomic conditions

Country	Households and employment				Economic profile					Non-standard employment		
	Household size*	Female employment rate	Employment gap (male rate–female rate)	Share of persons in dual-earner couples	GDP per capita (PPP 2000)	Unemployment rate	Employment by sector I	Employment by sector II	Employment by sector III	Low-wage work	Part-time work	Self-employment
	Average	%	Diff.	%	$	%	%	%	%	%	%	%
Denmark	2.8	71.4	8.9	80.3	28 907	4.5	3.6	26.0	70.3	10.4	11.6	6.4
Finland	2.7	65.4	4.6	69.7	26 010	9.1	5.0	28.9	66.0	10.6	8.5	12.4
Sweden	2.4	73.5	3.5	77.2	27 386	4.9	2.1	25.4	72.5	–	9.0	10.5
Ø	2.6	70.1	5.6	75.7	27 434	6.2	3.6	26.8	69.6	10.5	9.7	9.8
Ireland	3.8	54.0	22.0	46.1	30 101	4.0	6.8	29.5	63.8	18.5	21.6	13.8
UK	2.8	66.0	13.1	71.1	26 051	5.0	1.2	23.3	75.5	20.4	20.6	11.5
Ø	3.3	60.0	17.5	58.6	28 076	4.5	4.0	26.4	69.6	19.5	21.1	12.6
Austria	3.1	59.8	16.4	58.7	28 832	3.6	8.6	30.1	61.3	9.7	12.9	14.2
Belgium	3.1	50.7	17.9	68.7	26 832	6.6	2.1	25.1	72.8	13.3	14.4	12.7
Germany	2.8	58.7	14.1	67.1	25 822	7.4	2.3	36.2	61.5	19.4	16.4	10.1
France	3.0	55.2	13.9	62.2	26 229	8.4	3.4	26.3	70.3	15.3	9.1	8.7
Luxembourg	2.8	50.8	24.0	49.4	51 663	2.1	1.6	20.3	78.1	–	10.3	7.0
Netherlands	2.6	63.9	17.6	69.9	28 662	2.2	2.5	18.4	79.0	20.4	30.1	6.4
Ø	2.9	56.5	17.3	62.7	31 340	5.1	3.4	26.1	70.5	15.6	15.6	9.9

Greece	3.4	41.2	29.8	43.5	17426	10.8	13.4	22.6	64.1	17.6	8.2	37.1
Italy	3.4	41.1	27.6	44.7	26319	9.1	6.0	29.0	65.0	11.1	11.2	25.5
Portugal	3.8	61.0	15.5	67.3	18617	4.0	10.4	36.4	53.2	11.5	6.7	23.5
Spain	3.7	43.8	30.1	35.0	21576	10.3	8.9	29.4	61.7	18.3	10.2	20.1
Ø	3.6	46.8	25.7	47.6	20984	8.6	9.7	29.3	61.0	14.6	9.1	26.6
R^2 (Regime)	0.67	0.65	0.72	0.53	0.31	0.31	0.57	0.08	0.34	0.40	0.46	0.77

Note: * Households with at least one employed person.

Source (by column): ECHP 2001 [weighted] (1, 4, 7–12), OECD LFS 2001 (2, 3, 5, 6).

may prevent many women from taking advantage of those opportunities. For the Continental European cluster, we formulated a more or less inverse hypothesis. We find support for this in the case of the UK and some of the countries in the Continental cluster. Hence, the total difference between the two is not as pronounced as we would have expected.

There is also notable variation in the level of total employment. Compare, for instance, the levels of female employment in Austria and Belgium (59.8 and 50.7 per cent, respectively) or the UK and France (66.0 and 55.2 per cent, respectively). Despite these differences, the employment gap between men and women is similar in each of the two examples (Austria and Belgium: 16.4 and 17.9 per cent, UK and France: 13.1 and 13.9 per cent). Hence, the variation in the female employment rate is not a result of larger gaps between male and female employment. Rather, they simply mirror differences in the level of employment at large. When we look at who is at risk of in-work poverty, we have to take into account that there are differences in the size and composition of the working population.

In this context, it is intriguing to look at the level of low-wage work. Denmark combines the highest level of employment with the second-lowest level of low-wage work (there are no figures on low-wage work in Sweden). In the UK, which also has a rather high level of employment, more than one-fifth of all workers are at risk of low wages. A high level of decommodification and centralized bargaining lowers the risk of low-wage work in Denmark, while workers in the UK are subject to market forces. However, apart from this clear contrast between the UK and Denmark, no overall pattern emerges from the figures. There is noticeable variation within the Conservative cluster and the Southern cluster. Neither a clear influence of employment levels nor of minimum wage levels or bargaining mechanisms can be detected from these figures.

There is a more obvious relationship between low-wage work and part-time work. The share of part-time work parallels the share of low-wage work in a number of countries. The UK and Ireland and some of the Conservative countries (Germany, the Netherlands) rank highest in both characteristics. These countries exhibit a low degree of defamilization, which results in a high risk of women being in a marginalized labour-market position as part-time, low-wage workers. However, high low-wage rates in some countries of the Southern cluster indicate that other factors also influence the distribution of wages.

The self-employment rate shows large variation by welfare regime. The high incidence of self-employment in Southern European countries has been discussed as an expression of familialism (Flaquer, 2000). Particularly in Greece – and to a lesser extent in the other Southern European countries – a relevant share of all workers are employed by their families, which implies that market employment has not fully replaced the family as an economic basis. This is most evident in agriculture, but the situation also applies to other typically self-employed sectors such as hotels, restaurants and retail trade. Table 1.3 indicates higher levels of agricultural employment in all the Southern European countries, but also in Ireland and Austria. At the same time, these are the countries with the highest self-employment rates. We cannot, however, consider the relationship between self-employment and employment in specific service industries on the basis of a threefold industry classification. The differences in the incidence of self-employment are expected to be crucial to explaining the differences in in-work poverty: most poverty studies show that the self-employed, on average, are at higher risk of being poor.

INCIDENCE AND STRUCTURE OF IN-WORK POVERTY

Having observed differences in the incidence of low-wage work and self-employment, in female employment and in patterns of family living, we will now look at the respective variations in in-work poverty by welfare regime. The working poor are defined as working persons living in poor households. The definition of working is based on International Labour Organization (ILO) standards (working at least one hour per week). A person is considered to be poor when his or her equivalized (using the modified OECD-scale) net household income is below 60 per cent of the median. Table 1.4 contains working poor rates as well as rates by gender, age and education. As a reference point, we have also reported total poverty rates. Contrary to our expectations, the type of welfare regime explains variation in in-work poverty to a lesser degree than variations in poverty at large. However, as we expected, in-work poverty in the countries of the Social-Democratic cluster tends to be low, while the Southern cluster is characterized by high poverty rates. At the same time, variation within the Conservative regimes is large. In-work poverty rates in the Liberal countries are surprisingly low.[3]

Despite the fact that the latter results do not support all our hypotheses on between-cluster variation, the working poor rates very clearly support the thesis which was the starting point for this chapter – namely, that the 'working poor' are far from an Anglo-Saxon phenomenon alone. In fact, the Anglo-Saxon cluster has a working poor rate that is only slightly higher than the Nordic cluster and lower than the Continental European or the Southern European cluster! This also appears to be very much consistent with our idea that 'poverty in work' is not simply a problem which reflects

Table 1.4 Poverty and in-work poverty rate by socio-demographic characteristics (%)

Country	Total poor	Working poor	Gender		Age (in years)			Education (ISCED)		
			Male	Female	18–29	30–49	50–64	0–2	3	5–7
Denmark	13.4	5.0	3.4	4.4	12.8	2.5	1.2	3.9	4.1	3.5
Finland	14.2	7.1	5.4	6.6	11.5	4.5	6.0	8.3	7.6	2.7
Sweden	10.5	6.5	7.1	5.9	14.1	6.0	3.0	6.6	6.1	6.9
Ø	12.7	6.2	5.3	5.6	12.8	4.4	3.4	6.2	5.9	4.4
Ireland	18.4	7.0	8.8	5.1	3.4	9.9	6.4	11.5	5.8	3.1
UK	15.9	6.6	5.9	7.3	8.3	5.9	6.7	10.7	6.8	3.8
Ø	17.1	6.8	7.3	6.2	5.9	7.9	6.6	11.1	6.3	3.4
Austria	9.2	4.3	5.6	6.0	3.8	6.4	6.1	8.0	5.2	7.0
Belgium	11.9	5.7	3.7	4.3	4.7	4.0	3.4	5.9	5.4	2.1
Germany	10.5	6.8	4.0	5.5	10.0	3.8	3.2	9.1	4.6	2.1
France	17.4	8.9	8.8	6.8	8.7	7.7	8.1	13.7	7.5	3.2
Luxembourg	12.7	9.6	8.1	7.8	8.4	9.1	3.9	16.3	5.4	0.9
Netherlands	13.8	10.5	8.1	7.9	15.1	6.4	4.2	12.3	6.1	3.8
Ø	12.6	7.6	6.4	6.4	8.5	6.2	4.8	10.9	5.7	3.2
Greece	19.1	10.9	12.6	11.2	10.1	10.3	17.4	21.8	8.8	1.8
Italy	17.8	9.7	12.9	6.3	7.6	10.5	12.1	17.2	5.4	4.6
Portugal	17.7	8.9	12.7	10.0	8.4	12.2	13.6	15.0	2.9	1.1
Spain	17.4	8.3	10.6	8.2	5.9	10.8	11.1	16.2	5.9	2.6
Ø	18.0	9.4	12.2	8.9	8.0	11.0	13.5	17.5	5.8	2.5
R^2 (Regime)	0.64	0.37	0.73	0.46	0.39	0.70	0.82	0.67	0.02	0.13

Source: ECHP 2001 (weighted).

the size of the low-wage labour market, as is so often suggested or assumed. Rather, it is a problem that is associated with a multiplicity of institutional factors that influence household's capacity for optimal combined income packaging in an era in which multiple household incomes are often required to attain a decent standard of living. We hypothesized that these institutional factors are most favourably aligned in the Nordic countries and least favourably in the South. We assumed the institutional constellations in the Anglo-Saxon and Continental European countries to have mixed and sometimes contradictory effects. This, too, is borne out by our findings.

We can also look at the relevance of in-work poverty from a different angle, namely, are the poor likely to work or not? It is quite remarkable – and this is totally contrary to the perception of poverty in work being a typically Anglo-Saxon problem – that the 'working poor' make up a smaller share of the poor among the working-age population in the Anglo-Saxon cluster than in the rest of Europe, including the Nordic cluster (Table 1.5). In fact, close to half of the working-age poor in the Continental European cluster have a job themselves, and nearly three-quarters live in a household with at least one earner. Part of these differences can be explained by the variations in the poverty rates of the non-working population, which are also reflected in the poverty rates at large in Table 1.4. Given the low standard of social protection in the Anglo-Saxon countries, there is a much higher share of non-working poor.

In addition to variation at large, there is also variation in the specific poverty risks by gender, age and education. In some countries (Southern Europe, Ireland, but also France) men are at a higher risk of being poor than women; we find the opposite result in most other countries. This could be interpreted as a result of the role of female employment. The chance of being protected as second earners within the family context is likely to be higher in familialist countries. There are also clear differences in poverty risks by age which support this interpretation. In Social Democratic countries, mostly young people are at risk of being poor, while in the Southern European countries we find a negative age gradient. Early self-reliance puts Northern youngsters at risk of being poor, while their Southern counterparts are likely to be protected within the family context. Self-reliance is not an option since they have limited access to the labour market and a lack of claims in their own right owing to the fragmented social security system. At the same time, this increases the burden of the parents' generation, which results in an increased poverty risk among older age groups. Yet another pattern can be observed in the UK, which fits the Liberal ideal type best. Differences in in-work poverty by age are not pronounced. Prime age workers are also at a high poverty risk. One could argue that this is the

Table 1.5 Share of working persons among the poor (%)

Country	Working	Living in working households*	Difference
Denmark	48.6	62.2	13.6
Finland	36.6	62.3	25.7
Sweden	–	–	–
Ø	42.6	62.3	19.7
Ireland	30.4	56.0	25.6
UK	42.6	58.7	16.1
Ø	36.5	57.4	20.9
Austria	47.1	70.4	23.3
Belgium	38.0	61.3	23.3
Germany	37.1	71.9	34.8
France	65.6	79.8	14.2
Luxembourg	48.2	68.7	20.5
Netherlands	60.3	86.5	26.2
Ø	49.4	73.1	23.7
Greece	32.2	74.6	42.4
Italy	42.4	76.9	34.5
Portugal	33.2	67.2	34.0
Spain	51.6	83.3	31.7
Ø	39.9	75.5	35.7
R^2 (Regime)	0.25	0.54	0.56

Note: * Household with at least one worker.

Source: ECHP 2001 (weighted), basis: poor persons of working age.

result of a lack of protection for older workers. In contrast to the differences observed concerning the influence of age, there is a clear effect of higher education as a protection against poverty in all countries.

We have extensively discussed the differences in employment patterns and how these differences are likely to influence the likelihood of in-work poverty. Poverty rates for single-earner couples are significant everywhere in Europe, but are particularly high for the Continental and Southern clusters – which is consistent with our hypothesis (Table 1.6). Poverty at working age is clustered to a large extent among such single-earner couples – especially, again, in the Continental and Southern clusters. Despite the fact that single earnership is no less prevalent in the Anglo-Saxon cluster than it is on the Continent, poverty in work is somewhat less concentrated among single-earner couples there.

Table 1.6 Poverty rates and distribution of working poor by household type

Country	Poverty rates (%)					Distribution (share in %)				
	Single	Single parent	Single earner	Double earner	Others	Single	Single parent	Single earner	Double earner	Others
Denmark	15.8	12.4	10.7	1.9	11.1	29.9	7.0	27.0	28.5	7.7
Finland	9.6	9.8	6.8	4.0	21.6	24.7	5.8	15.8	30.4	23.3
Ø	12.7	11.1	8.8	3.0	16.4	27.3	6.4	21.4	29.5	15.5
Ireland	10.7	8.5	7.8	2.5	11.2	9.4	14.2	33.0	12.8	30.7
UK	11.5	11.0	11.3	3.7	7.6	20.3	13.9	26.3	32.0	7.6
Ø	11.1	9.8	9.6	3.1	9.4	14.9	14.1	29.7	22.4	19.2
Austria	5.4	8.3	5.7	2.4	5.1	14.6	10.8	27.2	23.2	24.2
Belgium	3.1	16.2	16.5	0.9	11.7	5.0	17.7	56.4	10.8	10.1
France	3.0	20.3	18.9	4.2	16.7	3.3	15.4	37.5	27.4	16.4
Germany	6.3	12.2	9.1	2.7	11.9	19.1	8.7	30.6	21.5	20.0
Luxembourg	8.1	22.8	16.8	7.9	27.6	12.5	11.5	24.1	48.3	3.6
Netherlands	7.2	12.7	13.1	5.1	14.9	9.5	10.9	38.5	22.8	18.4
Ø	5.5	15.4	13.4	3.9	14.7	10.7	12.5	35.7	25.7	15.5
Greece	4.2	6.3	13.2	6.6	20.0	1.5	4.2	35.5	24.4	34.3
Italy	2.9	10.6	19.2	2.3	12.1	1.7	9.0	57.6	9.1	22.7
Portugal	8.5	10.2	14.4	6.5	10.0	1.5	7.9	26.5	36.4	27.6
Spain	5.7	8.1	11.7	3.9	9.3	3.7	7.8	46.1	12.9	29.6
Ø	5.3	8.8	14.6	4.8	12.9	2.1	7.2	41.4	20.7	28.6
R^2 (Regime)	0.67	0.43	0.28	0.12	0.13	0.78	0.64	0.31	0.08	0.38

Source: ECHP 2001 (weighted).

Poverty rates for double-earner households (where double earnership is defined in a very broad sense; minimal employment by both partners qualifies as double earnership) are generally very low, confirming the view that double earnership, however minimal, offers in most cases very good protection against poverty. This is also the case in the Anglo-Saxon cluster, where low-paid and precarious work is more prevalent. To the extent that poverty prevails among double earners, it is mostly a problem when there are dependent children. However, because double-earner households make up such a significant share of the working-age population nowadays, poverty at working age is nevertheless concentrated to a significant extent among such households. The degree of cross-country variation in this respect is remarkably limited.

In Table 1.7, we look at poverty risks by employment patterns in a compressed form. We have differentiated between three different types of households that workers live in. We call the first 'fully-employed households' – that is, households in which all working-age members are working full-time. These could be single households but may also be dual-earner households or other households containing more than one adult. The second type consists of 'partially-employed households' – that is, households in which all the working-age members are employed, but not necessarily full-time. These households could be singles working part-time, but also dual-earner households where one partner works part-time. 'Non-fully-employed households' make up the third type. These are households in which not all the working-age members are working. From this perspective, we can clearly differentiate between what we might call underemployment[4] and insufficient earnings despite full employment as causes for in-work poverty. Although the typology covers up differences in detail, we can expect to find patterns which relate to the differences in the institutional framework which we have discussed so far.

When we compare the poverty risk by household type and the distribution of households, it becomes clear that a larger variation between countries can be observed in the latter. With few exceptions, all countries exhibit the same, non-surprising pattern of poverty rates, with fully employed households facing the lowest poverty risk and non-fully employed the highest. However, clear patterns related to welfare regime type emerge in the distribution of households. The large majority of the working poor in the Southern European countries and Ireland live in non-fully employed households (with the exception of Portugal). We could also count some Conservative countries with low employment rates (France, Belgium) among this group. In contrast, this share is fairly low in Denmark and the UK. These differences are mirrored by a respectively high or low share of working poor in fully employed households. Some of the results give us

Table 1.7 Poverty rates and distribution of working poor by household employment pattern

Country	Poverty rates (%)			Distribution (share in %)		
	Full-time	Full-time/ part-time	Not all members employed	Full-time	Full-time/ part-time	Not all members employed
Denmark	3.2	8.5	8.5	42.8	30.3	27.0
Finland	3.0	11.8	15.1	27.5	18.1	54.4
Sweden	–	–	–	–	–	–
Ø	3.1	10.2	11.8	35.2	24.2	40.7
Ireland	2.5	5.1	10.3	9.0	18.7	72.3
UK	4.0	7.7	12.2	31.1	37.4	31.5
Ø	3.3	6.4	11.3	20.1	28.1	51.9
Austria	3.6	3.9	5.7	39.0	19.2	41.8
Belgium	2.2	3.4	12.2	19.0	11.7	69.4
France	3.6	5.8	15.8	21.9	7.5	70.5
Germany	4.8	4.3	11.5	35.0	13.8	51.3
Luxembourg	4.4	11.1	14.8	24.1	21.1	54.8
Netherlands	6.0	11.3	17.5	21.8	47.9	30.3
Ø	4.1	6.6	12.9	26.8	20.2	53.0
Greece	6.1	10.8	13.7	20.6	8.5	70.9
Italy	3.4	2.0	14.9	12.5	2.3	85.2
Portugal	7.0	9.6	10.8	37.7	9.5	52.8
Spain	1.9	6.5	11.5	7.4	7.5	85.1
Ø	4.6	7.2	12.7	19.6	7.0	73.5
R^2 (Regime)	0.14	0.15	0.04	0.24	0.38	0.36

Source: ECHP 2001 (weighted).

reason to speculate about other, country-specific causes of in-work poverty. The high share of workers in fully employed households in Germany could be due to the lower level of wages in Eastern Germany. The same high share in Austria could be caused by the comparably large agricultural sector. As we have already mentioned, this is not the place to venture into such detailed explanations. We have shown, however, that the broad perspective of welfare regimes also offers helpful insights into the differences in the incidence – in particularly in the structure – of in-work poverty.

CONCLUSION

The purpose of this chapter has been to highlight the idea that 'poverty in work' comes in many different guises across advanced welfare states. A core claim is that 'poverty in work' is not simply a problem that reflects the size of the low-wage labour market, as is so often suggested or assumed. Rather, it is a problem that is associated with a multiplicity of institutional factors which influence a household's capacity for optimal combined income packaging in an era in which multiple household incomes are often required to attain a decent standard of living.

In a first step, we discussed why we expected to find differences in the extent and structure of in-work poverty. We argued that welfare state characteristics and labour market institutions not only have an impact on the level of wages and transfers, but also on the employment chances of individuals. The first factor determines the level of household income and thus the risk of being poor. The latter variable is crucial since it determines which persons are at risk for in-work poverty. Furthermore, we argued that the degree of defamilization has an impact on the composition of and employment patterns within households, which define the relationship between needs and resources. In a second step, we developed hypotheses regarding variations in in-work poverty by welfare regimes. The perspective of welfare regimes stresses the fact that welfare states are more or less coherent clusters of institutional arrangements which embody distinct values.

On the basis of (mainly) quantitative indicators, we provided evidence that the assumption of country clusters is also appropriate for categorizing institutional settings which we regard as relevant for the working poor. We hypothesized that institutional factors which determine a household's capacity for optimal household income packaging are most favourably aligned in the Nordic countries and least favourably so in the South. We expected the institutional constellations in the Anglo-Saxon and Continental European countries to have mixed and sometimes internally contradictory effects.

Despite the fact that our results do not support all our hypotheses on between-cluster variation, the working poor rates stress that the 'working poor' are far from an Anglo-Saxon phenomenon alone. In fact, we find that the Anglo-Saxon cluster has a working poor rate which is only slightly higher than that of the Nordic cluster and *lower* than that in the Continental European or the Southern European cluster. However, there are marked cross-cluster and cross-country differences in the composition of the working-age population. While a number of these are consistent with the hypotheses we have formulated, many remain to be better understood.

NOTES

1. Basically, the ECHP is an input-harmonized data source. However, the data from Sweden in particular differs in its basic setup as well as in the number and shape of its variables. Therefore, in some analyses, Sweden is omitted.
2. The differences in average household size reflect the high share of single adult households in the North, especially in Sweden (where this is in part a statistical artefact, since single youngsters above a certain age are assumed to represent independent households). Still, the gap between the South and the rest of Europe is striking: single adult households are a significantly smaller group in the South.
3. Various explanations could account for this result. Despite a low degree of defamilization, female employment rates in the UK are high, which increases the chances of multi-earnership. Specific benefit systems or tax credits for the working poor only exist at a relevant scale in the UK and Ireland (see Table 1.2). Ireland has experienced a phase of exceptional economic growth throughout the past ten years. However, it is beyond the scope of this chapter to regard such influences at the national level in detail. This section is meant to provide a provisional test of the hypothesis that variation in in-work poverty is related to variation between welfare regimes.
4. This term could imply that all persons of working age are expected to work. This is not, in fact, the case and it is not the conclusion which should be drawn from this table. However, it is intended to show that employment patterns differ strongly by welfare regime. On the one hand, this has to do with labour market conditions; on the other, with differences in the social expectations towards employment. For a discussion of groups who are not expected to work, see, for example, Spicker (1993: 111ff).

REFERENCES

Arts, W. and J. Gelissen (2002), 'Three worlds of welfare capitalism or more? A state-of-the-art report', *Journal of European Social Policy*, **12** (2), 137–58.

Atkinson, A.B., L. Rainwater and T.M. Smeeding (1995), *Income Distribution in OECD Countries. Evidence from the Luxembourg Income Study (LIS)*, Paris: OECD.

Berthoud, R. and M. Iacovou (2004), 'Introduction', in R. Berthoud and M. Iacovou (eds), *Social Europe. Living Standards and Welfare States*, Cheltenham: Edward Elgar, pp. 1–20.

Bertola, G., F.D. Blau and L.M. Kahn (2002), *Labor Market Institutions and Demographic Employment Patterns*, Working Paper 9043, Cambridge: National Bureau of Economic Research.

Bettio, F., J. Rubery and M. Smith (2000), 'Gender, flexibility, and new employment relations in the European Union', in M. Rossilli (ed.), *Gender policies in the European Union*, New York: Lang, pp. 123–58.

Blau, F. and L. Kahn (1996), 'International differences in male wage inequality: institutions versus market forces', *Journal of Political Economy*, **104**, 791–837.

Bonoli, G. (1997), 'Classifying welfare states: a two-dimensional approach', *Journal of Social Policy*, **26** (3), 351–72.

Card, D., F. Kramarz and T. Lemieux (1999), 'Changes in the relative structure of wages and employment: a comparison of the US, Canada and France', *Canadian Journal of Economics*, **32** (4), 843–77.

Dingeldey, I. (2001), 'European tax systems and their influence on family employment patterns', *Journal of Social Policy*, **30** (4), 653–72.

Esping-Andersen, G. (1990), *The Three Worlds of Welfare Capitalism*, Cambridge: Polity Press.
Esping-Andersen, G. (1996), 'Welfare states without work: the impasse of labour shedding and familialism in continental European social policy', in G. Esping-Andersen (ed.), *Welfare States in Transition; National Adaptations in Global Economies*, London: Sage, pp. 66–87.
Esping-Andersen, G. (1999), *Social Foundations of Postindustrial Economies*, Oxford: Oxford University Press.
Ferrera, M (1996), ' "The Southern Model" of welfare in social Europe', *Journal of European Social Policy*, **6** (1), 17–37.
Flaquer, L. (2000), 'Is there a Southern European model of family policy?', in A. Pfenning and T. Bahle (eds), *Families and Family Policies in Europe – Comparative Perspectives*, Frankfurt: Peter Lang, pp. 15–33.
Freeman, R. and R. Schettkat (2000a), *The Role of Wage and Skill Differences in US–German Employment Differences*, Working Paper 7474, Cambridge: National Bureau of Economic Research.
Freeman, R. and R. Schettkat (2000b), *Low Wage Services: Interpreting the US-German difference*, Working Paper 7611, Cambridge: National Bureau of Economic Research.
Gardiner, K. and J. Millar (2006), 'How low-paid employees avoid poverty: an analysis by family type and household structure', *Journal of Social Policy*, **35**, 351–69.
Gornick, J., M.K. Meyers and K.E. Ross (1997), 'Supporting the employment of mothers: policy applications across fourteen welfare states', *Journal of European Social Policy*, **7** (1), 45–70.
Iacovou, M. (2004), 'Patterns of family living', in R. Berthoud and M. Iacovou (eds), *Social Europe. Living Standards and Welfare States*, Cheltenham: Edward Elgar, pp. 21–45.
Immervoll, H. and D. Barber (2005), *Can Parents Afford to Work? Childcare Costs, Tax-Benefit Policies and Work Incentives*, OECD Social Employment and Migration Working Papers, No. 31, Paris: OECD.
Kahn, L. (2000), 'Wage inequality, collective bargaining and relative employment 1985–94: evidence from 15 OECD countries', *The Review of Economics and Statistics*, **82** (4), 564–79.
Korpi, W. (2000), 'Faces of inequality: gender, class, and patterns of inequalities in different types of welfare states', *Social Politics*, **7** (2), 127–91.
Lagarenne, C. and N. Legendre (2000), 'Les travailleurs pauvres en France: facteurs individuels et familiaux', *Économie et Statistique*, **335–5**, 3–25.
Leibfried, S. (1992), 'Towards a European welfare state? On integrating poverty regimes into the European Community', in Z. Ferge and J.E. Kolberg (eds), *Social Policy in a Changing Europe*, Frankfurt and Boulder, CO: Campus and Westview, pp. 245–79.
Lister, R. (1994), ' "She has other duties" – Women, citizenship and social security', in S. Baldwin and J. Faklingham (eds), *Social Security and Social Change. New Challenges to the Beveridge Model*, New York: Harvester Wheatsheaf, pp. 31–44.
Lucifora, C. (2000), 'Wage inequalities and low pay: the role of labour market institutions', in M. Gregory, W. Salverda and S. Bazen (eds), *Labour Market Inequalities: Problems and Policies of Low-Wage Employment in International Perspective*, Oxford: Oxford University Press, pp. 9–34.

Mandel, H. and M. Semyonov (2003), *Welfare Family Policies and Gender Earnings Equality: A Cross-national Comparative Analysis*, Luxembourg Income Study Working Paper No. 364, Luxembourg: LIS.

Marx, I. (2007), *A New Social Question? On Minimum Income Protection in the Postindustrial Era*, Amsterdam: Amsterdam University Press.

Marx, I. and G. Verbist (1998), 'Low-paid work and poverty: a cross-country perspective', in S. Bazen, M. Gregory and W. Salverda (eds), *Low-Wage Employment in Europe*, Cheltenham: Edward Elgar, pp. 63–86.

McLaughlin, E. and C. Glendinning (1994), 'Paying for care in Europe: is there a feminist approach?', in L. Hantrais and S. Mangen (eds), *Cross-National Research Papers*, Loughborough: European Research Centre, Leicestershire: University of Technology, pp. 52–69.

Millar, J. and A. Warman (1996), *Family Obligations in Europe*, London: Family Policy Studies Centre.

Moffitt, R.A. (2002), 'Welfare programs and labor supply', in A.J. Auerbach and M. Feldstein (eds), *Handbook of Public Economics*, Amsterdam: Elsevier, pp. 2393–430.

Moller, S., D. Bradley, E. Huber, F. Nielsen and J.D. Stephens (2003), 'Determinants of relative poverty in advanced capitalist democracies', *American Sociological Review*, **68** (1), 22–51.

Nickell, S and B. Bell (1995), 'The collapse in the demand for the unskilled and unemployment across the OECD', *Oxford Review of Economic Policy*, **11** (1), 40–62.

Nolan, B. (1994), 'Low pay and poverty', in B. Nolan and T. Callan (eds), *Poverty and Policy in Ireland*, Dublin: Gill and MacMillan, pp. 117–29.

Nolan, B. and I. Marx (2000), 'Low pay and household poverty', in M. Gregory, W. Salverda and S. Bazen (eds), *Labour Market Inequalities: Problems and Policies of Low-Wage Employment in International Perspective*, Oxford: Oxford University Press, pp. 100–19.

Organisation for Economic Co-operation and Development (OECD) (1996), *Employment Outlook*, Paris: OECD.

Organisation for Economic Co-operation and Development (OECD) (2004a), *Benefits and Wages. OECD Indicators*, Paris: OECD.

Organisation for Economic Co-operation and Development (OECD) (2004b), *Employment Outlook*, Paris: OECD.

Organisation for Economic Co-operation and Development (OECD) (2005), *Employment Outlook*, Paris: OECD.

Paugam, S. and H. Russell (2000), 'The effects of employment precarity and unemployment on social isolation', in D. Gallie and S. Paugam (eds), *Welfare Regimes and the Experience of Unemployment in Europe*, Oxford: Oxford University Press, pp. 243–64.

Scruggs, L. (2005), 'Welfare state entitlements data set: a comparative institutional analysis of eighteen welfare states', available at http://sp.uconn.edu/~scruggs/welproj.htm (accessed 26 April 2006).

Scruggs, L. and J. Allan (2006), 'Welfare-state decommodification in 18 OECD countries: a replication and revision', *Journal of European Social Policy*, **16** (1), 55–72.

Shipler, D.K. (2005), *The Working Poor. Invisible in America*, New York: Vintage.

Spicker, P. (1993), *Poverty and Social Security. Concepts and Principles*, London: Routledge.

Strengmann-Kuhn, W. (2003), *Armut trotz Erwerbstätigkeit. Analysen und sozialpolitische Konsequenzen*, Frankfurt and New York: Campus.
Trifiletti, R. (1999), 'Southern European welfare regimes and the worsening of the position of women', *Journal of European Social Policy*, **9** (1), 49–64.
Visser, J. (2004), 'Patterns and variations in European industrial relations', in European Commission, *Industrial Relations in Europe*, Luxembourg: Office for Official Publications of the European Communities, pp. 11–57.

2. The working poor in European welfare states: empirical evidence from a multilevel perspective

Henning Lohmann

INTRODUCTION

Recent comparative research at the European Union (EU) level shows that there is a great deal of variation in the extent of in-work poverty (Bardone and Guio, 2005). However, there is not much evidence to explain this variation. The few existing comparative studies are largely descriptive without going into the causes of the observed differences at the institutional level (see Marx and Verbist, 1998; O'Connor and Smeeding, 1995; Strengmann-Kuhn, 2003). In contrast to the research on the working poor, there is a large body of literature concerning country-specific differences in poverty in general. Many of these studies show that country-specific variations in poverty can be explained by differences in welfare state characteristics (see, for example, Brady, 2004; Gallie et al., 2000; Kenworthy, 1999; Moller, et al., 2003). In addition, studies on the incidence of low-wage work and the distribution of earnings stress the influence of labour market institutions (see, for example, Blau and Kahn, 1996; Lucifora et al., 2005; Rueda and Pontusson, 2000). However, it is important to recognize that each strand of research addresses a different concept: some studies focus on household incomes while others look at individual earnings. When the working poor are defined as workers who live in poor households, these two concepts are combined. Hence, variations in the incidence of in-work poverty cannot be explained from one perspective alone. Therefore, in this chapter, I hypothesize that welfare state measures and labour market institutions – in particular those affecting the mechanisms of wage-setting – both have an influence on in-work poverty. By using this approach, the chapter addresses the limitations of past research, namely, the disregard of institutional influences on the incidence and structure of in-work poverty.

In the following section, we discuss the respective influences in more detail and test them empirically in a comparison of 14 European countries.

Although this chapter is primarily interested in relationships at the macro level, it also considers the determinants of in-work poverty at the micro level. This multilevel perspective takes into account the way in which characteristics of the institutional framework alter individual poverty risks. Furthermore, we can control for country-specific differences in the composition of workers and their households in an encompassing manner which is often not possible when we only consider relationships at the macro level.

The chapter is organized as follows: the next section discusses the influence of the institutional framework on the incidence of in-work poverty. The third section examines poverty risk factors at the individual level. A description of data and methods used is given in the fourth section. All empirical analyses are based on data from the European Community Household Panel and macro data from sources such as the Organisation for Economic Co-operation and Development (OECD) and Eurostat. The fifth section presents the results of the empirical analyses. After a brief descriptive overview, the section will focus primarily on the causes for differences in the incidence of in-work poverty. The chapter ends with a concluding discussion.

WELFARE STATES, LABOUR MARKET INSTITUTIONS AND THE WORKING POOR

Welfare states differ according to their degree of decommodification and defamilization (Esping-Andersen, 1999). While decommodification describes the extent to which the well-being of a person is dependent on the market (Esping-Andersen, 1990), defamilization is concerned with the individual's dependence on the family (Lister, 1994; McLaughlin and Glendinning, 1994). In the first part of this section, I discuss how we can expect the degree of decommodification and defamilization to influence the extent of in-work poverty. In a further step, I discuss the influence of labour market institutions.

In technical terms, decommodification is defined as the level and availability of transfers to those outside the labour market (Esping-Andersen, 1990; Scruggs and Allan, 2006). As far as poverty in general is concerned, it is obvious that the degree of decommodification is related to the incidence of poverty, since the poverty risk of the jobless depends strongly on the availability and level of transfers (Atkinson et al., 1995; Förster and Pellizari, 2000; Kenworthy, 1999; Moller et al., 2003; Sainsbury and Morissens, 2002). With respect to the working poor, this relationship is less obvious. However, we can distinguish two relevant mechanisms. From the perspective of economic work incentives, we can argue that the level of transfers influences the level of wages that workers are willing to accept and thus the level of earnings. Apart from this indirect influence, there is also a direct influence on the level of household incomes. Transfers paid to unemployed household members increase the household income and thus decrease the risk of being poor for jobless and working individuals alike. Since both influences point in the same direction, we can expect the degree of decommodification to negatively influence the level of in-work poverty.[1]

As defined above, defamilization has to do with independence from one's family. This concept concerns women's independence from care obligations and a male main earner (Lister, 1994; Orloff, 1993), the independence of unemployed or low-paid adult children from their parents, and the independence of the elderly from their children (McLaughlin and Glendinning, 1994; Vogel, 1997). In terms of policies, defamilization is achieved via dual-earner policies such as care for children and the elderly (see Gornick et al., 1997; Korpi, 2000) as well as through policies which aim at the economic independence of young unemployed persons (see Paugam and Russell, 2000). These policies are relevant for an analysis of in-work poverty in a twofold manner. First, care obligations restrict female employment – or, more generally, restrict the possibility of having more than one earner per household – which is related to a higher risk of being poor (Büchel et al., 2003; Maître et al., 2003). Secondly, the situation of unemployed adults living together with other family members – in other words, a higher degree of intergenerational dependency – has an influence on the relationship of needs to earned incomes in these households. Larger households have larger needs and thus are more likely to be poor. Intergenerational dependency could, however, be interpreted in a positive way as well. Family solidarity protects jobless as well as low-paid family members from being poor. Thus, we can hypothesize two influences which point in opposite directions.

While dual-earner policies aim at the combination of work and family, many welfare states offer general support in the form of cash benefits or tax deductions in order to compensate for the higher needs and employment restrictions of families (see Korpi, 2000). These measures are expected to increase the income of family households and thereby to lower poverty. Strengmann-Kuhn (2003), for instance, demonstrates the poverty-reducing effect of child benefits in working households. There are, however, also potential disincentives to female employment that are likely to lower the level of earned incomes as they are observed in systems which tax couples jointly (Dingeldey, 2001). This adds to the ambiguous influence of defamilization on the incidence of in-work poverty.

Hitherto, the influence of institutions on in-work poverty has mainly been discussed with a focus on household income. Potential influences of labour market institutions, in contrast, refer to individual earnings. Recent research suggests that labour market institutions play a key role in explaining the extent of low-wage work as well as the distribution of wages (Blau and Kahn, 1996; Lucifora et al., 2005; Teulings and Hartog, 1997). In particular, institutional features like centralized and/or co-ordinated wage-setting and the strength of labour unions are likely to affect the incidence of low wages.

One measure of the strength of labour unions is union density. One would expect stronger unions to be better able to raise wage levels and therefore to reduce the share of low wages and the extent of poverty. This hypothesis is supported by results which show that union density is associated with reduced income inequality and that the upswing in income inequality in recent decades can partially be attributed to ongoing de-unionization (see Alderson and Nielsen, 2002; Freeman, 1993). However, recent research by Moller et al. (2003) suggests that union density has no significant influence on pre-tax/pre-transfer poverty (which is mainly determined by the distribution of earned incomes), although it does have an effect on poverty reduction via taxes and transfers.

It has been argued that union density is a weak indicator for the strength of unions, since bargaining coverage is often determined by other factors such as bargaining centralization or co-ordination. Previous results show that although de-unionization has taken place in many advanced economies, the negative effect on bargaining power is most visible in countries with decentralized bargaining systems such as the USA or the UK (Freeman, 1993; Lucifora, 2000; DiNardo et al., 1996). Furthermore, the distribution of wages is not only a function of union power, but also of the power balance between unions and employers' organizations mediated by governments. Therefore, the strength of corporatist arrangements is regarded as more powerful in explaining the influence of wage bargaining on wage inequality. The results of the study by Moller et al. (2003) show that wage co-ordination – which is used as indicator of corporatism – has a clear influence on the extent of pre-tax/pre-transfer poverty as well as on the degree of poverty reduction.[2] Thus, we can hypothesize that a higher level of bargaining centralization lowers the numbers of the working poor.

In addition to the bargaining system, minimum wages have been discussed as an institutional feature that aims at the reduction of poverty. In a certain sense, this discussion parallels the discussion on the relationship between low wages and poverty. It has been argued that only a certain share of low-wage earners who benefit from (rising) minimum wages live in poor households – implying that minimum wages have only a limited impact on poverty (see for the USA, Burkhauser and Finegan, 1988).[3] We can find similar results in recent studies which accompanied the introduction of national minimum wages in the UK and Ireland (see Manning and

Dickens, 2002; Nolan, 2000; Sutherland, 2001). However, if (higher) minimum wages have an influence on the working poor, it is assumed to be a positive one.

INDIVIDUAL AND HOUSEHOLD-RELATED POVERTY RISKS

Country-specific differences are not only explained by differences in the institutional framework. As previous research on poverty has shown, differences in aggregate poverty rates can, at least partly, be explained by differences in the composition of the population (see, for example, Frick et al., 2000; Jäntti and Danziger, 1994). The higher the share of people belonging to groups with a high poverty risk, the higher the total poverty rate. Thus, controlling for such differences provides insights not only into the individual causes of poverty, but also into how countries would differ given the same composition of the population.

Poverty research has established a number of individual and household-related factors which influence the risk of being poor. In broad terms, these can be classified as factors related to 'needs' and to 'resources'. Needs are imposed by a given household structure, as already discussed in the section above. In general terms, larger households have larger needs and these needs differ according to the age of the household members. Furthermore, the risk of being poor is influenced by the resources a person has at his or her command. Those resources which allow for successful participation in the labour market – such as education, labour market experience and occupation – are crucial. In addition to 'needs' and 'resources', there are 'restrictions' on labour market participation, such as care obligations for children or elderly people in a given household. These constraints are strongest for single-parent families, which belong to the groups who are most affected by poverty.[4]

The countries which are analysed in this chapter differ with respect to the size of their respective risk groups. However, the fact that the incidence of poverty risk factors is not exogenous must be taken into account. As far as the welfare state is concerned, two aspects are of specific relevance. First, it has been argued that the composition of households is influenced by the degree of decommodification and defamilization. Insufficient social security or unemployment benefits result in a need for the unemployed to live together with working family members and therefore have an influence on the size and structure of households. Second, as we discussed above, welfare state measures which aim at combining work and family have an influence on women's labour market decisions and thus on the average number of workers per household.

We can look at the assumed influence of labour market institutions in a similar way. As I argued above, labour market institutions are assumed to have an influence on the extent of low-wage work, which is one of the causes of in-work poverty. We can observe this influence either indirectly – at the aggregate level of labour market institutions – or at the individual level, by analysing the poverty risk of low-wage workers (see Lucifora, 2000; Strengmann-Kuhn, 2003). In the following analysis, we consider such influences both from the perspective of individual characteristics and from that of institutional differences. One crucial question in this analysis is whether the influences of the institutional framework remain significant after controlling for the composition of households, labour market participation and other characteristics at the individual level.

DATA AND METHODS

As discussed in the previous two sections, we can expect macro- as well as micro-level influences to explain the variance in in-work poverty. The following analysis regards these influences jointly using a multilevel approach. Referring back to the second section, I hypothesize that welfare state characteristics (degree of decommodification and defamilization) and labour market institutions – that is, *macro-level influences* – have an effect on the incidence of in-work poverty. The third section introduced a number of *micro-level influences* related to the needs, resources and restrictions of individuals and the households they live in. Furthermore, we can expect these micro influences to interact with macro influences (*cross-level interactions*). In other words, the strength of individual risk factors can be expected to differ according to the setup of the institutional framework. Along with micro-, macro- and cross-level influences, an additional aspect must be taken into account when comparing the extent of in-work poverty at the aggregate level. There are differences in the *composition of the working population* (for example, female employment, working time, size and structure of the households people live in), which explain part of the differences in aggregate poverty rates. We cannot regard these factors as exogenous; rather, they are to a large extent the consequence of welfare state measures. Hence, controlling for such micro-level differences already picks up part of the institutional differences.

Micro Data

The empirical analyses are based on the last wave (2001) of the European Community Household Panel (ECHP), which contains data on 15 EU countries (see Wirtz and Mejer, 2002). Sweden had to be excluded since its data differ fundamentally. Hence, the empirical analyses are based on a sample of 14 countries. The population in question is defined as workers living in private households, over 16 and below 65 years of age. The definition of working is based on International Labour Organization (ILO) standards (working at least one hour per week). The working poor are defined as workers who live in households with an equivalized (modified OECD-scale) net household income below 60 per cent of the median. Independent variables cover the needs, resources and restrictions of individuals which we discussed in the previous section as being decisive for the risk of being poor. Different needs are represented by a set of variables which record the number of persons living in each individual's household by age group (0–2, 3–5, 6–14 and 15+ years). To control for the specific risk of single parents and women after separation, marital status (dummy variable indicating separation or divorce) and gender are also included in the models. Education and occupation influence the ability to generate income through labour market participation. Education is included as a set of dummy variables (International Standard Classification of Education (ISCED) 0–2/3/5–7). Occupational variables differentiate between six different occupational groups. Furthermore, three different groups of workers are differentiated: low-wage workers, other workers and the self-employed or unpaid family members. A low-wage worker is a person who earns less than 67 per cent of the median hourly gross wage. The computation of the low-wage threshold is based only on dependent workers, since earnings data on self-employed workers is considered to be less accurate.[5] Thus, three dummy variables (low-wage worker, non-low-wage worker, self-employment/unpaid family member) control for differences in employment status and the level of remuneration. Furthermore, working time is included to control for income differences between full-time and part-time workers (< 29 hours). Since earned income from other household members is expected to prevent poverty, some models control for the number of employed household members. The respective variables record the number of additional workers in a person's household (apart form the person him/herself), partly differentiated by working time.

Macro Data

Table 2.1 provides an overview of the definition and sources of the macro indicators. Most indicators describe the situation in the year 2001. If no such information was available, the indicators refer to the most recent date before 2001. Since an Esping-Andersen-style decommodification index (see Scruggs and Allan, 2006) does not exist for all the countries included in this

Table 2.1 Indicators used in the analysis and sources of indicators

MICRO LEVEL		
Age; age-squared; education; number of children in household by age group; number of persons 17+ in household; marital status: divorced/separated; working time; number of employed household members by working time; type of employment: low-wage, self-employment, occupation (ECHP 2001)		
MACRO LEVEL		
Decommodification		
Level of transfers	Average net unemployment replacement rate as a % of average production worker wage (APW) in 2001	OECD 2002
Defamilization		
General family support	Family cash benefits (public expenditure as a % of GDP) in 1998	OECD Social Expenditure database (SOCX)
Dual-earner support	Family services (public expenditure as a % of GDP) in 1998	OECD Social Expenditure database (SOCX)
Intergenerational dependence	Average number of persons aged 17+ years per household (by country) in 2001	ECHP
Labour market institutions		
Bargaining centralization	Level of wage bargaining in 2000	Golden–Lange–Wallerstein 2006
Union density	Union members as a % of all employees in 2001	OECD LFS
CROSS-LEVEL INTERACTIONS		
Dual-earner support × Child (0–2 years) in household	See above	See above
Intergeneration dep. × Age	See above	See above
Barg. centralization × Low-skilled occup.	See above	See above

Table 2.2 Means and standard deviations of macro indicators

	Mean	s.d.	Min	Max
Unemployment replacement rate	63.9	16.7	27.6	81.6
Family services (expenditure)	0.71	0.61	0.11	2.23
Family cash benefits (expenditure)	1.43	0.64	0.29	2.40
No. of household members 17+ years	1.48	0.33	0.97	1.89
Bargaining level	3	1	1	5
Union density	35.5	20.4	9.6	77.8

Source: See Table 2.1, own computations.

chapter, the indicator simply reflects the level of unemployment benefits (as a percentage of the average wage of a production worker – APW). The respective information is taken from published figures from the OECD tax/benefit models (OECD, 2004).[6]

As we discussed in the previous section, the concept of defamilization covers different dimensions. Dual-earner support and general family support are measured by the level of public expenditure on family services and family cash transfers (both as a percentage of gross domestic product – GDP). The figures are taken from the OECD Social Expenditure Database (SOCX). The indicator of intergenerational dependence is the average number of persons older than 16 years of age living in a household (by country, computed on the basis of the ECHP). A high value for this indicator can be interpreted as a high level of intergenerational dependence because it is most likely to be caused by a higher share of young adults or elderly people living with their parents or children, respectively.

Information on the level of wage bargaining is taken from the Golden–Lange–Wallerstein data-set, which contains a large collection of different indicators dealing with corporatism and wage bargaining (see Golden et al., 2006). The indicator used differentiates between five levels of centralization: (1) plant-level wage-setting, (2) industry-level wage-setting without sanctions, (3) industry-level wage-setting with sanctions, (4) central wage-setting without sanctions, and (5) central wage-setting with sanctions. The missing countries have been coded according to information provided by the European Industrial Relations Observatory (EIRO). The strength of unions is measured according to trade union density (source: OECD Labour Force Survey database).

Table 2.2 provides information on the means and the variation of these macro indicators. I comment only briefly on these figures in order to give an impression of the total variation. Detailed information on these or similar indicators can be found in a number of comparative studies on welfare states and labour market institutions (see Lohmann and Marx in this volume). Average replacement rates vary from under 30 per cent of the APW (Italy, Greece) to about 80 per cent (Denmark, Luxembourg). There is only one country which spends more than 2 per cent of its GDP on family services (Denmark), but a few countries show a similar level of expenditure on family cash benefits (Austria, Belgium, Finland, Germany and Luxembourg). Expenditure on family services as well as on cash benefits is low in the Southern European countries. We can also observe clear differences in the average number of people of working age and above per household. There is a clear North–South divide, with Denmark at the bottom of the ranking and Spain (and as an exception, Ireland) at the top. In Denmark, an average working person lives together with one household member over 16 years of age, while the average is almost two additional household members in Spain and Ireland. As mentioned above, the indicator for bargaining level differentiates between five different levels. Union density ranges from almost 80 per cent (Finland, Denmark) to 9.6 per cent in France.

In addition, some of the models contain cross-level interaction effects. I hypothesize that higher spending on family services lowers the poverty risk associated with having young children. Intergenerational dependency can be seen as a factor which shifts the poverty risk from younger to older workers (owing to young unemployed and low-wage workers living with their parents). Centralized bargaining is expected to have an influence on the earnings differential by skills. Hence, additional models contain these respective interactions terms (see Table 2.1).

Multilevel Analysis

The ECHP provides data covering a period of eight years (1994–2001). Since country differences – and not differences over time – are the main focus of this chapter, I have used only the last wave of the panel (2001). One could make the criticism that changes over time – for example, owing to the economic cycle – are not recognized. Although there are differences in the economic conditions, the period from 1994 to 2001 was characterized by economic growth (however weak in some countries) and decreasing or stagnating unemployment rates in all countries (see OECD, 2006). Furthermore, variation in the macro indicators discussed above is rather low. More than 90 per cent of the variance of each indicator is between-country variance. The within-country variance of some indicators accounts for less than 3 per cent (spending on family services, union density). This does not mean that there are no signs of change in the institutional framework. As far as the averages across all countries are concerned, there is evidence of welfare state retrenchment (decreasing replacement rates) and de-unionization. But a model which took within-country and between-country variation into account would be dominated by the latter. For the purpose of focusing on within-country variation, a period of eight years seems too short. Therefore, the analyses consider only the latest year available.[7]

From the perspective of multilevel analysis, we can describe the panel wave used as two-level data with individuals nested into countries (see, for example, Snijders and Bosker, 1999). Not taking into account the clustering of observations would result in biased estimates and incorrect standard errors. There are two general approaches to dealing with this type of data. The first is to use dummy variables (fixed effects) for all countries in order to estimate country-specific intercepts. The second is to specify a country-specific random intercept. Although the first approach is feasible since the sample contains only 14 countries, it has the disadvantage that the country dummies pick up all country-specific variance, so that no further country-level variables can be added. However, it has the advantage that it clearly shows the differences between single countries. Furthermore, by adding individual-level variables, we are able to show how many of these differences can be explained by individual characteristics within each country. Hence, in a first step, I have estimated models with country dummies and different sets of individual-level variables. In a second step, I estimated random-intercept models which contain country-level as well as individual-level variables. In addition, cross-level interaction effects are included in order to test for country differences in the strength and/or direction of micro-level influences. Given the dichotomous nature of the dependent variable (poor/not poor) all the models are specified as logistic regressions.[8]

RESULTS: EXPLAINING CROSS-COUNTRY VARIATION IN IN-WORK POVERTY

Working poor rates differ from less than 5 per cent in Austria to almost 11 per cent in Greece (see Figure 2.1). In addition to working poor rates, the figure shows poverty rates for the working-age population and for the working-age population in working households (that is, households with at least one working member). General poverty research has often stressed that work protects against poverty. We can draw the same conclusion from this figure, since poverty rates in the working-age population are always higher than those of the working population. In many countries, however, the difference between the two rates is small. Hence, we can conclude that

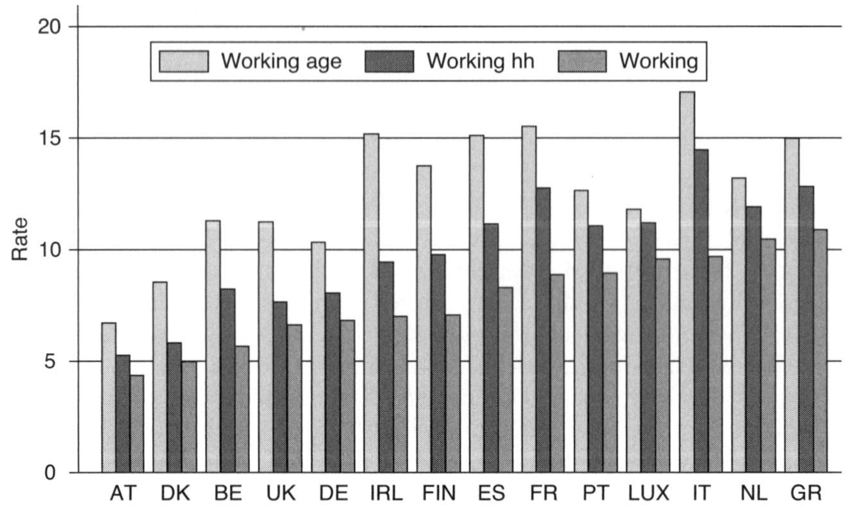

Notes: Working age: 17–64 years, working hh: persons living in a household with at least one worker.

Source: ECHP 2001, own computations.

Figure 2.1 Poverty rates by employment status (%)

although working lowers the risk of being poor, in most countries there is nevertheless a relevant risk of being employed but still poor.

The differences in these poverty rates are the starting point for the multivariate analysis. A series of logit models estimates the probability of being among the working poor. The sample includes only the working population (17–64 years). The results of these models are reported in Table 2.3 and in Figure 2.2. Model 1 contains just one dummy variable per country with Denmark as the country of reference. As the results show, the differences in the level of in-work poverty are significant in most cases (with the exception of Austria, Germany and Belgium).

Before we consider these country differences in more detail, we first discuss the individual risk factors. The size and the direction of the coefficients in Model 2 show which groups of the working population are affected by poverty. The results are mostly in line with results from general poverty research. There are differences according to age, education and marital status. As far as age is concerned, we find a U-shaped influence. The risk of being a member of the working poor is lowest for the middle age groups. Higher education lowers the risk of being poor. There are no significant differences between working men and women. However, the

Table 2.3 Coefficients (log odds) of logit models on risk of in-work poverty

	Model 1	Model 2
Country (ref.: DK)		
NL	0.896***	0.597***
BE	0.189	−0.174
FR	0.627***	0.181
IRL	0.392**	−0.712***
IT	0.800***	−0.079
GR	0.965***	−0.038
ES	0.642***	−0.404**
PT	0.748***	−0.038
AT	−0.025	−0.509***
FIN	0.359**	0.085
DE	0.114	−0.324*
LUX	0.652***	0.073
UK	0.412***	−0.064
Age		
In years		−0.077***
In years squared		0.001***
Gender (ref.: male)		
Female		−0.032
Education (ref.: ISCED 0–2)		
ISCED 3		−0.465***
ISCED 5–7		−0.627***
Marital status (ref.: else)		
Separated/divorced		0.467***
Number of children/persons in household (by age in y.)		
0–2		0.363***
3–5		0.279***
6–16		0.543***
17+		0.577***
Working time (ref.: 30+ hours)		
< =29 h		0.567***
Number of working hh members (by working time)		
< =29 h		−0.624***
30+ h		−1.188***
Employment status (ref.: employee, non-low-wage)		
Low-wage		0.973***
Self-employed		0.886***
Occupation (ref.: legislators, senior officials, managers)		
Professionals		0.070
Office clerks		0.234*

Table 2.3 (continued)

	Model 1	Model 2
Agricultural workers		1.669***
Service workers/others		0.727***
Workers/operators		0.739***
Labourers		0.986***
Intercept	–3.685***	−2.211***
n (persons)	53749	53749
log likelihood	–14931.3	−12223.2

Notes: Significant at p < 0.001 (***), p < 0.01 (**), p < 0.05 (*), p < 0.10 (+).

Source: ECHP 2001, working population in working age.

coefficient changes depending on whether or not we are controlling for employment variables (such as working time, low-wage work and occupation). Without controlling for these factors, working women are less likely to be poor than working men (results not reported). The fact that separation or divorce is often accompanied by economic strain is reflected by a higher poverty risk among this group.

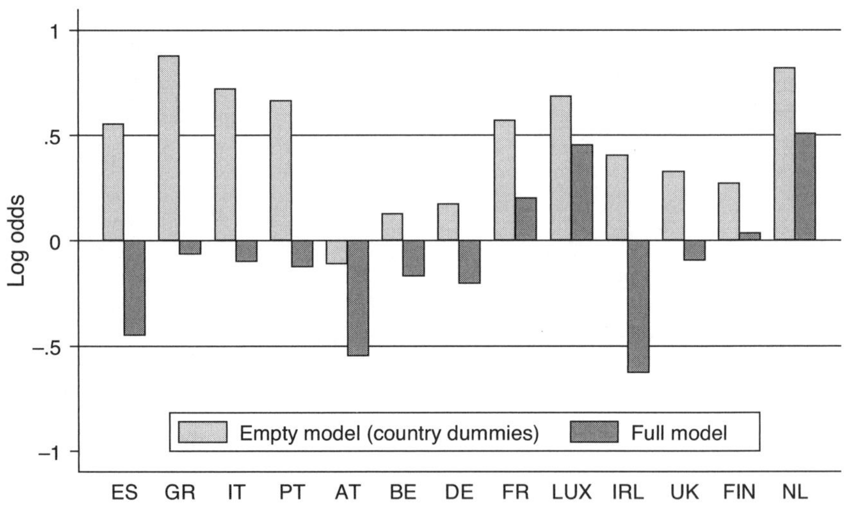

Source: See Table 2.3.

Figure 2.2 Results from logit models: country coefficients

Household context also strongly influences the risk of belonging to the working poor. The larger a person's household, the more likely he or she is to be poor. Differences between children of different age groups are rather small. While the number of household members reflects the needs of a household and – in the case of small children – potential restrictions for labour market participation, additional workers in a household are likely to lower the risk of poverty. Not surprisingly, this effect is strongest in the case of additional full-time workers. But even workers who live together with part-time workers (< 29 h) are also less likely to be poor.

As in the case of additional workers, the working time of the worker him/herself influences the person's risk of being poor. Part-time workers face a higher risk of poverty than full-time workers. Not surprisingly, low-wage workers are more likely to be poor. However, the poverty risk of (employed) low-wage workers does not differ largely from that of self-employed workers. To what extent this can be attributed to an under-reporting of earnings from self-employment cannot be differentiated on the basis of these results. When we look at occupation, agricultural workers are at the highest risk of being poor. Apart from this, there are clear differences between highly skilled and low-skilled workers. Professionals and other members of the service class are the least likely group to be poor.

We now return to the question of country differences. Looking at the country variables in Model 2, we come to different conclusions compared to those based on the results from Model 1 (see Figure 2.2). In many cases, the size of the country coefficient is largely reduced. This holds true in particular for Greece, Portugal and Italy. Hence, the different distributions and influences of the micro-level variables discussed above explain the differences in the extent of in-work poverty between these countries and Denmark. However, there are also cases where the differences have not only been reduced, but turned to the opposite (change of sign of the coefficient). The working populations in Ireland and Spain appear to have the lowest risk of belonging to the working poor when we control for all other variables in the model.

I argued above that the composition of the workers and the households they live in cannot be regarded as exogenous. On the contrary, household composition, employment patterns and the likelihood of low-wage work tend to be influenced by the institutional framework of a given country. To determine whether such individual and household-related factors make an impact on country differences let us consider a number of models which contain only subsets of the variables in the full model (M1) discussed above. The first contains only socio-demographic variables (age, gender, education, marital status); the second, information on the composition and employment patterns of households (number of children and adults, part-time work and number of working household members); the third contains only a variable on low-wage work; and the fourth model contains information on the structure of employment and the labour market (occupation and self-employment). It is interesting to see how these variables explain the differences between countries. Therefore, Figure 2.3 contains information on the absolute change of the country coefficients in these models compared with model M1. Although there are also changes in the variables themselves, these are not reported. However, none of the coefficients changes its sign, and most of the changes are small.

In most cases, household composition and employment have the strongest impact on the change in the country coefficient. It is particularly strong in the case of Ireland and Spain, but it is also strong in Greece and Italy. These countries are characterized by large households and a low degree of participation by additional household members in the labour market. As I argued above, these differences are very likely to be caused by differences in the institutional framework. Although the model controls for individual and household-related factors only, the reduction in the risk of being poor in comparison to that in Denmark can be – at least in part – attributed to institutional factors.

There are a few countries in which these variables for household composition and employment do not have the strongest impact on the country coefficient. In these cases, controlling for self-employment and occupations explains a larger amount of the country differences (Figure 2.3(d)). This is particularly true in the Southern countries, Austria and Ireland, a result which reflects the higher share of self-employed and agricultural workers in these countries. This could be attributed to a greater importance of familialism, but certainly also to economic factors. In addition, especially in the Southern European countries, socio-demographic variables (which include education) also result in a strong change in the country effect (Figure 2.3(a)). Again, one could argue that the educational distribution is influenced by institutional factors – although we have not discussed the setup of the educational system as being influential for the incidence and structure of in-work poverty. Finally, differences in the extent of low-wage work also explain part of the country-specific differences (Figure 2.3(c)). Compared with other factors, the extent to which this variable alters the country coefficients is rather small. On the one hand, the respective model controls for only one variable (low-wage work) while the others control for a combination of variables. On the other hand, it also provides evidence for the indirect relationship between low wages and poverty which has already been stressed in earlier research (see, for example, Marx and Verbist, 1998).

In a first step we have seen that part of the differences at the macro level can already be accounted for by differences in the composition of the population and in the influence of individual factors on the poverty risk. It has been argued that this can be attributed to differences in the institutional framework; however, these influences have not been shown directly in the analysis so far. This is the aim of the second step of the analysis (random effects models). Using macro-level indicators, we try to directly test the influences of institutional factors. The starting point for this analysis is the question of how much of the country-level variance is already explained by individual factors. As a first step, we regard an empty model. The estimation of variance components from this model indicates that only 5.6 per cent of the total variance is macro-level variance. If we include the same micro-level variables as before, this share is reduced to as little as 3.2 per cent.[9] The coefficients of this model hardly differ from those of the dummy variable model (results not reported). However, it is important to note that although we observe significant differences in the level of in-work poverty between countries, there is only a small fraction of variance that can be explained at the macro level.

Given the small amount of variance and the change in sign of some of the country dummies when controlling for individual-level characteristics, we first look at the influence of single factors at the macro level before we come to more complex models. These results are shown in the first column of Table 2.4. It reports coefficients from six different models (M3 a–f), each containing a single macro indicator. These bivariate models confirm our expectations about the influence of decommodification, defamilization and mechanisms of wage bargaining on the incidence of in-work poverty. A higher level of unemployment benefits, higher spending on family cash transfers and services, bargaining centralization and union density all lower the risk of in-work poverty.[10] In contrast, higher intergenerational dependency (measured by the average number of people at or above working age per household) increases the risk of in-work poverty. This would confirm the expectation that intergenerational dependency increases the needs of working households to an extent that is not compensated by the potential positive effects of income pooling.

It is not possible to evaluate the relative impact of single factors using the coefficients of logit models. Therefore, Table 2.4 also shows predicted probabilities from these models. Predictions are based on the minimum and maximum value of each variable; random intercepts are fixed at zero (for information on the means and standard deviations of these variables, see the previous section). The models predict a change of 2.2 to 6.6 percentage points in the risk of in-work poverty (difference between minimum and maximum values). From these figures, one could come to the conclusion

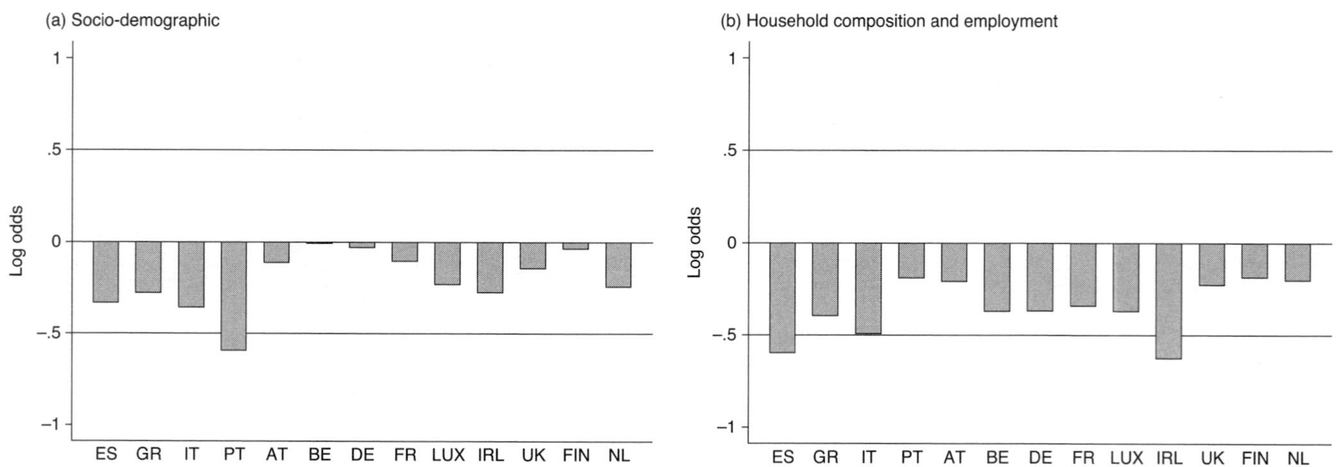
(a) Socio-demographic
Log odds
1
.5
0
–.5
–1
ES GR IT PT AT BE DE FR LUX IRL UK FIN NL
(b) Household composition and employment
Log odds
1
.5
0
–.5
–1
ES GR IT PT AT BE DE FR LUX IRL UK FIN NL

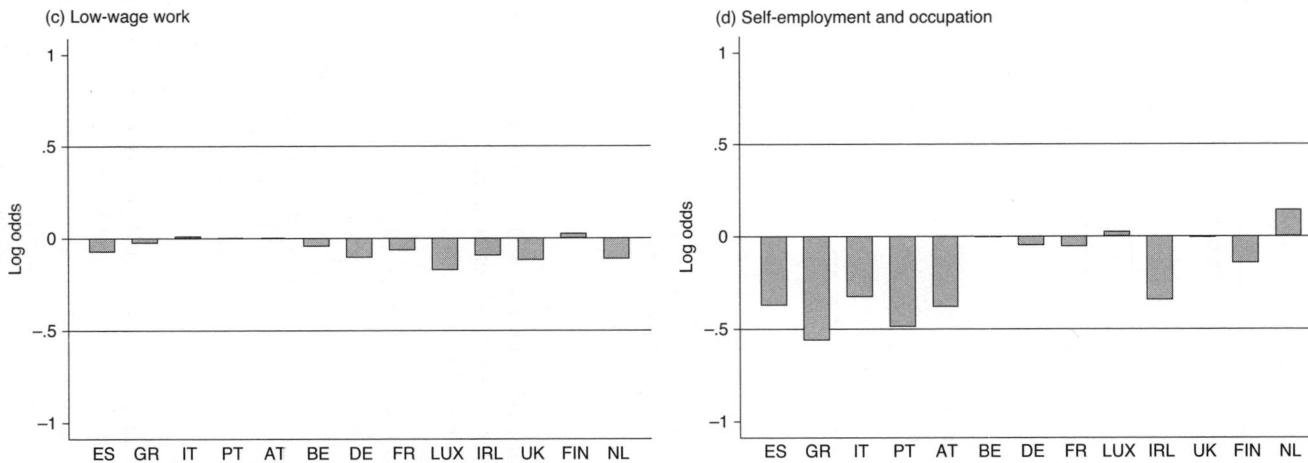

Notes: Subsets (a–d) are taken from the independent variables in Model 2 (see Table 2.3).

Source: Empty model (Table 2.3: Model 1), models a–d (not reported, but available from the author).

Figure 2.3 Results from logit models: change in country coefficients by controlling for different subsets of variables (comparison to empty model)

Table 2.4 Coefficients (log odds) of random intercept logit models on risk of in-work poverty

	Coefficients		Predicted probabilities (%)	
	Model 3 a–f[1]	Model 4 a–f[2]	min[3]	max[3]
Unemployment replacement rate	−0.013*	−0.001	11.1	5.8
Family cash benefits (expenditure)	−0.400***	−0.191*	12.2	5.6
Family services (expenditure)	−0.233	0.075	8.3	5.3
No. of hh members 17+ y.	0.681*	−0.282	5.2	9.3
Bargaining level	−0.082	−0.066	8.3	6.2
Union density	−0.012**	−0.006	9.7	4.5

Notes:
1 Coefficients of six bivariate models.
2 Macro-level coefficients of six multilevel models (micro-level variables as in Model 2, macro-level variables as in Model 3 a–f).
3 Prediction based on Model 3 a–f using minimum or maximum value of the corresponding indicator, random intercept fixed to zero.
Coefficients significant at $p<0.001$ (***), $p<0.01$ (**), $p<0.05$ (*), $p<0.10$ (+).

Source: ECHP 2001.

that welfare state characteristics and labour market institutions have a similar impact. However, we should keep in mind that these predictions are based on bivariate models. Hence, the estimates are likely to pick up the influence of unobserved characteristics as well.

This situation becomes quite clear when we control for micro-level influences. Adding macro-level variables does not alter the micro-level influences fundamentally. There are, however, large changes at the macro level (see Table 2.4, column 2). None of the coefficients turns out to be significant at the 5 per cent level. Furthermore, the direction of two coefficients – spending on family services and intergenerational dependency – is reversed. The latter is significant at the 10 per cent level. Here we see the ambiguous influence of intergenerational dependency. While larger households tend to be at a higher risk of being poor due to higher needs, the poverty risk is simultaneously lowered by income pooling. The multilevel model takes into account the structure of households at the micro level (see the coefficients for number of children and adults in the household in Table 2.3). Controlling for the structure of households, the dependency indicator turns out to be negative. This seems to confirm our expectation of the influence of income pooling.

The confirmation of our macro hypotheses depends strongly on the control of micro-level influences. Part of the variance at the macro level is already picked up by differences at the micro level. An interesting additional test would be one which showed whether or not poverty risks at the individual level differ given different institutional contexts: in other words, if one could find evidence for the significance of cross-level interactions. As discussed above, I assume that intergenerational dependency not only has an influence on the level of in-work poverty but also on the poverty risk by age. Furthermore, I hypothesize that centralized bargaining has an influence on the poverty risk of low-skilled workers. The third cross-level hypothesis refers to the influence of family services on poverty risk due to the restrictions imposed by very young children. There is no empirical evidence which supports the latter hypothesis; therefore, the results are not reported in detail. As seen above (Model 4), the main effect already points in the wrong direction. This is also the case if we include the respective interaction term. In this model, both coefficients point in the wrong direction and neither of the two coefficients is significant.

The results of the other two models are presented in Table 2.5. The first interaction term indicates that the risk of in-work poverty is, in fact, more closely related to higher age in countries where a larger number of persons over the age of 16 years live together in one household – which can be interpreted as a higher degree of intergenerational dependency. This confirms our expectation that in such countries, younger workers are protected within the household context while prime-age workers face additional burdens. Figure 2.4 shows this estimated relationship between age, intergenerational dependency and the risk of in-work poverty. Higher intergenerational dependency reduces the risk of in-work poverty in younger age groups, while it is increased in higher age groups. The sign of the second interaction term also points in the expected direction. Centralized bargaining reduces the poverty risk of low-skilled workers. However, neither the main effect nor the interaction effect is significant. Given the low number of countries, we can nevertheless take this evidence as weak support for the hypothesis that bargaining level has an influence on the poverty risk of low-skilled workers.

CONCLUSION

The aim of this chapter was to explain the variations in in-work poverty within Europe. The main focus has been on differences in the institutional

Table 2.5 Coefficients (log odds) of random-intercept logit models on risk of in-work poverty

	Model 5	Model 6
Macro level		
No. of household members 17+ years	−0.919**	
No. of household members 17+ y. *age	0.016**	
Bargaining level		−0.058
Barg. centralization* low-skilled occup.		−0.024
Micro level		
Age		
In years	−0.110***	−0.089***
In years squared	0.001***	0.001***
Gender (ref.: male)		
Female	0.037	0.033
Education (ref.: ISCED 0–2)		
ISCED 3	−0.431***	−0.440***
ISCED 5–7	−0.692***	−0.701***
Marital status (ref.: else)		
Separated/divorced	0.481***	0.466***
Number of children/persons in household (by age in years)		
0–2	0.479***	0.484***
3–5	0.374***	0.377***
6–16	0.577***	0.580***
17+	0.580***	0.577***
Working time (ref.: 30+ hours)		
< =29 h	0.615***	0.624***
Number of working hh members (by working time)		
< =29 h	−0.588***	−0.583***
30+ h	−1.263***	−1.263***
Employment status (ref.: employee, no low-wage)		
Low-wage	0.950***	0.955***
Self-employed	0.899***	0.907***
Occupation (ref.: legislators, senior officials, managers)		
Professionals	−0.176+	−0.175+
Office clerks	0.114	0.120
Agricultural workers	1.541***	1.546***
Service workers/others	0.576***	0.639***
Workers/operators	0.597***	0.593***
Labourers	0.861***	0.913***
Intercept **	−0.677	−1.784
intercept variance	0.120	0.133
n persons (countries)	53749 (14)	53749 (14)
log likelihood	−12524.7	−12535.9

Notes: Significant at p<0.001 (***), p<0.01 (**), p<0.05 (*), p<0.10 (+).

Source: ECHP 2001, working population in working age.

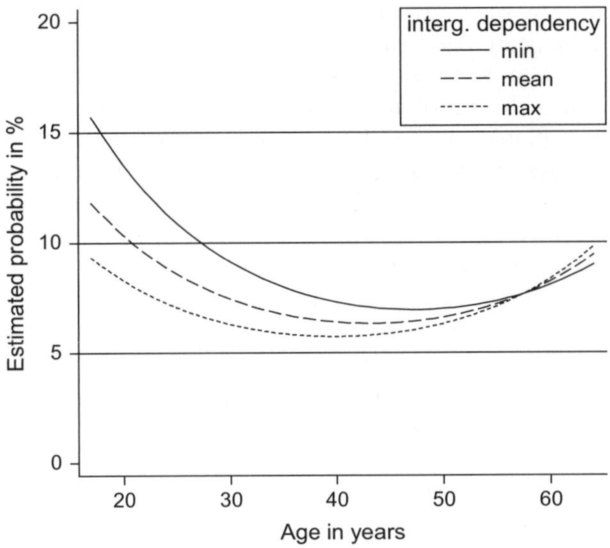

Notes:
* Prediction based on regression estimates (Model 5, Table 2.5) for male full-time worker (medium education, service occupation) living in a single-earner household with one child. Random intercept fixed to zero.
** Indicator: Number of persons 17+ years living in household (country average).

Figure 2.4 Predicted probability of in-work poverty by age and intergenerational dependency***

framework. In addition to the degree of decommodification and the mechanisms of wage-setting, I have argued that the degree of defamilization also has to be taken into account due to its influence on the composition and the needs of households in the working population. The chapter is based on a multilevel approach, combining the analyses of poverty risks at the micro level and of institutional influences at the macro level.

The empirical analyses have shown that micro- and macro-level influences are strongly interwoven. The distribution of micro characteristics cannot be regarded as exogenous, but rather as the result of welfare state characteristics and labour market institutions. Hence, controlling for micro factors already explains part of the between-country variance. We were able to show that household composition and employment patterns within households (number of workers, part-time/full-time work) largely account for the differences between countries. Furthermore, Southern European countries in particular differ as far as the structure of workers (self-employment, occupation) and educational distribution are concerned.

The level of low-wage work explains some of the differences between Northern European countries. Given that institutional differences are picked up via such compositional effects, it should not be surprising that the additional inclusion of macro indicators does not contribute significantly to the explanation of differences in in-work poverty.

However, if we regard country-specific differences from a strictly macro perspective, we find the expected relationships. A higher degree of decommodification, defamilization, wage bargaining centralization and union density have a negative influence on in-work poverty. The relationship between a high degree of decommodification and a low degree of in-work poverty is probably not only due to the opportunity for workers who are at a particular risk of being poor (for example, the low skilled) to opt out of the market. Transfers received by non-working household members also contribute to household income and to the reduction of poverty. The degree of defamilization has an ambiguous influence. On the one hand, higher intergenerational dependence increases the risk of being poor (owing to the higher needs of larger households); on the other hand, there is an influence of family solidarity which lowers the poverty risk. This interpretation is reinforced by the fact that the influence of age differs significantly according to the degree of intergenerational dependency. Younger workers are protected within the family; older workers face additional burdens. Interactions between the degree of dual-earner support and the poverty risk related to children and between wage-bargaining centralization and the poverty risk of low-skilled workers, however, did not prove to be significant.

This is not to say that differences in the level of earnings or in the incidence of low-wage work do not influence the incidence of in-work poverty. Individuals with a disadvantageous position in the labour market – such as part-time workers or low-wage workers – face a higher risk of in-work poverty. However, this risk is mediated within the household context. Hence, institutional factors which explain the incidence of low earnings have a less direct impact on in-work poverty. Drawing a conclusion from these results, we have to stress the fact that differences in in-work poverty must be explained from a perspective that not only takes into account institutional factors which alter the distribution of earned incomes, but also factors which affect the availability of transfers and the role of the family.

NOTES

1. It is difficult to judge the decommodifying or commodifying character of in-work benefits However, since such programmes exist at a relevant scale in only two countries in this comparison (UK and Ireland, see OECD, 2005), this issue will not be discussed further.

2. See Kenworthy (2003) for an extensive discussion of the indicators of wage co-ordination, wage-bargaining centralization and other indicators of corporatism.
3. I only discuss the direct distributional effects of minimum wages. There is a broad body of literature on the effects of minimum wages on employment and economic growth, which might have indirect distributional effects (for an overview, see Bazen, 2000).
4. Of course, there are other factors which negatively influence the income situation of single-parent households. Probably the most important is that the gender-specific division of labour is functional during marriage and turns out to be dysfunctional after a relationship breaks down.
5. Previous research has shown that the self-employed are more likely to be poor. As Strengmann-Kuhn (2003) shows by comparing deprivation and income-based poverty rates, this result is – at least in Northern and Middle European countries – driven by the underestimation of income within the group of self-employed.
6. The benefit level differs according to household type and previous level of income. Hence, the OECD publishes figures for a number of different constellations. The indicator used in this analysis has been calculated as the average of all group-specific indicators.
7. Models based on a panel wave from 1996 (the first year in which all 14 countries discussed in this chapter have been included in the ECHP) do not yield fundamentally different results. In addition, the models used in an earlier version of this chapter based on the full panel yield similar results (Lohmann, 2006). However, these models do not properly take the data structure into account. Therefore, we cannot rule out the possibility that the estimates are biased. In any case, these models underestimate the standard errors of the effects at the macro level.
8. There are different methods for estimating logistic regressions using random components for dichotomous dependent variables. In some cases, these methods yield substantively different results (see Guo and Zhao, 2000). In this paper, the estimation is based on numerical integration by adaptive Gauss quadrature using GLLAMM.
9. The macro-level-variance in the empty model is 0.196. It is reduced to 0.110 if all individual-level variables are included. The micro-level variance is set to 3.29. See Goldstein et al. (2002) on methods of variance partition in discrete response models.
10. Some of these coefficients are not significant. However, one should take into account the sample size of 14 countries.

REFERENCES

Alderson, A.S. and F. Nielsen (2002), 'Globalization and the great U-turn: income inequality trends in 16 OECD countries', *American Journal of Sociology*, **107** (5), 1244–99.

Atkinson, A.B., L. Rainwater and T.M. Smeeding (1995), *Income Distribution in OECD Countries. Evidence from the Luxembourg Income Study (LIS)*, Paris: OECD.

Bardone, L. and A.-C. Guio (2005), 'In-work poverty', *Statistics in Focus – Population and Social Conditions*, **2005** (5).

Bazen, S. (2000), 'Minimum wages and low-wage employment', in M. Gregory, W. Salverda and S. Bazen (eds), *Labour Market Inequalities: Problems and Policies of Low-Wage Employment in International Perspective*, Oxford: Oxford University Press, pp. 120–40.

Blau, F.D. and L.M. Kahn (1996), 'International differences in male wage inequality: institutions versus market forces', *Journal of Political Economy*, **104** (4), 791–837.

Brady, D. (2004), *The Welfare State and Relative Poverty in Rich Western Democracies, 1967–1997*, Luxembourg Income Study Working Paper Series No. 390, Luxembourg: LIS.

Büchel, F., A. Mertens and K. Orsini (2003), *Is Mothers' Employment an Effective Means to Fight Family Poverty? Empirical Evidence from Seven European Countries*, Luxembourg Income Study Working Paper Series No. 363, Luxembourg: LIS.

Burkhauser, R.V. and T.A. Finegan (1988), 'The minimum wage and the poor: the end of a relationship', *Journal of Policy Analysis & Management*, **8** (1), 53–71.

DiNardo, J., N.M. Fortin and T. Lemieux (1996), 'Labor market institutions and the distribution of wages', *Econometrica*, **64**, 1001–44.

Dingeldey, I. (2001), 'European tax systems and their influence on family employment patterns', *Journal of Social Policy*, **30** (4), 653–72.

Esping-Andersen, G. (1990), *The Three Worlds of Welfare Capitalism*, Cambridge: Polity Press.

Esping-Andersen, G. (1999), *Social Foundations of Postindustrial Economies*, Oxford: Oxford University Press.

Förster, M.F. and M. Pellizzari (2000), *Trends and Driving Factors in Income Distribution and Poverty in the OECD Area*, OECD Labour Market and Social Policy Occasional Papers No. 42, Paris: OECD.

Freeman, R.B. (1993), 'How much has de-unionization contributed to the rise in male earnings inequality?', in S. Danziger and P. Gottschalk (eds), *Uneven Tides: Rising Inequality in America*, New York: Russell Sage Foundation, pp. 133–63.

Frick, J.R., F. Büchel and P. Krause (2000), 'Public transfers, income distribution, and poverty in Germany and in the United States', in R. Hauser and I. Becker (eds), *The Personal Distribution of Income in an International Perspective*, Berlin and Heidelberg: Springer, pp. 176–204.

Gallie, D., S. Jacobs and S. Paugam (2000), 'Poverty and financial hardship among the unemployed', in D. Gallie and S. Paugam (eds), *Welfare Regimes and the Experience of Unemployment in Europe*, Oxford: Oxford University Press, pp. 47–68.

Golden, M., P. Lange and M. Wallerstein (2006), 'Union centralization among advanced industrial societies: an empirical study', Data-set available at www.shelley.polisci.ucla.edu/data, version dated 16 June 2006 (accessed 9 August 2006).

Goldstein, H., W. Browne and J. Rasbash (2002), 'Partioning variation in multilevel models', *Understanding Statistics*, **1** (4), 223–31.

Gornick, J., M.K. Meyers and K.E. Ross (1997), 'Supporting the employment of mothers: policy applications across fourteen welfare states', *Journal of European Social Policy*, **7** (1), 45–70.

Guo, G. and H. Zhao (2000), 'Multilevel modelling for binary data', *Annual Review of Sociology*, **26**, 441–62.

Jäntti, M. and S. Danziger (1994), 'Child poverty in Sweden and the United States: the effect of social transfers and parental labor force participation', *Industrial and Labor Relations Review*, **48** (1), 48–64.

Kenworthy, L. (1999), 'Do social-welfare policies reduce poverty? A cross-national assessment', *Social Forces*, **77** (3), 1119–39.

Kenworthy, L. (2003), 'Quantitative indicators of corporatism', *International Journal of Sociology*, **33** (3), 10–44.

Korpi, W. (2000), 'Faces of inequality: gender, class, and patterns of inequalities in different types of welfare states', *Social Politics. International Studies in Gender, State, and Society*, **7** (2), 127–91.
Lister, R. (1994), ' "She has other duties" – women, citizenship and social security', in S. Baldwin and J. Faklingham (eds), *Social Security and Social Change. New Challenges to the Beveridge Model*, New York: Harvester Wheatsheaf, pp. 31–44.
Lohmann, H. (2006), 'Working poor in Western Europe: what is the influence of welfare state provisions and labour market institutions?', paper presented at the Conference of the EuroPanel Users Network (EPUNet-2006), 8–9 May, Barcelona.
Lucifora, C. (2000), 'Wage inequalities and low pay: the role of labour market institutions', in M. Gregory, W. Salverda and S. Bazen (eds), *Labour Market Inequalities: Problems and Policies of Low-Wage Employment in International Perspective*, Oxford: Oxford University Press, pp. 9–34.
Lucifora, C., A. McKnight and W. Salverda (2005), 'Low-wage employment in Europe: a review of the evidence', *Socio-economic Review*, **3** (2), 259–92.
Maître, B., C.T. Whelan and B. Nolan (2003), *Female Partner's Income Contribution to the Household Income in the European Union*, ISER Working Papers 2003–43, Colchester: University of Essex.
Manning, A. and R. Dickens (2002), *The Impact of the National Minimum Wage on the Wage Distribution, Poverty and the Gender Pay Gap. Research Report for the Low Pay Commission*, London.
Marx, I. and G. Verbist (1998), 'Low-paid work and poverty: a cross-country perspective', in S. Bazen, M. Gregory and W. Salverda (eds), *Low-Wage Employment in Europe*, Cheltenham, UK and Lyme, USA: Edward Elgar, pp. 63–86.
McLaughlin, E. and C. Glendinning (1994), 'Paying for care in Europe: is there a feminist approach?', in L. Hantrais and S. Mangen (eds), *Cross-National Research Papers*, Loughborough: European Research Centre, Leicestershire: University of Technology, pp. 52–69.
Moller, S., D. Bradley, E. Huber, F. Nielsen and J.D. Stephens (2003), 'Determinants of relative poverty in advanced capitalist democracies', *American Sociological Review*, **68** (February), 22–51.
Nolan, B. (2000), *Low Pay in Ireland*. Denver, CO: Academic Books.
O'Connor, I. and T. Smeeding (1995): 'Working but poor: a cross-national comparison of earnings adequacy', *Journal of Income Distribution*, **5** (1), 91–110.
Organisation for Economic Co-operation and Development (OECD) (2004), *Benefits and Wages. OECD Indicators*, Paris: OECD.
Organisation for Economic Co-operation and Development (OECD) (2005), *Employment Outlook*, Paris: OECD.
Organisation for Economic Co-operation and Development (OECD) (2006), *Economic Outlook No. 79*, Paris: OECD.
Orloff, A.S. (1993), 'Gender and the social rights of citizenship: the comparative analysis of gender relations and welfare states', *American Sociological Review*, **58** (3), 303–28.
Paugam, S. and H. Russell (2000), 'The effects of employment precarity and unemployment on social isolation', in D. Gallie and S. Paugam (eds), *Welfare Regimes and the Experience of Unemployment in Europe*, Oxford: Oxford University Press, pp. 243–64.
Rueda, D. and J. Pontusson (2000), 'Wage inequality and varieties of capitalism', *World Politics*, **52** (April), 350–83.

Sainsbury, D. and A. Morissens (2002), 'Poverty in Europe in the mid-1990s: the effectiveness of means-tested benefits', *Journal of European Social Policy*, **12** (4), 307–27.

Scruggs, L. and J. Allan (2006), 'Welfare-state decommodification in 18 OECD countries: a replication and revision', *Journal of European Social Policy*, **16** (1), 55–72.

Snijders, T.A.B. and R.J. Bosker (1999), *Multilevel Analysis. An Introduction to Basic and Advanced Multilevel Modelling*, London, Thousand Oaks, CA and New Delhi: Sage.

Strengmann-Kuhn, W. (2003), *Armut trotz Erwerbstätigkeit. Analysen und sozialpolitische Konsequenzen*, Frankfurt and New York: Campus.

Sutherland, H. (2001), *The National Minimum Wage and In-Work Poverty*, DAE Working Papers Number MU0102, Cambridge: Department of Applied Economics, University of Cambridge.

Teulings, C. and J. Hartog (1997), *Corporatism or Competition? Labour Contracts, Institutions and Wage Structures in International Comparison*, Cambridge: Cambridge University Press.

Vogel, J. (1997), *Living Conditions and Inequality in the European Union 1997*, Eurostat Working Papers, Population and Social Conditions, E/1997-3, Luxembourg: Eurostat.

Wirtz, C. and L. Mejer (2002), 'The European Community Household Panel (ECHP)', *Schmollers Jahrbuch. Zeitschrift für Wirtschafts- und Sozialwissenschaften*, **122** (1), 143–54.

PART II

Country Chapters

3. When famialism fails: the nature and causes of in-work poverty in Belgium

Ive Marx and Gerlinde Verbist

INTRODUCTION

Gauging from comparative studies, including those which appear in this book, Belgium enjoys a relatively low incidence of low pay as well as a comparatively low poverty rate among its working-age population. Nevertheless, the 'working poor' constitute a significant proportion of the working-age population living in relative poverty. In this respect, Belgium is not atypical in the Continental European context (see Lohmann and Marx in this volume).

Belgium presents a particularly interesting case study when it comes to the particular nature and causes of in-work poverty as it manifests itself in the Continental European welfare states. Belgium bears many of the hallmarks of what Esping-Andersen has called the conservative welfare state model, in which the Christian Democratic 'subsidiarity principle' has institutionalized familialism in the sense of supporting the male-breadwinner/female-caregiver model. Belgium's labour market and welfare state remain geared towards the breadwinner: minimum wages are comparatively high, job security protection is elaborate, derived social security rights extensive; the tax system supports the sole breadwinner model, and so on.

On the surface, Belgium appears to epitomize the archetypal European welfare state caught in a 'welfare without work' conundrum. Because of its largely defensive response to economic change – partly in an effort to preserve breadwinner-type jobs – the country seems to have found itself trapped in a vicious circle of high spending on social transfers, high taxation and sluggish job growth – all to the detriment of women's employment chances, especially those of the least skilled. There is truth in this. At the same time, however, childcare provisions for working parents are extensive, making Belgium a case in point of what has been called 'optional familialism', where the caregiving family is supported, but at the same time families are also given the option of being (at least partially) unburdened from childcare responsibilities. In addition, over the past decades, Belgium has deployed a wide range of measures to improve the disposable income situation of single-earner households with low incomes as well as to boost multi-earnership. In that sense, the country presents a more complex case than it may appear to on the surface.

In this chapter, we first present the most up-to-date empirical evidence pertaining to low-wage employment and in-work poverty in Belgium. The remainder of the chapter looks at the institutional context in which in-work poverty arises in a Continental European welfare state setting like the Belgian one. In particular, we look at (1) the impact of wage-setting institutions, including minimum wage protection; (2) the impact of taxation and social security contributions, particularly as they affect low-wage workers and households; (3) the impact of child benefits and family provisions and (4) the impact of supply and demand-side policies intended to boost and support dual earnership. In the final section, we present our conclusions.

THE INCIDENCE AND CHARACTERISTICS OF LOW-WAGE WORK IN BELGIUM

The available empirical evidence suggests that Belgium has a comparatively compressed wage structure as well as a very low incidence of low pay. This is evident from calculations based on various sources, ranging from administrative data (social security databases) to empirical databases such as the European Community Household Panel (ECHP) or the Luxembourg Income Study (LIS). In the 1990s, around 12–13 per cent of all employees in Belgium who worked more than 15 hours per week received low pay (measured as two-thirds of the median gross hourly wage), compared with 15–16 per cent of workers in the EU-15 (calculation based on the ECHP 1996–2001; see European Commission, 2004).

These findings are confirmed for the beginning of the twenty-first century. Here, we present calculations based on data from the European Union Survey on Income and Living Conditions (EU-SILC) for Belgium in 2004. We have used individual data on gross and net wages as well as information on other socio-economic characteristics of individuals and their households. The income data refer to the year prior to the survey, namely, 2003.

We have used two definitions of low-wage work here. According to the broader definition, low-wage workers are those individuals whose yearly

Table 3.1 Share of low pay workers in the population, Belgium, 2003 (%)

Low-wage work defined as 2/3 of median	Percentage of individuals aged 16–64	Percentage of employees			
	Belgium	Belgium	Flanders	Wallonia	Brussels
Net wage of					
all employees	8.6	16.8	16.7	16.4	18.4
FYFT employees	2.1	4.1	3.6	4.5	6.0
Gross wage of					
all employees	10.0	19.6			
FYFT employees	3.8	7.4			

Source: Own calculations on EU-SILC 2004.

wage is less than two-thirds of the median net wage for everyone who works at least one hour per week and has a strict positive wage. The narrower definition considers only full-year full-time (FYFT) workers, with a low-wage worker earning less than two-thirds of median net wage of all FYFT workers. A FYFT-worker is someone who reports working full-time during a given 12-month period. By using this stricter definition, we have tried to eliminate the effect of part-time workers on the definition of low pay. The self-employed are excluded from both definitions.

Using the broad definition, 8.6 per cent of all individuals of active working age (16–64 years old) are low-paid workers (see Table 3.1); under the stricter FYFT definition, this number is only 2.1 per cent. These figures correspond, respectively, to 16.8 per cent and 4.1 per cent of all employees. We have also presented low-pay incidences based on gross instead of net wages. This results in a higher low-pay rate, especially for FYFT employees. The progressive rate structure of personal income taxes – and to a lesser extent, social insurance contributions – reduces inequality and compresses wage dispersion (see also Verbist, 2004). Hence, the incidence of low wages is higher when we use the gross wage definition. In the next part of this chapter, we focus on the two definitions of net wage.

The socio-economic situation differs considerably between the two major regions of the Belgian federal state, Flanders and Wallonia: employment rates in Flanders are substantially higher (65 compared to 56 per cent in Wallonia in 2006). Consequently, we might expect this to result in a different wage structure and a different incidence of low-paid workers. But apparently, the gap remains small: using the broad definition, the share of low-paid employees amounts to around 16.5 per cent in both regions; the gap is somewhat higher when we use the FYFT definition, with a lower

Table 3.2 Socio-economic characteristics of low-wage workers, Belgium, 2003

	All low-wage workers	FYFT low-wage workers	All employees	All 16–64 individuals
Gender				
Men	28.1	48.0	54.7	50.2
Women	71.9	52.0	45.3	49.8
Age category				
≤24 years	17.0	22.9	7.8	17.3
25–34 years	28.2	36.9	27.8	20.6
35–44 years	28.7	20.2	30.9	23.6
45–54 years	20.2	16.4	26.0	21.8
55–64 years	5.9	3.6	7.5	16.8
Education level*				
Low	29.0	30.3	20.1	31.0
Middle	46.4	49.4	39.9	38.7
High	24.6	20.3	40.0	30.3
Type of contract**				
Permanent job	76.3	80.1	89.5	–
Temporary job	23.7	19.9	10.5	–

Notes:
*Low-skilled: max. lower secondary education; middle: upper secondary or post-secondary non-tertiary; high: tertiary education.
**Refers to the situation at the time of the interview.

Source: Own calculations on EU-SILC 2004.

share found in Flanders (3.6 versus 4.5 per cent in Wallonia). The incidence of low-wage work is highest in Brussels.

When we look at the socio-economic characteristics of low-wage workers, there are some remarkable differences depending on whether we use the broader or the stricter definition (see Table 3.2). Under our broader definition, we find a very high share of female low-wage workers (71.9 per cent). But since there are many female part-time workers, this share shrinks to 52 per cent when we use the FYFT definition. Nevertheless, even under this stricter definition, women are still over-represented among low-wage workers, since their share among all employees is only 45.3 per cent.

Younger people (less than 25 years of age) are over-represented among low-wage workers, at 17 per cent (compared with 7.8 per cent of all employees). But despite this over-representation, prime-age individuals (25–55 years old) still make up around three-quarters of all low-wage workers.

Table 3.3 Household context of low-wage workers, Belgium, 2003

	All low-wage workers	FYFT low-wage workers	All employees	All 16–64 individuals
Position in household				
Reference person	32.3	31.9	56.3	49.0
Partner	49.7	34.0	31.9	31.5
Other	18.0	34.1	11.8	19.5
Household type				
One earner	31.3	36.1	33.5	34.3
Single	11.7	14.9	13.2	8.2
Lone parent	3.3	0.5	2.7	2.8
Couple, no children	5.9	7.2	6.3	7.2
Couple, children	6.0	4.5	7.7	10.7
Other, no children	2.5	6.1	2.3	3.2
Other, children	1.9	2.9	1.2	2.4
Two or more earners	68.7	63.9	65.2	45.8
Couple, no children	16.4	14.6	15.7	9.0
Couple, children	31.1	23.4	31.2	21.7
Other, no children	13.4	18.1	11.2	8.2
Other, children	7.8	7.7	7.1	6.9
Other	0.0	0.0	1.3	19.9

Source: Own calculations on EU-SILC 2004.

This figure is less when we use the FYFT definition, which reports a younger profile of low-wage workers. In general, the education level of low-wage workers is lower than average, with an especially high share of medium-skilled workers. Even though individuals with tertiary education are under-represented among the group of low-wage workers, they still make up 25 per cent of all, and 20 per cent of FYFT low-wage workers. The type of contract under which a worker is employed can be seen as an indicator of the vulnerability of his or her work status. With a share of around 20 per cent, low-wage workers are contracted in temporary – and, hence, probably more vulnerable – jobs almost twice as often as the average worker.

A highly relevant factor from a poverty perspective is the household context of the low-wage worker. Low-wage workers are relatively less likely to be heads of their households (reference person in the survey) than the average employee; more often, they are partners or have another position in the household (see Table 3.3). This last group is especially large when we use the FYFT definition. More than two-thirds of all low-wage workers live in dual-earner households. Under the FYFT definition, single earners are more prominent, especially in those households without children, indicating that households with children have relatively more part-time workers who earn low wages. It is striking that single parents represent 3.3 per cent of all low-wage workers and only 0.5 per cent of FYFT low-wage workers.

THE WORKING POOR

In-work poverty is comparatively less widespread in Belgium than it is elsewhere in Europe. Lohmann and Marx (in this volume) find a working-poor rate for Belgium of just under 6 per cent, the third lowest rate of the 15 countries included in their study. This finding is also in line with earlier studies (Marx and Verbist, 1998; Nolan and Marx, 2000), and these results are confirmed by the more recent EU-SILC data. Our definition of poverty risk conforms to that used in the other chapters of this book, namely, an income below 60 per cent of the median equivalized household income. This definition is currently used in the European Union for co-ordinating policy regarding social inclusion.

The incidence of poverty among low-wage workers amounts to 11.7 per cent when we consider all low-wage workers – and 5.8 per cent among FYFT low-wage workers – which is clearly above the average poverty risk for employees (3.9 per cent), but below the poverty risk for all individuals of active working age (12.8 per cent; see Table 3.4). This indicates that even a low wage is an important factor in protecting against income insecurity. Not only is the in-work poverty rate in Belgium small, but the working poor consist of low-wage workers only to a limited extent: out of all employed persons living in poverty, only 6 per cent are FYFT low-wage workers, and 50 per cent are low-wage workers according to our broader definition. Thus, the overlap between low pay and in-work poverty is small in Belgium.

Among the population at working age, the poverty risk in the Walloon region is, at 15.9 per cent, almost twice as high as it is in Flanders (8.8 per cent). Interestingly, this does not translate into similar regional differences in the poverty risk for low-wage workers: both regions have a poverty risk of around 10 per cent (broad definition) or around 4 per cent (FYFT definition). Low-wage poverty turns out to be most problematic in the Brussels capital region.

Male low-wage workers are faced with a significantly higher poverty risk than are women. Since women make up a high share of low-wage workers according to the broad definition, they account for half of the poor low-wage population. This is no longer the case when we apply our strict definition, which yields an almost 80 per cent share of men among poor

Table 3.4 Incidence and distribution of in-work poverty according to socio-economic characteristics, Belgium, 2003 (%)

	All low-wage workers		FYFT low-wage workers		All employees		All 16–64 individuals	
	Risk	Dist.	Risk	Dist.	Risk	Dist.	Risk	Dist.
All	11.7	100.0	5.8	100.0	3.9	100.0	12.8	100.0
Region								
Flanders	9.5	50.6	3.8	35.9	3.2	50.0	8.8	40.0
Wallonia	10.5	26.0	4.1	23.0	4.1	30.4	15.9	40.0
Brussels	31.7	23.4	20.6	41.1	9.8	19.6	26.2	20.0
Gender								
Men	19.8	47.5	9.5	78.1	4.1	56.8	11.8	46.0
Women	8.6	52.5	2.5	21.9	3.8	43.2	14.0	54.0
Age category								
≤24 years	13.9	20.1	2.3	9.2	7.3	14.4	16.6	22.4
25–34 years	11.5	27.7	6.0	37.7	3.8	26.4	10.9	17.6
35–44 years	11.0	27.0	8.9	30.9	4.1	32.4	12.6	23.1
45–54 years	11.4	19.7	5.0	14.0	3.3	22.0	10.5	17.8
55–64 years	10.9	5.5	13.1	8.2	2.5	4.8	14.6	19.1
Education level (*)								
Low	14.4	35.8	5.7	29.0	7.6	39.2	21.7	52.6
Middle	12.6	50.1	6.7	55.6	4.5	46.0	11.3	34.3
High	6.7	14.1	4.5	15.4	1.4	14.9	5.6	13.1
Type of contract								
Permanent job	10.7	69.3	4.8	65.8	3.1	69.5	–	–
Temporary job	15.2	30.7	10.0	34.2	11.4	30.5	–	–

Notes: (*) Low-skilled: max. lower secondary education; middle: upper secondary or post-secondary non-tertiary; high: tertiary education.

Source: Own calculations on EU-SILC 2004.

FYFT low-wage workers. The FYFT poverty risk also increases with age, indicating that low-wage work is less problematic for younger workers as far as income security is concerned. In contrast, however, among all employees, young workers have a higher poverty risk. Low- and medium-skilled workers face a higher poverty risk than highly skilled workers, and the working poor population consists mainly of medium-skilled workers.

The composition and the income configuration of a person's household are crucial determinants for his or her risk of poverty. Table 3.5 shows that the poverty risk among all 16–64-year-old individuals is highest among

Table 3.5 Incidence and distribution of in-work poverty according to household context, Belgium, 2003 (%)

	All low-wage workers		FYFT low-wage workers		All employees		All 16–64 individuals	
	Risk	Dist.	Risk	Dist.	Risk	Dist.	Risk	Dist.
All	11.7	100.0	5.8	100.0	3.9	100.0	12.8	100.0
Position in household								
Reference person	24.6	67.9	8.4	46.2	4.9	69.9	14.2	53.9
Partner	5.4	22.9	4.7	27.2	2.5	20.2	10.7	26.1
Other	6.0	9.2	4.5	26.6	3.3	9.8	13.2	20.0
Household type								
One earner		83.6		84.3		74.8		33.0
Single	34.4	34.2	6.4	16.3	5.4	18.0	7.6	4.8
Lone parent	22.0	6.2	0.0	0.0	9.2	6.3	16.5	3.6
Couple, no children	32.4	16.3	22.5	27.9	8.0	12.7	8.2	4.6
Couple, children	32.8	16.9	16.9	13.2	13.5	26.3	15.5	12.9
Other, no children	14.4	3.0	17.0	17.7	6.2	3.6	7.5	1.9
Other, children	42.7	7.0	18.8	9.2	25.0	7.9	27.6	5.2
Two or more earners		16.3		15.8		11.6		5.1
Couple, no children	2.1	2.9	0.0	0.0	0.4	1.5	0.3	0.2
Couple, children	3.3	8.8	0.0	0.0	0.7	5.5	1.5	2.6
Other, no children	0.9	1.0	0.0	0.0	0.2	0.5	0.7	0.5
Other, children	5.4	3.6	12.0	15.8	2.3	4.1	3.3	1.8
Other	0.0	0.0	0.0	0.0	41.9	13.6	39.9	62.1

Source: Own calculations on EU-SILC 2004.

individuals who live in households where no one is employed (39.9 per cent). But even households with one earner report an above-average poverty risk in the case of single parents (16.5 per cent), couples with children (15.5 per cent) and other households with children (27.6 per cent).

Among low-wage workers (broad definition), all single-earner households report an above-average poverty risk: around one third of singles and couples (with and without children) are at risk for poverty; for single parents this figure amounts to 22 per cent, and for other households with children it is as high as 42.7 per cent. When we restrict our analysis to FYFT low-wage workers, poverty risks are significantly lower than they are under the broad definition. Still, we find above-average poverty rates (around 20 per cent) for all non-single adult households with one wage earner. Apparently, for singles, a FYFT low wage offers better income protection than it does for multi-member households. The fact that solo parents report a zero poverty risk under the FYFT definition is mainly due to the fact there are very few single parents in this category (cf. Table 3.5).

In general, we can conclude that both the extent of low-wage work and in-work poverty remain limited in Belgium. In the next section, we identify and discuss the most important public policies which affect in-work poverty. We also present factors which may explain why, even though overall in-work poverty risks are low, some groups are more at risk than others.

LOW-WAGE WORK AND IN-WORK POVERTY: THE INSTITUTIONAL AND POLICY CONTEXT

Wage-setting Institutions and Minimum Wage Protection

Wage-setting in Belgium is a matter in which unions and employers have a large degree of autonomy. Although an initial round of bargaining at the national level sets the parameters every two years, actual wage bargaining takes place at the sectoral level, where collective agreements are negotiated in over a hundred parity commissions, some covering specific subsectors with only a few hundred workers. The role of central organizations, which are internally divided along ideological, sectoral and regional lines, is limited. Wage bargaining at the sectoral level has never given great weight to broader societal considerations such as employment growth and unemployment reduction. This stands in contrast to the solidaristic wage-setting regimes in the Nordic countries. Wage deals in high-productivity sectors like manufacturing tend to set the tone for wage increase demands in low-productivity sectors such as personal services; this situation may offer a partial explanation for Belgium's comparatively compressed wage structure. Another notable feature is Belgium's automatic wage indexation system, which guarantees that wages are automatically adjusted to price increases.

There is no statutory minimum wage in Belgium, but there is a nationwide, collectively agreed-upon minimum wage. It is this minimum wage which features prominently in calculations concerning such issues as work incentives and unemployment traps. At US$9.21, the Belgian gross minimum wage per hour in 2005 was below the statutory minimum wages that apply in its neighbouring countries (see Table 3.6). The gross earnings of a full-time Belgian minimum-wage worker amounted to 40 per cent of the average European gross wage in 2005, compared with 47 per cent in France, 46 per cent in the Netherlands and 35 per cent in the UK.

Table 3.6 Gross minimum wages (MW), 2000–2005

Country	Statutory MW per hour[1]		Relative MW levels[2]	
	2000	2005	2000 (%)	2005 (%)
Belgium	9.24	9.21	42	40
France	8.62	9.72	43	47
Ireland	8.26	9.24	53	53
Luxembourg	9.69	10.58	40	42
Netherlands	10.43	10.60	49	46
Poland	1.31	1.51	33	36
Spain	4.12	4.27	34	35
UK	7.88	9.47	32	35
USA	5.84	5.15	39	34

Notes:
1. US$ at 2005 market exchange rate and constant price.
2. Gross earnings of full-time MW-workers as % of gross average wages.

Source: Immervoll (2007).

However, this 'headline' minimum wage serves more of a benchmark purpose than anything else: it constitutes the absolute bottom line of the wage structure. 'Real' minimum wages (that is, pay scales for the youngest, least qualified and least experienced workers) are negotiated at the industry level. These tend to be considerably higher than the nationwide minimum wage. Figures published by the Belgian Ministry of Employment and Labour (Ministerie van Tewerkstelling en Arbeid, 2000) suggest that industry minimum wages are, on average, about 10 per cent higher than the nationwide minimum wage level. Industries where the lowest pay scales are 20 to 30 per cent higher than the nationwide minimum are not exceptional. There are even a few industries where the lowest pay scales are almost twice as high as the nationwide minimum. All the available evidence suggests that very few people actually work – or can work – for the nationwide minimum that features so prominently in the debate.

That said, minimum wages in Belgium have remained virtually stagnant in terms of real purchasing power over the past several decades, as has also been the case in many other Continental European countries – France being a notable exception (Immervoll, 2007; Marx, 2007). Relative to average wages, minimum wages have generally fallen – from 42 per cent in 2000 to 40 per cent in 2005 (Table 3.6). This raises the question of whether it would help to increase minimum wage protection, if the objective is to combat in-work poverty.

In-work poverty is routinely associated with low-paid work, although the actual link is in fact rather weak: our finding that only 6 per cent of all poor employees are FYFT low-wage workers confirms the results of other studies (see, for example, Marx and Verbist, 1998; Nolan and Marx, 2000). Given the limited overlap between low pay and poverty, any policy aimed at improving the earnings of the low-paid as a group will directly benefit only a minority of poor households and will have a substantial spillover effect, since a portion of the non-poor will also benefit. This is certainly true in the case of a minimum wage, even one which is highly effective in increasing the gross earnings of the low paid without having an adverse impact on employment levels. Even in the absence of negative effects on employment, most of the benefits would go to non-poor households simply because that is where most low-paid workers are found.

But, clearly, possible negative employment effects are a major concern in a country like Belgium, where the minimum wage is already comparatively high, The political consensus is that a substantial increase in the minimum wage is neither possible nor desirable (Marx, 2004). The idea here is that significant minimum wage hikes would simply be too harmful to employment and would effectively worsen Belgium's entrapment in 'welfare without work'. In particular, higher minimum wages are seen as an obstacle to women's employment chances and hence to the proliferation of dual earnership, especially among less-skilled couples.

The Impact of Taxes and Social Security Contributions on Income from Work and In-work Poverty

Belgium is often noted for its high level of taxes on wages. According to the Organisation for Economic Co-operation and Development (OECD) (2005), Belgium not only has the highest tax burden in the OECD on average and higher wages, but on low wage levels as well: the total of personal income taxes, employee social insurance contributions and employer social insurance contributions makes up 72 per cent of average gross wages, and 63 per cent of low wages (measured as 67 per cent of the average wage level), which is considerably higher than in most other countries (see Table 3.8). As Table 3.7 shows, in some cases, working households are literally taxed into poverty. Table 3.7 compares minimum wages with two poverty thresholds, calculated on the basis of 60 per cent of the median equivalent income (which was used in our calculation in the second section) as well as a more severe poverty measure of 50 per cent of this income concept. The gross minimum wage is sufficient to keep a household without children out of poverty (either a single person or a couple). But when there are children present, the gross minimum wage is below the 60 per cent poverty line; for

Table 3.7 Comparison of minimum wage (MW) levels with poverty lines, one earner households, 2003

	Gross MW	Net MW	Net income[1]	50% poverty line	60% poverty line
1 adult, no children	1163	925	1029	635	762
2 adults, no children	1163	1038	1155	953	1144
1 adult, 2 children	1163	1040	1378	1016	1220
2 adults, 2 children	1163	1114	1460	1334	1601

Note: 1. Net income includes net wage, holiday pay and end-of-year premium plus child benefits, all amounts on a monthly basis.

Source: Poverty lines calculated on the basis of EU-SILC 2004.

Table 3.8 Average tax rates (personal income tax plus employee social contributions) for full-time workers at minimum (MW), low (67% AW) and average wage (AW) level, 2000–2005 (%)

	2000			2005		
	MW	67% AW	AW	MW	67% AW	AW
Belgium	38.9	67.7	75.9	33.9	63.0	72.3
France	44.0	66.9	70.0	35.2	53.2	71.3
Ireland	16.8	19.6	32.3	12.3	18.7	26.1
Luxembourg	30.8	37.3	43.9	29.7	34.4	40.8
Netherlands	43.3	48.7	43.9	39.9	48.7	43.0
Poland	45.5	50.8	52.0	44.6	51.0	52.4
Spain	37.0	45.3	50.4	37.0	46.4	50.8
UK	16.9	31.0	35.4	17.7	33.1	37.3
USA	24.5	29.1	31.8	23.0	28.4	31.1

Source: Immervoll (2007).

a couple with two children, the gross minimum wage even falls below the stricter 50 per cent poverty line. Taxation aggravates the situation: a single-earner couple with no children would be taxed into poverty if it were not for additional wage components such as end-of-year premiums and holiday pay. For all household types except singles, the net minimum wage is below the 60 per cent poverty line. Solo parents move out of poverty thanks to child benefits and additional wage components, but these are not sufficient for a couple with two children.

Over the last years, Belgium has made efforts to reduce its tax burden on wages, especially for those at the lower end of the income distribution. Various measures have been taken. With the 2001 tax reform, a general tax cut was introduced along with a refundable low-wage tax credit. Also introduced were structural reductions of employee social insurance contributions for low-wage earners, as well as a variety of reductions in employers' social insurance contributions. One of the more recent measures intended to increase the net wages of low-wage workers is the so-called 'work bonus'. This was introduced in January 2005, replacing the structural reductions of employee contributions and the low-wage tax credit. The reduction can amount to 150 euros per month for a low-wage worker; it is tapered away as the wage level increases. In the case of people earning the lowest wages, this measure can reduce their employee social insurance contributions by half.

These measures have had some effect, given that the total tax burden on low wages fell from 68 per cent in 2000 to 63 per cent in 2005. As far as people earning the lowest wages are concerned, a similar decrease took place as the tax burden on Belgian minimum wages dropped from 38.9 per cent in 2000 to 33.9 per cent in 2005 (Table 3.8). However, poverty effects have been very limited up to now: a simulation showed, for instance, that poverty among beneficiaries of the work bonus decreased only from 5.6 to 5.2 per cent as a result of this measure (see Carpentier et al., 2006).

Direct Cash Child Support

We have seen that poverty in work is quite prevalent among single-earner households with children. In addition, Table 3.7 demonstrates that the net income of a single-earner minimum wage household with two children is not sufficient to keep the family out of poverty. This stresses the potential importance of child benefits in preventing in-work poverty, and it raises the question of whether households are adequately compensated for the extra financial burdens that children bring.

Child support in Belgium is distributed over a wide variety of measures. The most relevant of these are child benefits, child tax credits and childcare provisions. Compared with other countries, Belgium has a high level of family spending in the form of cash and tax benefits (see Figure 3.1). Both the child benefit system and the tax advantages for families with children are characterized by a high degree of universalism. This means that, in general, the amounts are not dependent on income level. There are only two exceptions to this: (1) certain groups of replacement income recipients receive a supplementary child benefit, and (2) some people's income is too low for them to fully take advantage of the child tax credit. This last point was

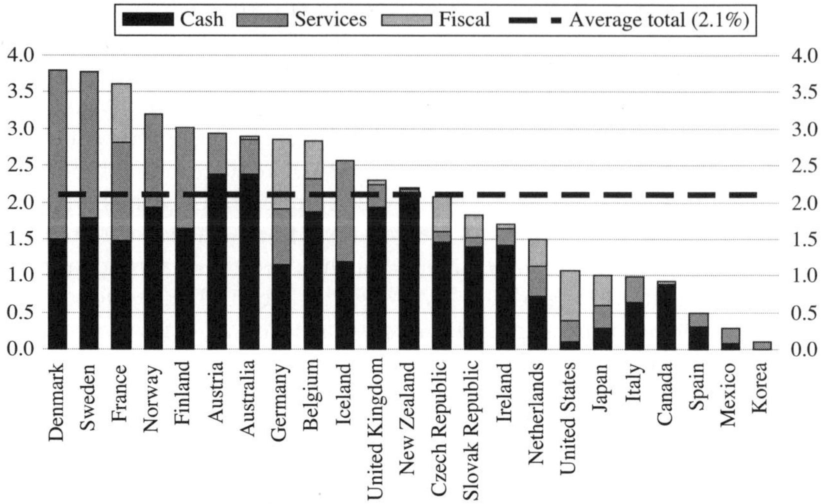

Note: Public support accounted here only concerns public support that is exclusively for families (for example, child payments and allowances, parental leave benefits and childcare support). Spending recorded in other social policy areas as health and housing subsidies are not included.

Source: OECD Social Expenditure Database (www.oecd.org/dataoecd/56/21/35632949.xls).

Figure 3.1 Family spending in cash, services and tax measures, % of GDP in 2001

partly remedied in the 2001 tax reform by making the non-used part of the child tax credit refundable up to a certain limit from fiscal year 2003 onwards.

Even though these two cash provisions for families with children are almost independent of income level, this does not mean that child benefits are uniform for all families with children: the Belgian system is characterized by a high degree of rank progressivity, meaning that benefit amounts increase substantially with the rank of the child in the household. The child benefit for a household with two children is, for instance, 2.84 times as high as the child benefit for a one-child family; for three children it is 5.34 times as high. Likewise, the child tax credit for a couple with two children is 2.70 times as high as the child tax credit for a single child, while for a family with three children it is 4.54 times as high (see Cantillon et al., 2006). The amount of the child benefit also increases with the age of the child. An argument in favour of this strong rank progressivity can be found in the fact that these provisions only partially cover the costs of having children. According to this view, strong rank progressivity should keep the increasing weight of non-covered costs that accompanies an increasing number of children bearable.

Thanks in part to the generosity of this system, child poverty in Belgium is at a relatively low level: less than 5 per cent of all children live in poor households – a figure that is comparable to that of the Nordic countries. Without these family cash transfers, almost 15 per cent of children would live in poverty (see Corak et al., 2005). However, we can see that over the past decades, even though child benefits have been adjusted to account for changes in purchasing power, they have not kept pace with welfare increases. Consequently, compared to national income or net wages, a creeping but steady welfare erosion of these amounts has taken place (Cantillon and Goedemé, 2006). This is especially problematic for families whose incomes are at the bottom of the distribution.

Institutional Support for Dual Earnership: Belgium's Optional Famialism

Belgium is habitually categorized as a 'conservative welfare state' where the male-breadwinner model still reigns supreme. In effect, it still carries many of the hallmarks of what Esping-Andersen has called the conservative welfare state model, in which the Christian democratic 'subsidiarity principle' has institutionalized familialism in the sense of supporting the-male-breadwinner/female-caregiver model. It is fair to say that in Belgium, the labour market and the welfare state remain heavily geared towards the breadwinner model: job security protection remains elaborate, derived social security rights are extensive, the tax system supports the sole-breadwinner model, and so on.

But as this and other chapters in this book show, single earnership has become a poverty risk in an era in which the average living standard – and hence the relative poverty threshold – are increasingly determined by the living standard of double-earner households. There are inherent limits to what breadwinner support policies (minimum wages, single-earner tax benefits and child benefits) can do to counteract this trend. The plain fact is that the best protection against poverty that a household can have is two working adults. Thus, policies that support dual earnership are of crucial importance. Today, Belgium is pursuing these policies at the demand side as well as the supply side.

Policies that facilitate the combination of work and caregiving

While Belgium's labour market and its welfare state remain geared towards the male-breadwinner model, childcare provisions for working parents are also quite extensive, making Belgium a case in point of what Knijn and Kremer (1997) have called 'optional familialism'. That is to say, the caregiving family is supported, but at the same time, families are also given the option of being (at least partially) unburdened from care responsibilities – hence facilitating their access to an earned income. Belgium has extensive childcare provisions, both in the form of institutionalized day-care centres as well as in the form of subsidized 'substitute mothers'. Gross fees are strongly income related as well as partially tax deductible, rendering childcare close to cost-free for those families with the lowest incomes. (The lowest daily gross rate is 1.33 euros, the highest is 23.75 euros.) In 2001, 30 per cent of children between the ages of 0 and 2 were enrolled in formal childcare – a substantially higher share than in countries such as Germany or the Netherlands. Belgium's maternal employment rate is around 70 per cent, which is at the level of Denmark, Sweden and Norway.

Nevertheless, bottlenecks remain. The main problem is localized scarcity of available childcare places. It is estimated that places are available for about one-third of all children under the age of 3 (Leitner, 2005). Waiting lists remain long, and this seems to be a particular problem in the larger cities. In addition, parents may find it very difficult to find institutionalized childcare outside regular working hours – that is to say, for evenings, weekends, holidays and so on. This may pose a particular barrier to less-skilled parents who take up jobs in the services sector, where hours are often irregular. Yet this is precisely the sector where the most job opportunities are available. It would seem, then, that further public investments in institutionalized childcare which broaden its availability and scope could have a substantial effect on the employment chances of less-skilled women.

Policies that boost the demand for less-skilled labour

There is a widely-held belief that unemployment rates – and, more broadly, non-employment rates – for less-educated women are bound to remain high unless more flexible, relatively low-paid jobs are 'allowed' to emerge in the domestic services sector. Such jobs could then provide many single-earner households with the additional income they need to escape poverty.

We have already discussed minimum wages and the limited scope for manoeuvring here: rapid downward adjustment is not a politically viable option. Yet the cost of labour – especially less-skilled labour – is generally perceived to be a major obstacle to more elevated levels of female participation, especially among less-skilled women. It is for this reason that successive Belgian governments have implemented measures which aim to reduce the cost of labour, particularly at minimum-wage level.

These have mainly taken the form of targeted reductions in employers' social security contributions: permanent but modest reductions applying to low-paid workers in general, and temporary but more substantial reductions for employers hiring people who have been unemployed for a long time as well as those from other segments deemed to be at high risk of unemployment. According to OECD (2003) figures, Belgium spends 0.69 per cent of its gross domestic product (GDP) on such programmes, compared to an OECD average of 0.18 per cent, making it a notable outlier. By far the most important measure currently in place is a permanent reduction of social security contributions on low wages. The reduction is highest at the minimum-wage level and decreases from there, becoming zero at around 130 per cent of the minimum wage.

It is not clear what effect these measures are having. Theoretical simulations suggest that reductions in employers' social security contributions will have a substantial impact on the employment of the less skilled. Empirical evaluation studies paint a different picture. There is no direct evaluation evidence available for Belgium, but there is evidence derived from similar schemes in France and the Netherlands which sheds doubt on the cost-effectiveness of such wage cost reduction schemes – particularly with regard to their impact on the employment chances of less-skilled women (see Marx and Verbist in this volume).

CONCLUSION

Comparative studies find that Belgium has a relatively compressed wage structure, including a fairly low incidence of low pay. Poverty rates among workers are also comparatively low in Belgium. Nevertheless, the 'working poor' constitute a significant proportion of the working-age population that lives in relative poverty. As is the case elsewhere in Continental Europe, this rarely has to do with the person in question being in a low-paid job. In fact, the overlap is very small indeed.

In-work poverty in Belgium – as elsewhere on the Continent – is principally a problem of single-parent households and single-earner couples with children. This may come as a surprise given the extent to which the breadwinner model is institutionally supported and protected in Belgium, especially if there are children.

The problem is that single earnership has inevitably become a poverty risk in an era in which the average living standard has come to be determined by the living standard of the double-earner household. There are inherent limits to what breadwinner support policies – minimum wages, single earner tax benefits and child benefits – can do to offset this fact. Apart from the fact that the spillover effects to non-poor households would be enormous, substantial increases in the minimum wage would be politically and economically unrealistic. Despite some erosion in recent years, Belgium retains a fairly generous, universal child benefits system.

Significantly higher cash benefits for families with children only seem realistically feasible for specific groups (such as solo parents); the same is true in the case of further tax and social security contribution reductions for low-income households.

There is no way around the fact that the best protection against poverty that a household can have is two working adults. It does not even matter much whether one or both partners have a low-wage or part-time job – what matters is that there are two incomes. Thus, policies that support dual earnership are of crucial importance. Today, Belgium is pursuing such policies on the demand side as well as the supply side, with mixed success.

Belgium offers extensive childcare provisions, both in the form of institutionalized day-care centres and in the form of subsidized 'substitute mothers'. Belgium's maternal employment rate is now at the level of the Nordic countries. Bottlenecks remain, however, in the form of localized scarcity and difficulties in finding institutionalized childcare outside regular working hours. The impact of efforts made on the demand side – particularly wage cost reductions for low-skilled workers – remains more elusive.

It clearly seems desirable that future efforts to combat in-work poverty should focus even more on boosting – and, more particularly, accommodating – dual earnership. However, this does not take away from the fact that important categories of the working poor – specifically single persons and solo parents – require targeted cash transfers in order to remain shielded from poverty. Although this chapter does not contain a longitudinal analysis, the evidence accumulated through other studies (see, for example, Layte and Whelan, 2003; OECD, 2001) strongly suggests that policy in Belgium cannot and should not rely on the assumption that in-work poverty is a predominantly transitory phenomenon. As always in the case of targeted measures, there is a potential trade-off between immediate need alleviation and long-term behavioural effects.

REFERENCES

Cantillon, B. and T. Goedemé (2006), 'De kinderbijslag in het werknemersstelsel: een terugblik in de toekomst. Reflecties bij 75 kinderbijslag', *Belgisch Tijdschrift voor Sociale Zekerheid*, **48** (1), 7–34.

Cantillon, B., G. Verbist and I. Segal (2006), 'Dekken de voorzieningen voor hoger onderwijs de studiekosten? Een doorlichting van de studiefinanciering in Vlaanderen', *Tijdschrift voor Onderwijsrecht en Onderwijsbeleid*, **2005–2006** (4–5), 368–88.

Carpentier, S., B. Cantillon, K. van den Bosch and G. Verbist (2006), 'Een analyse van de noodzakelijke voorwaarden om indicatoren beleidsanalytisch te gebruiken in het kader van de Belgische Nationale Actieplannen Sociale Insluiting', *Belgisch Tijdschrift voor Sociale Zekerheid*, **48** (3), 327–66.

Corak, M., C. Lietz and H. Sutherland (2005), *Impact of Tax and Transfer Systems on Children in the European Union*, EUROMOD Working Paper EM9/05, The Microsimulation Unit, University of Essex.

European Commission (2004), *Employment in Europe, Recent Trends and Prospects*, Directorate-General for Employment and Social Affairs, Luxembourg: Office of the Official Publications of the EC.

Immervoll, H. (2007), *Minimum Wages, Minimum Labour Costs and the Tax Treatment of Low-Wage Employment*, OECD Social, Employment and Migration Working Papers No. 46, Paris: OECD.

Knijn, T. and M. Kremer (1997), 'Gender and the caring dimension of welfare states: towards inclusive citizenship', *Social Politics*, **4** (3), 328–61.

Layte, R. and C. Whelan (2003), 'Moving in and out of poverty', *European Societies*, **5** (2), 167–91.

Leitner, S. (2005), 'Conservative familialism reconsidered: the case of Belgium', *Acta Politica*, **40**, 419–39.

Marx, I. (2004), 'Mass joblessness, the Bismarckian model and the limits to gradual adaptation: the case of Belgium', in G. Standing (ed.), *Minimum Income Schemes in Europe*, Geneva: International Labour Organization, pp. 219–41.

Marx, I. (2007), *A New Social Question? On Minimum Income Protection in the Postindustrial Era*, Amsterdam: Amsterdam University Press.

Marx, I. and G. Verbist (1998), 'Low-paid work and poverty: a cross-country perspective', in S. Bazen, M. Gregory and W. Salverda (eds), *Low-wage employment in Europe*, Cheltenham, UK and Lyme, USA: Edward Elgar, pp. 63–86.

Ministerie van Tewerkstelling en Arbeid (2000), *Het Federaal Werkgelegenheidsbeleid*, Brussels: Ministerie van Tewerkstelling en Arbeid.

Nolan, B. and I. Marx (2000), 'Low pay and household poverty', in M. Gregory, W. Salverda and S. Bazen (eds), *Labour Market Inequalities: Problems and Policies of Low-Wage Employment in International Perspective*, Oxford: Oxford University Press, pp. 100–119.

Organisation for Economic Co-operation and Development (OECD) (various years), *Employment Outlook*, Paris: OECD.

Organisation for Economic Co-operation and Development (OECD) (various years), *OECD Economic Survey*, Belgium, Paris: OECD.

Verbist, G. (2004), *Redistributive Effect and Progressivity of Income Taxes: An International Comparison across the EU using EUROMOD*, EUROMOD Working Paper EM5/04, The Microsimulation Unit, Cambridge University.

4. The different roles of low-wage work in Germany: regional, demographical and temporal variances in the poverty risk of low-paid workers

Marco Gießelmann and Henning Lohmann

INTRODUCTION

There is a long-standing discussion about the relationship between low wages and in-work poverty. In Germany, this relationship is obviously rather weak: empirical studies have shown that Germany, compared with other countries in the European Union (EU), is a country with a high proportion of low-wage workers – in particular when earned incomes are considered on a monthly basis. But although the low-wage sector is large (Eurostat, 2005), the poverty risk among workers used to be comparatively low (Strengmann-Kuhn, 2003). In this chapter, we explain this empirical phenomenon.

We show that individual low wages are often pooled with other earned incomes within a household, and consequently that living with other employed persons enables low-paid workers to avoid poverty. Then, by analysing the institutional framework, we show that Germany – and Western Germany in particular – can be regarded as a prime example of a modified male-breadwinner model (Lewis and Ostner, 1994) and that potential secondary earners are provided with the incentive to work part-time on a low-wage basis. From this perspective, we are able to explain the high proportion of low-wage workers and discuss whether low-wage work decreases rather than increases the household poverty risk (Becker, 2002). However, we should point out that an attempt to treat Germany as one macro unit fails: even though since reunification, Eastern Germany shares most elements of the institutional framework, it must be regarded as a different case owing to its tradition of dual earnership (Kurz, 1998) and to different economic conditions (Deutsches Institut für Wirtschaftsforschung et al., 2002).

As a consequence, alternative explanations for a high share of low-wage workers and a different interpretation of the role of low-wage work apply in Eastern Germany: while low-wage workers often provide an additional income in Western German households, in Eastern Germany they are usually primary earners. Thus, from a poverty perspective, low-wage work in Eastern Germany must rather be interpreted as a precarious form of employment. Of course, there are also precarious forms of (low-paid) employment in Western Germany. This is shown by analysing the characteristics of the working poor in (Western) Germany. In addition, we discuss whether these precarious forms of employment are becoming more widespread. We argue that employment-centred social policy alters the conditions for income pooling within households and thus the role of low-wage work and its relationship to in-work poverty. One sign of this development might be the increase in the proportion of low-wage work performed in both Eastern and Western Germany in recent years.

Our chapter ties in with studies showing that low-wage workers are not a high-risk poverty group in Germany (Hanesch et al., 2000; Strengmann-Kuhn, 2003) and that the household context is an important moderating factor in the effect of low-wage income on in-work poverty (Fritzsche and Haisken-DeNew, 2004; Göbel et al., 2005). Our hypothesis combines these findings. In addition, our approach explicitly associates empirical results with the configuration of the socio-political and economic framework. Consequently, we are able to discuss presumptions regarding the low in-work poverty rate in Germany and to provide a basis for a critical review of recent welfare state reforms in terms of the working-poor issue.

The chapter is organized as follows. After providing a short description of the data used, the second section of this chapter discusses different ways of measuring poverty and low wages. In particular, we explain our decision to refer to monthly rather than hourly wages. The third section provides an overview of the development of in-work poverty and low-wage work in Germany. In addition, we present the socio-demographic characteristics of the working poor in Germany. In the fourth section, we examine the household characteristics of German low-wage workers. The fifth section introduces the main features of the socio-political and economic framework in Germany. The focus of this introduction is on the differences between the Western and Eastern regions of reunited Germany. Given this background information, we discuss whether and how our empirical findings relate to the institutional and economic framework and explain how the role of low-wage work differs between Western and Eastern Germany. The conclusion of our chapter discusses recent changes in the institutional framework with regard to the role of low-wage work in German households.

DATA AND METHODOLOGY

The following analyses are based on data from the German Socio-Economic Panel (GSOEP), which we are using as a series of cross-sections. In order to correct for the under-/over-representation of certain socio-demographic groups in the GSOEP, we have used cross-sectional population weights, which are provided in the GSOEP Data, throughout our analyses (see Haisken-De New and Frick, 2005).

Our population consists of German workers in private households in the year 2004. Therefore, we refer predominantly to figures from this year but provide information about the underlying trends from 1991 to 2004 as well. The size of our sample is 11 161 in 2004 and varies between 7834 and 14 297 in the other years. Since the development of the economies and the dominant type of household model differs between Eastern and Western Germany, we will consider the two regions separately. However, poverty and low-wage thresholds are based on the German population at large.

We measure poverty on the basis of net disposable household income.[1] In order to account for variances in household needs, we have assigned a weight to each household according to its size and composition. Our calculation of these weights is based on the modified OECD equivalence scale. Dividing the net disposable income of a household by its specific weight, we arrive at the equivalized disposable household income. Throughout our analyses, this measure will be used as indicator of household welfare and is thus the basis for our calculation of the poverty threshold.[2]

A poor individual is defined as someone living in a household with an equivalized disposable income below 60 per cent of the population median. In this chapter, workers are regarded as persons between 17 and 64 years of age who work at least one hour per week. These concepts of 'poverty' and 'work' are fairly common and standard in research (especially in comparative research) on in-work poverty.

By contrast, a standard definition of 'low-wage work' has not yet been established. Studies differ with regard to the definition of wages (net vs gross, hourly vs monthly) and the definition of the working population (inclusion of part-time and marginal workers or not). As a consequence, the extent of low-wage work in Germany varies strongly across different studies. This is illustrated by our summary of several studies in Table 4.1, which report low-wage rates between 13.3 and 28 per cent.

Comparing the study by Hanesch et al. (2000) with the study by Strengmann-Kuhn (2003), we see that referring to gross (as opposed to net) incomes yields a higher low-wage rate. Because income taxes are progressive, they tend to flatten out wage disparities and thus reduce the share of low wages. Furthermore, monthly wages directly reflect variations in

Table 4.1 Low-wage concepts and results in different empirical studies

Study	Data	Analysed income	Reference Population	Low-wage threshold	Low-wage rate (GER)	EU-average
European Commision (2004)	ECHP (2000)	Hourly/gross	Employees working > 15 hours / week	2/3 of median	15.7	15.1
Brenke (2006)	SOEP (2003)	Hourly/gross	Employees	2/3 of median	20	–
OECD (1996)	SOEP (1994) / Country-specific (1993/1994)	Monthly/gross	Full-time employees and self-employed (West Germany only)	2/3 of median	13.3	11.6
Göebel et al. (2005)	SOEP (2003)	Monthly/gross	Employees	2/3 of median	28	–
Hanesch et al. (2000)	SOEP (1998)	Monthly/gross	Employees and self-employed	50% of median	24	–
Kalina and Weinkopf (2006)	SOEP (2004)	Hourly/gross	Employees in main occupation	2/3 of median in Eastern / Western Germany	21	–
Rhein et al. (2005)	IAB Employment Sample (2001)	Monthly/gross	Full-time employees	2/3 of mean	17.4	–
Strengmann-Kuhn (2003)	SOEP (1998) / ECHP (1996)	Monthly/net	Employees and self-employed	50% of median	21	16

working time. Therefore, low-wage rates calculated on the basis of monthly incomes are higher than those based on hourly earnings, as can be seen by the difference between the low-wage rates calculated by Brenke (2006) and Göbel et al. (2005). Since the income data of occasional and part-time workers are sometimes regarded as not reliable, some studies only analyse employees with a minimum number of working hours per month (European Commission, 2004). This restriction affects the incidence of low pay as well. Since persons who work only a few hours are more likely to earn low wages, the exclusion of such workers will result in a reduction of the low-wage rate.

Table 4.1 also indicates that the choice of how we define low-wage work has an effect on Germany's position in the European context. The high proportion of part-time workers in Germany (European Commission, 2004) has a stronger impact on the distribution of monthly wages than on those of hourly wages. Therefore, when analysing the net monthly wage of all workers, Strengmann-Kuhn (2003) shows Germany to be in a more exposed position than does the European Commission (2004), whose analysis is based on hourly gross earnings, only accounting for dependent employees working more than 15 hours per week.

We decided to use a similar concept of low-wage work to that used by Strengmann-Kuhn (2003). Workers who earn less than two-thirds of the median net monthly wage are defined as low paid. The computation of the threshold is based on all workers excluding the self-employed, but including part-time and marginal workers. If an employee has more than one job, only the main occupation is taken into account.[3]

The reason for our decision to use monthly wages is that this chapter focuses on the role of the household with regard to poverty prevention – that is, the effect of income redistribution within the household. Certainly, each individual's contribution to the household's welfare by means of his or her job is determined by two characteristics of that job: first, the level of the hourly wage and, second, the number of working hours. Whereas the monthly wage accounts for both factors, the hourly wage does not tell us anything about differences in the number of working hours. Therefore, from a poverty perspective, it is appropriate to refer to monthly net wages, as they clearly indicate the amount of welfare an individual adds to the household through his or her job.

In addition, it is worth pointing out that the overlap between low monthly-wage and low hourly-wage workers is large in Germany. An analysis of the composition of workers in Germany by type of income, carried out using data from the GSOEP (2004), reveals that our definition of (monthly) low-wage earners includes 75 per cent of all low hourly-wage workers.[4]

However, it is important to note that by making the decision to refer to monthly wages we do not directly address the prominent discussion about minimum wages, which is – at least in Germany – based on the hourly wage. This is important to note, since low hourly-wage and low monthly-wage workers might, despite the great overlap, differ in terms of their chances for avoiding poverty via income pooling.

OVERVIEW: IN-WORK POVERTY AND LOW-WAGE WORK IN GERMANY

Before we analyse the employment constellation of low-wage workers' households in the next section (and thereby explain why the in-work poverty rate in Germany is comparatively low), we provide a brief overview of the development of in-work poverty and low-wage work in Germany.

In a first step, we present a profile of the working poor in the year 2004 using a number of socio-demographic variables (Table 4.2).

As we can see from the first part of Table 4.2, the in-work poverty rate in Germany was 8 per cent in 2004. However, there are large differences in the in-work poverty risk between Eastern and Western Germany: in Eastern Germany, 15 per cent of all workers are poor, in Western Germany only 6 per cent. But although the level of in-work poverty differs, the socio-demographic structure of the working poor is similar between East and West: as additional analyses revealed, the regional difference in poverty risk affects all other socio-demographic groups – with a few exceptions – to the same extent. Therefore, we discuss further determinants of in-work poverty without referring to regional differences.

Table 4.2 reveals that employed women in Germany have a higher poverty risk than employed men. Albeit the majority of all workers are male, 55 per cent of the working poor are women. Furthermore, Table 4.2 shows that an employed woman without a partner is more than twice as likely to be poor as a woman with a partner (13 vs 6 per cent).[5] By contrast, the poverty risk of employed men is only weakly correlated with their partner status. Nine per cent of employed men without partners and as many as 6 per cent of those who have partners are poor.

According to our analysis, workers with children are over-represented among the working poor. Their poverty risk is 9 per cent. However, their risk is highly dependent upon their partner status: employed single parents have a poverty risk of 16 per cent, which is twice as high as that of workers who live with children in a dual-parent household (8 per cent).

With regard to our analysis of the age structure of the working poor, it becomes apparent that poverty is much more common among younger

Table 4.2 Socio-demographic characteristics of working poor and all employees in 2004 (%)

	Share of working	Share of all	Poverty risk
Region			
West Germany	66	82	6
East Germany	34	18	15
Both	100	100	8
Gender			
Men	45	52	7
Without partner	13	11	9
With partner	26	35	6
Other (partner status unknown)	7	6	9
Women	55	48	9
Without partner	20	12	13
With partner	23	31	6
Other (partner status unknown)	12	5	18
Children in household			
Without children (< 14 years)	64	70	7
With children (< 14 years)	36	30	9
Without partner	4	2	16
With partner	26	26	8
Other (partner status unknown)	6	2	22
Age			
< 31 years	40	22	14
31–40 years	21	28	6
41–50 years	23	27	7
51–64 years	15	23	5
Level of qualification			
No qualification	4	1	25
School degree (only)	33	14	17
Vocational qualification/ academic degree	62	83	6
Other	1	1	10
School degree (Casmin)			
No school degree	5	1	25
Secondary school degree	29	28	8
Intermediate school degree	35	35	8
Upper secondary degree	18	29	5
Other (including foreign grades)	13	7	15

Source: SOEP 2004 (weighted).

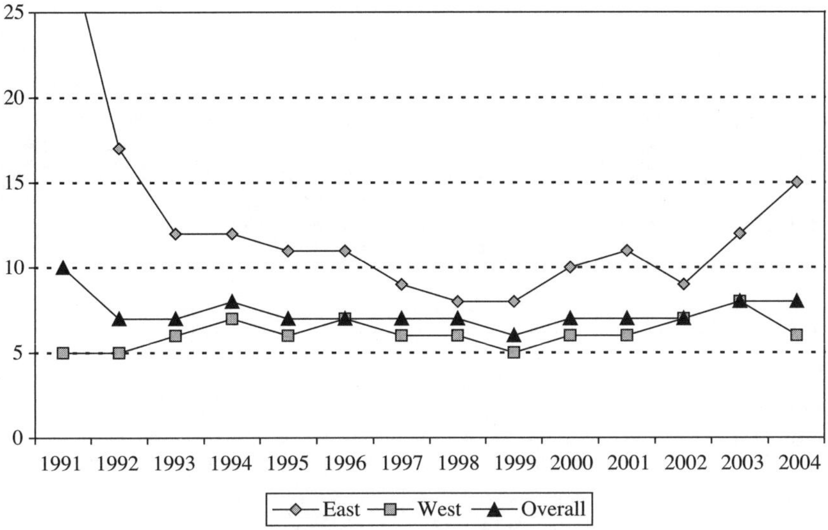

Source: SOEP 1991–2004 (weighted), see also Appendix.

Figure 4.1 In-work poverty rate in Western and Eastern Germany, 1991–2004 (%)

workers. Table 4.2 shows that individuals under 31 years of age make up nearly 40 per cent of the working poor in Germany. Consequently, with a poverty risk of 14 per cent, these workers are more than twice as likely to be poor as older employees.

Twenty-five per cent of workers who have neither a school degree nor a vocational qualification are poor. Since these individuals are weakly represented in the population, the difference in poverty risk among workers with a school degree is more meaningful: according to Table 4.2, workers without a vocational qualification are nearly three times as likely to be poor as those employees who have some form of vocational qualification (17 vs 6 per cent).[6] Another interesting point to note here is that having a vocational qualification has a much stronger effect on the poverty risk than type of graduation completed. As Table 4.2 reveals, the poverty risk between lower and upper secondary school graduates differs by just 3 percentage points.

As we have already reported, the level of in-work poverty differs substantially between Eastern and Western Germany. The following analyses about the development of in-work poverty and low-wage work therefore take regional differences into account. This enables us to gain a more comprehensive picture of the regional distinctions in the in-work poverty risk.

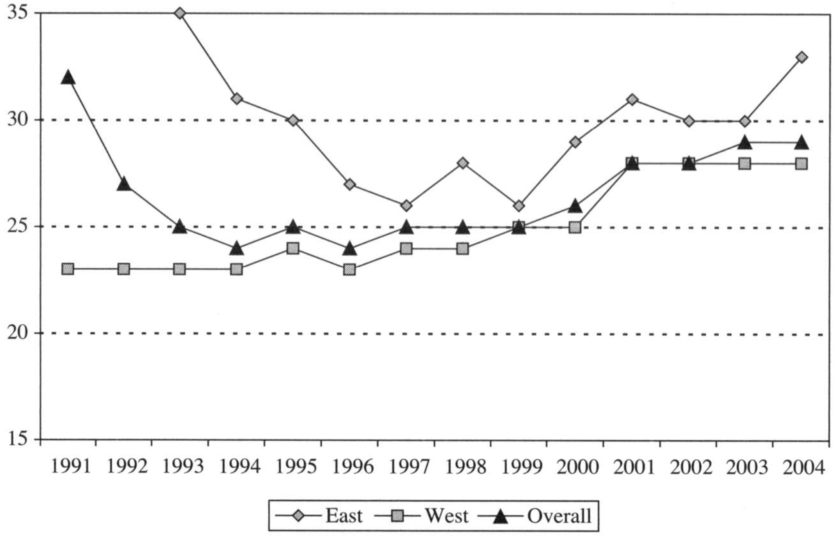

Source: SOEP 1991–2004 (weighted), see also Appendix.

Figure 4.2 Low-wage rate in Western and Eastern Germany, 1991–2004 (%)

Figure 4.1 shows the development of in-work poverty in Germany as a whole, in Western Germany and in Eastern Germany. The decline in the entire rate at the beginning of the observation period was caused by a strong decrease in in-work poverty in Eastern Germany between 1991 and 1993. From 1994 onward, both the Eastern and Western German rates decreased slowly, nearly converging in 1998 at a level of 6 per cent (Western Germany) and 8 per cent (Eastern Germany) respectively. From 1999 to 2003, the in-work poverty risk increased steadily, from 5 to 8 per cent in Western Germany and from 8 to 12 per cent in Eastern Germany. Comparing the 2004 rates with those of 2003, we find a slightly lower in-work poverty risk in Western Germany, whereas Eastern Germany experienced an increase of three percentage points.

Figure 4.2 shows the percentage of low-wage workers in Germany from 1991 to 2004. In Western Germany, the share of low-wage work has increased constantly, from 23 per cent in 1991 to 28 per cent in 2004. By contrast, it appears that the low-wage rate in Germany at large decreased from 32 to 24 per cent between 1991 and 1994. This was obviously caused by a rapid economic adjustment process in Eastern Germany after the process of reunification. In 1999, the Eastern and Western rates converged at a level of 25 and 26 per cent, respectively. Both rates increased

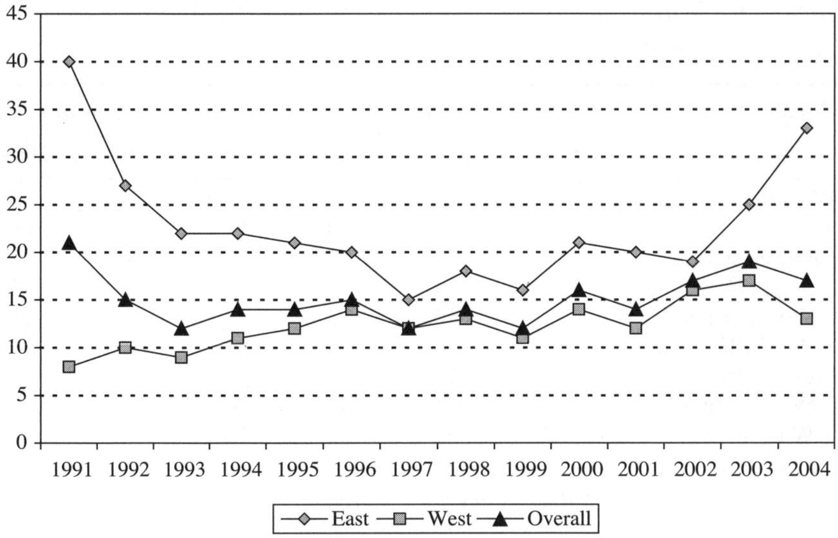

Source: SOEP 1991–2004 (weighted), see also Appendix.

Figure 4.3 In-work poverty rate of low-wage workers in Western and Eastern Germany, 1991–2004 (%)

between 2000 and 2004, with Eastern German employees again more likely to be low-paid than Western Germans (the Eastern German rate is 2 to 5 percentage points higher during that period).

It is not just the in-work poverty rate in 2004, but also its development during the period under observation which differs substantially between Eastern and Western Germany. The same situation applies to the trend of the low-wage rate. Furthermore, Figures 4.1 and 4.2 suggest a closer relationship between the low-wage rate and the in-work poverty rate in the case of Eastern Germany. This impression is confirmed by our statistical analysis of the correlations: the low-wage rate and the in-work poverty rate in Eastern Germany are correlated with a coefficient of r = 0.97. In Western Germany, by contrast, the respective coefficient is only r = 0.37. One could interpret this as a first clue about the different relationships between low wages and poverty in Eastern and Western Germany. Figure 4.3 further emphasizes this contrast: during the whole period under consideration, Eastern German low-wage workers were more likely to be poor than their Western German counterparts. The difference in the respective poverty rates ranged from 3 (2002) to 32 (1991) percentage points. Our assumption that low-paid workers generally manage to avoid poverty seems to be invalid for Eastern Germany. Consequently, the role of low-wage work

Table 4.3 Distribution and poverty rate of low-wage workers by household characteristics in Germany

Household type	Share (percentage)			Poverty risk (percentage)		
	1996	2000	2004	1996	2000	2004
Western Germany						
All	100	100	100	13	14	13
Single earner hh	23	27	29	32	34	32
Single hh	10	14	14	53	42	37
With partner	11	10	13	18	23	23
With other adult	3	3	3	31	37	27
Multi-earner hh	77	73	71	8	8	6
With partner	55	51	49	6	5	4
With other adult	22	22	22	14	13	9
Eastern Germany						
All	100	100	100	20	21	33
Single earner hh	31	30	36	28	46	42
Single hh	14	17	21	37	57	51
With partner	14	10	12	15	31	30
With other adult	4	3	3	–	–	–
Multi-earner hh	69	70	64	17	12	28
With partner	41	45	37	14	12	23
With other adult	27	25	26	21	11	29

Source: SOEP 1996–2004 (weighted).

appears to differ between Western German and Eastern German households.

In the section that follows, we will explain the results presented in this section by analysing the household context of low-wage workers in Germany. First, we explain the low poverty risk experienced by Western German low-wage workers. Then, by separately analysing Eastern German low-wage workers, we will explore whether the regional differences in the poverty risk of low-wage workers can be traced back to differences in household composition.

THE HOUSEHOLD CONTEXT OF LOW-WAGE WORKERS IN GERMANY

In the previous section, we showed that 87 per cent of all low-wage workers in Western Germany avoided poverty in 2004. This finding, of course, is based on the assumption that a household's income (as the sum of all market and transfer incomes that are accumulated within the household) and the respective amount of welfare are distributed equally among its members.

Low-wage workers in Eastern Germany, who had a higher risk of poverty throughout the whole period under consideration, are obviously less able to compensate for low wages. However, the difference in the low-wage rate between Eastern and Western Germany is rather small. In this section, we show how low-wage workers in Western Germany manage to avoid poverty. In addition, we explain why their Eastern German counterparts more often have an income below the poverty threshold.

Table 4.3 describes the household characteristics of low-wage workers in Germany. Furthermore, the table summarizes the way the relationship between low pay and poverty varies according to household structure. We calculated that in 2004, more than 70 per cent of all low-paid workers in Western Germany lived in multi-earner households, and hence were able to pool their income with at least one other earned income. By contrast, an additional analysis indicated that only about 50 per cent of non-low-paid workers have access to the income of an additional earner. Thus, low-paid workers are more likely than the average worker in Western Germany to live together with additional earners. Obviously, they avoid poverty by redistributing their respective earned incomes within the household context. This conclusion is underscored by the poverty rates for the two different types of households: low-wage employees with no other earners within the household appear much more likely to be poor (32 per cent) than employees who are able to pool their low income with another earned income (6 per cent). Thus, contributions of other incomes to the household actually help the majority of low-wage workers to avoid poverty.

A more detailed overview is achieved by further differentiating the household characteristics. It does appear that persons living with an employed partner make up half of the low-paid workers in Western Germany (2004: 49 per cent). With a poverty risk of 4 per cent in 2004, this group of low-wage workers had the lowest poverty rate. In contrast, 37 per cent of the low-wage workers who lived as singles fell below the poverty line in 2004. It may be somewhat surprising that single earners have a better chance of avoiding poverty if they live in couples. Obviously, single earners with partners often have indirect access to additional incomes, such as pensions or unemployment benefits. What is also intriguing about these results is that the largest group of low-wage workers – those living with an employed partner – face a poverty risk below the total Western German in-work poverty rate (6 per cent). Here, low wages may possibly be interpreted as additional incomes which can even act as protection against poverty.

Table 4.3 also shows that sharing a household with other employed people who are not the subject's partner is quite common among low-wage workers in Western Germany. The high percentage in this category (2004: 21 per cent) reflects the fact that low-paid workers without partners are often young individuals living with their parents. Although their poverty risk was greater than the overall in-work poverty risk in 2004 (6 per cent, Table 4.2), they still had a better chance of avoiding poverty than the average low-wage worker.

It does appear that the primary relationships found in Western Germany also hold true for low-wage workers who live in Eastern Germany. As we can see in Table 4.3, Eastern German low-wage workers living in multi-earner households also have a lower poverty risk than low-paid single earners (2004: 28 vs 42 per cent). However, compared to their Western German counterparts, Eastern German low-wage workers are more often single earners (2004: 36 vs 29 per cent). Furthermore, the contributions of other incomes have a smaller effect on the poverty risk of low-wage workers in the eastern parts of Germany: while the differences in the poverty risk between single earners in Eastern and Western Germany can be regarded as small (2004: 42 vs 32 per cent), Eastern German low-wage workers with employed partners were almost six times as likely to be poor as their Western German counterparts in 2004. Although the latter difference was less pronounced in 1996 and 2000, the relative difference in poverty risk between low-wage workers with and without an additional earner was greater in Western Germany in these years as well. In 1996 (2000), Western German low-wage workers without an additional earner were four (4.25) times as likely to be poor as their counterparts with an additional earner. In Eastern Germany, by contrast, the respective ratio was 1.6 (3.8).

Taken together, our findings explain the low poverty rate among low-wage workers in Western Germany. Based on the assumption that each household member has equal access to the household income, they reveal that low-wage workers generally avoid poverty by redistributing the members' earned incomes within the household context. This finding corresponds to the results of our analysis about the role of potential other sources of income for low-wage workers in Western Germany: only a minority of them – less than 10 per cent – have more than one job and thus access to a second own employment income (results not reported).

Differences between the poverty risks of low-wage workers in Eastern and Western Germany can, to some extent, be traced back to regional differences in the status of low-wage work in the household context. Furthermore, the results show that low individual pay translates into household poverty to a different degree for different household characteristics on the one hand, and between Eastern and Western Germany on the other. By demonstrating the importance of living arrangements in households for people in low-paid jobs, especially in Western Germany, single earners receiving low wages are identified as a high poverty-risk group. It becomes apparent that this group has grown steadily larger over the course of time: the share of single earners among low-wage workers in Western Germany has increased from 23 per cent in 1996 to 29 per cent in 2004 (Eastern Germany: 31 to 36 per cent).

In Eastern Germany, the effect of the household context on the poverty risk of low-wage workers is smaller. Living in a multi-earner household protects against poverty to a much lesser degree for Eastern than for Western low-wage workers. Thus, additional explanations other than income redistribution within the household context have to be taken into account in order to explain the regional differences in the poverty of low-wage workers. In addition, the high share of low-wage workers in both regions remains unexplained so far.

In order to clarify these issues, we will explain and classify our empirical findings in the next section by analysing Germany's institutional and economic framework. Explanations for the regional differences in the poverty risk of low-wage workers mainly have to do with the labour market situation, whereas the high share of low-wage workers in Western Germany can be interpreted as resulting from the configuration of the socio-political context. In addition, looking at our empirical results from a macro perspective will enable us to argue whether low wages might even act as a protection against poverty in Western Germany.

THE DIFFERENT ROLES OF LOW-WAGE WORK IN GERMANY

The preceding analysis showed that the majority of low-wage workers in Western Germany live together with other employed persons and thereby mostly avoid living in poverty. Thus, we explained empirically that a high low-wage rate on the one hand and a low in-work poverty rate on the other is not a contradiction in Western Germany. In Eastern Germany, by contrast, living together with other employed persons protects workers against poverty to a much lesser degree.

An additional analysis regarding the composition of low-wage workers using data from the GSOEP revealed that in 2004, 79 per cent of all low-wage workers in Western Germany were women. By contrast, the share of women among the entire working population was 48 per cent. In Eastern Germany, however, women accounted for only 65 per cent of low-wage (and 49 per cent of all) workers.

Our results concerning the household context of low-wage workers are obviously related to female participation in the labour market. Labour participation of women, in turn, can be regarded as dependent on cultural values on the one hand and on institutional variables on the other (Pfau-Effinger, 2004). Therefore, in order to interpret our empirical findings, in this section we analyse the cultural norms of gendered division of labour and the institutional framework in Germany. We also consider some features of the economic context – namely, the unemployment rate and the wage level. By describing these components, we show how the low in-work poverty risk of Western German low-wage workers and the regional differences in the poverty risk between Eastern and Western German low-wage workers relate to the configuration of the framework. From this macro point of view, we are also able to explain the high share of low-wage workers in Germany and to discuss whether low-wage work decreases rather than increases the household poverty risk in Western Germany.

Western Germany can traditionally be categorized as a society in which cultural norms and attitudes are oriented towards the male-breadwinner model of the family. This model prescribes that husbands hold regular full-time jobs and care for the material well-being of the family, whereas their wives are assigned the tasks of homemaking and caring for children (Lewis and Ostner, 1994). As in most European countries, this model became prevalent during the transition from the agrarian to the industrial society towards the end of the nineteenth century (Hinrichs, 1996; Pfau-Effinger, 2004). The allocation of gender-specific roles within the family was reinforced in West Germany after the Second World War. This can be explained by the domination of the Christian Democratic Party from 1949 to 1969, which is traditionally committed to a Catholic social doctrine (Esping-Andersen, 1999).

From the end of the 1960s, cultural ideas about female employment changed. This change was brought about by several developments which were all, more or less, related to the process of 'post-industrialization' – the transition from an industrial to a service society (Haller and Höllinger, 1994; Kaufmann, 2003; Pfau-Effinger, 2004): the expansion of the educational system, the emergence of the women's emancipation and the students' movements, the individualization of family forms and life courses and the creation of new fields of employment with jobs that were considered to be 'female'. Nevertheless, despite the fact that a change in female orientation towards employment took place, the idea that mothers are primarily responsible for childcare has prevailed in Western Germany to this day (Haller and Höllinger, 1994).

Attitudes and cultural norms are certainly important determinants of the dominant family model within a society. Nevertheless, previous research has shown that there are a number of institutional factors supporting the division of labour within households. Therefore, in the following paragraphs, we discuss the roles of taxation, the social insurance system, parental leave and childcare policies.

In Germany, the taxation of earned incomes is based on two prominent principles: first, married couples are regarded as a single economic unit. With regard to taxation, their incomes are added together, halved and then taxed as two separate incomes (Daly, 2000). Second, the taxation of income is progressive. Thus, assuming the existence of a primary earner, the income of a potential secondary earner is (virtually) taxed at a higher rate. Hence, the German system of taxation clearly privileges single-income couples and creates disincentives for potential secondary earners to take on employment.

However, Dingeldey (2000) argues that the principle of splitting also privileges couples whose individual incomes differ significantly. This is especially true if one earner works on the basis of a so-called 'marginal job'. Salaries from these jobs are exempt from joint taxation and taxed at a fixed rate of 30 per cent, as long as they do not exceed the amount of 400 euros (Bundesministerium der Justiz, 2006).[7] Summing up, it can be pointed out that secondary earners within couples are, on the one hand, provided with a disincentive to reduce the income gap with the primary earner (for example, by shifting from part-time to full-time employment) and, on the other hand, provided with an incentive to work marginally on a monthly low-wage basis.

The social insurance system in Germany is predominantly based on contributions and not financed by taxes. Thereby, the principle of equality between contribution and benefit applies (Kaufmann, 2003). Since contributions are compulsory and related to the (working) income, the extent of protection against life's risks largely depends upon employment. Thus, Germany can be regarded as a country with a relatively low degree of social security for persons who are not entitled by current or past employment (Esping-Andersen, 1990; Ullrich, 2005).[8] However, non-working dependants are entitled to many social security benefits and are thus released from the commitment to (own) employment via their relationship to the (employed) breadwinner (Pfau-Effinger, 2004).[9] Thus, it can be said that the German system of social security privileges those families who follow a single-earner model (Daly, 2000; Pfau-Effinger, 2004). It does not contain economic incentives for potential secondary earners to take on any more than marginal employment.

While Germany ranks high in international comparisons of parental leave policies (Daly, 2000), the coverage of public childcare in Western Germany is less extensive (Büchel and Spieß, 2002; Leibfried and Ostner,

1991): public childcare for children under 3 years of age is practically non-existent (coverage is below 3 per cent in Western Germany) and has not improved significantly since the early 1990s (Statistisches Bundesamt, 2004). For pre-school children (3–6 years), part-time childcare is a frequent solution: publicly funded childcare facilities are usually available until noon. The same goes for young pupils, since primary schools are required to care for their pupils until 1 p.m., but largely do not offer full-time childcare: only 8.3 per cent of all pupils aged 6 to 10 years were granted a full-time place in school or in an after-school care club (*Hort*) in Western Germany in 2002 (Riedel et al., 2005). Basically, therefore, children in Western Germany are supposed to stay in their parents' custody in the afternoon. As the role of the caretaker within the family is – in most cases – performed by women, mothers are often only able to work part-time.

Taking all these different aspects into consideration, we can sum up by saying that the configuration of the institutional framework in Germany supports part-time employment of the (female) partner of the (male) breadwinner. At the same time, it provides disincentives for women to work full-time. When we take the employment and family orientation of women into account as well, it is appropriate to think of Western Germany today as a society in which a modified (Dingeldey, 2000) or modernized (Pfau-Effinger, 2004) male-breadwinner model prevails. This model is based on a man who is employed full-time and a woman who works part-time. Naturally, due to the low number of working hours, part-time work is associated with a greater risk of low pay. Consequently, the role of low-wage work in Western Germany has to be interpreted as secondary employment within the household context. This explains the high proportion of low-paid workers in Western Germany, their above average appearance within the multi-earner household and, finally, their low in-work poverty risk.

In the previous section, we found that the poverty risk among low-wage workers with an employed partner is below the overall in-work poverty risk. Therefore, it might also be worth discussing whether low-paid female employment often even acts as a protection against poverty (see Becker, 2002). However, the role that additional earners play in preventing poverty ought not to be overestimated. Several studies dealing with female employment and attitudes towards it suggest that female participation in the labour market is strongly related to independence and self-realization (Haller and Höllinger, 1994; Kurz, 1998), motives which are pronounced in the higher education milieu. Consequently, supplementary female part-time work might be interpreted as a middle-class phenomenon, enhancing the welfare position of households which are – from a poverty perspective – not relying on this economic effect. The below-average in-work poverty risk of low-wage workers with employed partners must accordingly be interpreted as a mediated class (or education) effect. We are not able to clarify this issue definitively by means of our results. Thus, the question of whether low-wage work prevents poverty or indicates certain determinants of welfare still remains open.

Until now, our presentation of the framework has been restricted to Western Germany. In the previous section, we showed that low-wage employees in Eastern Germany are significantly more likely to be poor than their Western counterparts, despite the fact that the rate of low-wage employment is similarly high in both regions. This leads to the assumption that low payment has a different structure and different causes in Eastern Germany.[10]

In this section we were already able to reveal that Eastern German low-wage workers are more likely to be single earners than their Western German counterparts. However, the difference is rather small and does not fully explain the regional variances in poverty risk. In order to provide an exhaustive explanation, we need to consider the fact that context and (gender) culture differ between Eastern and Western Germany.

After reunification, West Germany's institutional framework was imposed upon the Eastern Federal States (Kaufmann, 2003). The only institutional feature that now differs is the childcare system, which, in the East, still contains some elements of the former German Democratic Republic (GDR) system and consequently provides options for full-time childcare (Dingeldey, 2000). By contrast, the economic context reveals large differences between the two regions (Deutsches Institut für Wirtschaftsforschung et al., 2002). First, compared with Western Germany, firms (especially industrial businesses) are, on average, younger, smaller and, consequently, less productive. Second, Eastern Germany still faces infrastructural deficits and thus attracts very few investors. Third, since the ageing and shrinking of the population are proceeding faster than in Western Germany, the Eastern German economy suffers from a comparatively low demand for goods and services. Accordingly, Table 4.4 reveals that the wage level in Eastern Germany has been significantly lower than that of Western Germany since reunification (see also Görzig et al., 2004). In 1991, the average Eastern German hourly wage (4.63 euros) was less than half as high as the average wage in Western Germany (10.81 euros). Wage levels then converged steadily up until 1995. From 1995 to 2001, the difference remained relatively stable, with the average Eastern German wage amounting to between 67.6 and 71.4 per cent of that in Western Germany. In 2001, the wage gap was again reduced by about 3 percentage points and has remained relatively stable in subsequent years.[11]

The difference in the average hourly wage between Eastern and Western Germany can be regarded as significant throughout the whole period under

Table 4.4 Hourly gross wages in Eastern and Western Germany (1991–2004)

Year	Mean wage		Wage gap (percentage)
	Western Germany	Eastern Germany	
1991	10.81	4.63	42.8
1992	11.87	6.27	52.8
1993	12.49	7.73	61.9
1994	12.87	8.63	67.1
1995	13.56	9.51	70.1
1996	14.05	9.50	67.6
1997	14.00	9.93	70.9
1998	14.22	9.73	68.4
1999	14.22	9.86	69.3
2000	14.36	10.25	71.4
2001	14.43	10.77	74.6
2002	15.12	11.07	73.2
2003	15.61	11.50	73.7
2004	15.82	11.82	74.7

Source: SOEP 1991–2004 (weighted).

consideration. As a consequence, at any given point in time, primary earners in particular have had a greater low-wage risk. Thus, the aggregation of two low-wage incomes within a household is more probable in Eastern Germany, and the sum of two Eastern German earned incomes is less likely to reach the poverty threshold defined on the basis of the joint distribution. Consequently, the poverty risk of low-paid workers with working partners in Eastern Germany is higher than it is in Western Germany. Along with the higher proportion of single earners among low-wage workers in East Germany (which is interpreted below), this explains the difference in poverty risk between Eastern and Western German low-wage workers.

It may seem surprising that the difference in wage levels between Eastern and Western Germany does not result in a significant difference in the low-wage risk. This can be traced back to the fact that female full-time employment is more common in Eastern Germany. Consequently, employed women are at a lower part-time risk and therefore also at a lower low-wage risk compared with Western Germany.

Whereas after the Second World War the (modified) male-breadwinner model was established in West Germany, the dual-earner model became predominant in the GDR (Braun and Nowossadeck, 1992). The comprehensive provision of state-run childcare facilities allowed for high labour participation among women. The reasons for this were economic as well as ideological in nature: on the one hand, the GDR system suffered from a labour shortage; on the other hand, the emancipation of women is a traditional socialist claim (Kurz, 1998).

The socio-political framework of the former GDR and the cultural imprint under the socialist regime have shaped current attitudes towards female employment in Eastern Germany (Braun and Nowossadeck, 1992; Kurz, 1998). But despite the strong orientation towards female employment and the provision of day-care facilities, many couples in Eastern Germany fail to take on two jobs. This is indicated by the fact that the share of single earners among the low-paid is larger than in Western Germany. Obviously, in Eastern Germany, the dual-earner model has eroded. One possible reason for this development is that the high orientation towards employment among Eastern German women conflicts with many components of the institutional framework (Braun and Nowossadeck, 1992; Dingeldey, 2000), which is now – as mentioned above – the same one that exists in Western Germany. Another reason might be the high share of unemployed persons in the East. During the observation period, individuals in Eastern Germany were nearly twice as likely to be unemployed as individuals in Western Germany (Bundesagentur für Arbeit, 2006).

In summary, it does appear that although the low-wage rates are similarly high in Eastern and in Western Germany, the causes are different: whereas low-wage jobs in Western Germany are often supplementary incomes that help families to increase their welfare, the high share of low-wage work in Eastern Germany reflects the inequality of incomes between the two regions. Low-wage work in Eastern Germany consequently has the role of a primary employment within the household context. A low wage received by a primary (and especially by a single) earner is, as a matter of course, more strongly associated with household poverty than a low wage received by a secondary earner. When we also consider the high unemployment rate in Eastern Germany, this explains our findings about the high in-work poverty risk of low-wage workers in Eastern Germany.

SUMMARY AND PERSPECTIVE

We have shown that in Western Germany, the modified male-breadwinner model is the dominant type of family model. This can be traced back to cultural norms, on the one hand, and to the configuration of the institutional context, on the other. Thus, low-paid jobs are widespread, and in most cases are a supplementary source of income for households in Western Germany.

This situation is also reflected in our data: in 2004, 28 per cent of all workers in Western Germany received a low wage. The vast majority of them – 71 per cent (2004) – lived together with additional earners and had an average in-work poverty risk of only 6 per cent (2004). A low-wage worker who lived with an employed partner even had a below-average in-work poverty risk – that is, 4 per cent (2004).

The role of low-wage work in Eastern Germany is different. Since cultural norms are oriented towards female full-time employment, and childcare provision supports the double-earner model, low-paid jobs are not primarily linked to part-time and secondary employment. Rather, the high proportion of low-wage work (2004: 33 per cent) expresses a generally lower wage level in Eastern Germany as compared to Western Germany. The high unemployment rate in Eastern Germany is reflected by the empirical fact that low-paid jobs are more often the sole source of income (in contrast to Western Germany, only 64 per cent of workers live with additional earners) and that low-wage workers are much more likely to receive state transfers. Consequently, the poverty risk among low-wage workers (2004: 33 per cent) and the general in-work poverty risk (2004: 15 per cent) are higher than they are in Western Germany (13 per cent and 6 per cent, respectively).

But the problem of low-paid jobs being the main source of income is obviously not only an Eastern German issue. This is revealed by our analysis of the composition of the working poor in Germany, which indicates that region of residence is a decisive, but not the sole determinant of in-work poverty. Furthermore, in an additional analysis, we found that although the poverty risk of low-wage workers is small, the vast majority of poor employees in Western Germany – 63 per cent – are low paid.

Young people who are at an early stage in their careers often receive low hourly wages – which can be explained by the fact that wage systems are mostly organized in terms of age and seniority. In addition, it might be argued that entry into some professions takes place via internships and part-time jobs. Consequently, workers under 31 years of age are – with a poverty risk of 14 per cent (2004) – over-represented in the group of the working poor. Persons who, due to a lack of educational and/or vocational qualification, only have access to simple and unspecialized job opportunities have a greater risk of being low-paid as main earners as well. Thus, their poverty risk is well above average.

In addition, our analysis has revealed that women without partners have, compared with their male counterparts, a high in-work poverty risk (13 per cent). This can largely be traced back to the fact that women are more often single parents, who have an above-average in-work poverty risk of 16 per cent. Also, it should be noted that the modified male-breadwinner model creates economic dependencies within couples (Lewis and Ostner, 1994). As Daly (2000) argues, the high level of decommodification among women depends upon marriage with a male breadwinner. In the case of separation or divorce (which is, in many cases, associated with a shift from being a secondary to a primary earner), an expansion of (formerly) part-time employment is likely not to be possible. Given the fact that women more often assume custody of children after separation, this might explain the high poverty risk of women without partners (Andreß et al., 2006).

The high in-work poverty risk of single parents can be traced back to restrictions in the childcare system. Single parents in gainful employment often have to make do with part-time work and are consequently at a high risk of low pay. Since they are main earners by definition, their low payment situation is a precarious one. Consequently, a diversification of lifestyles – which implies the realization of family models with only one adult – is not compatible with the configuration of the socio-political framework: from the point of view of single parents, the institutional context in Western Germany is misspecified.

As studies reveal, there is a trend towards alternative living arrangements and single-parent families in Germany (see Brüderl, 2004). This development, in turn, increases the incidence of precarious low-wage employment. Apart from a pluralization of lifestyles, there are other reasons for assuming that the role of low-wage work is beginning to be redefined in Western Germany. The increasing unemployment rate in Western Germany during the period under consideration (from 6.2 per cent in 1991 to 9.4 per cent in 2004; Statistisches Bundesamt, 2004) reveals that Germany is facing a decline in the percentage of employed persons. Therefore, it might have become more difficult for a low-wage worker to pool his or her income with that of another earner. This affects the in-work poverty issue, since the impact of low-wage work on poverty risk depends upon the household context. Indeed, our analysis (Table 4.3) indicates that the number of low-paid earners who do not have access to a partner's earned income has increased steadily, from 23 per cent in 1996 to 29 per cent in 2004. In addition, we can assume that an increasing unemployment rate affects the poverty risk of non-low-wage employees as well.

Furthermore, the high unemployment rate indicates a lower demand for labour in general and consequently a decrease in bargaining power for dependent employees. This loss is strengthened by social policy which increasingly stresses the importance of labour market participation by lowering the level of unemployment benefits: for instance, a recent reform in unemployment policies ('Hartz 4 – Reform') has abolished the status-based system of unemployment assistance in favour of a system similar to the former social assistance programme, which places more conditions on the granting of benefits (Becker and Hauser, 2006).

In addition, we can observe a decline in union power in recent years (in part, this development can also be traced back to shifts in the bargaining position of unions brought about by a high unemployment rate): union density as well as collective bargaining coverage have decreased in the last few years (Ellguth and Kohaut, 2005). The erosion of the latter is partly driven by so-called 'opt-out' clauses, which were initially introduced to help firms which suffered from negative economic conditions (Bispinck, 2004). Since there is no general minimum wage in Germany, lower wage boundaries are set by collective agreements. Hence, the decline in bargaining coverage is expected to result in a decrease in lower wage boundaries. Furthermore, a larger dispersion of wages is being discussed as means to create a higher demand for low-skilled labour (Bonin et al., 2003).

Owing to the low demand for labour and increased labour market pressures, former standard full-time earners are being forced to make do with atypical employment and low-wage jobs (Hoffmann and Walwei, 1998). In addition, the unemployed are largely being channelled into low-paid employment. The steadily increasing low-wage rate in Western Germany (Figure 4.2) could be interpreted as support for this assumption. As a consequence, part-time and low-wage jobs often lose their status as supplementary sources of income and become the main source of income within the household. An increase in poverty among the group of low-paid employees (from 10 to 13 per cent) and workers in general (from 5 to 6 per cent) can be observed since the end of the 1990s, and might already reflect this change in the role of low-wage work.

Taking all these different aspects into consideration, we can assume that changes in the economic context and the institutional framework, resulting in an increase in the poverty rate in Germany in recent years (Bundesministerium für Gesundheit und Soziale Sicherung, 2005), have also raised the poverty risk of the employed population. First signs of an erosion of the dominant role of low-wage work have already been indicated by our analysis. Therefore, a comprehensive review of recent changes in the configuration of the welfare state and the labour market and its consequences on the incidence and structure of in-work poverty appear to be important issues for further research.

NOTES

1. In the GSOEP, this information is collected via the so-called 'income-screener' question ('If you take a look at the total income from all members of the household, how high is the [disposable] monthly household income today?').
2. For a discussion about the implications of different equivalent scales see Becker (2002).
3. The net income in the primary job is also collected using an 'income-screener' question in the GSOEP. However, we have used a modified version of the respective variable with imputed values in case of item non-response (see Frick and Grabka, 2005).
4. In detail, we found that 18 per cent of all workers in Germany receive a low wage according to both definitions. Eleven per cent earn a low monthly wage and 6 per cent a low hourly wage alone. Thus, with a total of 24 per cent, we found a higher share of low hourly-wage workers than Kalina and Weinkopf (2006), whose results are based on identical data and the same threshold (see Table 4.1). This variance in results can be explained by differences in the definition of the working population: Kalina and Weinkopf included only workers who are primarily employed and consequently excluded students, pensioners, and so on with supplementary (and consequently low-paid) jobs.
5. The category 'other' includes predominantly (adult) children. Their above-average in-work poverty risk may seem surprising, but it obviously reflects the fact that an early entry into the labour market is more common in lower classes.
6. Nevertheless, employees with a vocational qualification still represent the largest group among the working poor in Western Germany.
7. During the period under consideration, the exact conditions of a marginal job have changed several times with respect to the upper limit of wage and number of working hours. Nevertheless its basic feature, the flat tax rate, has always remained.
8. Compared with other so-called 'residual' welfare states, benefits such as social assistance payments and housing benefits, which are granted independent of past or current employment status, are high in Germany (Esping-Andersen, 1990; Kaufmann, 2003). Therefore, our valuation here is based on the difference in the level of coverage between people with and without employment.
9. As far as health care is concerned, for example, family members of a single earner are generally covered without any additional contributions (Dingeldey, 2000). However, this regulation only applies to non-working family members or those who work marginally. Another important example is that of retirement pensions, whose level is determined by the duration and amount of contributions to the pension insurance fund (Kaufmann, 2003). In the case of death, titles to benefits are partially transferred to married partners ('survivorship annuity'; Daly 2000).
10. The high share of Eastern German low-wage workers who receive social assistance payments or unemployment benefits (about 25 per cent, own calculations with GSOEP 2004), reinforces this impression.
11. These results partially explain the development of the difference in in-work poverty rates between Eastern and Western Germany (Figures 4.1 and 4.3), which was – at least until 2002 – approximately mirrored by the development of the difference in the wage levels. However, the increase in the in-work poverty rate in Eastern Germany between 2002 and 2004 remains unexplained.

REFERENCES

Andreß, H.-J., B. Borgloh, M. Bröckel, M. Gießelmann and D. Hummelsheim (2006), 'The economic consequences of partnership dissolution. A comparative analysis of panel studies from five European countries', *European Sociological Review*, **22**, 533–60.

Becker, I. (2002), 'Frauenerwerbstätigkeit hält Einkommensarmut von Familien in Grenzen', *Vierteljahreshefte zur Wirtschaftsforschung*, **71** (1), 126–46.

Becker, I. and R. Hauser (2006), *Verteilungseffekte der Hartz-IV-Reform: Ergebnisse von Simulationsanalysen. Forschung aus der Hans-Böckler-Stiftung, 69*, Berlin: Edition Sigma.

Bispinck, R. (2004), 'Kontrollierte Dezentralisierung der Tarifpolitik – Eine schwierige Balance', *WSI Mitteilungen*, **57** (5), 237–45.

Bonin, H., W. Kempe and H. Schneider (2003), 'Household labor supply effects of low-wage subsidies in Germany', *Journal of Applied Social Science*, **123** (1), 199–208.

Braun, M. and S. Nowossadeck (1992), 'Einstellungen zur Familie und zur Rolle der Frau', in P. Mohler and W. Bandilla (eds), *Blickpunkt Gesellschaft 2. Einstellung und Verhalten der Bundesbürger in Ost und West*, Opladen: Westdeutscher Verlag, pp. 127–40.

Brenke, K. (2006), 'Wachsender Niedriglohnsektor in Deutschland – Sind Mindestlöhne sinnvoll?', *Wochenbericht des DIW Berlin*, **15/16**-2006, 197–205.

Brüderl, J. (2004), 'Die Pluralisierung partnerschaftlicher Lebensformen in Westdeutschland und Europa', *Aus Politik und Zeitgeschichte*, 2004/**B19**, 3–10.

Büchel, F. and C. Spieß (2002), *Form der Kinderbetreuung und Arbeitsmarktverhalten von Müttern in West- und Ostdeutschland*, Schriftenreihe des Bundesministeriums für Familie, Senioren, Frauen und Jugend; Bd. 220, Stuttgart: Kohlhammer.

Bundesagentur für Arbeit (2006), *Arbeitsmarkt 2005. Arbeitsmarktanalyse für Deutschland, West- und Ostdeutschland*, Amtliche Nachrichten der Bundesagentur für Arbeit, Nürnberg: Bundesagentur für Arbeit.

Bundesministerum der Justiz (2006), *Sozialgesetzbuch Viertes Buch: SGB IV*.

Bundesministerium für Gesundheit und Soziale Sicherung (2005), *Lebenslagen in Deutschland. Der 2. Armuts- und Reichtumsbericht der Bunderegierung*, Bonn: Bundesministerium für Gesundheit und Soziale Sicherung.

Daly, M. (2000), *The Gender Division of Welfare: The Impact of the British and German Welfare States*, Cambridge: Cambridge University Press.

Deutsches Institut für Wirtschaftsforschung, Institut für Arbeitsmarkt- und Berufsforschung, Institut für Weltwirtschaft, et al. (eds) (2002), *Fortschrittsbericht wirtschaftswissenschaftlicher Institute über die Entwicklung in Ostdeutschland*, Halle (Saale): Institut für Wirtschaftsforschung.

Dingeldey, I. (ed.) (2000), *Erwerbstätigkeit und Familie in Steuer- und Sozialversicherungssystemen: Begünstigungen und Belastungen familialer Erwerbsmuster im Ländervergleich*, Opladen: Leske + Budrich.

Ellguth, P. and S. Kohaut (2005), 'Tarifbindung und betriebliche Interessenvertretung: Aktuelle Ergebnisse aus dem IAB-Betriebspanel', *WSI Mitteilungen*, **58** (7), 398–409.

Esping-Andersen, G. (1990), *The Three Worlds of Welfare Capitalism*, Princeton, NJ: Princeton University Press.

Esping-Andersen, G. (1999), *Social Foundations of Post-Industrial Economies*, Oxford: Oxford University Press.

European Commision (2004), *Employment in Europe 2004: Recent Trends and Prospects*, Luxembourg: Office of the Official Publications of the EC.

Eurostat (2005), 'In-work poverty: new commonly agreed indicators at the EU level', *Statistics in Focus – Population and Social Conditions*.

Frick, J.R. and M.M. Grabka (2005), 'Missing income data in the German SOEP: incidence, imputation and its impact on the income distribution', *Allgemeines Statistisches Archiv*, **89**, 49–61.

Fritzsche, B. and J.P. Haisken-DeNew (2004), *Lebensstandarddefizite bei erwerbstätigen Haushalten ('Working Poor')*, Forschungsprojekt des Bundesministeriums für Gesundheit und Soziale Sicherung (Endbericht), Essen: RWI.

Göbel, J., P. Krause, and J. Schupp (2005), 'Mehr Armut durch steigende Arbeitslosigkeit: Niedriglöhne überwiegend als Zusatzeinkommen im Haushalt', *Wochenbericht des DIW Berlin*, **72** (10), 175–83.

Görzig, B., M. Gornig and A. Werwatz (2004), *East Germany's Wage Gap: A Non-parametric Decomposition Based on Establishment Characteristics*, Discussion Papers No. 451, Berlin: DIW.

Haisken-De New, J.P. and J.R. Frick (2005), *DTC – Desktop Companion to the Socio-Economic Panel Study*, Berlin: DIW.

Haller, M. and F. Höllinger (1994), 'Female employment and the change of gender roles: the conflictual relationship between participation and attitudes in international comparison', *International Sociology*, **9** (1), 87–112.

Hanesch, W., P. Krause and G. Bäcker (2000), *Armut und Ungleichheit in Deutschland: Der neue Armutsbericht der Hans-Böckler-Stiftung, des DGB und des partätischen Wohlfahrtsverbandes*, Hamburg: Rowohlt.

Hinrichs, K. (1996), 'Das Normalarbeitsverhältnis und der männliche Familienernährer als Leitbilder der Sozialpolitik: Sicherungsprobleme im sozialen Wandel', *Sozialer Fortschritt*, **45** (4), 102–7.

Hoffmann, E. and U. Walwei (1998), *Längerfristige Entwicklung von Erwerbsformen in Westdeutschland, IAB Kurzbericht No. 2*, Nürnberg: Institut für Arbeitsmarkt- und Berufsforschung.

Kalina, T. and C. Weinkopf (2006), *Mindestens sechs Millionen Niedriglohnbeschäftigte in Deutschland: Welche Rolle spielen Teilzeitbeschäftigungen und Minijobs? IAT-Report*, Wuppertal: Institut für Arbeit und Technik.

Kaufmann, F.-X. (2003), *Varianten des Wohlfahrtsstaats: Der deutsche Sozialstaat im internationalen Vergleich*, Edition Suhrkamp 2301, Frankfurt am Main: Suhrkamp.

Kurz, K. (1998), 'Hausfrau oder Berufsfrau? Einstellungen zur Rolle der Frau in Ost- und Westdeutschland', in P. Mohler and W. Bandilla (eds), *Blickpunkt Gesellschaft 4. Soziale Ungleichheit in Deutschland*, Opladen: Westdeutscher Verlag, pp. 173–220.

Leibfried, S. and I. Ostner (1991), 'The particularism of West German welfare capitalism', in M. Adler (ed.), *Edinburgh Education and Society Series: The Sociology of Social Security*, Edinburgh: Edinburgh University Press, pp. 164–86.

Lewis, J. and I. Ostner (1994), *Gender and the Evolution of European Social Policies, ZeS-Arbeitspapier Nr. 4*, Bremen: ZeS.

Organisation for Economic Co-operation and Development (OECD) (1996), *OECD Employment Outlook*, Paris: OECD.

Pfau-Effinger, B. (2004), *Development of Culture, Welfare States and Women's Employment in Europe*, Aldershot: Ashgate.

Riedel, B., T. Gadow, E. Van Santen, K. Fuchs, M. Schilling and H.R. Leu (2005), *Zahlenspiegel 2005. Kindertagesbetreuung im Spiegel der Statistik*, Deutsches Jugendinstitut, Universität Dortmund.

Rhein, T., H. Gartner and G. Krug (2005), *Aufstiegschancen für Geringverdiener verschlechtert, IAB Kurzbericht No. 3*, Nürnberg: IAB.

Statistisches Bundesamt (2004), *Statistiken der Kinder- und Jugendhilfe. Tageseinrichtungen für Kinder am 31.12.2002*, Wiesbaden.

Strengmann-Kuhn, W. (2003), *Armut trotz Erwerbstätigkeit: Analysen und sozialpolitische Konsequenzen*, Frankfurt: Campus.
Ullrich, C.G. (2005), *Soziologie des Wohlfahrtsstaates: Eine Einführung*, Frankfurt am Main: Campus-Verlag.

APPENDIX

Table 4.A1

Year	In-work poverty rate			Low-wage rate			In-work poverty rate of low-wage workers		
	Western	Eastern	Overall	Western	Eastern	Overall	Western	Eastern	Overall
1991	5	30	10	23	64	32	8	40	21
1992	5	17	7	23	43	27	10	27	15
1993	6	12	7	23	35	25	9	22	12
1994	7	12	8	23	31	24	11	22	14
1995	6	11	7	24	30	25	12	21	14
1996	7	11	7	23	27	24	14	20	15
1997	6	9	7	24	26	25	12	15	12
1998	6	8	7	24	28	25	13	18	14
1999	5	8	6	25	26	25	11	16	12
2000	6	10	7	25	29	26	14	21	16
2001	6	11	7	28	31	28	12	20	14
2002	7	9	7	28	30	28	16	19	17
2003	8	12	8	28	30	29	17	25	19
2004	6	15	8	28	33	29	13	33	17

5. The silent transformation of the Dutch welfare state and the rise of in-work poverty

Erik Snel, Jan de Boom and Godfried Engbersen

INTRODUCTION: WELFARE STATES AND IN-WORK POVERTY

Until recently, scholars argued that different welfare state regimes create different kinds of poverty. The typical face of poverty in liberal welfare states such as the USA is that of the working poor. The relatively large number of working poor in the USA is a consequence of the central characteristics of a liberal welfare state (Esping-Andersen, 1990). The combination of marginal social protection and low minimum wages creates a situation in which vulnerable people are often forced to work but remain poor (Jencks, 2005; Neubeck, 2006). On the other hand, because of the low wage levels in the USA, there is ample low-skilled and low-paid work available for those people who depend on this segment of the labour market. Such jobs are often lacking in the more developed welfare states of the European continent. As a result, there are many US citizens who work but are nevertheless poor. Moreover, working poor individuals often have to combine several low-paid jobs in order to make ends meet – a situation that has been vividly described in ethnographic studies about the American working poor (Ehrenreich, 2002; Newman, 1999; Venkatesh, 2006).

The typical face of poverty in the European welfare states – especially those on the European continent – is rather different. Continental European or 'corporatist' welfare states tend to become 'welfare states without work' (Esping-Andersen, 1996). Because of the higher levels of social security in these countries – mostly in the form of a social safety net for all citizens – those who do not work or are unable to work can generally rely on social security or means-tested social assistance. The relatively high legal minimum wages in the Continental European welfare states protect the working population but also make labour relatively expensive. As a consequence, low-skilled labour becomes unprofitable and tends to be excluded from the formal labour market. In short, the Continental European welfare states have high levels of social security but tend to exclude vulnerable groups – especially low-skilled workers – from the labour market. The corresponding typical face of poverty in countries like the Netherlands is (or was) that of 'persistent state dependency': the Dutch poor mostly did not work, but lived on social benefits (Engbersen, 1995; Engbersen et al., 2006).

The risk of this kind of comparison of welfare state regimes (liberal versus conservative welfare states), however, is that they tend to be static and often overlook institutional changes within separate countries. Indeed, Esping-Andersen insists that the characteristics of welfare state regimes are so much anchored in historical institutions that fundamental changes are hardly thinkable (the axiom of 'path dependency' or 'institutional immobility'; Esping-Andersen, 1996; Pierson, 1994; 2000).[1] Others point out fundamental changes that have taken place in contemporary welfare states. In the case of the Netherlands, Visser and Hemerijck (1996) argued that small reforms in labour conditions, monetary policies and social security have resulted in significant changes in social security: less social protection, less generous social benefits and more 'activating' labour market policies (cf. Hemerijck and Visser, 2006). Gilbert (2002) observed a transformation of the welfare states in both the USA and Europe, from the traditional welfare state to an 'enabling state'. Universal and unconditional social security systems that offered protection from the social risks of the free labour market ('decommodification') were typical for the 'old' welfare state. The new enabling state, on the other hand, emphasizes the promotion of work rather than social protection. The central aim of the enabling state is to prevent social exclusion and to stimulate citizens to work (= 'social inclusion'). Social security contains financial incentives and sanctions that stimulate benefit claimants to return to the labour market. Universal and unconditional social benefits are gradually replaced by selective arrangements for a more restricted group of households that are really unable to provide for their own incomes through formal work (Gilbert, 2002: 43–7).

Gilbert's argument is *not* that US and European welfare states are converging, but rather that they are developing in a similar direction: less social protection and more emphasis on 'activating' measures and promotion of work. Such institutional reforms are visible in the Netherlands as well. As early as the late 1980s – at the height of the economic crisis – social benefits were actually reduced (by an average of 10 per cent) and subsequently frozen for many years. The problem, however, as it was then perceived, was excessive dependence on disability benefits (often referred to as the 'Dutch disease'). In 1987, a drastic revision of the Dutch Disability Insurance Act (Dutch acronym WAO) was issued, the first of a whole series of revisions in the WAO, which ended in 2006 with the repeal of the WAO and the introduction of a new act: Work and Income According to Labour Capacity. The name of this new act clearly shows its intention: people with health limitations are expected to work and earn their own income as far as their health enables them to do so. Partial disability benefits are only possible when people still work. This drastic policy change began in the mid-1980s with the removal of the measure stipulating that people with partial health limitations could receive a full disability benefit. Another drastic policy change which was initiated during those years was the gradual reduction of the duration of unemployment benefits. All these changes were intended to reduce persistent benefit dependence and to stimulate the resumption of work. However, in the early 1990s, it became clear that the welfare state reforms had thus far failed to achieve this objective. A new round of even more drastic adjustments to the Dutch social security system followed. These new policy interventions were inspired by a new definition of the problem. The problem of the Dutch welfare state was not only a financial one – the burden of many and persistent social benefits – but one of uncontrollability. The new social security reforms of the 1990s were therefore primarily aimed at influencing the behaviour of social benefit claimants, social security institutions and all the societal organizations surrounding the Dutch social security system. Van der Veen (1999) describes the new social security reforms of the 1990s as the transition from a *social right paradigm* to an *incentive paradigm*.

The successive changes in the Dutch social security and social assistance systems in the 1990s are too numerous to describe extensively here (see Aarts et al., 2002; Teulings et al., 1997; Van der Veen, 1999; Visser and Hemerijck, 1996). However, we can give some examples:

- *Disentanglement of the implementation of social security*. Interest groups such as employers and trade unions were disconnected from the social security system because they were held responsible for the enormous increase in social security dependence that occurred in the late 1980s.
- *Privatization of risks*. The risks of illness, incapacity and unemployment were 'returned' to employers – first by the differentiation of employer contributions (in case of incapacity or unemployment), and later by repealing all collective social protection for ill employees. Employers are now obliged to pay wages to sick employees during the first year (later the first two years) of their illness. The idea

was that employers would be more active in stimulating sick employees to resume work if they themselves were responsible for the employees' wages during the period of illness.

- *Further reduction of the level and duration of benefits.* During the 1990s, the level of disability and unemployment benefits was reduced further – from 80 down to 70 per cent of the claimant's former income. The duration of unemployment benefits is continuously being reduced. There is still no time limit on disability and social assistance benefits, although there is more pressure on benefit claimants to resume work.
- *More selective access to social benefits.* By using stricter criteria, the influx of employees with minor health limitations being covered under the Disablement Insurance Act was reduced. Under the new Work and Income According to Labour Capacities Act, partially incapacitated persons are denied access to the disability scheme altogether. They can receive income support only when they work. If not, they have to rely on (means tested) social assistance. Another example of more selective access to social security was when the right of social assistance for young people was replaced during the 1990s by the obligation to work (the so-called Juvenile Work Guarantee Scheme).
- *More conditional social benefits.* Unconditional social rights were gradually replaced by more conditional benefits – specifically, the condition to find work. A first example is widow's pensions: widows (of working age) are now obliged to find employment. Successive reforms of the Dutch Social Assistance Act, in particular, implied stricter requirements for single parents to find new employment. In the 1980s, single parents with children under 18 years of age were not obliged to work. Since 1996, however, only single parents with children under 5 have been exempted from labour market participation. With the new Work and Social Assistance Act, any single parent – irrespective of the child's age – is obliged to work (or at least to look for work or improve his or her labour market chances through education). Employees with minor health limitations and social assistance claimants in general were also confronted with stricter regulations aimed at promoting work (for instance, the use of financial sanctions or interruption of benefits).
- *'Activating' labour market policies.* Whereas in the 1980s, the Netherlands was heavily criticized for its markedly passive labour market policies, which created massive and persistent unemployment (Therborn, 1986), during the 1990s there was a fundamental change in the direction of 'activating' labour market approaches. In

> particular, the cabinets of Social Democrats and Liberals (the so-called 'purple coalition') that ruled the Netherlands during the second half of the 1990s heavily emphasized work resumption (the cabinet's motto was 'Work, work, work'). One instrument for promoting work was extensive subsidized work programmes, which provided thousands of (often persistently) unemployed people with low-paid 'additional' employment.

In our view, the successive reforms that have taken place in the Dutch social security system from the mid-1980s until now have resulted in a silent transformation of the Dutch welfare state. Many of the reforms described above were implemented by the cabinet of Social Democrats and Liberals that was in power from 1994 until 2002. The Conservative cabinet that followed radicalized the social security reforms even further by issuing the new social assistance and disability acts that we already mentioned. However, these new reforms, which took place after 2002, are not included in our empirical analysis, since our empirical data only cover the period from 1985–2001.

Our main argument in this chapter is that the institutional reforms in the Dutch social security system that have been implemented since the late 1980s have implied a fundamental change in the nature of income poverty in the Netherlands. Until then, poor people in the Netherlands were predominantly (persistent) social benefit claimants. We will argue that the described social security reforms in the Netherlands – especially the stricter regulations to promote resumption of work by single mothers, employees with minor health limitations, and long-term unemployed persons in general – resulted in an increase in in-work poverty. As a result of the more selective and activating social security system that developed during the 1990s, social benefit claimants were pushed into the labour market. Labour market participation, however, does not necessarily imply an escape from financial poverty. In particular, (former) benefit claimants with weak labour market positions (in terms of employment or household characteristics) tend to remain poor even though they participate in the labour market. Our main hypothesis, therefore, is that the expected increase in in-work poverty is a consequence of the fact that people with weak labour market positions (low-skilled or part-time workers, people working in precarious service jobs, singles or single parents living in one-earner households) are being pushed from the social security system into the labour market.

However, we should also consider the possibility that the (expected) rise in in-work poverty in the Netherlands is *not* related to institutional reforms in the Dutch welfare state and social security system. The increase in in-work poverty in the Netherlands could also stem from the more general economic and demographic developments that took place in the Netherlands in the (late) 1990s – such as an increase in low-paid work, part-time work, insecure low-paid service jobs, self-employment, increased female labour market participation, or an increasing number of singles, single parents and, more generally, of one-earner households.

This chapter analyses the development of in-work poverty in the Netherlands over the period from 1985–2001 by using statistical data from the Dutch Socio-Economic Panel. Our research questions are threefold (1) How did in-work poverty in the Netherlands develop during this period? (2) Who are the working poor in the Netherlands? (3) How can we explain the increase in in-work poverty in the Netherlands? The next section of this chapter outlines the empirical data and methodologies used in our analysis. The third section describes the development of in-work poverty in the Netherlands. The fourth examines the composition of the Dutch working poor population, in terms of their labour market characteristics, and their individual and household characteristics. In the fifth section we discuss our findings and our central hypothesis that the rise of in-work poverty in the Netherlands is directly related to the institutional reforms of the Dutch social security system in the last decades.

DATA AND METHODS

Database

The data used in our analyses are taken from the Dutch Socio-Economic Panel (DSEP), which existed from 1984 to 2002. Here we use the data from 1985[2] until 2001. In the first year DSEP still contained a limited number of respondents, making its data less reliable. In 2002, there was a major change in the method of income measurement. Unlike all previous years, information about household incomes was not derived from the survey, but directly from administrative data. Since this significantly influenced the outcomes, we decided not to use 2002 data in our analyses. The DSEP is an annual survey among 5000 households (around 10 000 adult individuals) and gives a consistent description of the socio-economic situation of households and individuals and – as a panel study – of changes in this situation.

Here, we make particular use of the data about household incomes and various background characteristics of the households and individuals involved. However, using statistical data collected over such a long period almost inevitably implies that the methods of data collection change over the years. From 1984 through to 1989, the survey was held twice a year and asked for the current monthly income of households. These monthly incomes were then converted to annual incomes. From 1990 onwards, the DSEP became an annual survey and asked (among many other things) for the household income in the previous year.

As a consequence, the DSEP now contains two different figures based on income data that were collected in 1989 (in the 1989 wave based on monthly incomes in that year and in the 1990 wave based on annual incomes in the previous year). Although this is not completely unproblematic, we decided not to change this situation – for instance, by regarding the 1990 wave as the 1989 wave (that is, the year the income data refer to, and so on for all following years). There were basically two reasons for this. First, all the other variables used in the analysis (including household composition and even some income components) refer to the year the survey was held. Second, we do not want to remove ourselves from the community of researchers using the DSEP and their customary way of interpreting DSEP data. However, the reader should keep in mind that our income data for the years after 1989 actually refer to the household income in the previous year.

Definitions and Measurements

Being poor is defined here as living in a poor household. To establish whether or not a household is poor, we use the poverty threshold that is widely accepted in international comparative poverty research. A household is considered to be poor when its equivalized disposable household income[3] is less than 60 per cent of the median disposable income of all households in that year. In our analyses, we used the standard variable 'equivalized disposable household income' in DSEP. The equivalence factors used in DSEP differ from those used in other research – namely, 1 for the first adult in the household, 0.38 for each additional adult, and 0.15–0.30 for underage children, depending on their age and position in the household.

The population used in our analyses is adults of working age (15–64 years of age), with the exception of two specific categories. The first of these are households with negative disposable incomes (which appear frequently among self-employed persons). Second, and consistent with most Dutch poverty research, students were also excluded from the analyses. The reason for doing so is that when we only consider the (mostly low) incomes of students they will generally be considered as 'poor' (and when they have a small job, they will be considered as working poor). However, we do not consider students to be poor because they are aware that being a student involves having a low income and choose this position in order to obtain much higher incomes later in their careers. In our perception, including both negative household incomes and students would result in an overestimation of the magnitude of poverty in a country. In our analyses, 'working' is defined as working at least one hour a week.

THE DEVELOPMENT OF IN-WORK POVERTY IN THE NETHERLANDS (1985–2001)

This section describes the development of poverty and in-work poverty in the Netherlands from the mid-1980s until 2001. During these years, as we already mentioned, the Dutch economy was characterized by two major periods. In the late 1980s, the Netherlands faced a severe economic crisis and a large and persistent unemployment rate. The 1990s – particularly the second half of the 1990s – brought an economic recovery, economic prosperity and constant job growth. In the international literature, this period in Dutch economic history became known as the 'Dutch miracle' (Visser and Hemerijck, 1996). One crucial feature of the booming economy during these years was the strong increase in labour market participation. The number of employed persons (working at least 12 hours a week) increased from around 5.5 million in 1990 to 7 million in 2001; an increase of 25 per cent in only 12 years (see Table 5.A1 in the Appendix). Here we will describe what these changes in the economic tide implied for the development of income poverty – particularly of in-work poverty – in the Netherlands.

Figure 5.1 shows the development of the total poverty population (individuals between 15 and 64 years of age) in the Netherlands from 1985 to 2001. The figure shows that the size of the Dutch poverty population in the 1990s was considerably larger than in the 1980s. However, we should add that this outcome is strongly influenced by the relative poverty measurement (60 per cent of the annual median income) used in our analysis.[4] More importantly, since our focus is on the development of in-work poverty, Figure 5.1 shows a gradual shift within the Dutch poverty population from non-working poor to working poor (see also Table 5.A2 in the Appendix). In the mid-1980s, less than 3 per cent of all Dutch individuals of working age were poor *and* working. In 1990, 4.3 per cent of the Dutch population of working age belonged to the working poor. In 2001, the last year under examination, this figure had increased to 6 per cent. At the same time, the share of the non-working poor (as a percentage of the total population of working age) remained constant (it fluctuated between 4 and 6 per cent with no discernible trend). As a result of both tendencies, the ratio between the

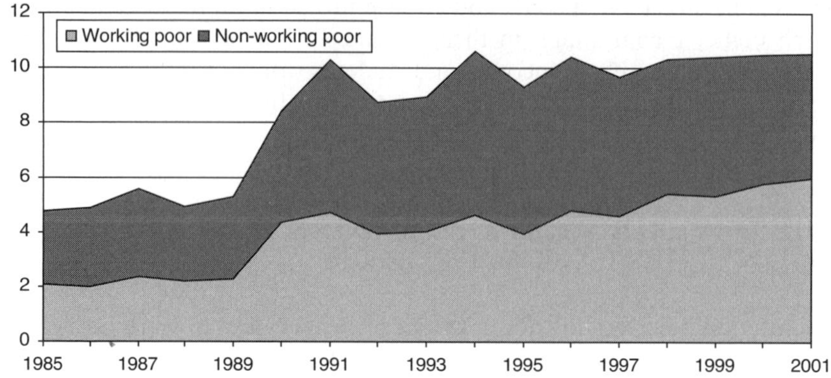

Note: Persons 15–65 years of age not including students.

Source: Dutch Socio-Economic Panel Survey 1985–2001; own computations.

Figure 5.1 Working and non-working poor persons in the Netherlands (% of total population)

two categories changed. Up until the mid-1990s, the majority of the Dutch poverty population of working age (15–64 years, students not included!) was not working. However, since the late 1990s, there has been a significant shift in the Dutch poverty population. Beginning in 1998, the majority of the Dutch poverty population was actually working. In 2001, not less than 57 per cent of all adult members of poor Dutch households were working. Although more recent empirical data are not available, we expect that the number of working-poor individuals in the Netherlands will have increased further after 2001, because the transformation of the Dutch welfare state (less social protection, more emphasis on work promotion) was even more pronounced after that.

The conclusion can be that the economic boom and constant job growth that occurred in the Netherlands in the late 1990s went hand in hand with an increase in in-work poverty and a shift in the Dutch poverty population (from non-working to working poor). However, the increase in in-work poverty may just be the result of strongly increased labour market participation during these years. After all, with more people at work – as was the case in the Netherlands during this period – the number of working poor automatically increases even when the poverty risk for working people remains constant. If this is the case, the increase in in-work poverty in the Netherlands can simply be attributed to economic developments – especially to increased labour market participation during those years. But as Figure 5.2 makes clear, this is only one part of the story, because the

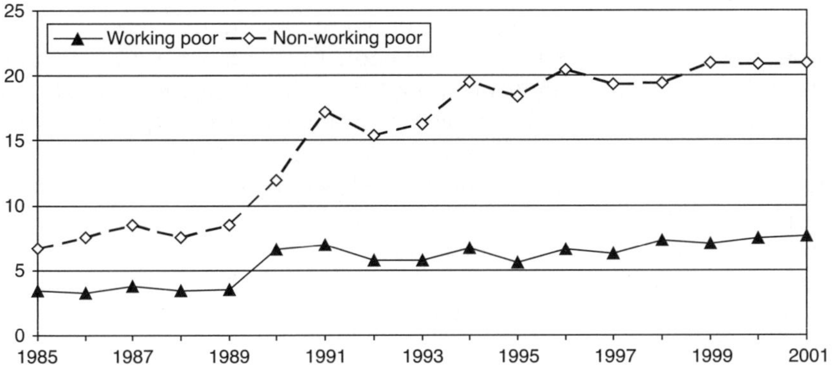

Note: Persons 15–65 years of age not including students.

Source: Dutch Socio-Economic Panel Survey 1985–2001; own computations.

Figure 5.2 Poverty risks of working and non-working persons in the Netherlands (%)

poverty risk of employed persons (or the in-work poverty rate) also increased from a level of less than 4 per cent in the late 1980s to between 5 and 6 per cent from the early to mid-1990s, and to at least 7 per cent since 1998. The latter figure implies that one in every 14 working individuals in the Netherlands lives in a poor household. We can also conclude that the poverty risk for working people in the Netherlands almost doubled between the late 1980s and 2001 (and may have increased even further after that). Figure 5.2 also shows that the poverty risk for non-working people is significantly higher than that of working people and has also increased in the last decades; but this does not negate the fact that there has also been a significant increase in in-work poverty in the Netherlands since the mid-1990s.

To summarize our findings thus far, we can say that since the mid-1990s – that is, in a period that saw a booming economy, strongly increased labour market participation, and institutional reforms in the Dutch social security system – there has been a significant shift in the Dutch poverty population. Whereas until the mid-1990s, the majority of the Dutch poverty population was not working, since 1998 at least half (up to almost 60 per cent in 2001) of the Dutch poverty population was working. In our perception, these figures reveal a significant change in the character of the Dutch welfare state and social security system. Until recently, the typical face of poverty in the Netherlands was that of the non-working poor living off social benefits. Since the mid-1990s, a new face of poverty has arisen in the Netherlands: individuals who are working – partly because they have been pushed from social security or social assistance back into the labour market – but are nevertheless poor. Furthermore, we have established that this increase in in-work poverty in the Netherlands is not only the result of increased labour market participation during those years (which, when the in-work poverty risk for working people remains constant, automatically results in more in-work poverty). In addition, working people now face a greater risk of income poverty – up to a point where shortly after the turn of the millennium, one in every 14 working adults (students not included) lived in a poor household. Although we do not have more recent empirical data, this number may have increased even further in recent years.

WHO ARE THE WORKING POOR?

Who are the working poor? This section of the chapter describes the main labour market (employed versus self-employed individuals, working hours, occupational class), individual and household characteristics (gender, age, household composition and number of incomes in the household, educational levels) of the working poor in the Netherlands. We also analyse to what extent these labour market, individual and household characteristics of the working poor have changed in recent decades.

Labour Market Characteristics

As international research shows, self-employed persons experience a higher in-work poverty risk than employees (Bardone and Guio, 2005). An alternative explanation for the rise of in-work poverty in the Netherlands in the 1990s may therefore be that the number of self-employed persons living below the poverty threshold increased. However, Figures 5.3(a) and 5.3(b) do not support this assumption. Although Figure 5.3(b) shows that self-employed persons in the Netherlands have a higher poverty risk than employees, the figure also makes clear that the poverty risks of both categories tend to converge. Whereas the poverty risk of the self-employed has tended to decline, the poverty risk of employees increased in recent decades (from little more than 2 per cent in the mid-1980s to around 7 per cent in the last three years under examination). Although self-employed persons are still over-represented in the Dutch in-work poverty population, this over-representation has been on the decline. As a result, as Figure 5.3(a) shows, the self-employed are a declining, not a growing share of the Dutch in-work poverty population.

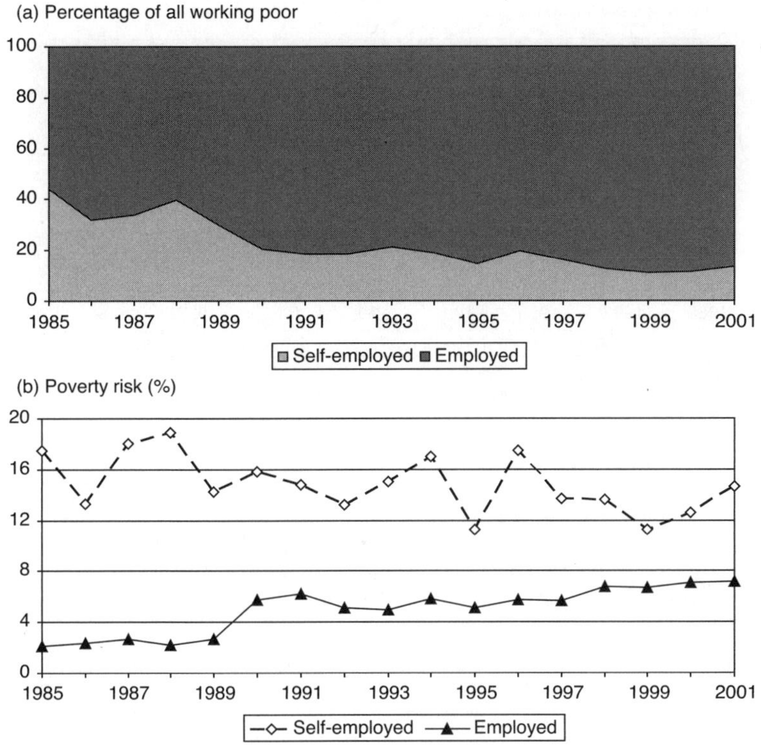

Note: Persons 15–65 years of age not including students.

Source: Dutch Socio-Economic Panel Survey 1985–2001; own computations.

Figure 5.3 Employment, self-employment and in-work poverty

Another issue is part-time work. The Netherlands has experienced a strong increase in part-time work in recent decades, especially because of the huge influx of women into the labour force and the fact that many female Dutch workers work part-time (Visser, 2002). The so-called '1.5 breadwinner model' (the man works full-time, the wife works part-time) has become more or less the standard in the Netherlands. One could assume that the increase in in-work poverty in the Netherlands is the result of the large increase among women working in part-time jobs – especially because in our analysis, anyone who works at least one hour a week is defined as 'working'.[5] On the other hand, part-time work is not necessarily related to in-work poverty. Part-time workers (or low-paid workers in general) living in households with more than one

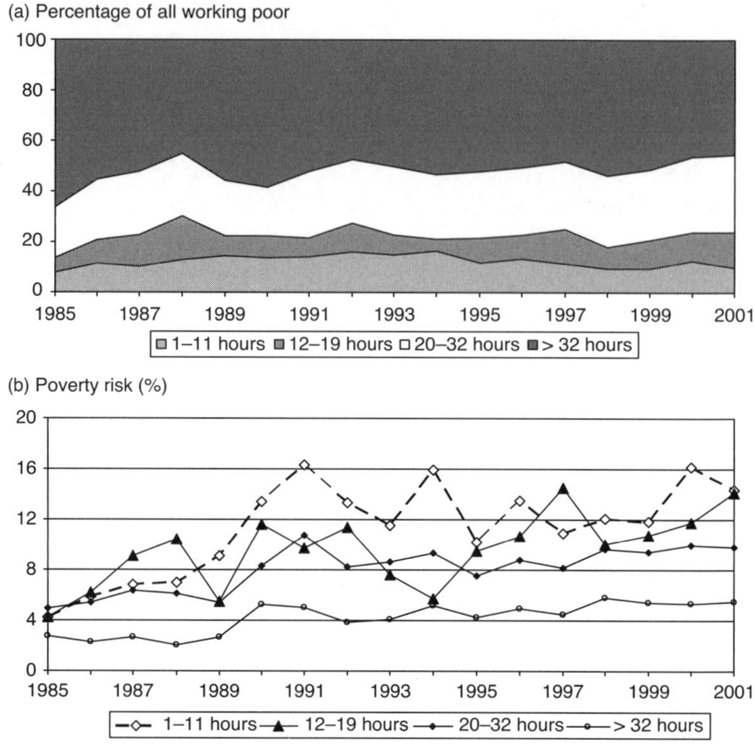

Note: Persons 15–65 years of age not including students.

Source: Dutch Socio-Economic Panel Survey 1985–2001; own computations.

Figure 5.4 Part-time work and in-work poverty

income have the possibility of pooling multiple incomes and are often not poor.

As Figure 5.4(a) shows, the increase in in-work poverty in the Netherlands in the second half of the 1990s was not the result of an increase in part-time work. In all years, full-time workers (people working at least four days a week) were the largest subcategory among the working poor. Between 1985 and 1993, the share of full-time workers among the working poor was quite constant (it declined with some fluctuations, from 55 to 53 per cent). In the following years, the share of full-time workers among the working poor fell further, to 45 per cent in 2001. Nevertheless, full-time workers are still the largest subcategory among the working poor. Figure 5.4(b) makes clear that the risk of in-work poverty is obviously related to the number of working hours. People working in small part-time jobs (less than 20 hours a week) have a larger poverty risk than people working in more significant part-time or full-time jobs (more than 20 hours). In particular, the in-work poverty risk for people working between 12 and 19 hours a week has exploded since the mid-1990s (from almost 6 per cent in 1994 to 14 per cent in 2001). However, the share of this subcategory among the working poor is too small to explain the overall increase in the in-work poverty risk in the Netherlands in the late 1990s.

The fact that in-work poverty appears to be unrelated to part-time work is not really surprising. Many part-time workers – especially those with small part-time jobs – are women from non-poor households who earn some income in addition to their spouses' earnings. These households are not poor, and the extra incomes from the wives' part-time jobs make them even less poor. However, we can assume that part-time work is strongly related to in-work poverty when there is only one income earner in the household (see Figure 5.8(a) and (b)).

A final labour market characteristic that is relevant in relation to in-work poverty is occupational class. It has been argued that structural changes in Western economies – in short, the shift from industrial to post-industrial employment – have also resulted in the rise of precarious and often low-paid service jobs. Esping-Andersen (1993: 25) even mentioned the rise of what he called the new 'post-industrial service proletariat'. These precarious new service jobs are concentrated in urban economies and are often filled by women, immigrants, and other population categories with weak labour market positions (Sassen, 1991; Snel et al., 2007). The increase in precarious, low-skilled service work may be another possible explanation for the increase in in-work poverty in the Netherlands. We measured the occupational class of the working poor using the class scheme developed by Esping-Andersen (1993). What is crucial to this approach is that he distinguishes two separate occupational hierarchies: the Fordist hierarchy (ranging from managers, clerical and sales occupations to skilled and unskilled manual workers) and the post-industrial hierarchy (ranging from professionals, technicians and semi-professionals to skilled and unskilled service workers). Here, we 'collapsed' Esping-Andersen's class scheme into four basic categories: Fordist high, post-industrial high, Fordist low, and post-industrial low occupations. The latter two categories consist of skilled and unskilled manual or service workers.[6]

If the increase in in-work poverty in the Netherlands was indeed the result of an increase in precarious, low-skilled service work, we would expect this subcategory of the occupational structure to (a) account for a significant and increasing share of the Dutch in-work poverty population, and (b) have high and increasing in-work poverty risks. However, neither appears to be

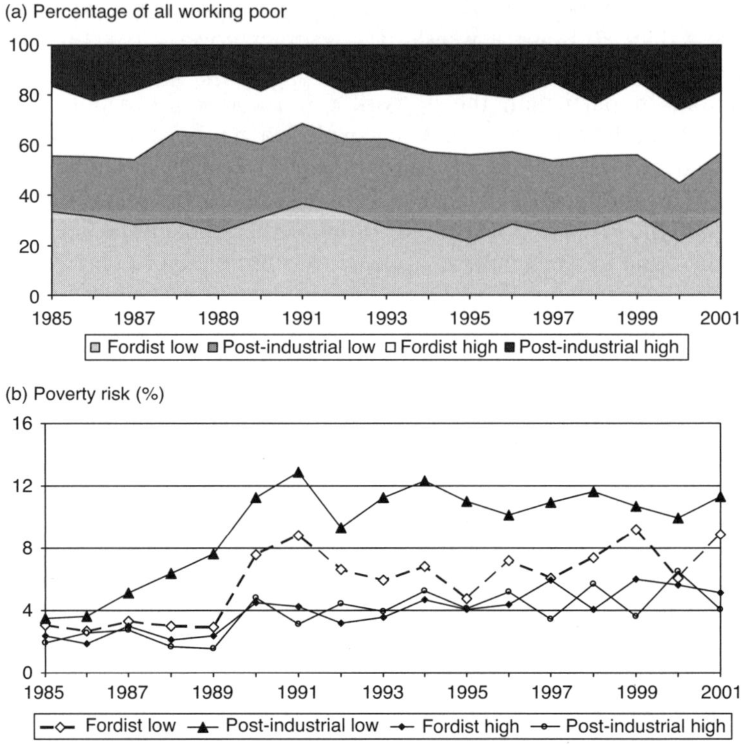

Note: Persons 15–65 years of age not including students.

Source: Dutch Socio-Economic Panel Survey 1985–2001; own computations.

Figure 5.5 Social class and in-work poverty

the case. In 2001, for instance, skilled or unskilled manual workers ('Fordist low') formed a larger share of the Dutch working poor than skilled and unskilled service workers ('post-industrial low'; 30 versus 26 per cent). The relatively high share of persons working in managerial, clerical and sales occupations (25 per cent) among the working poor is also remarkable. Moreover, almost half of the Dutch working poor are persons working in higher Fordist or higher post-industrial occupations. As Figure 5.5(b) shows, the in-work poverty risks are indeed highest in the lower post-industrial occupations, but they are only marginally different from the in-work poverty risks in the low-skilled Fordist occupations. Moreover, the poverty risks of low-skilled service workers are not increasing. Overall, changes in the occupational class structure (especially the rise of precarious service jobs) do not explain the increase in in-work poverty in the Netherlands.

More generally, we can say that the labour market characteristics discussed thus far reveal little about the causes for the increase in in-work poverty in the Netherlands. This is less surprising than it seems to be at first glance. Increases in self-employment, part-time work and the number of low-qualified service jobs may result in an increase in the number of low-paid workers. However, having a low (individual) income is not the same as poverty, because poverty is measured at the household level. When people with low earnings live in non-poor households and can pool their own small incomes with those of their spouses, they are not necessarily poor. In other words, the individual and household characteristics of the working poor may be more significant than their labour market characteristics.

Individual and Household Characteristics

In this section, we will describe four individual and household characteristics of the working poor: gender, household type, number of incomes in the household and educational level. We will start with in-work poverty and gender. One of the most important socio-economic developments in the Netherlands in recent decades has been the strong increase in female labour market participation. The female employment rate (that is, the number of employed women in relation to all women of working age) increased from 30 per cent in 1985 to 54 per cent in 2001 (see Table 5.A1 in the Appendix). More female labour market participation can contribute to in-work poverty when the new female labour market participants are over-represented in low-paid, precarious and part-time jobs. As we mentioned before, many Dutch women do indeed work in part-time jobs. However, part-time and low-paid work contributes to in-work poverty primarily when there is no possibility of pooling various incomes within the household; that is, in single-earner households.

As Figure 5.6(a) reveals, in-work poverty in the Netherlands is, to a large extent and increasingly, a female issue. This is a surprising outcome insofar as earlier research showed that in-work poverty in most European countries is predominantly a male phenomenon. The reason is that low-paid male workers are often single earners (the traditional breadwinner), whereas many low-paid female workers do not live in poor households (Bardone and Guio, 2005). However, this is different in the Netherlands. Since the early 1990s, at least 60 per cent of the Dutch working poor are women. Moreover, since the early 1990s, the in-work poverty risk for women has also been at least twice as high as it is for men (Figure 5.6(b)).

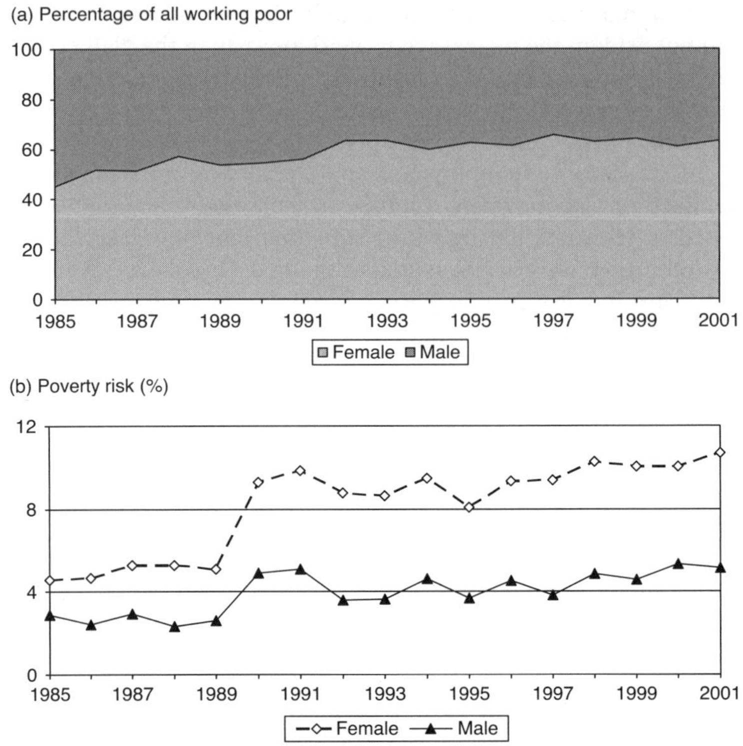

Note: Persons 15–65 years of age not including students.

Source: Dutch Socio-Economic Panel Survey 1985–2001; own computations.

Figure 5.6 Gender and in-work poverty

For the time being, we may conclude that the increase in in-work poverty in the Netherlands indeed seems to be related to the increase in female labour market participation. Not only do more women work (and thus have a chance of becoming working poor) but, more importantly, the in-work poverty risk for women also increased during the 1990s (Figure 5.6(b)). Both tendencies contribute to the increase in in-work poverty in the Netherlands. Later we will find, however, that gender has no direct influence on a person's odds of in-work poverty.

Another important factor is the household situation of the workers. As we argued before, low wages and part-time work only result in more in-work poverty in the case of singles and single parents who do not have the possibility of pooling various incomes within their households. Figures

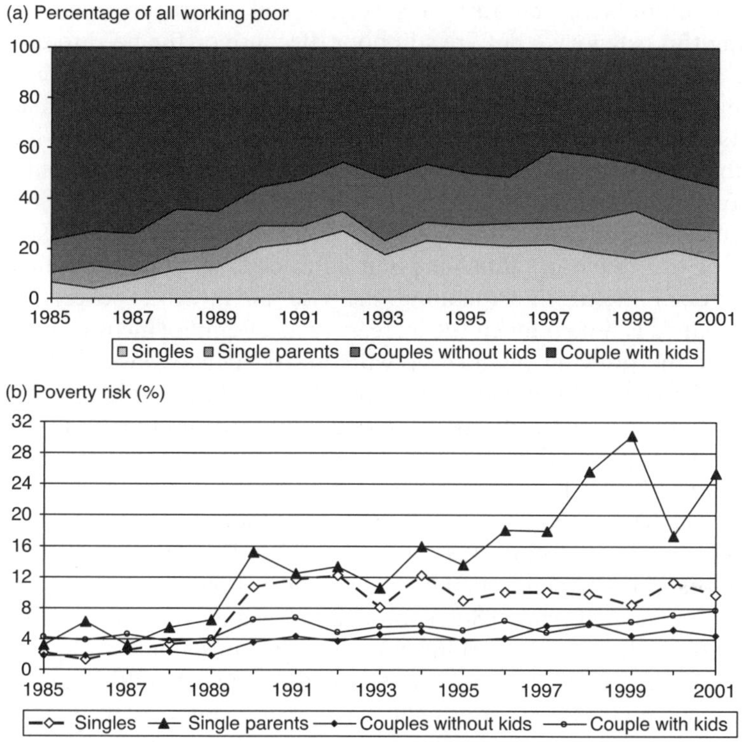

Note: Persons 15–65 years of age not including students.

Source: Dutch Socio-Economic Panel Survey 1985–2001; own computations.

Figure 5.7 Household composition and in-work poverty

5.7(a) and (b) show the household composition of the working poor and the in-work poverty risks of various household categories. As Figure 5.7(a) shows, couples with children are still by far the largest subcategory among the working poor, although this category has shrunk over the years. The shares of singles and single-parent families among the working poor, on the other hand, have increased over the years, although all figures fluctuate heavily each year. In the late 1990s, one in three or four working poor individuals was either single or a single parent. Moreover, as Figure 5.7(b) shows, the in-work poverty risk for single parents jumped higher in recent years (especially after 1996). Single parents were also an important category at risk of poverty in the 1980s and early 1990s, but then they were mostly not working. In recent years, more and more single parents do work – undoubtedly because of stricter social security regulations concerning this category – but are still poor. Because of the need to combine work and caregiving, single parents can often work only part-time. For single parents, working part-time for a low wage almost automatically results in in-work poverty because almost by definition, they fail to have the possibility of pooling multiple incomes in one household. As a result of all this, one in three or four single parents in the late 1990s were working but nevertheless poor.

All of our outcomes thus far point more or less in the same direction. The crucial factor in explaining the rise of in-work poverty in the Netherlands is not so much the increases in self-employment or part-time work or the growing number of workers (particularly women) in low-qualified service jobs as such, but rather the fact that working people with weak labour market positions live in households without other adults with whom they can pool their incomes. To test whether this is true, we analysed the relationship of in-work poverty to the number of income earners in a household. The outcomes support our expectation that in-work poverty is strongly concentrated in single earner households – either families with a traditional (mostly male) single breadwinner or households of singles and single parents. As Figure 5.8(a) shows, the large majority (up to 80 per cent in 1999) of the Dutch working poor live in households with only one income earner. However, this is not something new. Single-earner households made up the large majority of the working poor in all the years under examination (1985–2001). Figure 5.8(b) shows, however, that the in-work poverty risk for single-earner households increased considerably during the 1990s (from 12 per cent in 1990 to 19.4 per cent in 2001). In other words, almost one in five working adults in single earner households is poor!

In our view, this development is directly related to the institutional reforms in the Dutch social security system described earlier in this chapter. Single earners are often working individuals with marked weak labour positions. This applies both to traditional male breadwinners (often immigrants) and to modern single-earner households (singles, single parents). In the 1980s and early 1990s, it was usually accepted that these individuals, who had few prospects on the formal labour market, lived off of social security. Beginning in the mid-1990s, many of these individuals with weak labour market positions were pushed into the labour market. But given their insufficient qualifications, they were unable to escape from poverty. As a result, they now work but are nevertheless poor.

A final individual characteristic covered in our analysis is the educational level of the working poor. For several reasons, we assumed that in-work poverty was strongly related to low-skilled work. First, given the shift from Fordist to post-industrial work, we expected to see an increase in in-

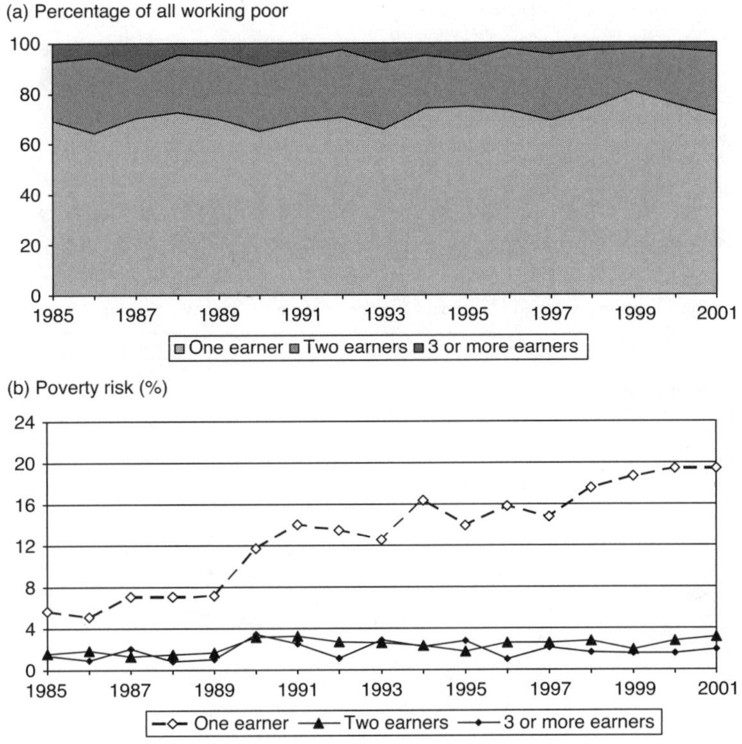

Note: Persons 15–65 years of age not including students.

Source: Dutch Socio-Economic Panel Survey 1985–2001; own computations.

Figure 5.8 Number of income earners in the household and in-work poverty

work poverty because low-skilled work is less protected in the service industries than in the highly unionized industrial sector. Second, because of the institutional changes in the Dutch social security system, working people with weak labour market qualifications are less sheltered by social security and more often obliged to participate in the labour market – even when their income-earning capacities are limited. However, as becomes clear from Figure 5.9(a), a surprisingly large number of working poor individuals have at least an intermediate educational level (up to 66 per cent in 2001). We can thus conclude that in-work poverty in the Netherlands is certainly not restricted to the least educated workers.

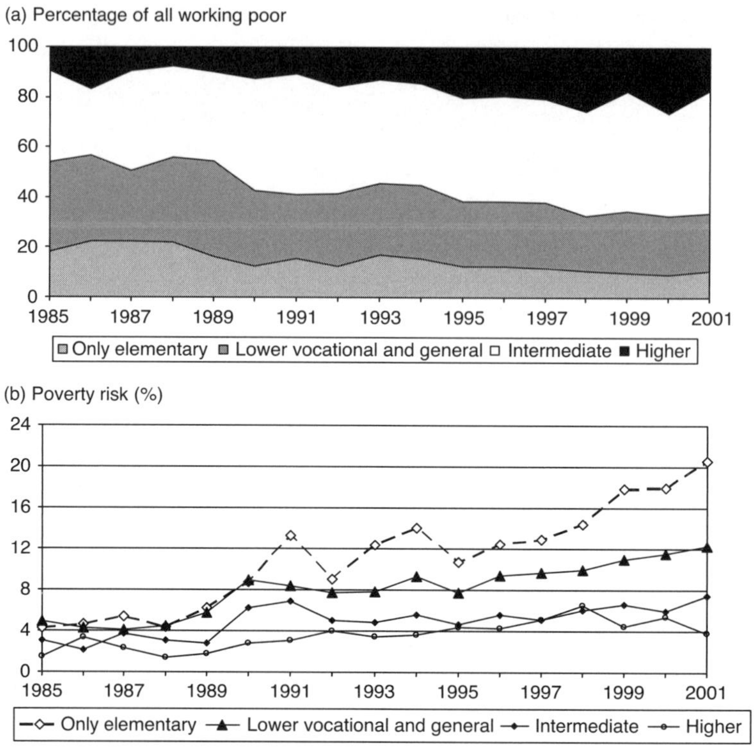

Note: Persons 15–65 years of age not including students.

Source: Dutch Socio-Economic Panel Survey 1985–2001; own computations.

Figure 5.9 Educational levels and in-work poverty

On the other hand, as Figure 5.9(b) shows, the in-work-poverty risks of low-educated workers (with only an elementary education) are significantly higher than the in-work poverty risks of all other categories. Moreover, the in-work-poverty risks of low-educated workers more than doubled between 1990 and 2001 (from 8.7 per cent to 20.5 per cent). The in-work poverty risks of workers with lower vocational or general educations also increased, albeit to a lesser extent.

Multivariate Analysis

Our description thus far has shown that self-employed persons, people working in part-time jobs and low-skilled service jobs, women, singles, single parents – and one-earner households in general – and low-educated workers are over-represented among the working poor. However, these are strongly overlapping categories. For instance, women can be over-represented among the working poor because they work in part-time jobs more often. The multivariate analysis (logistic regression) in Table 5.1 shows what factors make a difference for a person's odds of in-work poverty and what factors do not. We used the data from the last cross-section (2001) and included all variables discussed thus far in the model, plus two additional variables (age and number of children in the household). The most interesting finding in Table 5.1 is that gender as such does not make a difference. Taking all other factors into account, women do not belong to the working poor more often than men do. Nor does the number of children in a household make a difference. All other factors show significant effects on the odds of in-work poverty.

Table 5.1 starts with the labour market characteristics discussed before. The odds of in-work poverty are around 2.5 (=1/0.397) times higher for self-employed individuals than they are for employees. Working hours also make a great difference. People with small part-time jobs (up to 20 hours a week) have an almost four times greater chance of experiencing in-work poverty than full-time workers (at least 32 hours a week). But even more significant, part-time jobs (20–31 hours a week) greatly increase people's odds of in-work poverty. Our expectation that working in lower service jobs increases the odds of in-work poverty appears to be wrong: the in-work poverty risk of workers in lower Fordist jobs is not significantly different. The odds of in-work poverty for individuals working in higher Fordist or post-industrial jobs are less than half of those for the low-Fordist reference category.

Household characteristics also make a significant difference for a person's odds of in-work poverty. Single parents belong to the working poor almost twice as often as the reference category of couples with children. This is what we expected; however, single persons belong to the working poor much less often than the reference category of couples with children. The most important factor, however, is the number of income earners in the household. The odds of in-work poverty for households with two or more income earners are less than 10 per cent of those for households with only one adult income earner. Educational level also makes a huge difference: in-work poverty appears to be heavily concentrated within the group of workers with the lowest educational level (only elementary education). Having a lower vocational or general education decreases the odds of in-work poverty by more than 50 per cent (compared with the reference category of workers with only elementary education). The odds of in-work poverty for people with a higher

Table 5.1 In-work poverty risks in the Netherlands (2001) (logistic regression coefficients, standard errors, p values, odds ratios)

Variable	coef.	s.e.	p	odds ratio
Constant	3.708	0.570	0.000	40.760
Labour market characteristics				
Employment status (Ref: self-employed)				
Employed	−0.924	0.274	0.001	0.397
Working hours (Ref > 32 hours)				
Small part-time (< 12 hours)	1.344	0.322	0.000	3.833
Middle part-time (12–19 hours)	1.384	0.271	0.000	3.992
Large part-time (20–31 hours)	0.894	0.195	0.000	2.446
Occupational class (Ref: Fordist low)				
Post-industrial low	−0.115	0.218	0.597	0.891
Fordist high	−0.787	0.211	0.000	0.455
Post-industrial high	−0.821	0.240	0.001	0.440
Individual and household characteristics				
Gender (Ref: male)				
Female	0.179	0.187	0.338	1.196
Household situation (Ref: couple with kids)				
Couple without kid(s)	−0.412	0.311	0.186	0.663
Single adult	−0.828	0.312	0.008	0.437
Single parent	0.598	0.273	0.029	1.818
Number of income earners (Ref: one earner)				
Two income earners	−2.708	0.189	0.000	0.067
Three or more income earners	−3.866	0.373	0.000	0.021
Educational level (Ref: only elementary)				
Lower general or occupational	−0.876	0.307	0.004	0.416
Middle general or occupational	−1.074	0.279	0.000	0.342
Higher occupational	−1.738	0.344	0.000	0.176
University	−1.487	0.413	0.000	0.226
Number of children	0.119	0.118	0.315	1.126
Age	−0.080	0.008	0.000	0.923
N	4039			
−2 Log likelihood	1382.931			
Pseudo-R2 (Nagelkerke)	0.332			

Source: Dutch Socio-Economic Panel Survey 2001.

vocational or university education are only one-fifth of those for the reference category of workers with the lowest educational level. Finally, age also makes a difference. The effect of age is negative: the in-work poverty risk is higher for younger persons.

DISCUSSION

In this study, we showed that the major economic boom and constant job growth in the Netherlands in the second half of the 1990s (the so-called 'Dutch Miracle') went hand in hand with an increase in in-work poverty. Between 1990 and 2001 – at the height of the economic boom – the in-work poverty risk increased from 6.6 to 7.7 per cent. In the 1980s and early 1990s, the majority of all poor adults of working age (15–64 years) were not working. Ever since 1998, more than half – up to 57 per cent in 2001 – of the Dutch poverty population in the working age was actually working. In this chapter, we argued that the rise of in-work poverty in the Netherlands is partly the natural result of increased labour market participation during those years (leading to more in-work poverty even when working people's odds of being poor remain constant). However, this is only part of the story. In addition, working people in the Netherlands now face a greater risk of income poverty, up to a point where one in 14 working adults (students with odd jobs not included) live in poor households. In our perception, these figures reveal a significant change in the character of the Dutch welfare state. Until recently, the typical face of poverty in the Netherlands was that of the non-working poor living off social benefits. Since the mid-1990s, a new face of poverty has emerged: individuals who are working – partly because they were pushed from social security or social assistance back into the labour market – but are nevertheless poor. In-work poverty is no longer typical only for liberal welfare states such as the USA, but has become 'normal' in the Netherlands as well.

Our main hypothesis in this study was that the rise of in-work poverty in the Netherlands is not so much the consequence of economic and demographic developments (more self-employment, more part-time and flexible work, the rise of low-skilled service work, more female labour market participation, individualization, more single-parent families, and so on), but of institutional reforms in the Dutch welfare state (more selective access to social security, reduction of the duration and levels of social benefits, activating labour market policies and more obligations to work). However, in our statistical analysis, we had no possibility of directly linking the level of in-work poverty in the Netherlands to these changes in the Dutch welfare state. Instead, we examined changes in the composition of the in-work poverty population in terms of both their labour market characteristics and their individual and household characteristics.

As far as labour market characteristics are concerned, we examined the employment status, the number of working hours and the occupational class of the working poor. We found that all these factors are significantly related to a person's odds of in-work poverty. Self-employed persons, people working in small part-time jobs (less than 20 hours a week) and people working in skilled and unskilled Fordist or post-industrial occupations (note: not only low-skilled service jobs!) have significantly higher odds of in-work poverty than employees, people working more than 20 hours a week and people working in higher Fordist or post-industrial occupations. However, we argued that the increase in in-work poverty in the Netherlands since the mid-1990s cannot be attributed to changes in these labour market characteristics. The in-work poverty risks for self-employed persons, part-time workers and workers in low-skilled Fordist and post-industrial jobs have not increased over the years (since the early 1990s). Increases in self-employment, part-time work and the number of low-qualified service jobs may have resulted in a rising number of low-paid workers but, as we have argued, having an (individual) low income is not necessarily related to poverty measured at the household level. People with low-paid work who live in households with other income earners and pool their income with that of a spouse are generally not poor.

We also examined various individual and household characteristics (gender, household composition, the number of income earners in the household, and educational levels) of the working poor. A remarkable outcome is that gender as such does not explain a person's odds of in-work poverty. Although in-work poverty in the Netherlands – in contrast to other countries – appears at first to be a predominantly female phenomenon (during the 1990s, at least 60 per cent of the working poor were female), gender as such does not make a difference. Taking all other factors into account (part-time work, working in low-skilled service work, educational level, household composition and number of incomes in the household) there were no gender differences in the odds of in-work poverty.

All the other individual and household characteristics covered in the analysis do make a difference, however. The odds of in-work poverty among single parents are almost twice as high as the odds of couples with children. The odds of in-work poverty for households with two or more income earners are less than 10 per cent compared with the in-work poverty risk of households with only one income earner. In-work poverty also turned out to be related to educational qualifications: low-skilled working individuals have a much higher in-work poverty risk than working people with more human capital. Moreover, we saw that the in-work poverty risks of single parents, one-earner households and low-skilled working individuals increased during the 1990s. In other words, the point is *not* that there were more single parents, single-earner households and low-skilled workers during the 1990s, but that belonging to one or more of these categories resulted in an increasing risk of in-work poverty.

Behind these statistical categories, there are both new and traditional groups who are at risk with regard to in-work poverty: on the one hand, there are single parents who face the difficult combination of having to provide an income and taking care of the children alone and, on the other hand, there is the traditional male breadwinner who has to maintain a whole family with one single income. For both at-risk groups, however, it is first and foremost the case that low-educated individuals have a high poverty risk. Well-educated single parents or single breadwinners generally have sufficient human capital to avoid financial poverty (for single parents in the Netherlands this is documented by Hooghiemstra and Knijn, 1997). Low-qualified or unskilled single parents or single breadwinners – many of whom come from immigrant backgrounds – are especially unable to earn labour incomes that are sufficient to keep themselves out of poverty.

Finally, we assumed that the increased in-work poverty risks of these vulnerable social categories (single parents and other single earners, workers with health limitations and/or limited human capital) are related to the institutional changes in the Dutch social security and social assistance systems we described earlier in this chapter. Up until the early 1990s, these groups with limited chances in the labour market had more or less been given up on. It was generally accepted that these groups have few possibilities on the labour market and would therefore depend on social benefits indefinitely. However, this changed during the 1990s when new social policies emphasizing activation and labour market participation were put in place. As a result of successive social security reforms, vulnerable social categories were pushed into the labour market and urged to earn their own incomes. However, as our study makes clear, labour market participation does not always imply an escape from financial poverty.

NOTES

1. Esping-Andersen (1996: 265), for instance, states that 'the alignment of political forces conspire just about everywhere to maintain the existing principles of the welfare state'.
2. We do not use the 1984 data because in this year income data were collected in the April survey while in all other years (in the period 1985–89) the household income was measured in the October survey. Because this may have distorted the information (periodical increase of wages, seasonal unemployment), we excluded the 1984 wave from our analysis.
3. The disposable household income refers to summed up income of all household members minus income transfers (such as paid alimony), income tax, expenses for income insurances, and so on. To make it more complex, there was another significant change in the method of income measurement in 1990. Until then, DSEP asked for the *net* monthly household income. Starting 1990, DSEP asked for the *gross* annual household income. In all years, this figure was converted into a (net) disposable household income by subtracting paid taxes et cetera.

4. The outcomes in Figure 5.1 differ considerably from other research findings about income poverty in the Netherlands in the 1980s and 1990s. Other studies usually find that income poverty in the Netherlands was much higher in the 1980s than in the 1990s (cf. Engbersen et al., 2000; SCP/CBS, 2005; Vrooman and Hoff, 2004). There are two explanations for the differences in outcomes. (1) The population examined in the analysis: this analysis is not about all Dutch households or individuals, but only about individuals of working age. (2) The definition of poverty: Dutch poverty research usually uses poverty measures that are more stable over the years. The relative poverty measure used here (60 per cent of the annual median income) tends to be less stable, especially in times of economic growth. When household incomes increase, so does the poverty threshold and *thus* the number of individuals or households below the poverty line. We have nevertheless used a relative poverty threshold in this analysis in order to make our outcomes comparable with the outcomes in other chapters of this book.
5. In official Dutch statistics, only persons who work at least 12 hours a week are counted as workers.
6. Unlike in Esping-Andersen's classification, we have also included sales personnel in shops and on markets in the category of 'Fordist low occupations'. In classifying the occupations of the DSEP respondents in terms of Esping-Andersen's classification of occupational categories, we gratefully made use of a classification scheme drawn up by Professor Robert Kloosterman (University of Amsterdam). To our knowledge, this classification scheme has not been published. The authors thank their Amsterdam colleague Professor Kloosterman for allowing us to make use of his work.

REFERENCES

Aarts, L., P. de Jong en R. van der Veen (2002), *Met de beste bedoelingen: WAO 1975–1999, Trends, onderzoek en beleid*, Doetinchem: Elsevier Bedrijfsinformatie.

Bardone, L. and A.C. Guio (2005), 'In-work poverty', *Statistics in Focus. Population and Social Conditions*, **2005** (5), 1–10.

Engbersen, G. (1995), 'The road to anomia? Poverty regimes and life chances', in B. Unger and F. van Waarden (eds), *Convergence or Diversity*, Aldershot: Avebury, pp. 200–225.

Engbersen, G., J.C. Vrooman and E. Snel (eds.) (2000), *Balans van het armoedebeleid. Vijfde jaarrapport armoede en sociale uitsluiting*. Amsterdam: AUP.

Engbersen, G., K. Schuyt, J. Timmer and F. van Waarden (2006), *Cultures of Unemployment. A Comparative Look at Long-Term Unemployment and Urban Poverty*, 2 rev edn, Amsterdam: AUP.

Ehrenreich, B. (2002), *Nickel and Dimed: Undercover in Low-wage America*, London: Granta Books.

Esping-Andersen, G. (1990), *The Three Worlds of Welfare Capitalism*, Cambridge: Polity Press.

Esping-Andersen, G. (1993), 'Post-industrial class structures: an analytical framework', in. G. Esping-Andersen (ed.), *Chancing Classes. Stratification and Mobility in Post-Industrial Societies*, London: Sage, pp. 7–31.

Esping-Andersen, G. (1996), 'Welfare states without work: the impasse of labor shedding and familialism in Continental European social policy', in. G. Esping-Andersen (ed.), *Welfare States in Transition: National Adaptations in Global Economies*, London: Sage, pp. 66–87.

Gilbert, N. (2002), *Transformation of the Welfare State. The Silent Surrender of Public Responsibility*, Oxford: Oxford University Press.

Hemerijck, A.C. and J. Visser (2006), *How Welfare States Learn*, position paper for NWO Shifts in Governance programme, Den Haag-Amsterdam.
Hooghiemstra, E. and T. Knijn (1997), 'Onder moeders paraplu: alleenstaande ouders op de armoedegrens', in G. Engbersen, E. Snel and C. Vrooman (eds), *De kwetsbaren. Tweede jaarrapport armoede en sociale uitsluiting*, Amsterdam: Amstendam University Press, pp. 103–22.
Jencks, C. (2005), 'What happened with welfare', *The New York Review of Books*, **52** (20), 76–86.
Neubeck, K.J. (2006), *When Welfare Disappears: The Case for Economic Human Rights*, London: Routledge.
Newman, K.S. (1999), *No Shame in my Game. The Working Poor in the Inner-City*, New York: Russell Sage Foundation.
Pierson, P. (1994), *Dismantling the Welfare State? Reagan, Thatcher, and the Politics of Retrenchment*, Cambridge: Cambridge University Press.
Pierson, P. (2000), 'Increased returns, path dependency, and the study of politics', *American Political Science Review*, **94** (2), 251–68.
Sassen, S. (1991), *The Global City: New York, London and Tokyo*, Princeton, NJ: Princeton University Press.
Snel, E., J. Burgers and A. Leerkes (2007), 'Class position of immigrant workers in a post-industrial economy', *Journal of Ethnic and Migration Studies*, **33** (8), 1323–42.
Social and Cultural Planning Bureau and Netherlands Statistics (SCP/CBS) (2005), *Armoedemonitor 2005*, Den Haag: SCP.
Therborn, G. (1986), *Why Some People Are More Unemployed than Others. The Strange Paradox of Growth and Unemployment*, London: Verso.
Teulings, C., R. van der Veen and W. Trommel (1997), *Dilemma's van sociale zekerheid. Een analyse van tien jaar herziening van het stelsel van sociale zekerheid*, Den Haag: VUGA.
Van der Veen, R. (1999), 'Institutionele veranderingen, sociale bescherming en sociale ongelijkheid', in G. Engbersen, J.C. Vrooman and E. Snel (eds), *Armoede en verzorgingsstaat. Vierde jaarrapport armoede en sociale uitsluiting*, Amsterdam: AUP, pp. 65–82.
Venkatesh, S. (2006), *Off the Book: The Underground Economy of the Urban Poor*, Cambridge: Harvard University Press.
Visser, J. (2002), 'The first part-time economy of the world: a model to be followed?', *Journal of European Social Policy*, **12** (1), 23–42.
Visser, J. and A. Hemerijck (1996), *A Dutch Miracle: Job Growth, Welfare Reform and Corporatism in the Netherlands*, Amsterdam: Amsterdam University Press.
Vrooman, J.C. and S. Hoff (eds) (2004), *The Poor Side of the Netherlands. Results from the Dutch Poverty Monitor*, The Hague: Social en Cultureel Planbureau. www.scp.nl/english/publications/books/9037701833/The_poor_side_of_the_Netherlands.pdf (accessed 27 November 2007).

APPENDIX

Table 5.A1 Number of working people, employment and unemployment rates in the Netherlands (1985–2001)

	Employed persons (1000s)	Employment rate*			Unemployed persons** (1000s)	Unemployment rate		
		Overall	Males	Females		Overall	Males	Females
1985	4811	49	67	30	–	–	–	–
1986	5040	–	–	–	–	–	–	–
1987	5257	52	70	35	–	–	–	–
1988	5378	53	70	36	453	7.7	7.4	8.3
1989	5477	54	70	37	407	6.9	6.4	7.8
1990	5644	55	71	39	358	5.9	5.4	6.8
1991	5790	56	72	41	334	5.4	4.9	6.3
1992	5885	57	72	41	336	5.3	4.9	6.1
1993	5925	57	71	42	415	6.5	6.0	7.3
1994	5920	57	70	42	486	7.5	7.0	8.3
1995	6063	58	72	44	464	7.0	6.4	8.1
1996	6185	59	72	45	440	6.6	5.8	7.8
1997	6384	60	74	47	375	5.5	4.8	6.5
1998	6587	62	75	49	287	4.1	3.7	4.8
1999	6768	63	76	51	221	3.1	2.7	3.7
2000	6917	64	77	52	188	2.6	2.3	3.1
2001	7062	65	77	54	146	2.0	1.8	2.3

Notes:
* Employment rate: working persons (at least 12 hours a week) as a percentage of the total population of working age (15–65 years).
** Unemployed persons: registered as job seekers and available at least 12 hours a week.

Source: Netherlands statistics (statline).

Table 5.A2 Working and non-working poor in the Netherlands (1985–2001)

	Poor as % of total population in working age			Share of poverty population %		Poverty risk %	
	Working poor	Non-working poor	All Poor	Working poor	Non-working poor	Working poor	Non-working poor
1985	2.1	2.7	4.8	43.3	56.7	3.5	6.7
1986	2.0	2.9	4.9	41.0	59.0	3.2	7.5
1987	2.3	3.2	5.6	42.0	58.0	3.8	8.5
1988	2.2	2.7	4.9	44.4	55.6	3.4	7.6
1989	2.3	3.0	5.3	43.3	56.7	3.5	8.5
1990	4.3	4.1	8.4	51.6	48.4	6.6	11.9
1991	4.7	5.6	10.3	45.7	54.3	7.0	17.2
1992	4.0	4.8	8.7	45.3	54.7	5.7	15.4
1993	4.0	5.0	9.0	44.7	55.3	5.8	16.3
1994	4.6	6.0	10.6	43.6	56.4	6.7	19.5
1995	3.9	5.4	9.3	42.3	57.7	5.6	18.4
1996	4.8	5.6	10.4	46.0	54.0	6.6	20.5
1997	4.6	5.1	9.7	47.7	52.3	6.2	19.3
1998	5.4	4.9	10.3	52.6	47.4	7.3	19.4
1999	5.3	5.1	10.4	51.3	48.7	7.0	21.0
2000	5.8	4.7	10.5	55.2	44.8	7.5	20.9
2001	6.0	4.6	10.6	56.8	43.2	7.7	20.9

Note: Persons 15–65 years of age not including students.

Source: Dutch Socio-Economic Panel Survey 1985–2001; own computations.

Table 5.A3 Mean and median equivalized disposable household incomes (in Dutch guilders) and % of poor households in the Netherlands (1985–2001)

Year	Reference period	Mean	Median	60% of median	Poverty rate %
1985	Monthly income in 1985	22057	19598	11759	4.8
1986	Monthly income in 1986	22655	20183	12110	4.9
1987	Monthly income in 1987	23213	20795	12477	5.6
1988	Monthly income in 1988	24085	21530	12918	4.9
1989	Monthly income in 1989	25052	22507	13504	5.3
1990	Annual income in 1989	24180	21993	13196	8.4
1991	Annual income in 1990	26838	24567	14740	10.3
1992	Annual income in 1991	27321	25208	15125	8.7
1993	Annual income in 1992	27684	25585	15351	9.0
1994	Annual income in 1993	30279	27687	16612	10.6
1995	Annual income in 1994	28950	26773	16064	9.3
1996	Annual income in 1995	30652	28137	16882	10.4
1997	Annual income in 1996	31799	29635	17781	9.7
1998	Annual income in 1997	32631	30782	18469	10.3
1999	Annual income in 1998	34169	32204	19322	10.4
2000	Annual income in 1999	35203	33038	19823	10.5
2001	Annual income in 2000	37078	34674	20804	10.6

Note: Persons 15–65 years of age not including students.

Source: Dutch Socio-Economic Panel Survey 1985–2001; own computations.

6. In-work poverty in a transitional labour market: Sweden, 1988–2003

Björn Halleröd and Daniel Larsson

INTRODUCTION

The labour market is a society's main provider of economic resources, and the link between poverty and such factors as unemployment, early retirement, and so on is indisputable. Employment is therefore naturally seen as the main cure for poverty, while family and income transfer systems constitute an alternative support network in cases where employment fails. However, the working poor challenge this view, since their very existence implies that the labour market creates jobs with wages that are too low and/or employment contracts that are not secure enough to keep people out of poverty. Thus, if a substantial share of the poor are working poor, we need to reconsider the traditional view of the relationship between employment and poverty.

In this chapter, we examine the relationship between labour market position and in-work poverty in Sweden. We look at the period from 1988 to 2003 with special emphasis on three time periods: the late 1980s, the mid-1990s and the early years of the second millennium. These periods of time represent three distinctive situations. In the late 1980s, the Swedish labour market was characterized by a high employment rate and an extremely low unemployment rate. At the beginning of the 1990s, this situation changed radically, with skyrocketing unemployment and a shrinking employment rate. By the turn of the millennium, the economy was solidly back on track. However, at this point, the country's economic policy was focused on low inflation rather than on full employment. The employment rate was still lower than in the late 1980s, and the unemployment rate had stabilized at around 5 per cent of the labour force – figures that in the 1980s would have been seen as totally unacceptable.

Our aim is, first, to analyse the degree to which poor Swedes are working as well as the variation in in-work poverty between the late 1980s and the beginning of the new century. Second, we wish to analyse to what degree the working poor are poor because of their inferior labour market position.

That is, are the working poor poor because they are mixing periods of employment with periods of unemployment, because they are underemployed (prevented from working full time) or because they share households with spouses who are suffering from unemployment problems? Third, we also analyse the relationship between in-work poverty and labour market position – that is, class position and occupational sector – again looking at changes over time.

A WELFARE STATE AND LABOUR MARKET IN TRANSITION

Sweden is often depicted as the prime example of a social democratic welfare state regime (Esping-Andersen, 1991), the Scandinavian model or a comprehensive welfare system (Korpi and Palme, 1998; 2004). Despite different labels, the cornerstone of the Swedish welfare state model has traditionally been the wage solidarity policy, the general and generous income maintenance system, the high employment rate and low unemployment. The ideal outcome of this model is that most people are working, wages are sufficiently high to keep those who are working out of poverty, and income losses during temporary periods of unemployment, sickness, and so on are replaced via income maintenance programmes. Even though the Swedish welfare state model still functions according to these principles, there have been a large number of more or less profound changes during the time period studied here (Esping-Andersen, 1999; Hajighasemi, 2004).

Sweden was affected – as were most other countries – by economic problems that followed in the wake of the two oil crises in the 1970s, and during the 1980s, a series of deregulations took place. The wage solidarity policy, upheld with centralized wage bargains between the Swedish Labour Confederation (LO) and the Swedish Employers' Confederation (SAF), was undermined as early as 1983, when the largest trade union organizing industrial workers sidestepped the confederation and bargained directly with their branch employers (Canova, 1994; Edin and Holmlund, 1995; Elvander, 1988). In 1990, the Swedish Employers' Confederation made a declaration stating that in principal, it did not take part in central bargaining, and it was not until 1997 that the unions once again sat down with the central confederations of industrial employers to discuss the conditions and the future of the labour market (Benner and Vad, 2001; Elvander, 2003). The partial dismantling of centralized wage setting is probably one reason why wage dispersion has increased during the past decades (Björklund and Freeman, 1997; Blau and Kahn, 1996; Nordström-Skans et al., 2006). Another important transformation in the Swedish model was the deregulation of the financial market during the 1980s, starting with the upheaval of state regulation of interest rates, and followed by the deregulation of foreign exchange control, which was completed in 1991. Deregulation was combined with an expansive financial policy which, among other things, entailed that expansion of welfare state efforts continued throughout the 1980s. By the late 1980s, the Swedish economy was severely overheated, and it was obvious that the economy was in need of a cooling down. However, attempts to give the Swedish economy a soft landing failed, and in the early 1990s the bubble burst. After this, the country experienced negative growth rates for three years in a row. The economic crises triggered a series of welfare state retrenchments at the same time that the labour market faced a major restructuring (Magnusson, 2006). Unemployment increased from about 2 per cent to 8 per cent in just two years, and the employment rate fell from about 83 per cent in 1990 to 72 per cent in 1994 (Statistics Sweden Labour Force Survey). At the same time, the proportion of temporary employment increased from about 10 per cent at the beginning of the 1990s to around 16 per cent in the late 1990s (Aronsson et al., 2000). Other important consequences of the crisis were cutbacks in the social insurance system, restructuring of the public sector and increasing taxes (SOU, 2001).

From the mid-1990s onward, the Swedish economy recovered. Public finances, which had virtually collapsed at the beginning of the decade, were restored, and since that time, Sweden has experienced an economic growth rate that, from a European perspective, must be seen as fairly high. However, the country's policy priorities have changed from fighting unemployment to fighting inflation (Lindvall, 2004), a line of action that is upheld via an independent national bank and a strict budget process. The level of unemployment is still much higher than was the case before the crisis, and the employment rate has not recovered to the pre-crisis level.

WHO ARE THE POOR, WHO IS WORKING, AND WHO ARE THE WORKING POOR?

Most people probably have a rather straightforward understanding of what it means to be working and poor. What we see in front of us is a person who goes to work every day, works full-time, but still cannot make ends meet. However, if we look at the ways in which the working poor are defined in the literature, it is easy to see that things are a bit more complex. Poverty typically refers to a person's income situation during a particular time span – usually one year, one month, or in some cases one week. A person is commonly considered to be poor if she or he lives in a household that has an annual income below the poverty line,[1] while employment usually refers to another time frame. According to Peña-Casas and Latta (2004), a poor person is considered to be working poor if he or she has worked at least one month during the past 12 months (which is their broad definition). A similar definition is used by Kim (1998). A more common approach, also used by Peña-Casas and Latta, is to define a person as working if she or he has worked for at least six months during the past 12-month period (Bardone and Guio, 2005; Klein and Rones, 1989; Mosisa, 2003). There are also examples where a person is defined as working poor if he or she lives in a poor household with one working person (Nightingale and Fix, 2004). The different ways in which the working poor are distinguished from the non-working poor reflect a substantial definitional problem – that is, what kind of phenomenon are we actually investigating?

The most clear-cut example of 'working poor' is a person who lives in a single-adult household without children and works full-time, but at a wage that is too low to lift him or her above the poverty line. In this case, wage-setting in combination with taxation is both the cause of and the cure for the problem – increased minimum wages and/or lowered taxation will solve it. One can, of course, suspect that such a policy will turn some of the working poor into non-working poor, as their work will be priced out of the market, but it will nevertheless solve the working poor problem. However, the definitions of in-work poverty referred to above also include people who are poor because they are temporarily unemployed, cannot find full-time jobs, have spouses who are unemployed or retired early, and so on. Thus, the working poor problem could, after all, be an unemployment problem – which is something that has fundamental policy implications, changing the focus from wage-setting to job creation. The problem can be tackled from two different angles. First, we could apply stricter definitions of in-work poverty and collect data that allow for strict co-ordination of the measurement of income and employment. Second, we could turn the issue into an empirical rather than a definitional question. That is, we could investigate to what degree the working-poor individuals have an unemployment history, whether they share a household with persons who are unemployed, and so on. In this chapter, we will try to apply both strategies.

WHAT CAN WE EXPECT?

Theories of labour market segmentation that divide the labour market into core and periphery have long been discussed (Atkinson, 1984; Barron and Norris, 1976; Ellingsaeter, 1998; Gallie et al., 1998). This is not the place to discuss this area of research in detail: we simply point out some of the features that are often connected with a peripheral or secondary labour market and in-work poverty. Work in the periphery is typically characterized by low skill levels, short-term contracts, part-time work and, consequently, low pay (Kalleberg, 2003). A trend towards a more segmented labour market – which also implies the growth of what we can call peripheral jobs – ought to have consequences for in-work poverty, because a growing share of the workforce will have low wages and at the same time be exposed to unemployment, labour market insecurity and part-time jobs. Considering the fact that the development of the Swedish labour market has led to greater wage dispersion, higher unemployment and a larger share of temporary employment positions, we can expect a trend towards increasing in-work poverty.

However, we can also assume that the effect of labour market segmentation on in-work poverty is influenced by business cycle changes and changes in the demand for labour power. If we assume that the peripheral sector is characterized by numerical flexibility, then we can also assume that it is first and foremost these types of jobs that disappear when unemployment goes up. Increasing unemployment should therefore typically reduce the kind of jobs that are associated with in-work poverty, which in turn should lead to a decrease in in-work poverty (Peña-Casas and Latta, 2004). Hence, when unemployment goes up, it is possible that the working poor will be transformed into non-working poor. From this perspective, we could assume that the unemployment shock that hit Sweden in the early 1990s in fact led to a decrease in in-work poverty.

In-work poverty is closely related to gender in two ways. First, the division between a primary and a secondary labour market is related to gender inequality, such that men are more likely to be on the primary and women more likely to be on the secondary labour market (cf. Ellingsaeter, 2000; SOU, 2004). Hence, women are more often found in low-wage occupations, and are more likely to work part-time, and should therefore be more exposed to in-work poverty. However, this should primarily be a problem for women living in single-adult households. Households with more than one adult usually have more than one wage earner – especially in countries like Sweden that have a comparatively high female employment rate. This is one of the main reasons why the relationship between low wages and in-work poverty is so surprisingly weak (Bardone and Guio, 2005; Peña-Casas and Latta, 2004). It can also be argued that it has become more important for families to have dual earners in order to prevent in-work poverty, especially when the main provider is in the low-paid service sector (Gallie et al., 1998). Thus, the family situation is important for the in-work poverty risk, and we can expect that single-adult households and couples with only one wage earner will be most exposed to in-work poverty.

The discussion above brings us to the point of formulating hypotheses about the development of in-work poverty in Sweden.

1. Considering the general development of the labour market, we can expect a growth in peripheral jobs to lead to an increase in in-work poverty over time.
2. We can expect in-work poverty to often be related to previous unemployment experience and a generally vulnerable labour market position.
3. We expect in-work poverty to mainly be a single-earner household problem. In-work poverty among couples is therefore expected to most often be a consequence of one partner's unemployment.
4. We assume that the deep labour market crisis of the 1990s especially hit people whose position in the labour market was peripheral. Despite the assumed underlying trend towards increasing in-work poverty, we therefore expect to see a decrease in in-work poverty during the mid-1990s, because the working poor were pushed out of the labour market and transformed into non-working poor.

DATA AND OPERATIONALIZATION

We have used data from Statistics Sweden's annual Survey of Living Conditions for the years 1988–89, 1994–95 and 2002–03. The data represent a population-based random sample of the Swedish population from the age of 16 and upwards. Data are collected via face-to-face interviews. Data on income are gathered from the general income register and contain information on all types of incomes, transfers and taxes connected to the respondent and, when relevant, the respondent's partner (regardless of whether the two are married or only cohabiting). Income data on respondents who live with their parents are problematic, since they are technically defined as households of their own. This means that we know nothing about their parent's incomes and hence are unable to construct a realistic picture of household income. From a European perspective, Swedish children leave their parental homes early, and more than two-thirds of those in the age group between 20 and 24 have formed households of their own (Vogel, 2005). In order to handle this problem, we have limited our data-set to respondents who are between 20 and 64 years of age, and we have furthermore excluded all respondents who share a household with their parents. Because we are, after all, studying a relatively uncommon phenomenon, we have decided to merge data from two consecutive years into one data-set. Information on the data-sets is shown in Table 6.1.

Table 6.1 The Survey of Living Conditions: sample size and response rate

Year	The random sample	Total working sample	Response rate	The final working sample*
1988–98	16741	13295	79.4	8366
1994–95	14969	12005	80.2	8477
2002	14945	11956	80.0	8059

Note: * Individuals 20–64 years of age not including single individuals living with their parents.

We have measured poverty via the conventional 60 per cent of median income measure – that is, a person is poor if he or she lives in a household that has an equivalent disposable household income that is less than 60 per cent of the median income.[2] A person is considered to be working if he or she has received any wage income, from an employer or from a self-owned company, during the year. This means that employed individuals who for various reasons – for example, long-term illness or parental leave – do not receive any wage from their employers are defined as not working. We have also excluded those who were out of work at the time of the interview. By doing so, we have minimized to some degree the problem caused by the fact that some of the working poor are only working for part of the year – which most likely means that if they are poor, it is because they lack work, not because they are working poor. There is also a practical reason for excluding this category. Basic survey information on employment conditions is, for obvious reasons, missing for this category. Even though our strategy for defining those who are working largely excludes people who are only loosely attached to the labour market, we have also included individuals who were unemployed or out of work for other reasons during parts of the observation year. This means that some of the observed in-work poverty is actually caused by unemployment and weak labour force attachment.

Wages are, of course, a central variable when analysing in-work poverty. However, using annual wages in our analysis is problematic, since they depend not only on the salary, but also on the time each individual spends working. Thus, the variable we ideally want to look at is wage per hour. The problem is that we do not have direct information about hourly wages, only annual wage income. But we do have information about working hours per week, which means that we can calculate a proxy for hourly wage by dividing the annual wage income by 52 to get weekly income and then dividing the weekly income by the number of working hours per week. This gives us a reasonably correct estimate for respondents who work the whole year and who do not significantly change their working hours during the year, for example due to unemployment. The problem is, of course, that – as is the case with annual wage – we still underestimate the hourly wage for those who have been unemployed, on parental leave or have not been working for any other reason during parts of the year. We also underestimate the hourly wage for those who, for example, moved from a full-time job to a part-time job, at the same time as we overestimate the hourly wage for those who made the opposite move. However, even though our proxy for hourly wage has a number of shortcomings, it nevertheless provides a more accurate picture of the relationship between wage-setting and in-work poverty, since the main reason for low annual wages – especially among women – is a limited number of working hours. We have used the most common threshold to distinguish low wages from non-low wages, that is, we define those whose wage is less than two-thirds of the median wage income as low-wage earners (Peña-Casas and Latta, 2004).

In addition to hourly wage, we have also used a number of indicators to measure a peripheral labour market position. First, we measured unemployment experience during the past five years. We have divided the indicators into three categories: (1) no unemployment, (2) unemployed less than six months and (3) unemployed more than six months. Second, we measured the occurrence of part-time work, distinguishing between full-time (more than 30 hours per week) and part-time (30 hours or less per week). Most Swedish part-time workers have a weekly work time between 20 and 30 hours. Only around 1 per cent work less than 20 hours per week. For that reason, we have not distinguished between 'long' and 'short' part-time. Third, we measured the type of employment contract, where we distinguished between regular contracts with no time limit and temporary, time-limited employment contracts.

General labour market position is indicated by Statistic Sweden's socio-economic class code, which closely resembles the well-known EGP (Erikson–Goldthorpe–Portocarero) class schema (Bihagen and Halleröd, 2000; Erikson and Goldthorpe, 1993). This class schema has 10 categories and distinguishes between self-employed and employees, blue-collar and white-collar workers, service and production workers, skilled and unskilled workers (for white-collar, different degrees of skill). Because people are regarded as poor if they live in a household that has an income below the poverty line, it seems justified to analyse the households' class position rather than that of individuals. The household class schema used here is based on the highest class position in the family (Erikson, 1984). For the employed, we follow the hierarchy from unskilled, blue-collar, service worker (lowest) to higher white-collar worker. Hence, if the husband is a skilled, blue-collar production worker and the wife is a middle range white-collar worker, the household is classified as belonging to the latter category. Construction of household class for the employed is relatively straightforward and theoretically justifiable (Bihagen, 2000). Classification is more complex when it comes to the self-employed. Here, we have chosen the following strategy. If either spouse is self-employed with employees, the household is categorized as such. If one of the spouses is self-employed without employees and the other spouse is a blue-collar worker or lower white-collar worker, the household is categorized as self-employed. However, if the other spouse is a middle range or higher white-collar worker, the household is categorized this way. Although this is, to some degree, an arbitrary decision, it can be justified by the fact that self-employed individuals without employees have the same living conditions in many respects as blue-collar workers and lower white-collar workers (Halleröd, 1997).

Family characteristics are measured according to six different household types. First, we have distinguished between single adults and couples. Thereafter, we separated households with and without children. Finally, we have divided two-adult households between those in which the respondent's spouse is working and those in which she or he is not working. This categorization of household types allows us to analyse the relationship between in-work poverty and single-earner households.

LABOUR MARKET ATTACHMENT AND POVERTY

Table 6.2 shows that the poverty rate for the total population (20–64 years of age) has increased from somewhat over 5 per cent in 1988–89 to more than 9 per cent in 2002–03. The poverty rate has increased in most of the groups specified in the table. The poverty rate among the self-employed is extremely high, especially in 1988–89 and 1994–95, when more than 20 per cent of the self-employed fell below the poverty line. This figure decreases over time, and in 2002–03 it was down to 15 per cent – still high, but lower than previously. However, it is important to keep in mind that the poverty rate among the self-employed is probably overestimated. Studies using direct measures of consumption of goods and services have shown, for example, that the poverty risk among the self-employed is about the same as among blue-collar workers (Halleröd, 1997). The figures for the employed are substantially lower. In 1988–89, less than 2 per cent of the employed were poor. This figure has increased somewhat over time, to just above 3 per cent in 2002–03. More than half of the poor in the late 1980s were working poor – that is, employed or self-employed – a figure that fell to just above 40 per cent in the mid-1990s and down to around one-third in

Table 6.2 Poverty rate and distribution of the poor in relation to employment status (population 20–64 years old)

	1988–89			1994–95			2002–03		
	Percentage of the population	Poverty rate	Percentage of the poor	Percentage of the population	Poverty rate	Percentage of the poor	Percentage of the population	Poverty rate	Percentage of the poor
Employed	75.6	1.8	26.9	65.4	2.6	21.7	68.0	3.2	23.0
Self-employed	7.3	20.2	28.7	7.2	22.1	20.6	6.0	15.4	10.7
Total in-work	82.9	3.5	55.6	72.6	4.5	42.3	74.9	4.3	33.7
Unemployed	2.5	7.3	3.5	9.7	12.5	15.8	6.1	20.8	13.5
Students	2.9	13.1	7.4	5.4	28.6	19.9	6.2	37.3	24.5
Early retired	5.1	8.0	8.0	6.1	4.8	3.8	6.6	12.3	8.6
Old age retired	0.8	20.4*	0.7	0.8	1.4	0.1	1.4	6.8	1.0
Homemakers	3.6	14.7	10.2	3.1	19.1	7.6	2.1	27.7	6.2
Others	2.2	28.9	12.2	2.3	35.5	10.4	3.0	39.1	12.5
Total out of work	17.1	13.4	44.4	27.6	16.2	57.6	25.4	24.6	66.2
Total	100	5.2	100	100	7.7	100	100	9.4	100

Notes:
* The general retirement age was 65 but some employee categories have negotiated a lower old age retirement age. Because this is rather unusual, the n for old age retired is very small (58) and the figures should be interpreted with care.
Individuals 20–64 years of age not including single individuals living with their parents.

Source: Survey of Living Conditions.

the early 2000s. Thus, a substantial fraction of the poor are working. At the same time, it seems clear that the proportion of the poor who are working has declined over time. However, it is predominantly among the self-employed that we can observe a decline. Figures for the employed are considerably more stable, and the employed make up around one-fourth to one-fifth of all poor people.

The poverty rate among those who are out of work is, of course, much higher. It is also in this category that we see a very substantial increase, from 13 per cent in the late 1980s to almost 25 per cent in the early 2000s. The proportion of the unemployed who are poor increased during the entire period, from about 7 per cent in 1988–89 to 20 per cent in 2002–03. Another group worth looking at is students. The poverty rate in this group increased from almost 14 per cent in 1988–89 to 37 per cent in 2002–03, an increase which occurred in tandem with a substantial expansion of tertiary education and increasing difficulties for young people in finding employment.

The data presented in the following tables are restricted to the employed and self-employed. Table 6.3 shows the fraction of the employed population in different categories. The fraction earning a low hourly wage hovers around 16 per cent. Hence, our data do not indicate a growth in low-wage jobs over time. The share that has experienced unemployment at some time during the past five years increased between 1988–89 and 1994–95, but remained fairly stable between 1994–95 and 2002–03. Part-time work – another indicator of a peripheral labour market position – has decreased over time, a development that most likely has a negative impact on in-work poverty. This can be explained by the fact that a larger share of the female labour force worked full time at the beginning of the new century compared to the late 1980s. (About 75 per cent of employed women worked full time in 1988–89 compared to 87 per cent in 2002–03. The corresponding figures for employed men are 96 per cent in 1988–89 and 97 per cent in 2002–03).

The proportion of unskilled blue-collar households within both production and services is decreasing over time. This is also the case for skilled blue-collar households within the production sector. The only increase among blue-collar workers is found among skilled blue-collar service workers. The proportion that hold middle-range white-collar and higher white-collar positions has increased, indicating an upgrading of skills during the period (Åberg, 2003).

Regarding household types, only small changes have occurred. The proportion of single adults with children has increased. We can also see that among cohabitants, it has become more common to have a spouse who is not employed – a change that occurred between 1988–89 and 1994–95, and which reflects the drop in the employment rate and the increasing unemployment during this period. Furthermore, the proportion of young people

Table 6.3 Socio-demographic profile of the employed in Sweden (%)

	1988–89	1994–95	2002–03
Low hourly wage	16.6	15.7	15.8
Unemployment experience during last five years			
Not unemployed	87.7	83.4	83.4
Unemployed less than six months	8.6	9.3	10.3
Unemployed more than six months	3.5	7.3	6.3
Full-time/part-time employment			
Full-time (> 30 hours per week)	85.6	88.0	92.5
Part-time (30 or less hours per week)	14.4	12.0	7.5
Temporary work	6.7	9.5	9.9
Household class position			
Unskilled blue collar – service	9.9	10.1	8.0
Unskilled blue collar – production	5.7	4.1	3.7
Skilled blue collar – service	4.2	4.7	6.2
Skilled blue collar – production	11.5	10.7	8.6
Lower white collar I	5.3	4.3	4.0
Lower white collar II	10.1	9.4	8.8
Middle-range white collar	22.0	23.2	25.5
Higher white collar	17.1	19.5	22.8
Self-employed – no employees	6.8	6.2	5.3
Self-employed – with employees	7.4	7.9	6.9
Household types			
Single adult	20.0	20.5	20.4
Single adult with children	3.6	3.9	5.0
Cohabiting, no child, spouse not employed	5.7	7.7	7.7
Cohabiting, no child, spouse employed	28.9	27.7	28.1
Cohabiting with child, spouse not employed	4.0	7.3	5.0
Cohabiting with child, spouse employed	37.6	32.9	33.8
Age			
20–24	8.3	5.0	4.4
25–30	14.4	14.2	13.2
31–50	54.9	55.6	51.7
51–64	22.4	25.1	30.6
Gender			
Men	52.2	52.3	52.5
Women	47.8	47.7	47.5

Note: Individuals 20–64 years of age not including single individuals living with their parents.

Source: Survey of Living Conditions.

on the labour market (20 to 24 years old) has decreased at the same time that the oldest group (50 to 64 years old) increased. No changes have occurred during the period as far as the gender composition of the employed population is concerned.

Table 6.4 presents the poverty rates among the employed. The poverty risk for people earning low wages increased between 1988–89 and 1994–95, only to decrease again in 2002–03, when about 18 per cent of low-wage earners were poor. Thus, even though the in-work poverty risk is rather high, the majority of low-wage earners are not poor. However, the other side of the coin shows that a large majority of the working poor are low-wage earners. This leads us to the conclusion that far from all low-wage earners are poor but, at the same time, low wages are almost a prerequisite for in-work poverty.

During the past five years, a large (but, over time, decreasing) majority of the working poor have had no unemployment experience at all. In the late 1980s, the difference in poverty rate between those with unemployment experience and those without unemployment experience was, by all measures, small. But this difference has increased over time, and we can conclude that in-work poverty is related to an increasing extent to vulnerable labour market positions. However, it is important to remember that even in 2002–03 a vast majority – more than two-thirds – of the working poor had no unemployment experience whatsoever. The proportion of poor people increased both among those employed full-time and those with part-time employment. Because the fraction of part-timers has decreased, this development has led to a situation in which almost 90 per cent of the working poor work full-time. The proportion who are poor also increased both among individuals with regular work and those doing temporary work. The increase for those with regular jobs is quite small, while the increase among those doing temporary work is substantial. Moreover, the proportion of the working poor who had temporary jobs doubled between 1988–89 and 1994–95.

The incidence of in-work poverty has increased in almost all class categories. The most noticeable increase is among blue-collar service workers, which is in line with our theoretical assumptions. However, in-work poverty is most common among the self-employed, and in 1988–89 the self-employed made up more than 50 per cent of all working poor – a figure that had decreased to around one-third in 2002–03. The high incidence of in-work poverty among the self-employed is most certainly an effect of measurement problems. It is not known at this stage whether the change over time is caused by improved conditions for the self-employed or whether it is the measurement problems that have decreased. What we do know is that in-work poverty is becoming an increasing problem for the employed.

Table 6.4 Poverty rate of the employed and socio-demographic profile of the working poor in Sweden (%)

	1988–89		1994–95		2002–03	
	Poverty rate	Percentage of the poor	Poverty rate	Percentage of the poor	Poverty rate	Percentage of the poor
Low hourly wage						
Yes	14.5	69.7	22.5	78.6	17.8	66.1
No	1.3	30.3	1.1	21.4	1.7	33.9
Unemployment experience during last five years						
Not unemployed	3.3	84.9	4.0	74.6	3.5	69.0
Unemployed less than six months	4.1	10.1	7.4	15.2	6.8	16.3
Unemployed more than six months	4.9	4.9	6.4	10.3	9.9	14.7
Full-time/part-time employment						
Full-time (> 30 hours per week)	1.6	72.7	2.2	75.1	4.1	89.0
Part-time (30 or less hours per week)	3.5	27.3	5.5	24.9	6.3	11.0
Temporary work contract						
Yes	5.0	9.8	8.8	18.5	10.3	23.9
No	3.3	90.2	4.1	81.5	3.6	76.1
Household class position						
Unskilled blue collar – service	4.4	12.6	6.4	14.2	8.7	16.5
Unskilled blue collar – production	2.8	4.6	3.2	2.9	5.1	4.4
Skilled blue collar – service	2.7	3.3	3.9	4.1	8.0	11.8
Skilled blue collar – production	1.1	3.5	1.8	4.3	2.7	5.4
Lower white collar I	1.4	2.1	2.1	2.0	4.4	4.2
Lower white collar II	1.0	2.9	1.2	2.5	2.0	4.1
Middle-range white collar	0.9	5.8	1.5	7.9	1.5	9.2

Higher white collar	0.9	4.4	1.1	4.9	1.7	9.3
Self-employed – no employees	14.3	27.8	24.2	33.5	18.6	23.2
Self-employed – with employees	14.3	33.0	13.5	23.6	7.4	12.0
Household types						
Single adult	6.4	36.9	7.9	36.1	6.9	33.1
Single adult with children	2.3	2.5	4.4	3.8	3.9	4.6
Cohabiting, no child, spouse not employed	4.1	6.7	4.1	6.9	4.3	7.7
Cohabiting, no child, spouse employed	1.6	13.8	2.6	15.9	2.2	14.7
Cohabiting with child, spouse not employed	9.7	11.3	8.0	13.0	11.3	13.2
Cohabiting with child, spouse employed	2.6	28.8	3.3	24.4	3.4	26.7
Age						
20–24	4.9	11.7	12.8	14.3	14.4	14.8
25–30	3.4	14.1	3.9	12.3	4.4	13.7
31–50	3.1	48.7	4.0	49.5	4.3	51.7
51–64	3.9	25.5	4.3	23.9	2.7	19.7
Gender						
Men	3.5	53.5	4.6	52.9	4.1	50.9
Women	3.4	46.5	4.5	47.1	4.4	49.1
Total	3.5	100.0	4.5	100.0	4.3	100.0

Note: Individuals 20–64 years of age not including single individuals living with their parents.

Source: Survey of Living Conditions.

Looking at different household types, we see that in-work poverty is most common among single-adult households without children and among the fairly small group of cohabitants with children but with only one wage earner. Rather surprisingly, we do not find a particularly high incidence of in-work poverty among single parents. The pattern is fairly stable over time. More interesting, though, is that in-work poverty seems to have become a problem for the young people on the labour market. In 1988–89, only about 5 per cent of the youngest age group on the labour market were poor, compared with about 15 per cent in 2002–03. There are no differences in in-work poverty between men and women.

The results so far can be summarized as follows. In-work poverty in Sweden is a quantitatively small, but growing problem among employees. Low hourly wages are perhaps the clearest characteristic of the working poor. It is otherwise difficult to identify clear-cut features of the working poor. Contrary to what one might believe, the majority of the working poor work full-time and do not have any experience of recent unemployment episodes. Most working poor individuals are not employed on temporary contracts, even though in-work poverty is associated to an increasing extent with time-limited work contracts. We can observe an increase in in-work poverty among blue-collar service workers, which is in line with assumptions about a growing peripheral labour market. In-work poverty is also, as expected, more common in single-earner households. The working poor are increasingly found among the younger section of the labour force. There are no significant differences between women and men.

MULTIVARIATE ANALYSIS

In the multivariate analysis, all the factors discussed above are integrated and analysed simultaneously in a logistic regression model. In-work poverty is such a rare phenomenon that in order to carry out the analysis, we have been forced to collapse several of the independent variables into fewer categories so as to avoid having too many empty cells. The need to do this is also underpinned by the fact that complicated interaction effects between gender on the one hand and hourly wage, part-time work and household type on the other have necessitated a separate analysis for men and women. Therefore, the class variable has been collapsed into four categories: blue-collar service workers, blue-collar production workers, white-collar workers and the self-employed. The different household types have also been condensed into four categories: single-adult households, couples with only one wage earner, couples without children and couples with children. This means that single-adult households also include single adults

Table 6.5 Poverty risks among employed Swedes (odds ratios)

Variable	1988–89		1994–95		2002–03	
	Men	Women	Men	Women	Men	Women
Low hourly wage	0.94***	**0.97*****	0.93***	**0.97*****	0.97***	**0.98*****
Unemployed 1–6 months during past five years	0.98	0.73	0.40	1.53	1.17	1.11
Unemployed more than 6 months during past five years	0.50	0.81	0.17**	0.58	1.62	1.46
Part-time worker	1.97	3.00***	2.08	2.91***	1.80	1.03
Temporary work contract	1.58	2.03*	1.20	1.50	1.68	1.84*
Reference group: white-collar worker						
Blue-collar service worker	1.59	1.41	2.20	2.08*	2.68**	1.90*
Blue-collar production worker	1.14	0.29	1.42	0.67	0.97	1.28
Self-employed	16.21***	10.58***	2.79	**9.55*****	4.60***	3.47***
Reference group: couples without children						
Single adult	5.69**	12.15***	6.43**	**2.24***	3.17***	2.30**
Couple – spouse not working	11.30***	8.15***	8.81**	0.95	3.76***	2.58**
Couple with child(ren)	2.20	1.23	3.77	0.44	1.49	1.65
Age (log)	0.77	0.92	0.50**	0.65**	0.74*	0.75*
Constant	0.15*	0.02***	1.8	0.27*	0.34	0.20**

Notes:
*** $p < 0.001$, ** $p < 0.01$, * $p < 0.05$.
Bold figures indicate significant differences ($p < 0.05$) between men and women.
Individuals 20–64 years of age not including single individuals living with their parents.

Source: Survey of Living Conditions.

with children. The reason for this is that there are very few single adult men with children, and hardly any of them are poor. Hourly wage is included in the analysis as a continuous variable. Age is also included as a continuous variable, but in order to capture the curvilinear association with in-work poverty, we have used a log transformation.[3]

The odds ratios from the multivariate analysis are shown in Table 6.5. There is, as expected, a negative odds ratio of less than 1 for the association between hourly wage and poverty: that is, the higher the wage, the lower the poverty risk. The negative effect is significantly stronger for men than for women, which possibly reflects the fact that men are still the main breadwinners in most households (Halleröd, 2005). Now, if in-work poverty is a low-wage problem, and if we were able to measure hourly wage in an accurate way, all occurrences of in-work poverty should be explained by this variable and the part-time indicator. However, because a number of other variables in the model remain significant, this is not the case.

The impact of employment experience is, in most cases, insignificant. Moreover, the only significant result is very hard to understand, since it goes in the wrong direction: those who experienced more than six months of unemployment in 1994–95 had a lowered risk of in-work poverty. One possible explanation is that individuals with unemployment experience who managed to establish themselves on the labour market in the midst of the Swedish unemployment crisis constitute a highly select group. Part-time work does have an impact on the poverty risk for women at the first two points of observation. The effect is not significant in 2002–03, which might reflect the decrease in part-time work among women. We can also see that women with temporary work contracts have an increased risk of in-work poverty, at least at the first and last points of measurement. We analysed class position using white-collar workers as a reference category. The highest in-work poverty risk is found among the self-employed. There are, as we mentioned above, reasons to be careful when interpreting these results. The only other results that are significant are the estimates for female blue-collar service workers in 1994–95 and for all blue-collar service workers in 2002–03. The household variable confirms that in-work poverty is mainly a problem for single-earner households. There is also a significant age effect for the last two measurement points, showing that it is predominantly the younger section of the labour force that is affected by in-work poverty.

Table 6.6 presents estimated in-work poverty probabilities for different categories of blue-collar workers. The estimates are based on the regression model presented in Table 6.5. The first example is a person earning the median wage for an unskilled, blue-collar service worker. It is also assumed that he or she is cohabiting, has at least one child and is 40 years old. Hence, this is a typical example of a low-wage earner. The in-work poverty risk for this example is negligible for both men and women in 1988–89. It is a bit higher for women in 1994–95, and for both men and women in 2002–03. However, it remains low throughout the observed period. The in-work poverty risk increases if we instead suppose that our example is living in a single-adult household. In fact, the estimated probabilities for this category come close to the actual average for each of the measurement years, which means that the in-work poverty risk is also relatively low for a category that,

Table 6.6 Estimated probabilities of in-work poverty (%)

	1988–89		1994–95		2002–03	
	Men	Women	Men	Women	Men	Women
Blue-collar service worker, median wage for unskilled service worker, couple with children, 40 years old	0.3	0.3	0.2	2.0	1.4	2.3
Blue-collar service worker, median wage for unskilled service worker, single adult, 40 years old	1.6	3.6	1.0	4.3	4.4	5.0
Blue-collar service worker, median wage for unskilled service worker, single adult, 26 years old	2.2	3.9	2.1	6.7	6.0	6.8
Blue-collar service worker, low wage (60% of median for all wage earners), single adult, 26 years old	9.1	6.3	22.5	12.6	17.3	11.8
Blue-collar service worker, median wage for the working poor, single adult, 26 years old	11.9	4.9	61.2	17.1	28.7	12.5

Note: Estimates based on logistic regression models in Table 6.5.

beforehand, could easily have been perceived as being highly exposed to in-work poverty. The risk increases more if we assume that our example is 26 years old instead of 40, but the estimates are still clearly below the actual poverty rate for the total population, and much lower than for the out-of-work section of the population (see Table 6.2). In the fourth example, we assume that our hypothetical person is a low-wage earner, earning only 60 per cent of the median hourly wage. The in-work poverty risks are now increasing substantially. The increase is more pronounced among men, reflecting the stronger income effect in this group. This result emphasizes that in-work poverty is truly a low-wage problem. Now, if we return to our data and check the actual hourly wages among the working poor, we find that in most cases, these individuals earn incomes far below the low-income threshold. Thus, in the last example, we have given our sample individual the median wage for the working poor for each year and for men and women, respectively. In 1988–89, the difference between a low wage and the actual median wage for men is quite small; for women experiencing in-work poverty, the actual median wage is in fact higher than the threshold, which leads to a slightly lower estimate. In 1994–95, the situation looks very different, especially for men. The median income for men who are working and poor is only 28 per cent of the median for all wage earners, which simply cannot be a correct measure of hourly wages in a highly regulated labour market such as the Swedish one. The most probable explanation for this is that since the Swedish labour market was particularly bad at this time – with many people experiencing unemployment during part of the year – a fairly large section of the population that we have identified as being in work had, in reality, been out of work during parts of the year. Thus, even though our data do not allow us to confirm that low income among the working poor is caused by unemployment, our best guess is that a large share of the working poor, predominantly men, were in fact unemployed in 1994–95. In 2002–03, wages – especially among men experiencing in-work poverty – are also very low, probably concealing an unemployment problem. Hourly wages among women in in-work poverty are generally higher than among men. Because women occupy low-wage positions to a much larger extent than men do, it is more likely that in-work poverty among women is a low-wage problem.

One way of getting a grip on the problem is to analyse to what degree the working poor earn extremely low hourly wages. Our calculation shows that the median hourly wage for a blue-collar worker in 2002–03 was around 115 crowns per hour. This is well in line with statistics on wages within the private sector. Official statistics also confirm Sweden's compressed wage structure, and the hourly wage for the lowest quartile is just around 12 per cent lower than the overall median (SCB, 2007). Now, if we first make the not particularly bold assumption that any hourly wage that falls below 50 per cent of the median for a blue-collar worker is in fact a measurement error that, in most cases, is caused by non-observed unemployment, then we can, in a second step, exclude this group from the analysis and thereafter calculate new figures for in-work poverty. If we do this, we find a slight decrease in 1988–89, from the already low 1.8 per cent to 1.2 per cent. For the two later observations, the decrease is more substantial. In 1994–95, in-work poverty decreased from 4.5 per cent to 1.4 per cent, and in 2002–03, the figure decreased from 4.3 per cent to 2.2 per cent. There is also a clear difference between women and men, and correcting for extremely low hourly incomes nearly eradicates in-work poverty among men. Thus, we can conclude that in-work poverty in Sweden is a very small problem, and to the extent that it exists at all, it is a problem for women with low-wage incomes. However, we can also conclude that higher unemployment and less secure employment conditions are creating poverty among what seems to be a growing section of the population that has a peripheral attachment to the labour market. A higher demand for labour power will therefore lead to a situation in which people who are poor because they are not working are transformed into people who are not poor because they are working.

CONCLUSIONS

In this chapter, we have analysed in-work poverty in a transitional labour market. Three periods have been studied: the first representing a booming economy with extremely low unemployment (1988–89); the second, an economy in crisis with skyrocketing unemployment and a changing labour market (1994–95); and the third, a period of economic recovery and stabilization, but with a labour market that was markedly changed compared with the first period (2002–03). We have used data from the Swedish Survey of Living Conditions and have empirically defined the working poor as those who received any wage income during the year and who were working when interviewed, but nevertheless had an annual equivalent disposable household income below the poverty line.

The basic assumption was that a transformation of the labour market took place during the period under investigation, implying segmentation between core positions and peripheral positions on the labour market, and that the extent of in-work poverty can largely be explained by this development. Our results show that in-work poverty in Sweden is an increasing but relatively uncommon phenomenon. The in-work poverty rate in the late 1980s was about 3.5 per cent. In the mid-1990s, the figure had increased to 4.5 per cent, and in the early 2000s the figure was marginally lower, 4.3 per cent. These figures included the self-employed – a group with an extremely high in-work poverty rate, and one that is, at least to some degree, attributable to measurement problems. If we looked solely at employees, we saw that only 1.8 per cent were among the working poor in the late 1980s. The corresponding figure in the mid-1990s was 2.6 per cent, and in the early 2000s, 3.2 per cent. Thus, there was a trend towards increasing in-work poverty, but the figures were on a very low level.

Our analysis revealed a close connection between low hourly wages and in-work poverty. We also saw a connection between temporary employment contracts and in-work poverty which was growing stronger over time. In addition, part-time work was related to in-work poverty – but only among women (very few men were working part-time). The connection between blue-collar service jobs and in-work poverty also strengthened over time. Overall, these results indicate that the transformation of the labour market – with greater wage dispersion, more temporary work contracts and a growing low-skilled service sector – has resulted in the growth of in-work poverty. The central issue in relation to these results is whether this development has led to an increase in low-paid jobs, and, therefore, to increased in-work poverty – or whether a more insecure labour market has led to more unemployment and, in turn, to increased poverty. This issue is of great policy importance, since the first option should reasonably lead to a policy that focuses on increased wages among low-wage earners, while the second option ought to lead to a policy focusing on the fight against unemployment, which could possibly be facilitated through lower minimum wages.

In our empirical analysis, we have done our utmost to define the working population as strictly as our data allow. Ideally, we wanted a situation in which we could analyse poverty among people who had been employed during the whole year, without any unemployment spells or any longer periods out of work (owing to, for example, long-term illness or parental leave). This ideal situation would enable us to be certain that in-work poverty, whenever it occurs, is caused by low hourly wages or by too few working hours. However, this ideal situation was not achieved, which means that some of the working poor might simply be poor because they were out of work. Our in-depth analysis suggested this as well, and our conclusion is that the majority of the working poor were poor because they had been partly out of work during the observation year, and that in-work poverty as a consequence of low wages is, by all measures, a very small problem in Sweden. Instead, we have seen an increase in poverty caused by less secure labour market conditions, and if we look at those who are working, there are, on any given day, a number of people who have recently been or are about to be without work. This group is increasing as unemployment increases, and it is among this category that we predominantly find those who we defined as the 'working poor' at the outset of this study. This result suggests that, at present, Swedish policy-makers should be more concerned about unemployment than about low wages.

NOTES

1. The measurement of income is often confined to a relatively short period such as monthly or weekly income, while poverty is conceptualized in terms of annual income – a fact that further complicates the relationship between employment and poverty.
2. The poverty line relates to the median income in the total population 16 to 84 years of age. Children living together with their parents are, for reasons mentioned above, not included in the calculation.
3. The variable is calculated as the natural logarithm of age minus 19.

REFERENCES

Åberg, R. (2003), 'Unemployment persistency, over-education and employment chances of the less educated', *European Sociological Review*, **19** (2), 199–216.

Aronsson, G., T. Lindh and M. Dallner (2000), *Flexibla inkomster och fasta utgifter: en studie av ekonomisk stress och hälsa bland korttidsanställda*, Stockholm: Arbetslivsinstitutet.

Atkinson, J. (1984), 'Manpower strategies for flexible organizations', *Personnel Management*, **115**, 28–31.

Bardone, L. and A.-C. Guio (2005), 'In-work poverty', in Eurostat (ed.), *Statistics in Focus – Population and Social Conditions*, Luxembourg: Eurostat.

Barron, D.R. and G.M. Norris (1976), 'Sexual divisons and the dual labour market', in D.L. Barker and S. Allen (eds), *Dependence and Exploitation in Work and Marriage*, New York: Longman.

Benner, M. and T.B. Vad (2001), 'Sweden and Denmark. Defending the welfare state', in S. Schmidt (ed.), *Welfare and Work in the Open Economy*, New York: Oxford University Press.

Bihagen, E. (2000), *The Significance of Class*, Umeå: Department of Sociology, Umeå University.

Bihagen, E. and B. Halleröd (2000), 'The crucial aspects of class: an assessment of the relevance of class in Sweden from the 1970s to the 1990s', *Work, Employment and Society*, **14**, 307–30.

Björklund, A. and R.B. Freeman (1997), *Generating Equality and Eliminating Poverty, the Swedish Way*, Stockholm: Univ. Swedish Institute for Social Research.

Blau, F.D. and L.M. Kahn (1996), 'International differences in male wage inequality: Institutions versus market forces', *Journal of Political Economy*, **104**, 791–837.

Canova, T.A. (1994), 'The Swedish model betrayed', *Challenge*, **37** (3), 36–40.

Edin, P.-A. and B. Holmlund (1995), 'The Swedish wage structure: the rise and fall of solidarity wage policy?', in R.B. Freeman and L.F. Katz (eds), *Differences and Changes in Wage Structures*, Chicago, IL, and London: University of Chicago Press.

Ellingsaeter, A.L. (1998), 'Labour market restructuring and polarization processes: the significance of political-institutional factors', *Economic and Industrial Democracy*, **19**, 579–603.

Ellingsaeter, A.L. (2000), 'Scandinavian transformations: labour markets, politics and gender division', *Economic and Industrial Democracy*, **21**, 335–59.

Elvander, N. (1988), *Den svenska modellen: löneförhandlingar och inkomstpolitik 1982–1986*, Stockholm: Allmänna förl. i samarbete med FA-rådet.

Elvander, N. (2003), 'Avtalsrörelsen 2001: Den nya lönebildningsregimen på prov', *Ekonomisk Debatt*, **31**, 15–27.

Erikson, R. (1984), 'Social class of men, women and families', *Sociology*, **18**, 501–14.

Erikson, R. and J.H. Goldthorpe (1993), *The Constant Flux; A Study of Class Mobility in Industrial Societies*, Oxford: Clarendon Press.

Esping-Andersen, G. (1991), *The Three Worlds of Welfare Capitalism*, Oxford: Polity Press.

Esping-Andersen, G. (1999), *Social Foundations of Postindustrial Economies*, Oxford: Oxford University Press.

Gallie, D., M. White, Y. Cheng and M. Tomlinson (1998), *Restructuring the Employment Relationship*, New York: Oxford University Press.
Hajighasemi, A. (2004), *The Transformation of the Swedish Welfare System: Fact or Fiction? Globalisation, Institutions and Welfare State Change in a Social Democratic Regime*, Huddinge Stockholm: Södertörns högskola Almqvist & Wiksell International distributör.
Halleröd, B. (1997), 'Fattigdom och materiell deprivation: En empirisk analys', in J.V. and L. Häll (eds), *Välfärd och ojämlikhet i 20-års perspektiv 1975–1995*, Örebro: Statistiska Centralbyrån, Rapport 91.
Halleröd, B. (2005), 'Sharing of housework and money among Swedish couples: do they behave rationally?', *European Sociological Review*, **21**, 273–88.
Kalleberg, A.L. (2003), 'Flexible firms and labor market segmentation – Effects of workplace restructuring on jobs and workers', *Work and Occupations*, **30**, 154–75.
Kim, M. (1998), 'The working poor: lousy jobs or lazy workers', *Journal of Economic Issues*, **32**, 65–78.
Klein, B.W. and P.L. Rones (1989), 'A profile of the working poor', *Monthly Labor Review*, **112**, 3–13.
Korpi, W. and J. Palme (1998), 'The paradox of redistribution and strategies of equality: welfare state institutions, inequality, and poverty in the western countries', *American Sociological Review*, **63**, 6661–87.
Korpi, W. and J. Palme (2004), 'New politics and class politics in the context of austerity and globalization: welfare state regress in 18 countries 1975–1995', *American Political Science Review*, **97**, 425–46.
Lindvall, J. (2004), *The Politics of Purpose: Swedish Macroeconomic Policy after the Golden Age*, Göteborg: Dept. of Political Science Statsvetenskapliga institutionen Univ.
Magnusson, L. (2006), *Håller den svenska modellen? Arbete och välfärd i en globaliserad värld*, Stockholm: Norstedts akademiska förlag.
Mosisa, A.T. (2003), 'The working poor in 2001', *Monthly Labor Review*, **126**, 13–19.
Nightingale, D.S. and M. Fix (2004), 'Economic and labor market trends', *Future of Children*, **14**, 49–59.
Nordström-Skans, O., P.-A. Edin and B. Holmlund (2006), *Wage Dispersion Between and Within Plants: Sweden 1985–2000, Working Paper*, Uppsala: Department of Economics.
Peña-Casas, R. and M. Latta (2004), *Working Poor in The European Union*, Luxembourg: European Foundation for the improvement of Living and Working Conditions.
SCB (2007), 'Genomsnittlig timlön. Statistikdatabasen, Statistic Sweden', www.ssd.scb.se/databaser/makro/start.asp (accessed 21 February 2007).
SOU (2001), *Välfärdsbokslut för 1990-talet*, Stockhom: Statens offentliga utredningar.
SOU (2004), *Den könsuppdelade arbetsmarknaden. Betänkande av utredningen om den könssegregerade svenska arbetsmarknaden*, Stockholm: Statens offentliga utredningar.
Vogel, J. (2005), 'Välfärdsmätning och social rapportering', in SCB (eds), *Ungdomars etablering, Generationklyftan 1980–2003 – Rapport 108*, Örebro: Statistic Sweden.

7. 'Much ado about nothing?' Institutional framework and empirical findings on the working poor phenomenon in Finland from 1995 to 2005

Ilpo Airio, Susan Kuivalainen and Mikko Niemelä

INTRODUCTION

Comparatively speaking, Finland is a country with little poverty. This situation changed, however, in the 1990s. During the years from 1990 to 1993, Finland experienced a deep economic recession; the gross domestic product (GDP) declined by 13 per cent and unemployment rose to 18 per cent (see, for example, Kiander and Virtanen, 2002). Following the recession, income inequality and poverty increased, and poverty became a political and societal concern (Kuivalainen et al., 2005). Poverty was no longer seen as a problem limited to a small, marginalized group; rather it was publicly realized that poverty also touches those who were traditionally thought to be well secured against poverty – the working population. In Finland, discussion of the working poor became particularly prominent in 2003, after the publication of Barbara Ehrenreich's book *Nickel and Dimed* in Finnish (Ehrenreich, 2003). Although a great deal of discussion took place, there was hardly any empirical research conducted on the issue. Therefore, the discussion was – and still is – based on loose ground. One might ask whether the worry over in-work poverty in Finland has simply been 'much ado about nothing' – especially because studies conducted in the late 1990s indicated that poverty indisputably affects the unemployed, particularly the long-term unemployed, and that work is the best guarantee against poverty (see, for example, Kangas and Ritakallio, 2005; Riihelä et al., 2002).

There are only a few studies that have focused on in-work poverty in Finland. These studies show that poverty among the employed population increased from the early 1990s up until early 2000 (Airio, 2005a; Airio and

Niemelä, 2004; Kauhanen, 2005). In 2000, approximately 5 per cent of the working population was poor (Airio and Niemelä, 2004; Kauhanen, 2005). Based on present evidence, it appears that poverty among the employed has returned as a new, old social risk (cf. Taylor-Gooby, 2004). In this chapter, we examine whether poverty among the employed has also continued to grow during the 2000s.

This chapter provides analyses of poverty among working people in Finland from the mid-1990s until 2005. It describes the main features of Finnish government policies and changes in labour market institutions, welfare state provisions and household structures. The first part of the chapter provides information about the institutional framework in Finland. Our goal here is, on the one hand, to point out those features that have explained the low poverty status of the employed in comparison to many other countries up to now (Airio, 2005b; Peña-Casas and Latta, 2004) and, on the other hand, to discuss those changes that are most likely to result in an increase in in-work poverty. The second part of the chapter presents empirical analyses of the development of in-work poverty in Finland from 1995 until 2005. Thus, this chapter aims to provide an understanding of recent developments against the background of the institutional framework. We explore the changes in the incidence and structure of the working poor in Finland during the past 10 years.

THE INSTITUTIONAL FRAMEWORK

Labour Market Institutions

The economic situation of paid employees is related to labour market policy. Labour market policy can be seen as one of a number of regulatory policies whose goals include influencing the distribution of market incomes (Ringen, 1987). In his book *Small States in World Markets*, Peter Katzenstein (1985) argues that democratic corporatism is the most viable solution for small states in the international economy. Because small states lack the power that large states have to influence world markets, co-operation between political and economic organizations is crucial, on both economic and social issues.

In Finland, centralized income policy bargaining – based on so-called social corporatism – has served as the central means for achieving economic and social policy goals since the 1960s. It has had great significance first and foremost in income distribution, and consequently for the economic situation of employed people. Neither the economic depression nor the high unemployment of the early 1990s broke the social corporatism in

Finland. Labour organizations still pursue centralized and moderate pay settlements. Finland continues to have one of the highest rates of union membership in the industrialized world, with nearly 80 per cent of its employees organized in trade unions (OECD, 2004a). However, there are some signs that local collective bargaining is playing an increased role.[1] As in many other countries, the union density rate has fallen since the early 1990s; a recent study shows that union density in Finland has declined by more than 10 percentage points during the past 10 years (Böckerman and Uusitalo, 2005).

Wage-setting established through social corporatism has a significant effect from the point of view of economic well-being, since it sets wages at sufficient income levels. There is no minimum wage legislation as such in Finland, but the minimum tariff wages established in each collective agreement set an effective floor for wages. Finnish labour law stipulates that the minimum provisions of collective agreements be extended to non-signatory parties as well, provided that the collective agreement is considered to be adequately representative. Since agreements are sectoral, the minimum wage provisions vary from industry to industry (EIRO, 2005; Vartiainen, 1998). Earnings inequality in Finland continues to be at one of the lowest levels among the Organisation for Economic Co-operation and Development (OECD) countries, and in contrast to most OECD countries, it has not increased significantly since the beginning of the 1980s (Kauhanen, 2005: 31; OECD, 2004a: 141). Nonetheless, income inequality as a whole has increased in Finland during the past decade. This phenomenon is mainly the result of increased capital income among the highest income deciles on the one hand, and stagnated income within the lowest income deciles on the other (see, for example, Moisio, 2006; Sauramo, 2002).

The discussion on labour market adjustment has recently turned in another direction from Katzenstein's (1985) proposal of developing social corporatism. There is a clear tendency towards increasing labour market flexibility – namely, with regard to wages and working hours. In principle, this translates into efforts to increase the share of low-paid and temporary employment. The share of low-wage workers has increased in Finland: in 1991, the share of low-wage workers was approximately 7 per cent, whereas in 2000, it had increased to 11 per cent (European Commission, 2004; Marx and Nolan, 1999: 5). There has been considerable debate about the need for removing barriers to low-paid and low-productivity work in order to increase employment (see, for example, Holm and Vihriälä, 2002). The issue of developing low-productivity employment is prominent.[2] Certainly, developing low-productivity employment might be one way to tackle unemployment, but whether it improves the economic well-being of people who are currently unemployed is not evident.

The other significant reason for the low level of in-work poverty in Finland is related to high female employment – and more generally, to the commitment to full employment. These characteristics are typical for the Nordic countries (for example, Esping-Andersen, 1990). Female labour market participation is high compared to the rest of the OECD countries. The majority of employed women work full-time, and for these reasons, most working-age families contain two earners (Peña-Casas and Latta, 2004: 36). During the recession years, the female employment rate decreased in Finland; this was particularly evident among mothers with young children, and even more so among single parents. However, since the mid-1990s, the female employment rate has increased again, although the levels have not reached those of 1990.

The 1990s witnessed the replacement of lifelong full-time work with flexible work, and the common trend has been the proliferation of atypical work. In 2003, temporary work accounted for about 16 per cent of all employees (OECD, 2004b). When temporary work is full-time, it does not necessarily hamper the workers' economic well-being. Problems are more likely to arise from the insecurity and uncertainty caused by fixed-term contracts. The fragility associated with temporary employment exposes the employee to financial troubles more often than permanent employment does (Kauhanen, 2002: 96).

A notable characteristic of the Finnish labour market has been the low proportion of part-time work compared with most European countries. Earlier studies have shown that during economic recessions, the number of people working part-time tends to increase (see, for example, Rubery, 1989). This was also the case in Finland: as opportunities for full-time work became scarce, people began looking for part-time work. During the recession, part-time work became more typical, and its prevalence has continued to increase after the recession: in 1990, the proportion of people working part-time was about 8 per cent; in 2004, it reached 11 per cent (OECD, 2005). However, this share is still low from an international perspective.

Atypical forms of work became more common during the 1990s as the share of part-time and temporary employment grew faster than total employment. This development has had an effect on poverty among employees during the latter part of the 1990s. According to studies (Airio and Niemelä, 2004; Kauhanen, 2005), poverty increased most among atypical workers during the period from 1995 until 2000; furthermore, the risk of poverty among the employed is highest for atypical workers. Taking recent developments in the labour market institutions into account, we have some grounds to assume that poverty among employees will have increased during the 2000s, particularly due to increased part-time employment.

Welfare State Provisions

The main objective of the welfare state has been the alleviation of poverty (for example, Ringen, 1987: 143). The Nordic countries have been characterized by high levels of social security (Esping-Andersen, 1990; Kautto et al., 1999). Since income is one of the main determinants of poverty, social protection schemes are important. The three most significant types of social protection schemes are social assistance, unemployment security and family benefits. We shall now look at these three forms of security in order to illuminate the relationship between welfare state provisions and in-work poverty in Finland.

As in other Western countries, the notion of welfare state retrenchment has also become prominent in Finland. In particular, cuts in social security were carried out during the economic recession (see Kosunen, 1997). After the economic recession, policy interest turned to the promotion of employment and employability, and there has been an ideological shift. 'Making work pay' has become the main principle in social policy (Kuivalainen et al., 2005). Since Prime Minister Paavo Lipponen's first government (1995), policy-makers have stressed the need for schemes to be changed so that work is the primary means of earning a living, and that work always guarantees a better income than living on benefits. A number of benefits – particularly unemployment security and social assistance schemes – have been reformed in order to promote employment and to diminish negative incentives to work.

Unemployment schemes have been reformed with the particular aim of increasing active participation in the labour market and employment among the recipients of benefits.[3] Changes have been made in entitlement and eligibility rules. In principle, the outcome of these reforms should be such that on the one hand, a higher share of the recipients of unemployment benefits will receive income from earnings and thus their economic situation will be better than it was previously; but, on the other hand, poverty among the unemployed will have increased due to the cuts made in unemployment benefits.

The Finnish social assistance benefit (*toimeentulotuki*) is payable to all persons whose income is insufficient – irrespective of their employment status – to guarantee a minimum standard of living. In the past, the Finnish social assistance scheme has been characterized by strict means-testing (Eardley et al., 1996). However, recent legislative reforms have made means-testing more moderate (Kuivalainen, 2004). A new three-year pilot law was introduced in 2002 (HE155/2001). According to this law, 20 per cent of a person's earnings are disregarded, up to a total of 100 euros per month per household. The programme was extended at the beginning of 2005.

Work-related expenses have been taken into account in social assistance for a long time. The amendment to the Finnish social assistance schemes which was made in 1998 clarified these rules, allowing for more work-related expenses to be taken into account. Changes implemented in social assistance schemes have aimed to promote the integration of their recipients into the labour market and to encourage working. On the whole, these reforms imply that there should be a greater share of working households receiving social assistance. Nevertheless, statistics show that the share of the employed among social assistance recipients is low, and it has not increased since the 1990s – quite the contrary. Furthermore, an evaluation study has shown that the social assistance reforms have not increased the use of social assistance among the working population (Hiilamo et al., 2004).

Family support is an important resource for many working-age families with children. On the one hand, family benefits provide financial support to families with children. On the other, family support in the form of childcare provisions facilitates labour market participation, thus playing an important role in the economic situation of families. For working families with children, the most important type of social security transfers are family benefits.[4] The child benefit (*lapsilisä*) is a tax-free allowance paid to every family with a child under the age of 17, irrespective of their income. A monthly supplement is paid to single parents. Single parents are guaranteed a maintenance benefit (*elatustuki*) in case the absent parent defaults on his or her obligations. During the 1990s, small cuts were introduced in the field of family policy, but eligibility and entitlement rules remained more or less unchanged (see Hiilamo, 2002). This situation has continued into the 2000s as well.

In Finland, childcare policy is part of the system of universal welfare state provisions, and all parents of young children up to school age have guaranteed access to a subsidized childcare place. Since 1996, the parents of all children under school age have been entitled to municipal day care for their children. Childcare services are highly subsidized, and the level of payment is determined according to income; therefore, families with low earnings are also able to afford daytime childcare. Childcare is also guaranteed after school. Parents who do not use day-care facilities are entitled to a Child Home Care Allowance (*kotihoidontuki*) payment. The parents of a small child have the right to take unpaid care leave from their work until the child is 3 years old. There have been some significant improvements made to the child home care allowance. Since 2005, pensions accrue on the basis of the child home care allowance, and the level of the allowance has increased significantly.

The aim of taxation policy has been to reduce the tax rate. All three governments which have been in power since the mid-1990s have emphasized tax relief for payroll taxation, particularly for low and middle-income families. Recent studies show that the taxation of wage income has decreased (OECD tax database; Kurjenoja, 2004). Thanks to recent tax relief, Finland has reached the average European level in terms of wage taxes for people in the below-average income bracket (Kurjenoja, 2004).

Overall, the Finnish welfare system has been effective in reducing poverty among the population (Ritakallio, 2002). The economic recession did not change this: in 2000, market-based poverty was still reduced by 70 per cent. The recent developments in welfare state provisions have attempted to make work pay. This employment-friendly policy, together with changes in taxation policy, has probably led to improved financial conditions for low-income workers. Furthermore, the efforts to reconcile work and the family are likely to have had similar effects. Overall, we have good grounds to assume that poverty among the employed is still rather low.

Household and Individual Characteristics

Earlier studies have shown that both household and individual factors contribute to poverty, and more so to in-work poverty. According to Strengmann-Kuhn (2004), the household plays a significant role in explaining poverty among the employed. The size and composition of the household, as well as the number of earners in a family, have a significant impact on its risk of poverty. The two Finnish studies on in-work poverty (Airio and Niemelä, 2004; Kauhanen, 2005) have shown that of all household types, single-parent families have the highest risk of poverty. Couples with children also have a high poverty risk, and the risk rises linearly with the number of children. As such, the situation is similar to that in most European countries (Peña-Casas and Latta, 2004). The number of earners in a family has a significant impact on its poverty status. The risk of poverty has been found to be the smallest among those households with two earners, and highest among households with no earners.

As far as individual characteristics are concerned, the most important one relates to employment status. Individuals who have permanent, full-time jobs are the best protected against economic poverty. Part-time employees have a much higher risk of poverty than people in full-time employment (Airio and Niemelä, 2004). Evidently, poverty among the employed is related to the number of months in work per year – that is, work intensity (Kauhanen, 2005: 28–9). In Finland, women comprise a greater share of the working poor. This is mainly due to the greater share of women who are employed part-time or under fixed-term contracts (Kauhanen, 2005). The increased rate of part-time employment among women may reflect an increased poverty rate.

Merja Kauhanen (2005) also studied the factors which contribute to a person's ability to move out of in-work poverty. Her results indicate that the individual's age and level of education exert the greatest influence. Individuals who were young and possessed a higher level of education were more likely to exit from in-work poverty.

On the whole, demographics statistics have not shown any momentous changes in family types since 1995. Overall, the demographic structure in Finland is beneficial in terms of economic security (Kangas and Ritakallio, 2005). Taking into account the high labour demand during the 2000s and the decreased unemployment rate – especially among the young – we can assume that poverty among the employed has not increased drastically.

PURPOSE OF THE STUDY, DATA AND METHODS

The purpose of the empirical section of this chapter is to explore the changes in the incidence and structure of the working poor in Finland from 1995 until 2005. There are three main research objectives: (1) The incidence of poverty in different labour market positions, (2) the incidence and the structure of in-work poverty among different population groups, and (3) the incidence of poverty based on work intensity and work stability.

We hypothesize that the incidence of in-work poverty has not risen significantly during the 10 years of our observation period, and that the share of the working poor has remained low – particularly from an international perspective. These assumptions can be justified by the facts presented in the previous section, which demonstrate that changes in welfare state provisions and taxation policies have very much favoured the well-being of the working population. Yet, a more detailed analysis could reveal groups that have high rates of in-work poverty, even though the 'big picture' might look comforting. For example, earlier studies have shown that the risk of being among the working poor differs between population groups. Hence, there might be population groups that have very high in-work poverty rates – and these groups could have witnessed a worsened situation during the observation period. This could particularly be the case among groups which have a precarious position in the labour market, such as part-time workers, or in households where the relative number of workers is inadequate, such as single-earner households.

Data

The data-sets used in this study are cross-sectional surveys which were compiled in the Department of Social Policy at the University of Turku in 1995,

Table 7.1 Data-sets of the study

Year	Sample size	Effective response rate (%)	Non-weighted N
1995	3000	65	1859
2000	4001	62	2400
2005	4001	63	2391

2000 and 2005 (see Table 7.1). The surveys included a broad set of questions dealing with material standards and economic resources, attitudes towards redistribution and the welfare state, and people's views of their own circumstances. Every year, random samples were collected from the population register, and the data-sets represent the total Finnish-speaking population between the ages of 18 and 70. The data-sets are weighted so as to be representative in terms of age and gender.

A non-response analysis did not reveal any systematic bias associated with such traditional background variables as age, education, gender and socio-economic position. As a rule, underprivileged groups such as the unemployed are under-represented in the survey data. The distribution of the background variables in the data-sets is proportional to their distribution in the whole population, and the proportion of unemployed persons included in the data works relatively well: it is the same as in the whole population. Overall, the numbers of non-weighted cases are quite large. However, in the analyses for certain subgroups, the number of non-weighted cases may be rather small. As a result, care should be taken when interpreting the results, which are based on a small number of cases. Therefore, in the next section, percentages which are based on fewer than 10 cases are marked with asterisks.

Methods

We define the working poor as workers who live in poor households. Here, workers are defined based on questionnaire responses regarding the respondent's labour market status. Many studies have shown that any given picture of poverty is highly dependent on the way in which poverty is defined – and, in particular, on the way in which poverty is measured. In addition, in cases where the overlap between different poverty indicators has been explored, the correlation between indicators has been rather small (for example, Bradshaw and Finch, 2003; Kangas and Ritakallio, 1998; Niemelä, 2005; Saunders et al., 2002). This phenomenon may be explained by the multidimensional nature of poverty: different indicators simply

Table 7.2 Poverty measures

Measure	Criterion
Low income	All those whose disposable household income is less than 60% of median equivalized disposable household income (modified OECD equivalence scale)
Consensual deprivation	All those who involuntarily lack at least three commodities regarded as necessities by the majority of the whole population

Notes:
Necessity items in 1995: medical services (96% of the population regard as necessity), a hot meal every day (95%), washing machine (88%), dental examination once a year (82%), vacuum cleaner (80%), modern dwelling (78%), public transportation according to one's need (77%), householders' comprehensive insurance (66%), not more than two persons in each bedroom (59%), a haircut every third month (59%), daily paper (53%) and freezer (52%).

Necessity items in 2000: medical services (97%), a hot meal every day (96%), washing machine (88%), dental examination once a year (83%), vacuum cleaner (83%), modern dwelling (80%), public transportation according to one's need (72%), householders' comprehensive insurance (70%), a haircut every third month (62%), telephone (57%), not more than two persons in each bedroom (57%), freezer (55%) and television (51%).

Necessity items in 2005: medical services (97%), a hot meal every day (97%), washing machine (91%), vacuum cleaner (87%), dental examination once a year (85%), modern dwelling (84%), public transport (76%), householders' comprehensive insurance (74%), freezer (61%), a haircut every third month (59%), telephone (57%), not more than two persons in each bedroom (57%), a hobby or leisure activity (51%).

provide different results, but none of these results are wrong in and of themselves; they are merely limited. Therefore, one possible option for obtaining a comprehensive picture of poverty would be to make use of many different approaches simultaneously (for example, Bradshaw and Finch, 2003; Kangas and Ritakallio, 1998; Muffels et al., 1992). This type of research strategy yields a wider picture of which sectors of the population are more vulnerable to specific forms of economic hardship.

In this chapter, we analyse poverty using measures of low income and consensual deprivation (see Table 7.2). Looking at trends in in-work poverty based on different indicators, there is good reason to expect that the analysis will show somewhat different trends. Since the mid-1990s, income inequality has increased in Finland. It is widely known that relative income poverty is closely linked to income inequality, and thus researchers have questioned whether low income alone is actually a valid indicator of poverty (Ray, 1998; see also Pryke, 1995). Previous studies on the development of low income have shown that since the mid-1990s, the number of people earning low incomes has increased at the same time that income inequality has increased. In addition, researchers have pointed out that this increase has been dramatic for the unemployed, but that there has also been a slight increase or at least steady development in other labour market positions (see, for example, Niemelä, 2005; Riihelä et al., 2002).

On the other hand, previous studies have shown that when economic hardship is measured more directly – for example, using different deprivation indexes or subjective assessments of an individual's or household's financial situation, the trend in the late 1990s looks completely different. These studies indicate that there has been a trend towards decreasing poverty and deprivation in Finland since the mid-1990s (see, for example, Airio and Niemelä, 2004; Kangas and Ritakallio, 2005). Because trends in low income are so closely linked to trends in income inequality, we have used consensual deprivation as a control measure in this chapter. Based on previous studies, our assumption is that different measures will show somewhat different trends. However, we can also expect that different measures will yield quite similar results regarding the position of the employed relative to people in other labour market positions.

We measured low income using standard methods. The income data used in the analysis is based on questionnaire responses and measures monthly net income. Using income data based on the monthly questionnaire, we find a higher poverty rate compared with that shown by income data from the annual register. It is important to keep this in mind when analysing the results. We used the relative income method to estimate the low-income threshold. In order to test the sensitivity of the findings, we applied three alternative low-income cut-offs (40, 50 and 60 per cent of the median net income). Because of space considerations, in the subsequent comparisons, we only showed the results produced using 60 per cent of the median equivalent income. In order to make the different households comparable, we divided the household incomes by the number of consumption units in each household. The equivalence scale from which we derived the consumption units was the modified OECD scale, with one slight adjustment: while in the modified OECD scale, all persons over 13 years of age are defined as adults, here we defined all persons over 17 years of age as adults. In all other cases, the values of the parameters are the same as in the OECD scale.

The consensual deprivation approach was formulated by Mack and Lansley. This approach defines poverty as 'an enforced lack of socially perceived necessities' (Mack and Lansley, 1985: 39), and it aims to reveal whether people are living below the minimum publicly accepted standard. In this approach, the necessities of life were defined by public opinion, and people were then regarded as poor based on their ability (or inability) to maintain the standard of consumption perceived as necessary by the majority of the population. As in some earlier studies (Gordon and Townsend, 2000; Kangas and Ritakallio, 1998; 2005), the criterion for poverty was set at an involuntary lack of three or more necessities in the household of the respondent.

RESULTS

Table 7.3 provides a picture of what consensual deprivation and low-income measures can tell us about the financial circumstances in different labour market positions. As we discussed in the previous section, to some extent, different indicators show different trends in poverty between the years 1995 and 2005. Among the whole population, the low-income rate has increased by almost four percentage points, while the rate of consensual deprivation has decreased by five percentage points.

Regardless of the indicator used, employed people are in the best financial situation. The employed had the lowest poverty rates in all cross-sectional points of observation. However, as we expected, there are some differences in the trend for in-work poverty. There is a clear decrease in poverty as measured by consensual deprivation. However, when we use low income as a measurement, the trend is slightly different. While in the late 1990s, the low-income rate among working people increased – as it did in the whole population – in the early 2000s, the relative position of employees has improved and their risk of poverty in relation to whole population has decreased.

It is hardly surprising that unemployment is the most important factor associated with poverty. Regardless of the indicator used, the risk of poverty is radically higher for unemployed persons than it is for the employed or the retired. The only exception here is the low-income rates of students, which are even higher than those of the unemployed. During the late 1990s, unemployed persons were the only group whose financial positions worsened according to both indicators. Even though their situation has improved slightly during the early 2000s, they are still in the most disadvantaged position.

Overall, Table 7.3 indicates that in-work poverty is not a widespread socio-political problem in Finland. In fact, one could say that the picture is completely the opposite: the working population is in the best financial position in Finland, or at least their poverty is a marginal problem – especially if we compare their situation to that of the unemployed. Even though in-work poverty does not seem to be a widespread issue in general, knowing which groups face the greatest risk of belonging to the working poor does have an important socio-political significance. Table 7.4 presents a picture

Table 7.3 Poverty risks by labour market status in Finland according to low-income and consensual deprivation measures (%)

Labour market status	Low income			Consensual deprivation		
	1995	2000	2005	1995	2000	2005
Employed	6.1	7.8	7.0	8.4	4.2	3.6
Unemployed	35.5	56.9	55.0	29.0	31.7	25.7
Retired	14.5	16.8	18.9	8.1	6.5	7.7
Student	45.5	59.1	70.3	21.9	13.0	17.7
Other	15.8	22.6	22.6	15.3	7.8	13.0
Total	15.8	19.1	19.6	13.2	8.3	8.2

Source: Surveys of the Department of Social Policy at the University of Turku (weighted).

of the incidence of working poor individuals in different population groups, and Table 7.5 shows the structure of in-work poverty in Finland from 1995 until 2005. The background factors we explored are education, age, household type, number of children in the household and gender.

There has been a lot of discussion in Finland about the extent to which it pays to invest in education. According to our examination of in-work poverty, measures of both low income and consensual deprivation show a clear result: the higher the level of education, the lower the risk of poverty. Thus, both the incidence and the structure of in-work poverty indicate that the overall picture is clear: education seems to pay very well.

When we examine the working poor at different stages of life, the vulnerable situation of younger age groups is evident. The youngest age group, in particular, is over-represented among the working poor. Furthermore, the incidence of poverty in the youngest age group is the highest regardless of the indicator used. Both indicators show that the poverty rates for the youngest age group have increased during the early 2000s. These results are quite as we expected. Unstable labour market positions in the form of part-time and temporary work are more common in younger age groups than they are in others. In this respect, however, we should mention the limitations of the cross-sectional data. It is possible that for younger age groups, low-wage jobs may play a positive role as an entry into the labour market (cf. Kauhanen, 2005). However, the panel data and a dynamic approach would be needed in order to test that hypothesis.

Household type as well as family size have traditionally been important factors in explaining poverty. Moreover, it has been argued that changes in family structure – that is, the increasing trends towards single-parent families and single households, and the decrease in dual-earner households – is

Table 7.4 Poverty risk of different population groups in Finland according to low-income and consensual deprivation measures (%)

Characteristic	Low income			Consensual deprivation		
	1995	2000	2005	1995	2000	2005
Total	6.1	7.8	7.0	8.4	4.2	3.6
Education						
Basic level	10.3	12.3	13.2	11.7	6.3	6.0
Vocational/college	6.2	8.6	7.9	8.2	4.2	4.6
University	0.0	2.0*	2.4*	8.4*	2.1*	0.7*
Age						
–24	15.9*	14.6*	32.3	26.0	10.2*	12.8*
25–34	6.7	4.9	5.6	10.4	4.4	4.0
35–44	4.7	10.6	5.8	6.6	4.9	2.4*
45–54	6.4	6.9	5.9	6.8	3.5	3.3
55–	7.2*	6.0	4.9	3.4*	1.2*	3.0*
Household type						
Single	3.7*	5.4	6.0	16.9	8.1	4.9
Couple	2.0*	3.4	5.6	6.1	2.0*	4.6
Couple with children	7.3	8.5	5.5	5.2	3.2	2.3
Lone parent	8.1*	26.3	23.1	29.9	10.7*	6.4*
Number of children						
None	5.5	6.0	6.2	9.6	8.1	4.2
1	5.4	7.1	6.3	8.3	2.0*	2.2*
2	6.8	7.1	8.8	5.8	3.2*	1.5*
3 or more	12.8	23.7	9.6	7.1*	10.7*	4.9*
Gender[1]						
Female	3.8*	10.6	12.8	21.6	10.0	5.9
Male	6.2*	7.7*	8.8	17.1	6.6*	4.5*

Notes:
1 Single and lone parent households.
* Unweighted number of cases less than 10.

Source: Surveys of the Department of Social Policy at the University of Turku (weighted).

one of the most important internal challenges of contemporary welfare states (Esping-Andersen, 2002; Taylor-Gooby, 2004). Our results indicate that single parents and single households occupy the worst financial positions among all household types. Our assessment of the structure of in-work poverty shows that single parents are over-represented among the working poor using both indicators. Moreover, when measured according

Table 7.5 The structure of in-work poverty in Finland according to low income and consensual deprivation measures (%)

Characteristic	Low income			Consensual deprivation			Share of total working population		
	1995	2000	2005	1995	2000	2005	1995	2000	2005
Education									
Basic level	42.2	31.1	28.5	36.9	30.2	26.6	27.5	20.3	16.5
Vocational/ college	57.8	63.1	61.7	58.8	58.6	68.2	59.5	57.3	55.3
University	0.0	5.8*	9.7*	4.3*	11.2*	5.2*	12.9	22.4	28.3
Age									
–24	12.9*	8.2*	22.9	17.1	11.0*	19.4*	5.5	4.8	5.5
25–34	25.3	13.8	17.8	30.0	23.3	23.2	24.2	21.7	21.1
35–44	24.4	40.1	24.1	26.4	35.3	18.2*	33.2	29.5	28.0
45–54	28.2	29.1	23.7	23.1	27.1	25.9	28.5	32.6	28.9
55–	9.2*	8.8	11.5	3.3*	3.4*	13.4*	8.5	11.4	16.5
Household type									
Single	11.0*	13.6	19.6	32.7	35.2	27.1	16.1	17.4	20.1
Couple	9.5*	15.6	25.1	18.5	16.4*	35.4	26.0	32.6	28.0
Couple with child.	72.5	55.3	40.6	32.2	37.5	30.4	53.3	45.9	47.8
Lone parent	7.0*	15.5	14.8	16.6	10.9*	7.1*	4.6	4.1	4.1
Number of children									
None	41.1	42.8	52.1	55.7	58.3	69.8	48.6	55.2	58.2
1	19.2	17.0	14.8	23.1	16.5*	10.4*	23.0	18.6	16.2
2	19.1	16.7	20.9	12.6	11.9*	7.3*	18.2	18.5	16.6
3 or more	20.7	23.4	12.2	8.6*	13.3*	12.5*	10.2	7.6	8.9
Gender[1]									
Female	50.1*	65.6	56.5	66.5	67.9	53.6	61.8	58.2	46.5
Male	49.9*	34.4*	43.5	33.5	32.1*	46.4*	38.2	41.8	53.5

Notes:
1 Single and lone parent households.
* Unweighted number of cases less than 10.

Source: Surveys of the Department of Social Policy at the University of Turku (weighted).

to consensual deprivation, single households are over-represented as well. However, there are some differences between the indicators regarding the incidence of in-work poverty. During the period from 1995 until 2005, the incidence of consensual deprivation among single parents decreased from

30 to 6 per cent. On the other hand, their low income rate increased from 8 to 23 per cent. However, it should be noted that in the case of lone parents, the number of non-weighted cases is very small, and this may account for these dramatic differences. In addition, although the trends according to poverty measures differ remarkably in absolute terms (percentage points), the relative differences as well as the rankings between household types have been constant.

In general, childless couples and couples with children have the lowest poverty rates. Consensual deprivation among childless couples has decreased if we compare the years 1995 and 2005. However, low-income rates have increased slightly. On the other hand, regardless of the poverty indicator used, the financial position of families with children has improved. An examination of the number of children in a household sheds additional light on the situation of families with children. These results show that in the latter part of the 1990s, the incidence of low income increased substantially in families with three or more children. This result reflects the deterioration of family policy allowances that occurred in the late 1990s (see Hiilamo, 2002). The situation of larger families improved from the early 2000s until 2005, at the same time that improvements in child allowances took place and Child Home Care Allowance payments were instituted. However, the overall picture shows that a clear relationship exists between the number of children in a household and the incidence of low income (see also Airio and Niemelä, 2004; Kauhanen, 2005).

In international literature, a case has been made for the feminization of poverty (Pearce, 1978). However, in Finland, family allowances and public childcare have allowed for high rates of female labour market participation. Previous study results on Finnish poverty have shown that the thesis of the feminization of poverty does not hold true in Finland – on the contrary, Finnish poverty is rather masculine (for example, Kangas and Ritakallio, 2005). However, the results show that women have higher in-work poverty risks than do men, and they are over-represented among the working poor (see also Kauhanen, 2005). As far as the incidence of in-work poverty is concerned, consensual deprivation decreased for both genders during the period from 1995 until 2005. On the other hand, low-income rates have increased for both sexes. While the increase in the low-income rate was about two and a half percentage points for men, the increase for women was nine percentage points. In order to explore the interaction between household structure and gender, we applied a multivariate analysis (not presented here). The applied regression model indicated that these gender differences can be explained by the fact that single parents are more likely to be women than men. When we controlled for this interaction, the results showed that there were no statistically significant gender differences at all.

Table 7. 6 Poverty risk of Finnish working population by work intensity and stability according to different poverty measures (%)

Characteristic	Low income			Consensual deprivation		
	1995	2000	2005	1995	2000	2005
Work intensity						
Full-time worker	5.9	6.1	5.3	7.7	3.7	3.0
Part-time worker	12.1	22.7	21.5	15.6	8.3	9.3
Work stability						
Permanent	3.5	6.0	4.6	6.6	3.3	2.4
Temporary	10.4	11.5	10.7	11.9	6.5	6.9
Work intensity (household)[1]						
No full-time workers	21.9	29.0	30.7	13.8	9.8	9.0
One full-time worker	10.3	11.2	9.8	8.7	2.3*	7.3
Two full-time workers	2.3	3.0	2.2	2.4*	1.9*	1.5*
Work stability (household)[1]						
No permanent jobs	15.5	19.3	16.6	11.2	9.0	9.5
One permanent job	8.7	8.3	9.7	9.0	3.6	3.8
Two permanent jobs	2.8*	3.3	2.1*	1.1*	1.0*	1.1*

Notes:
1 Childless couples and couples with children.
* Unweighted number of cases less than 10.

Source: Surveys of the Department of Social Policy at the University of Turku (weighted).

Table 7.6 explores work intensity and work stability and their relationship to poverty. First, it looks at work intensity by comparing the poverty rates of full-time and part-time workers. Second, it investigates work stability by analysing the differences between individuals with permanent jobs and those who are employed temporarily. Finally, it focuses on intra-household work intensity and stability among childless couples and couples with children.

The differences between full-time and part-time workers are clear. Regardless of the poverty indicator used, part-time workers have much higher poverty rates than full-time workers. Trends in the development of poverty differ as well. While the low-income rate among part-time workers has increased, the financial situation of full-time workers improved slightly during the period from 1995 until 2005. However, consensual deprivation has decreased among both groups. Differences between these groups arise when we focus on the development during the early 2000s. Both measures indicate that the poverty rates of full-time workers have decreased, while part-time workers' financial situation has worsened.

The differences in poverty rates between workers employed in permanent and temporary jobs are also obvious: those who are employed temporarily have higher poverty rates than those who hold permanent jobs. If we compare the years 1995 and 2005, consensual deprivation indicates that poverty has decreased among both groups. The consensual deprivation indicator also shows that there were some differences in the development of poverty in the early 2000s. While consensual deprivation increased among persons employed in temporary jobs, the financial situation of those in permanent jobs improved slightly. The trend shown by low income is different: while the low income rate of people in a temporary jobs has been somewhat constant, there is an increasing trend toward low income for those in permanent jobs.

The examination of intra-household work intensity and stability shows that the poverty rate among those households that have two full-time workers is considerably lower than those that have only one or where there is no full-time worker. Unsurprisingly, those households that do not include any full-time workers have the highest poverty rate regardless of the indicator used. In addition, even though their rate of consensual deprivation has decreased, the low-income estimates show that the financial situation for this group has worsened during the past 10 years. In the case of people in permanent work, the picture is very similar to that of full-time workers: those couples whose members both hold permanent jobs have lower poverty rates than the other groups. Regardless of the poverty measure used, households in which neither member of the couple has a permanent job have the highest poverty rates. Overall, Table 7.6 indicates that differences between full-time and part-time workers tend to be larger than the differences between people holding permanent and temporary jobs. In line with previous studies (Airio and Niemelä, 2004; Kauhanen, 2005), Table 7.6 shows that Finnish in-work poverty is also clearly linked to work intensity and stability, and this is particularly true if instances of part-time and temporary work accumulate in the same household. Although the public debate has implied that poverty among the working population is increasing, it is only among part-time employees where we can witness such a development.

CONCLUSIONS

This chapter has provided information about the institutional framework as well as empirical results regarding the working poor phenomenon in Finland during the period from 1995 until 2005. The main result of our study is that in-work poverty is not a widespread socio-political issue in

Finland. In fact, our results indicate quite the opposite. In-work poverty is a marginal problem, especially if we compare the situation of the working population with that of the unemployed. While in many countries, the working population is being confronted with poverty more often than before, the situation in Finland is different.

As far as the changes during the past 10 years are concerned, it appears that the changes in the labour market and welfare state provisions that took place at the end of the 1990s and in the early 2000s have not given rise to a dramatic increase in in-work poverty. The development of poverty for working people has been rather constant: the increase in income poverty has been very modest. And if we use the consensual deprivation measure, the situation is even more positive: consensual deprivation decreased during the research period. Thus, the overall picture is such that in-work poverty is relatively low in Finland.

One explanation for the low poverty rate among the employed in comparison to that in many other countries lies in the power of social corporatism and trade unions in Finland. Neither the economic depression nor the high unemployment that occurred in the early 1990s broke social corporatism. Second, the comparatively high female employment rate and large share of dual-earner families also explain the low poverty rate among the employed in Finland.

Third, as the results presented in this chapter indicate, work really does guarantee a better income than living on benefits. Employment-friendly policies, together with changes in taxation policy, have meant positive development for the employed as well as for low-income workers. On the whole, however, these policies together with activation policies have only had a limited effect on reducing unemployment. Therefore, the anti-poverty power of these policies has remained weak, because the root cause of Finnish poverty is long-term unemployment. The clear policy prescription is that anti-poverty policies should focus on improving the financial position of the unemployed. The high poverty rates among the unemployed indicate that the level of means-tested labour market support is too low to guarantee a minimum standard of living.

This chapter has approached poverty using two different measures simultaneously. The advantage of this approach is that it provides a wider picture of the different forms of economic hardship (Bradshaw and Finch, 2003). Even though in some cases, the indicators yielded different results concerning the incidence and trends of poverty, the core result was that regardless of the indicator used, younger age groups, single parents, single households as well as families with many children have the highest risk of in-work poverty. There are also clear signs that unstable labour market positions such as part-time and temporary work are associated with higher poverty rates. This is particularly true if more than one person in the same household is in this type of unstable work position. Previous studies (for example, Kauhanen, 2002; 2005) have shown that women and younger age groups are concentrated more in part-time employment and fixed-term contracts. Thus, labour market instabilities are linked to gender and stage of life differences as well.

Cross-sectional data is limited in its usefulness when it comes to studying the working poor. As Esping-Andersen (2002: 6–7) has argued, the core welfare issue is not so much how many people are low paid at any given moment, but how many are likely to remain persistently low paid. For example, our results indicate that the incidence of poverty for the youngest age group has been higher than in any other group. However, we must remember that low-wage jobs may also play a positive role by providing an entry into the labour market. Based on cross-sectional data alone, we do not know whether or not this is the case; we therefore require a diagnostic methodology which focuses on dynamics as well.

To summarize our findings, Finland has traditionally been a country with a low rate of in-work poverty from a European standpoint, and during the 10-year time span of our analysis, income poverty has increased only slightly. The institutional setting that protects the working-age population from poverty is functioning well in Finland. Some might say that the recent discussion of in-work poverty in Finland could be described as 'much ado about nothing' – because there has been an almost non-existent change in income poverty, while consensual deprivation has decreased by half during the past 10 years. In the future, research should be qualitative and concentrate on issues like how in-work poverty affects people's lives, how the dynamic processes of in-work poverty function, and whether there are specific professions where it is common for workers to have difficulties achieving an adequate living standard. Answers to these questions would put the in-work poverty problem in Finland into perspective and prompt further discussion.

NOTES

1. The income policy settlement for 2005–07 included an understanding on improving local collective bargaining to meet the needs of both employers and the workforce. This local partnership package signifies a new departure in Finnish income policy settlements.
2. For instance, beginning in 2003, the government started an experiment which abolished employer contributions for all private employers in targeted high unemployment regions for three years (HE120/2002). According to an evaluation study, the reduction in payroll taxes did not have a significant effect on employment (Korkeamäki and

Uusitalo, 2005). The experiment was extended in 2005 and will continue until 2009 (HE170/2005). In 2006, a new form of low-wage support was made available to employers who employ persons aged 54 or older whose monthly salary is lower than 2000 euros (HE146/2005).

3. For example, the adjusted unemployment benefit (*soviteltu päiväraha*) was set in 1994. The adjusted benefit is presently calculated in such a way that the full benefit is reduced by 50 per cent of the recipient's earnings or other income over a calendar month or four-week period.
4. There are no separate, specific tax credit systems for low-income families in Finland.

REFERENCES

Airio, I. (2005a), 'Working poor in the EU countries', paper for the workshop 'Working Poor in Western Europe', Centre for Empirical Research in the Economic and Social Sciences, Cologne, 4–5 November.

Airio, I. (2005b), 'Saako yhdellä palkka riittävän turvan köyhyyttä vastaan?', *Talous & Yhteiskunta*, **2/2005**, 18–22.

Airio, I. and M. Niemelä (2004), 'Turvaako työ köyhyydeltä? Tutkimus työssä olevien köyhyydestä vuosina 1995 ja 2000', *Janus*, **12** (1), 64–79 (with English summary: 'Does work secure from poverty? A study of working poor in Finland 1995 and 2000').

Böckerman, P. and R. Uusitalo (2005), *Union Membership and the Erosion of the Ghent System: Lessons from Finland*, Discussion papers 213, Helsinki: Labour Institute for Economic Research. Available at http://www.labour.fi (accessed 15 October 2005).

Bradshaw, J. and N. Finch (2003), 'Overlaps in dimensions of poverty', *Journal of Social Policy*, **32** (4), 513–25.

Eardley, T., J. Bradshaw, J. Ditch, I. Gough and P. Whiteford (1996), *Social Assistance in OECD Countries: Volume I Synthesis Reports. Department of Social Security Research Report No. 46*, London: HMSO.

EIRO (European Industrial Relations Observatory) (2005), *Minimum Wages in Europe*. Available at http://www.eiro.eurofund.eu.int/2005/07/study/tn0507101s.html (accessed 1 February 2006).

Ehrenreich, B. (2003), *Nickel and Dimed: On (Not) Getting by in America*, New York: Henry Holt and Company.

Esping-Andersen, G. (1990), *The Three Worlds of Welfare Capitalism*, Cambridge: Polity Press.

Esping-Andersen, G. (ed.) (2002), *Why Do We Need a New Welfare State?* Oxford: University Press.

European Commission (2004), *Employment in Europe*, Luxembourg: Office for Official Publications of the European Communities.

Gordon, D. and P. Townsend (eds) (2000), *Breadline Europe. The Measurement of Poverty*, Bristol: Policy Press.

HE 155/2001, Hallituksen esitys eduskunnalle laiksi toimeentulotuesta annetun lain 11 ja 15 § väliaikaisesta muuttamisesta.

HE 120/2002, Hallituksen esitys Eduskunnalle laiksi työnantajan sosiaaliturvamaksusta vapauttamisesta kunnissa vuosina 2003–2005.

HE 146/2005, Hallituksen esitys Eduskunnalle laiksi väliaikaisesta työnantajan matalapalkkatuesta.

HE 170/2005, Hallituksen esitys Eduskunnalle laiksi työnantajan sosiaaliturvamaksusta vapauttamisesta eräissä kunnissa vuosina 2003–2005 annetun lain muuttamisesta.

Hiilamo, H. (2002), *The Rise and Fall of Nordic Family Policy? Historical Development and Changes During the 1990s in Sweden and Finland*, Research report 125, Helsinki: National Research and Development Centre for Welfare and Health.

Hiilamo, H., J. Karjalainen and A. Parpo (2004), Tavoitteena kannustavampi toimeentulotuki, Tutkimus toimeentulotuen lakimuutoksista, Tutkimuksia 139. Helsinki: Stakes (with English abstract 'Incentives and social assistance – a study of legislative amendments related to social assistance').

Holm, P. and V. Vihriälä (2002), 'Matalan tuottavuuden työn tuki. Tarpeellinen keino työllisyyden parantamiseksi', Pellervon taloudellisen tutkimuslaitoksen työpapereita No. 57. Helsinki (with English summary: 'Subsidies for low-productivity work – a useful means to improve employment in Finland', Pellervo Economic Research Institute. Working Papers No. 57.

Kangas, O. and V.-M. Ritakallio (1998), 'Different methods – different results? Approaches to multidimensional poverty', in H.-J. Andress (ed.), *Empirical Poverty Research in a Comparative Perspective*, Ashgate: Aldershot, pp. 167–203.

Kangas, O. and V.-M. Ritakallio (2005), *Different Methods, Different Trends – Poverty in Finland in the 1990s*, Series A:15/2005, Turku: Publications of the Department of Social Policy, University of Turku.

Katzenstein, P.J. (1985), *Small States in World Markets. Industrial policy in Europe*, Ithaca, NY, and London: Cornell University Press.

Kauhanen, M. (2002), *Määräaikaiset työsuhteet ja toimeentulon riskit*, Sosiaali- ja terveysturvan tutkimuksia 69, Helsinki: Kela (with English summary *Temporary Employment and Risks of Inadequate Income*, Social Insurance Institution, Studies in Social Security and Health 69. Helsinki).

Kauhanen, M. (2005), *Työssäkäynnin ja taloudellisen syrjäytymisen dynamiikka*, Työpoliittinen tutkimus 276, Helsinki: Työministeriö (with English summary: *The Dynamics of Employment and Economic Exclusion*, Ministry of Labour: Helsinki).

Kautto, M., M. Heikkilä, B. Hvinden, S. Marklund and N. Ploug (eds) (1999), *Nordic Social Policy, Changing Welfare States*, London: Routledge.

Kiander, J. and S. Virtanen (2002), *1990s Economic Crisis: The Research Programme on the Economic Crisis of the 1990s in Finland: Final Report*, Helsinki: Valtion taloudellinen tutkimuskeskus.

Korkeamäki, O. and R. Uusitalo (2005), *Sosiaaliturvamaksukokeilun vaikutus työllisyyteen. Arviointiprojektin raportti*, Sosiaali- ja terveysministeriön monisteita 2005:7, Helsinki: STM (with English summary: *Employment Effects of an Experiment with Social Security Contributions. Report of Evaluation Project*, Stencils of the Ministry of Social Affairs and Health 2005:7, Helsinki. Available at http://stm.fi/Resource.phx/publishing/store/2005/06/te1118305896453/passthru.pdf (accessed 16 October 2005).

Kosunen, V. (1997), 'The recession and changes in social security on the 1990s', in M. Heikkilä and H. Uusitalo (eds), *The Cost of Cuts. Studies on Cutbacks in Social Security and their Effects in the Finland of the 1990s*, Helsinki: National Research and Development Centre for Welfare and Health.

Kuivalainen, S. (2004), *A Comparative Study on Last Resort Social Assistance Schemes in Six European Countries. Research report 146*. Helsinki: Stakes.

Kuivalainen, S., I. Airio, H. Hiilamo and M. Niemelä (2005), 'Suomalainen köyhyyspolitiikka', in J. Saari (ed.), *Köyhyyspolitiikka – johdatus sosiaalipolitiikan ytimeen*. Helsinki: STKL, pp. 63–121.
Kurjenoja, J. (2004), *Finland and Wage Taxes. International wage Tax Survey 2004. Tax Payers Association of Finland*. Available at http://www.veronmaksajat.fi/uploads/q6p9hrh.pdf (accessed 16 October 2005).
Mack, J. and S. Lansley (1985), *Poor Britain*, London: George Allen and Unwin.
Marx, I. and B. Nolan (1999), *Low Pay and Household Poverty*, Working Paper 216, Luxembourg: Luxembourg Income Study.
Moisio, P. (2006), 'Suhteellinen köyhyys Suomessa', *Yhteiskuntapolitiikka*, **71** (6), 639–45.
Muffels, R., J. Bergman and H.-J. Driven (1992), 'A multi-method approach to monitor the evolution of poverty', *Journal of European Social Policy*, **2** (3), 193–213.
Niemelä, M. (2005), *Trends on the Relationship between Low Income and Low Expenditure in Finland 1966–2001. Reports from the Department of Social Policy, Series C:16/2005*, Turku: University of Turku.
Organisation for Economic Co-operation and Development (OECD) (2004a), *Employment Outlook 2004*, Paris: OECD.
Organisation for Economic Co-operation and Development (OECD) (2004b), *Labour Force Statistics 1983–2003*, Paris: OECD.
Organisation for Economic Co-operation and Development (OECD) (2005), *Employment Outlook 2005*, Paris: OECD.
Organisation for Economic Co-operation and Development (OECD) Tax database. Available at http://www.oecd.org/document/60/0,2340,en_2649_37427_1942460_1_1_1_37427,00.html (accessed 1 November 2005).
Pearce, D. (1978), 'The feminization of poverty: women, work, and welfare', *Urban and Social Change Review*, **11** (February), 28–36.
Peña-Casas, R. and M. Latta (2004), *Working Poor in the European Union*, Luxembourg: European Foundation for the Improvement of Living and Working Conditions.
Pryke, R. (1995), *Taking the Measure of Poverty. A Critique of Low-Income Statistics: Alternative Estimates and Policy Implications, Research Monograph 51*, London: Institute of Economic Affairs.
Ray, D. (1998), *Development Economics*, Princeton, NJ: Princeton University Press.
Riihelä, M., R. Sullström and M. Tuomala (2002), *On Economic Poverty in Finland in the 1990s*, Discussion paper 264, Helsinki: VATT.
Ringen, S. (1987), *The Possibility of Politics. A Study in the Political Economy of the Welfare State*, Oxford: Clarendon.
Ritakallio, V.-M. (2002), 'Trends of poverty and income inequality in cross-national comparison', *European Journal of Social Security*, **2** (4), 151–77.
Rubery, J. (1989), 'Precarious forms of work in the United Kingdom', in G. Rodgers and J. Rodgers (ed.), *Precarious Jobs in Labour Market Regulation*, Genova: ILO.
Saunders, P., J. Bradshaw and M. Hirst (2002), 'Using household expenditure to develop income poverty line', *Social Policy & Administration*, **36** (3), 217–34.
Sauramo, P. (ed.) (2002), *Kriisistä nousuun – miten kävi kansalaisille? Palkansaajien tutkimuslaitos*, Helsinki: Edita.
Strengmann-Kuhn, W. (2004), 'Working poor in Europe: a partial basic income for workers?', in G. Standing (ed.), *Promoting Income Security as a Right: Europe and North America*, London: Anthem Press, pp. 253–68.

Taylor-Gooby, P. (ed.) (2004), *New risks, new welfare: the transformation of the European Welfare State*, Oxford: Oxford University Press.
Vartiainen, J. (1998), *The Labour Market in Finland: Institutions and Outcomes, Publications Series 1998/2*, Helsinki: Prime Minister's Office.

8. Two countries in one: the working poor in Italy

Ferruccio Biolcati-Rinaldi and Federico Podestà[1]

INTRODUCTION

Within the framework of a comparative analysis of in-work poverty, the Italian case can be of interest not only as a classic example of a Southern European welfare regime, but also because of its high level of internal heterogeneity. Southern Italy – also called the Mezzogiorno – experiences incidences of poverty and in-work poverty that are much higher than those in the Northern and Central regions of Italy. Such a difference is an unavoidable point of departure which has already been highlighted by many scholars (Kazepov, 1998; Negri and Saraceno, 1996; Sgritta and Innocenzi, 1993) and can be a useful analytical tool for better grasping the Italian experience. This is the intention of this chapter, and one that is rhetorically expressed in the title. In other words, we want to study how it is possible – within one historical and political unit – that social and economic processes can diverge so dramatically.

The chapter comprises six sections. Following the introduction, the second section presents the Italian welfare regime in its historical perspective, while the third treats the different elements of this welfare regime (work, state, and family) analytically. On this basis, the fourth section develops some working hypotheses that are then compared with the empirical analysis and findings of the fifth section. In the last section, we attempt to sum up our findings in a comprehensive picture of in-work poverty problems as they relate to the Italian case.

FROM THE GOLDEN AGE TO THE CURRENT CRISIS

Italy is a prototypical example of the Mediterranean welfare system (found in Italy, Greece, Spain and Portugal). This can be confirmed by observing the socio-economic developments that occurred in the post-Second World War era. The family constituted the core of the institutional balance of the Italian welfare system during the Golden Age (1950s and 1960s). While state intervention has constantly been characterized by a weak welfare effort, the family has permanently assumed an important role in providing social protection. More precisely, all (or almost all) obligations to support and care for weaker and more dependent subjects (children and old people) fall to the nuclear family. Against this backdrop, the Italian family developed sharp distinctions between the roles of men and women. Men exercised (and substantially continue to exercise) the role of breadwinner via stable participation in the labour market, while women played (and partly continue to play) a key role as unpaid caregivers in households (Esping-Andersen, 1996; Ferrera, 1996; Millar and Warman, 1996; Saraceno, 2003).

This type of institutional architecture worked well during the Golden Age. At the macro level, it allowed Italy to obtain good economic performance and maintain sufficient social stability. At the micro level, the male breadwinner was able to keep himself and members of his family above the poverty level (D'Apice and Fadda, 2003): the average one-income family model was extremely widespread, and statistical dispersion from this average family income was particularly low. There are two reasons for this: on the one hand, in the 1950s and 1960s, women's economic dependence on men was nearly absolute (Sorensen and McLanahan, 1987) and, consequently, two-income families were extremely rare. On the other hand, during the same period, the highest risk for poverty was among those families of the Mezzogiorno that lacked even a single income earner (Becchi Collidà, 1979).

Economic and socio-demographic transformations which occurred in the last decades have resulted in a profound crisis of the Mediterranean welfare model. Certainly, one crucial aspect of this crisis concerns high levels of in-work poverty. At the end of the 1990s, countries belonging to this cluster exhibited the highest incidence in the EU-15 of active poor, working poor and employed poor[2] individuals (see Table 8.1; see also the chapter by Lohmann and Marx in this volume). A helpful tool for understanding this pattern can be found in the inability of the Mediterranean welfare system to create work for women and young people (Esping-Andersen, 1996; 2002). This means that the adult man is often the only worker in the family.

On the one hand, while women aim to change their role in the family – and more generally, in society – through more stable and considerable participation in the labour market, the Mediterranean welfare states have remained frozen in the traditional male breadwinner mould, forcing

Table 8.1 Rates of active poor, working poor and employed poor in the EU in 1999 (%)

	PT	GR	IT	ES	LU	EU15	FR	NL	UK	AT	FI	BE	DE	IE	SE	DK
Working poor	15	14	10	9	9	7	7	7	7	6	6	5	5	5	5	4
Active poor	15	16	15	14	10	10	11	7	10	7	8	8	8	8	6	4
Employed poor	10	9	8	7	9	6	6	6	7	4	4	4	5	4	3	3

Source: Peña Casas and Latta (2004).

women to confront major difficulties in combining their non-paid household activities with their paid professional activities (Hemerijck, 2002). As a result, Southern European countries exhibit the lowest rates of female employment and, in turn, the highest rates of couples with one job in Europe. Conversely, these countries show the lowest rate of couples with two jobs. In 1999, the share of couples in Europe with one job was 36.4 versus 59.0 per cent for couples with two jobs, while the figures were very different in Greece (52.7 and 43.5 per cent, respectively), Spain (55.5 and 38.4 per cent) and Italy (49.8 and 43.5 per cent; Iacovou, 2003).

On the other hand, the evolution of labour market institutions has generated significant disparities between generations. The labour markets of the Southern European countries are currently marked by an acute insider–outsider contrast: while adult men continue to enjoy stable job positions, new entrants to the workforce, such as young people, are faced with difficulties in finding employment. This situation is associated with a postponement of the transition to adulthood. More precisely, more and more young people continue to live in their parental homes for longer and longer periods of time (Schizzerotto and Lucchini, 2004; Sgritta, 2001). Such a trend can obviously increase the risk of poverty for workers living in the family.

Before we formulate any specific hypotheses, we must develop a more detailed overview of the recent evolution of the Italian welfare regime. In doing so, we first look at the development of the welfare state and the labour market. Second, we describe the consequences they have for the family. This discussion will be developed while taking into account the most evident differences between Italy's North-Central and Southern regions.

THE ITALIAN WELFARE REGIME

Italian social programmes are built around the post-war male-breadwinner model. In practice, this has meant that the Italian welfare state is very oriented towards occupational insurance schemes and, more precisely, pension biased. Throughout the post-war period, pensions progressively managed to receive the lion's share of social spending. At the beginning of the 1950s, pension expenditure represented 45 per cent of Italy's total outlays for income maintenance programmes, equal to spending for family allowances. But over the next three decades, pension spending increased to the point that by 1980, it accounted for 80 per cent of all outlays, while spending on family allowances decreased to about 10 per cent, and sickness, disability and unemployment insurance made up the remaining 10 per cent (Ferrera, 1984).

Accordingly, pensions remained the core of the welfare policy agenda in the retrenchment era. During the 1990s, Italian policy-makers realized several pension reforms in order to prevent increases in retirement costs from undermining public finances. These reforms did not alter the architecture of the Italian welfare state. Social insurance schemes targeted at people with stable job positions, such as adult men, remain predominant. In contrast, women and young people – who face career instability and precarious employment – are largely excluded from public social protection programmes.

In addition, the state scarcely appears to be supporting the family in terms of fighting poverty and providing childcare. With respect to family allowances, the spirit of recent political reforms has been to promote means-testing. In fact, such policies are specifically geared towards families facing economic hardship, and take the form of specific allowances for rent, school textbooks and child support for large families with more than three underage children, as well as a maternity allowance (D'Apice and Fadda, 2003). With regard to childcare, we can say that the results of the Italian system are still underdeveloped compared to those of most non-Mediterranean European countries. In fact, although Italy has one of the highest proportions of children aged 3–6 years using childcare arrangements (95 per cent), it has one of the lowest percentages of children younger than 3 years old who use childcare services (6 per cent; Del Boca and Pasqua, 2002). Obviously, women with children younger than 3 years of age will face great difficulties in combining their non-paid household activities with their paid professional work. Nevertheless, such difficulties are dealt with differently by women in various regions in the country. This is because the structure of the subsidies and the number of available childcare spaces are set by the local governments. For example, during the mid-1990s, crèches for 0–3-year-olds were available at a rate of almost 12 per cent in the Northern regions; in the Southern regions, the rate was around 2 per cent (Del Boca and Pasqua, 2002). Obviously, this difference entails important disparities in female workforce participation rates between these two geographical areas (see below).

Looking at the main indicators, the Italian labour market shows some similarities to most European countries, but also some peculiarities. There are similarities with regard to both changes and levels of unemployment during the last decades. Since the end of the 1970s, Italy as well as the rest of Europe have suffered from a constant increase in the rate of unemployment. Moreover, the difference between the Italian rate and the overall European unemployment rate for the period from 1980 to 1995 was less than one percentage point (10.3 and 9.4 per cent, respectively; OECD, various years). Finally, since the mid-1990s, both Italy and Europe as a whole have seen a progressive decrease in unemployment. However, Italy stands out with regard to its employment rate. Its figures have consistently been significantly lower than the European average as far as this indicator is concerned. In 1999, the Italian employment rate was the lowest in the European Union, and seven percentage points less than the European average (56.1 and 64.3 per cent, respectively; Eurostat, various years).

However, both Italy's similarities with other European countries and its peculiarities underlie marked disparities across groups of individuals competing in the labour market and important imbalances across genders and Italian regions. Several features confirm this pattern. We start with the individual disparities. Italy's distinctiveness originates from low levels of employment caused by a strong disparity between men and women. In fact, although the Italian male employment rate remains lower than the European average (69.4 and 72.7 per cent, respectively, in 2003), that gap is less than in the case of the female employment rate. Here, the difference between the Italian and European averages amounts to more than 13 percentage points (42.7 and 56.0 per cent, respectively in 2003; Eurostat, various years). This situation is essentially due to two main factors. The first concerns the structure of the Italian welfare regime: As we have seen, the low supply of public childcare service is a factor which accounts for the great difficulties faced by Italian women with children – and, in particular, children younger than 3 years of age – in combining their non-paid household activities with their paid professional work. This has important consequences for women's decision to work and, consequently, for the Italian employment rate. These women's difficulties are then exacerbated by the limited supply of part-time employment, which does not accommodate the low degree of flexibility that exists in the hours of childcare services. As a consequence, Italian mothers are often forced to choose between not working at all or working full-time, neither of which may be their preferred option (Del Boca and Vuri, 2005).

The second factor has to do with the sharp contrast between the North-Central and Southern regions of Italy. The country's inability to create work for women largely explains the extremely low female employment rate in the Southern regions, which was only 27.1 per cent in 2003. If we take into account that in the same year the female employment rate in North-Central Italy was 51.1 per cent, it is easy to understand the impact of the Southern regions' figures on the national average (42.7 per cent; ISTAT, 2004). The employment status of women who live in Italy's South can be partly explained by the highly limited supply of public childcare services compared to that in Italy's North-Central regions. Nevertheless, the main cause of these women's situation must be traced to the very limited opportunities supplied by the labour market in the Southern regions. Unable to find a job, more and more women who live in these regions tend to leave the workforce and spend their time exclusively on non-paid household activities (Villa, 2004).

Let us now consider unemployment. Although the Italian unemployment rate follows a pattern quite similar to the European average, it also reveals some important peculiarities which underlie further differences between North-Central and Southern Italy, as well as other social disparities. First, Italian unemployment is at its highest for young people. In 2003, the unemployment rate for 15–24-year-olds in the labour force was three times that of the total working-age population (27.1 and 8.8 per cent, respectively). Second, in 2003, the percentage of jobless people in Southern Italy and on the islands of Sardinia and Sicily (17.2 and 19.4 per cent, respectively) was much higher than in the rest of the country (North-west: 4.2 per cent; North-east: 3.3 per cent; Centre: 6.6 per cent); ISTAT, various years). Therefore, if we look at these two phenomena in combination, we can see that the youth unemployment results are essentially a problem in Southern Italy. Whereas in Northern and Central Italy, the bulk of the jobless are unemployed workers – that is, dismissed workers – in the South, the largest group (50.0 per cent) is composed of first-time job seekers (Caroleo and Mazzotta, 1998).

To summarize, the high unemployment rate among young people and the low female employment rate constitute the main structural characteristics of the Italian labour market. Nevertheless, these problems are essentially concentrated in the South of Italy. This means that, while in the North-Central regions, women are moving closer to male models of labour participation, and youth unemployment is moving into line with European standards, in Southern Italy these two groups tend to remain excluded from the job market. Obviously, this geographical division must be considered when we investigate the difference between insiders and outsiders in the Italian labour market. This is particularly true because these different employment patterns have important consequences for the income formation of families living in different areas of the country. Nevertheless, before describing these disparities, let us illustrate some characteristics of the Italian family.

The traditional family structure continues to play a crucial role in the lives of individuals in Italy – and in Mediterranean Europe in general – in contrast to in other developed countries. Although new household forms are arising, individuals continue to adopt habitual behaviours in terms of family formation and social reproduction. In the first place, marriage remains the preferred way for Italian men and women to create a family. The quota of unmarried cohabiting people in Italy is very low: 6 per cent between the ages of 16 and 29 (Sgritta, 2001). In addition, marriage still plays a crucial role in two other aspects over the course of life: social reproduction and leaving the parental home. First, children are very rarely born to unmarried couples. Second, leaving the parental home and marriage are almost perfectly synchronized. For instance, more than 80 per cent of Italian women born in the 1960s left their families directly to get married (Ongaro, 2001).

All these factors contribute to explaining an apparently paradoxical aspect of the Italian family: although Italy exhibits one of the lowest fertility rates in Europe, it has larger average household sizes compared with other European countries. This is essentially because in Italy, there are few people living alone. This implies that most Italian workers live in traditional families comprising a married couple with or without children. Thus, the risk of belonging to the working poor in Italy is strictly correlated with the ability of one's family members to produce income and, consequently, to have a job.

SOME WORKING HYPOTHESES

Based on this overview of the past and current structure of the Italian welfare regime, we can now formulate some hypotheses as a guideline for the empirical analysis.

We have seen that Italian welfare regime development has been characterized by a consistent structure of work, welfare and family systems. The labour market is a dualistic one, with a sharp contrast between insiders (adult men) and outsiders (young people and women). The welfare state tends to reinforce this distinction with a system that is oriented towards occupational insurance schemes and which makes only weak efforts to improve family allowances or the childcare system. The pattern is completed by a family system that – particularly in the case of its female members – works as a provider of care and protection, thanks to a strong structuring of gender roles.

Such a design starts to suffer in a changing economy that demands more work, that is, in an economy that expects higher labour market participation from families and individuals. At least, in the Italian case, this change took place without any welfare compensation. In fact, there has been a contraction of the existing system without any restructuring in favour of the traditional outsider categories. In this context, it is possible to formulate two different series of hypotheses. At the macro level – as we discussed in the second section – we can expect to see higher in-work poverty rates, compared with the other non-Mediterranean countries, owing to Italy's difficulties in reforming its original design. This is particularly true for the Mezzogiorno, where every aspect of the problems – unemployment, lack of policies supporting families, sharp gender division of domestic and non-domestic work, and so on – is exaggerated. Moreover, in the Southern regions there are many families with breadwinners in unstable positions in the labour market, so that even the traditional model does not apply.

As far as the micro level is concerned, let us begin from the following point. Poverty can be conceptualized as a relationship between resources (income from work, social transfers, and so on) and needs (number of members, but also care load). Looking at resources – on the basis of the previous argument – we can expect lower in-work poverty rates for families who are able to extend insider status to members other than the breadwinner, that is, for households containing more workers and retired persons. We can also expect higher in-work poverty risks for families where outsiders (young people and women) are not able to escape their situation. With regard to needs, it is necessary to consider not only the household dimension, but also the care load, which can affect resources by preventing people from participating in the labour market and reducing their career perspectives – this is indeed the case for women in Italy. This is the 'trap' side of the coin of family solidarity. The other is the 'resource' side: the care given by a (female) member to another (old or very young) member of the family can be an effective way to solve an urgent family problem.

The situation we have just described will differ between the North-Central regions and the Mezzogiorno. Here, the challenge is to find out whether this is simply a problem of scale (for example, since there is more unemployment, there will be more in-work poverty) or of possible interactions. In order to clarify this point, we will specify our hypotheses concerning young people.

Let us develop two facets mentioned in the previous sections of this chapter with respect to the difference between North-Central and Southern Italy in terms of the labour market: (1) Italy shows one of the highest rates in Europe of couples with one job and one of the lowest rates of couples with two jobs; (2) more and more young Italian people are continuing to live in their parental homes for longer and longer periods. The first facet is connected to the Italian labour market's inability to ensure high levels of female employment. Nevertheless, as anticipated, the difference between female employment rates in the Southern and Northern-Central regions of Italy is extremely high. Clearly, this means that the disparities in terms of the respective rates of couples with two jobs and couples with one job are extremely high as well. In fact, in the South of Italy, the proportion of couples with two jobs is only 28 per cent, while in Northern Italy it is more than 50 per cent (ISTAT, 2003). As Villa (2004) highlights, this disparity increases further if we take the presence of children into account. Specifically, it is more probable that couples with children will be single-income families in the South than in the North-Central regions. Obviously, all these facts suggest some hypotheses about the risk of belonging to the working poor in Italy.

Nevertheless, before we continue looking at this aspect, let us develop the fact that more and more young Italians are continuing to live for longer and longer periods in their parental homes. While at the EU-15 level, the percentage of young people in the age group between 16 and 30 who remain with their parents amounts to 44.7 per cent, in Italy this rate is 65.1 per cent (Vogel, 1997). Lack of work is often invoked as an explanation for why Italian young people stay with the family for so long. In Italy, 90 per cent of unemployed 20–30-year-olds depend totally on parental support (Esping-Andersen, 2002). Nevertheless, even this argument must be redefined with respect to the differences between the macro areas of the country. In fact, there is a radical difference between North-Central and Southern Italy regarding the conditions of young people who live with their families. In the Northern regions, a large proportion of these young people (60 per cent of men and 50 per cent of women) already have jobs; while in the South, this number is only 32 per cent (for men and women combined). As we have already seen, it is more difficult for young people in the South to find jobs, although when they do find work they tend to leave the parental home. Apparently, the opposite is the case in the North-Central regions (Sgritta, 2001). If so, this fact must be taken into account when formulating hypotheses about the working poor. We can therefore specify that, while in North-Central Italy the presence of young people in their parents' home can be a situation which increases family income, in the South it tends to decrease equivalent family income.

From this hypothetical framework, we derived some research questions which structured our analysis: how many working poor people are there in Italy? Are the numbers increasing or decreasing? Who are the working poor, and what factors are associated with in-work poverty?

THE WORKING POOR IN ITALY IN THE ECHP DATA

The empirical analysis is based on data from the Italian section of the European Community Household Panel (ECHP) which covers the period from 1994 to 2001 (Eurostat, 2003).[3] For the key variables, we have followed the standard definitions adopted throughout this book. Poverty status is based on current monthly income;[4] the poverty line is set at 60 per cent of the median income, and the modified OECD scale is used. The analysis is restricted to individuals 15–64 years old who are normally or currently working as defined by the International Labour Organization's main activity status.[5] For the eight years we considered, the mean working poor rate was 10.2 per cent (Table 8.2, section A). But this rate was very different from region to region: the mean rate in the South (23.0 per cent) was more than five times the mean rate in the North-Central regions of Italy (4.5 per cent). Over time, the figures remained substantially stable – except in the South, where it is possible to detect a two-stage trend: a tendency towards decreasing poverty from 1994 (23.6 per cent) to 1998 (20.6 per cent) and an increasing tendency from 1998 to 2001 (23.5 per cent). As far as the overall poverty rate is concerned, we can make similar comparisons (Table 8.2, section B). From another point of view, we can see that approximately one-fifth of the poor were working, and the incidence of workers among the poor was very similar in the different Italian regions (Table 8.2, section C). Over time, these figures remained quite steady, except in the North-Central region, where there was an almost continuous decrease in workers among the poor from 1994 (24.5 per cent) to 2001 (17.8 per cent). In sum, one worker in 10 is poor (but the numbers vary across regions) and two poor people in 10 are workers (all over Italy). Over the years (1994–2001), these ratios remained unchanged at the national level with some differences at the regional level: the in-work poverty rate – like the overall poverty rate – increased (after decreasing) in the South. It did not change much in the North-Central regions, and here it was even less a work-related problem, owing to the sharp decrease in workers among the poor population.

These estimates provide us with a measure of the gap between North-Central and Southern Italy and require a comparative analysis of these two regions. The gap becomes even clearer when we look at the incidences of in-work poverty among different social groups living in the North-Central

Table 8.2 Poverty and work in Italy

		1994	1995	1996	1997	1998	1999	2000	2001
(A) Poverty rate among working population									
%	North-Centre	5.1	4.7	4.5	5.1	4.1	4.6	4.1	3.5
	South	23.6	23.7	23.2	22.2	20.6	23.0	24.3	23.5
	Italy	10.6	10.5	10.4	10.4	9.4	10.4	10.4	9.7
N	North-Centre	5 613	5 467	5 362	4 992	4 809	4 696	4 489	4 183
	South	2 363	2 422	2 471	2 272	2 241	2 132	2 022	1 879
	Italy	7 976	7 889	7 833	7 264	7 050	6 828	6 511	6 062
(B) Poverty rate among population									
%	North-Centre	8.3	8.1	8.9	9.4	8.5	8.8	8.7	8.2
	South	33.0	34.0	33.6	33.0	31.7	34.4	35.8	34.2
	Italy	17.2	18.0	18.3	18.2	17.2	18.3	18.8	17.8
N	North-Centre	13 889	13 376	13 221	12 456	11 998	11 601	10 986	10 097
	South	7 867	8 193	8 097	7 455	7 140	6 852	6 464	5 930
	Italy	21 756	21 569	21 318	19 911	19 138	18 453	17 450	16 027
(C) Working rate among poor population									
%	North-Centre	24.5	23.5	20.2	21.4	19.0	20.7	19.6	17.8
	South	20.8	20.3	20.6	20.0	19.7	20.3	20.9	21.7
	Italy	21.9	21.2	20.5	20.5	19.5	20.4	20.5	20.6
N	North-Centre	1 143	1 079	1 204	1 245	1 069	1 108	1 057	908
	South	2 578	2 758	2 773	2 612	2 369	2 552	2 551	2 216
	Italy	3 721	3 837	3 977	3 857	3 438	3 660	3 608	3 124

Source: Own calculations on European Community Household Panel, Italy, waves I–VIII, weighted data.

regions compared to in the South. The difference is impressive (Figures 8.1 and 8.2): For example, in 2001, the in-work poverty risk of the group with the highest incidence in the North-Central regions (the risk among households where at least one member is unemployed is 11.4 per cent) was almost the same as that in the group with the lowest incidence in the South (high/medium-qualified workers, 12.0 per cent).[6] Moreover, in the North-Central region, some group differences (gender, permanent/fixed-term contract, presence of one or more retired people in the household whose pension contributes to the household income) are not statistically significant (according to a Pearson chi-squared test with a significance level set at 0.001). We also found household typology to be one of these factors: while in the North-Central regions, in-work poverty never exceeds 5 per cent in different household types (and the differences between them are not statistically significant), in the Mezzogiorno, couples with children have a higher in-work poverty risk compared with singles, couples without

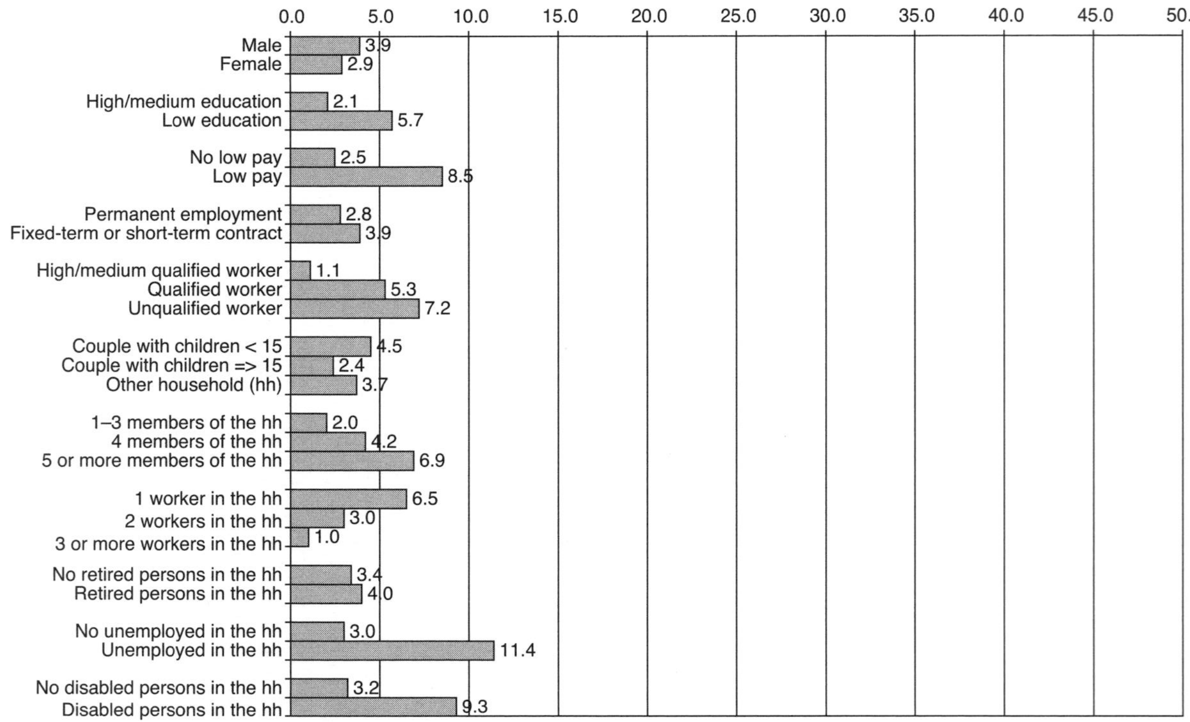

Source: Own calculations on European Community Household Panel, Italy, wave VIII, weighted data.

Figure 8.1 In-work poverty incidence among different groups in North-Centre Italy, 2001 (%)

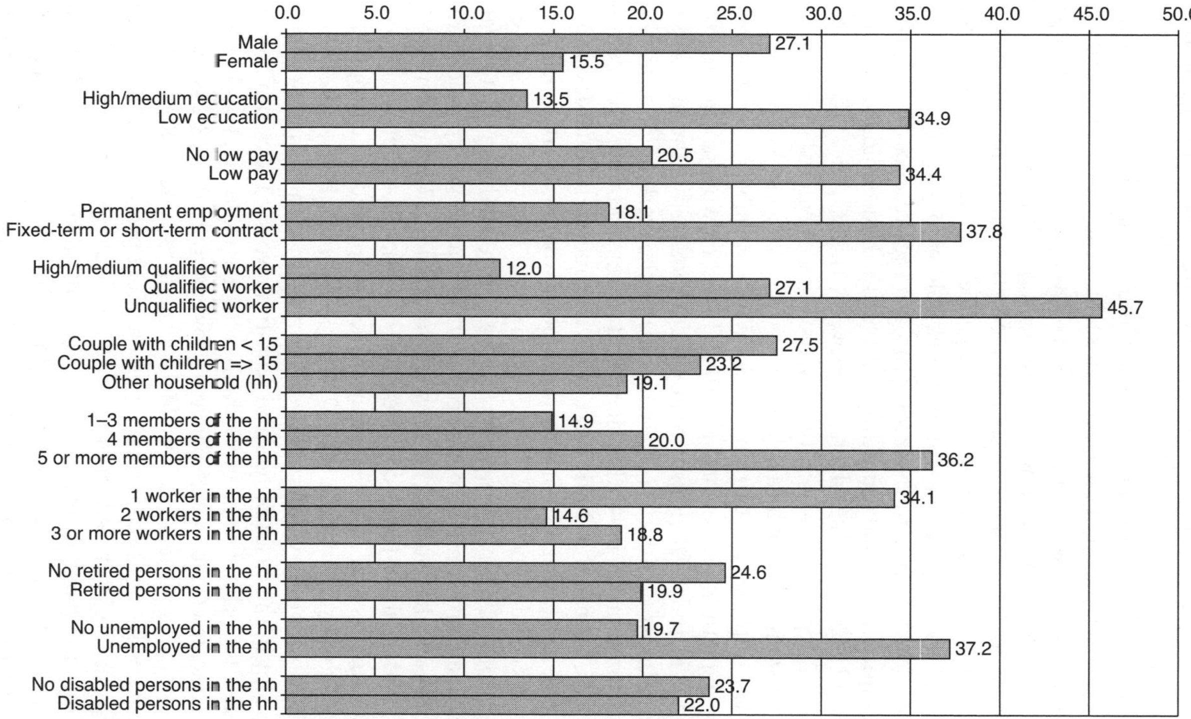

Source: Own calculations on European Community Household Panel, Italy, wave VIII, weighted data.

Figure 8.2 In-work poverty incidence among different groups in South Italy, 2001 (%)

children and other households (19.1 per cent). If at least one of the children is aged less than 15 (27.5 per cent), the risk seems to be even higher compared to the situation where all the children are 15 years of age or older (23.2 per cent).

The other variables show an identical pattern: the groups which are more at risk are the same, but on a different scale in each of the two regions. For instance, workers with low educations have a higher incidence of poverty compared to workers with high/medium education levels – but these contrasts are at different levels in the North-Central regions (5.7 vs 2.1 per cent) and in the South (34.9 vs 13.5 per cent). The only exception is the presence of a disabled person in the household who requires extra care: the poverty risk is higher in the Mezzogiorno, but the presence of a disabled person does not seem to make any difference for the household, while in the North-Central regions it does. Here, the poverty risk is almost three times higher (9.3 vs 3.2 per cent) – as if the North-Central regions' smaller families could least afford such a care load.[7]

What is the outcome of such processes? Which variables are significant in forming a picture of in-work poverty? In other words, who are the working poor in Italy? Obviously, regional composition is the first aspect to consider: almost two-thirds (65.9 per cent) of the working poor lived in the Southern regions in 1994; this share had increased to 69.8 per cent in 1998 and to 75.1 per cent in 2001. Next, let us consider individual-level variables. In 1994, most of the Italian working poor were male (70.1 per cent) with low levels of education (79.9 per cent); most of the working poor were 40–49 years old (28.3 per cent). As far as job-related risk factors are concerned, one-third seems to be the proportion that shows up repeatedly: 34.2 per cent of the working poor were low paid, 37.3 per cent were employed under short-term contracts (in 1998); 32.4 per cent were unqualified workers and 36.7 per cent were self-employed. The proportion of the poor working part-time was 17.4 per cent. For almost all of these variables, in-work poverty differs between the North-Central and Southern regions (except in the cases of age and part-time work): the South has the higher share of working poor individuals who are male (62.4 vs 74.0 per cent), low-educated (75.8 vs 82.5 per cent), low-paid (23.0 vs 38.2 per cent), under fixed-term contracts (13.7 vs 44.7 per cent) or unqualified (25.1 vs 36.1 per cent). Self-employed individuals were more prevalent in the North-Central regions (50.1 per cent) compared to the South (30.0 per cent). Over time, the situation partially changed: the share of high/medium-educated, non-low-paid, full-time or permanently employed, high/medium-qualified and qualified workers increased. In the case of these same variables – except for the final one – it is possible to envisage a convergence between the North-Central regions and the Mezzogiorno.[8]

We now move on to the household-level variables. In 1994, most of the working poor lived in young families (couples with at least one child aged less than 15: 41.9 per cent), in large households (five or more members: 60.1 per cent), with only one member working (48.2 per cent) and without retired persons in the household (89.4 per cent). This is especially true for the working poor living in the Mezzogiorno; it is also important to note that the share of mature families (couples with one or more children, all aged 15 or older) is almost double in the South (40.1 per cent) compared with in the North-Central regions (24.2 per cent; see Table 8.3). As far as risk factors connected to household structure are concerned, 41.6 per cent of the working poor lived in families with at least one unemployed member, 9.6 per cent in households with at least one child aged 0–2 years, 21.2 per cent in families with at least one member who was severely hampered in his or her daily activities by some physical or mental health problem, illness or disability. It is interesting to note that a work-related risk factor (unemployment) affects working poor composition more in the South (22.2 vs 51.3 per cent), while care-related risk factors – infants (13.6 vs 7.7 per cent) and above all disability (27.3 vs 17.7 per cent) – affect the Northern-Central working poor more significantly. Over time, the same changes took place, specifically from 1994 to 1998: the share of large households and of families with unemployment and disability decreased; at the same time, the share of households containing only one worker increased.

It is also interesting to note the income structure of the working poor. From what we have seen above, we know that the share of the working poor who are low paid and live in households where they are the only workers is higher in the South than it is in the North-Central regions. This does not imply that the Southern breadwinner is more frequently a low-paid worker. More specifically, while this is partially true, the difference is made up by additional workers who more often also hold low-paying jobs. In 1994, the only worker in a working-poor family had a slightly higher probability of being low paid in the South (27.1 per cent) compared with in the North-Central region (23.7 per cent), while for workers in households where additional members held jobs, the gap was much higher (51.6 vs 22.4 per cent). In the following years it is possible to find similar patterns. This information has obvious implications for remedying in-work poverty, at least in the Mezzogiorno: the problem is not only to find additional jobs for the families, but also good – that is, not low-paid – jobs.

In the last part of the analysis, we will move towards a multivariate framework, developing a random-effects logistic regression model for the probability of being among the working poor in Italy during the period from 1994 to 2001 (Powers and Xie, 2000: 177–88).[9] The intent – mainly

Table 8.3 Working poor composition in Italy (1994, 1998 and 2001) (%)

Household characteristic	1994			1998			2001		
	North-Centre	South	Italy	North-Centre	South	Italy	North Centre	South	Italy
Couple with children < 15	36.9	44.5	41.9	30.7	41.6	38.0	41.4	40.2	40.8
Couple with children => 15	24.2	40.1	34.7	38.6	40.0	38.8	23.4	36.9	33.3
Other household (hh)	38.9	15.4	23.4	30.7	18.4	23.2	35.2	22.9	25.9
[N]	[252]	[486]	[743]	[192]	[445]	[650]	[145]	[436]	[583]
1–3 members of the hh	17.3	12.1	13.9	25.3	16.9	19.4	28.9	20.1	22.3
4 members of the hh	32.0	23.0	26.0	44.8	34.1	37.1	39.5	30.9	33.3
5 or more members of the hh	50.8	64.9	60.1	29.9	49.0	43.5	31.6	49.0	44.4
[N]	[277]	[536]	[820]	[192]	[445]	[650]	[145]	[436]	[583]
1 worker in the hh	36.3	54.0	48.2	53.6	61.3	58.4	50.2	60.9	58.0
2 workers in the hh	40.2	25.1	30.1	35.5	24.1	27.5	43.8	25.0	30.0
3 or more workers in the hh	23.6	20.9	21.7	10.9	14.7	14.1	6.0	14.1	12.0
[N]	[277]	[536]	[820]	[192]	[445]	[650]	[145]	[436]	[583]
No retired persons in the hh	85.6	91.4	89.4	80.3	88.5	86.2	71.7	81.6	79.2
Retired persons in the hh	14.4	8.6	10.6	19.7	11.5	13.8	28.3	18.4	20.8
[N]	[277]	[536]	[820]	[193]	[445]	[650]	[145]	[435]	[583]
No unemployed in the hh	77.8	48.7	58.4	74.7	57.1	63.1	81.3	65.1	68.9
Unemployed in the hh	22.2	51.3	41.6	25.3	42.9	36.9	18.7	34.9	31.1
[N]	[277]	[536]	[820]	[192]	[445]	[650]	[145]	[436]	[583]
No children 0–2 years in the hh	86.4	92.3	90.4	92.3	88.8	89.7	87.5	89.4	88.9
Children 0–2 years in the hh	13.6	7.7	9.6	7.7	11.2	10.3	12.5	10.6	11.1
[N]	[277]	[536]	[820]	[192]	[445]	[650]	[145]	[436]	[583]
No disabled persons in the hh	72.7	82.3	78.8	86.6	94.4	92.2	85.6	93.6	91.7
Disabled persons in the hh	27.3	17.7	21.2	13.4	5.6	7.8	14.4	6.4	8.3
[N]	[277]	[536]	[820]	[192]	[445]	[650]	[145]	[436]	[583]

Source: Own calculations on European Community Household Panel, Italy, waves I, V, VIII.

explorative – is to obtain a global picture of the determinants of in-work poverty and to consider whether such a picture changes significantly in the North-Central regions as compared to the Mezzogiorno. There are many results (see Table 8.4), but they can be organized quite easily around the following dichotomies: work/life course and individual/household. The overall presentation tells a story of wide-ranging similarities between the two Italian regions, with few but noteworthy differences.

The most important (and common) factor is work, both at the individual and household levels. The scale of the problems in the two regional labour markets is very different – both in terms of unemployment (see the third section above) and low-paid workers (who were much more prevalent in the South (16.7 per cent) than in the North-Central regions (6.3 per cent) in 2001 according to ECHP data) – but the mechanisms leading to in-work poverty seem to be the same. At the household level, it is the shortage of resources (workers and retired people) and the excess of needs (family members) that results in poverty of similar strengths in the different regions: workers living in families with five or more members have a probability of being poor that is three times higher (the odds ratio is 3.245 in the North-Central regions and 3.827 in the South) than that of workers in four-member families. Conversely, the probability is much lower if there are two or even three or more workers in the household instead of one. The odds ratio for a household with two workers is 0.266 in the North-Central regions and 0.165 in the South (three workers: 0.085 and 0.077). The effect of the number of workers can largely be traced back to women's participation to the labour market. At the individual level, job quality makes the difference in both regions. In the case of a low-paid job, the effect is particularly strong, both in the North-Central regions (the odds ratio is 3.925) and in the South (3.584). It is also noteworthy that the risk of poverty for an unqualified worker is much higher in the Mezzogiorno (4.281) compared with the North-Central regions (2.183).

When we look at course of life, the picture is much more heterogeneous. First, it is the course of a household's life – and not the individual's – that matters: the risk of poverty does not vary significantly according to a worker's gender and generation. What counts is the course of family life, but only in the Mezzogiorno. In the Northern and Central regions, the only difference we see is between couples with children (and the other households) and couples without children, who run a significantly lower risk of poverty (0.454). In the Southern regions, every other family form runs a significantly lower risk of poverty compared to couples with one or more children who are all aged 15 or older. From the point of view of this analysis, the variation between young and mature couples with children is particularly interesting. In the North-Central regions they run similar

Table 8.4 Random-effects logistic regression model for the probability of being working poor in Italy, 1994–2001

Variables	North-Centre			South		
	Odds Ratio	Coef.	Std. Err.	Odds Ratio	Coef.	Std. Err.
Constant	–	−5.196	0.224***	–	−3.647	0.188***
Male	1.000	0.000	–	1.000	0.000	–
Female	1.047	0.046	0.111	0.909	−0.094	0.103
15–29 years old	0.984	−0.015	0.148	1.244	0.202	0.124
30–39 years old	0.814	−0.205	0.144	0.893	−0.113	0.118
40–49 years old	0.819	−0.199	0.131	0.961	−0.039	0.104
50–64 years old	1.000	0.000	–	1.000	0.000	–
High/medium education	1.000	0.000	–	1.000	0.000	–
Low education	1.870	0.626	0.106***	2.709	0.996	0.094***
Employee, no low wage	1.000	0.000	–	1.000	0.000	–
Employee, low wage	3.925	1.367	0.146***	3.584	1.276	0.102***
Self-employed	2.932	1.075	0.105***	1.876	0.629	0.090***
Full-time job	1.000	0.000	–	1.000	0.000	–
Part-time job	2.493	0.913	0.140***	2.524	0.926	0.118***
High/medium qualified workers	1.000	0.000	–	1.000	0.000	–
Qualified workers	1.841	0.610	0.118***	2.739	1.007	0.101***
Unqualified workers	2.183	0.781	0.153***	4.281	1.454	0.120***
Couple without children	0.454	−0.787	0.227***	0.328	−1.111	0.172***
Couple with children <15	0.908	−0.095	0.126	0.677	−0.388	0.096***
Couple with children => 15	1.000	0.000	–	1.000	0.000	–
Other households (hh)	1.143	0.134	0.127	0.460	−0.776	0.118***
1–3 members of the hh	0.249	−1.386	0.118***	0.336	−1.087	0.100***
4 members of the hh	1.000	0.000	–	1.000	0.000	–
5 or more members of the hh	3.245	1.177	0.130***	3.827	1.342	0.095***
1 worker in the hh	1.000	0.000	–	1.000	0.000	–
2 workers in the hh	0.266	−1.323	0.101***	0.165	−1.799	0.083***
3 or more workers in the hh	0.085	−2.456	0.154***	0.077	−2.561	0.125***
No retired persons in the hh	1.000	0.000	–	1.000	0.000	–
Retired persons in the hh	0.535	−0.624	0.123***	0.311	−1.167	0.117***
No unemployed in the hh	1.000	0.000	–	1.000	0.000	–
Unemployed in the hh	1.713	0.538	0.108***	1.859	0.620	0.069***
No children 0–2 years old in the hh	1.000	0.000	–	1.000	0.000	–

Table 8.4 (continued)

Variables	North-Centre			South		
	Odds Ratio	Coef.	Std. Err.	Odds Ratio	Coef.	Std. Err.
Children 0–2 years old in the hh	0.936	−0.065	0.142	1.079	0.076	0.101
No disabled persons in the hh	1.000	0.000	–	1.000	0.000	–
Disabled persons in the hh	1.672	0.514	0.132***	1.235	0.211	0.118
Log Likelihood			−4054.4808			−6665.4353
Number of observations			31693			20175
Number of individuals			7007			4460
Wald chi2(19)			859.54			1682.02
Prob > chi2			0.0000			0.0000

Note: Significant at $p < 0.001$ (***), $p < 0.01$ (**), $p < 0.05$ (*).

Source: Own calculations on European Community Household Panel, Italy, waves I–VIII, unweighted data.

risks of poverty, while in the South, mature families run a higher risk – as anticipated above (see the fourth section) – owing to the interaction between the availability of jobs and the length of time that Italian youth remain in the parental home in the different regions. While some young people living in the North-Central regions do not seem eager to leave their parental homes even when they find a job, their counterparts in the South are held back from establishing their own families because of the difficulties they encounter in the labour market. In this way, what can be a resource in the North-Central regions becomes a burden in the Mezzogiorno.

Another interesting regional difference is related to the course of household life: a co-variation between the presence of a person in the household who requires special care and poverty risk exists in the North-Central regions but not in the South, as we saw above at the bi-variate level.[10] This is probably due to the different effects of family solidarity and the position of the household on the labour market in the North-Central region as compared to the South (see Table 8.3). What in ordinary times is just a needs-load (the family), in an emergency – such as when physical or mental health problems, illnesses or disabilities appear – can become a resource, one that is paradoxically easier to activate in the Mezzogiorno.

A COMPREHENSIVE PICTURE

Do we really have two countries in one? In other words, how is it possible to have markedly diverging economic and social processes existing inside the same historical and political unit?

During the eight years we studied, the mean in-work poverty rate in the South (23.0 per cent) was more than five times the mean rate in the North-Central regions of Italy (4.5 per cent), and such a gap persists when we look at the specific rates of population groups living in the two regions. Moreover, there are no signs of convergence: in the North-Central regions, there is an almost continuous decrease in the number of workers among the poor, whereas the share of working poor living in the Southern regions increased from 65.9 per cent in 1994 to 75.1 per cent in 2001. It is easy to conclude that in-work poverty is mostly concentrated in the Mezzogiorno.

This situation does not represent anything new; instead, it is the result of a persistent dualism in Italian society. As we have seen, Italy's post-war economic development was sustained by a welfare regime that was shaped by the male-breadwinner model. In this context, poverty was mostly an out-of-work problem resulting from weak economic development in the Southern regions which were unable to make the model work. Nowadays, poverty and the in-work poverty gap can be explained by a differential development of the traditional model. In the Northern and Central regions, development has been sustained by higher economic growth and a better-functioning local welfare system: the borders between insiders and outsiders in the labour market have become more permeable, fostering employment for young people and activity for women. In the South, however, we see an inertia effect: the breadwinner model has presumably spread, but with few modifications, so that there are few additional workers and – as we have seen – when they do exist, they are often forced to work in low-paying jobs.

We can take a further analytical step by looking at the processes behind these changes. In the empirical analysis, two main factors appear: income formation processes and the course of family life. The multivariate model in the previous section shows how the presence of additional workers (women and young people) or of unemployed persons and pensioners – as well as the type of work (low paid or not, employee or self-employed, full/part-time) – all lead to similar outcomes across the Italian regions. A sort of scale mechanism seems to be at work: economic development – via work and welfare (pension) – has the same influence on the financial situation of the families who live in the North-Central regions rather than in the Mezzogiorno, so that the development differential translates into a family wealth differential.

The same is not true in the case of the course of family life, where such simple translation mechanisms do not apply. In some instances, the course of family life can exacerbate the regional difference – as it does in the case of mature families, that is, couples with children older than 15. Italian families are characterized by children who remain in the parental home longer than in other European countries, but with the labour markets at different levels of development, what can be a resource in the North-Central regions instead becomes an additional burden in the Mezzogiorno – so that for workers living in these families, the risk of being poor is even higher than it is for workers with younger children.

In other instances, however, the course of family life can actually reverse the usual in-work poverty risk faced by people living in different regions – as in the case of families where one member is severely hampered in his or her daily activities by some physical or mental health problem, illness or disability. There is consistent evidence that such a care load does not raise a family's poverty risk in the South, but does so in the North-Central regions. Here, it seems that the rigid balance between people working for the family and people living in the family does not permit activating any additional caregiving potential, so it is easier for a crisis to develop under such circumstances. But what may function as a resource for the Mezzogiorno's families in the short run, in the long run can become a trap which lowers outsiders' labour market participation and career perspectives.

NOTES

1. Although this chapter is the result of joint work, the different parts can be attributed as follows: Ferruccio Biolcati-Rinaldi wrote the first, fifth and final sections, while Federico Podestà wrote the second and third sections; the fourth section was written jointly. We would like to thank Sophal Ear for his comments on this chapter.
2. Defined as follows. Active poor: working or looking for work for at least six months in the previous year. Working poor: working for at least six months in the previous year. Employed poor: employee for at least six months in the previous year (Peña Casas and Latta, 2004).
3. We preferred the Eurostat ECHP to the Bank of Italy Survey on Household Income and Wealth because the former is a full panel instead of a partial one (Banca d'Italia, 2006).
4. The definition of poverty is based on current monthly income and not on previous year's income, because in such a longitudinal analysis, we find it important that all variables refer to the same points in time. For a discussion of the problem see Atkinson et al. (2002: 105–8).
5. In these analyses, we assume that self-employed income data are sufficiently reliable. This assumption, especially in the Italian case, would deserve appropriate empirical investigation.
6. Some variables need to be specified. North-Central regions: Piemonte, Valle d'Aosta, Liguria, Lombardia, Trentino-Alto Adige, Veneto, Friuli-Venezia Giulia, Emilia-Romagna, Toscana, Umbria, Marche, Lazio. Southern regions: Abruzzo, Molise, Campania, Puglia, Basilicata, Calabria, Sicilia, Sardegna. High/medium education:

ISCED 3–7; low education: ISCED 0–2. Low-paid worker: an employee who earns less than two-thirds of the median gross hourly wage. High/medium-qualified workers: legislators, senior officials and managers, professionals, technicians and associate professionals, clerks; qualified workers: service workers and shop and market sales workers, skilled agricultural and fishery workers, craft and related trades workers, plant and machine operators and assemblers; unqualified workers: elementary occupations. Part-time job: working less than 30 hours per week (in one's main job). Disabled person: a person declared to be severely hampered in his or her daily activities owing to any physical or mental health problem, illness or disability.

7. Four variables (age, full/part-time, employee/self-employed, 0–2-year-old child in the household) are not statistically significant in either North-Central or Southern Italy.
8. In the case of in-work poverty, the substantive interpretation of such diachronic changes is particularly difficult. In fact, the alternative to working poor status might not only be to be working and non-poor, but also to be non-working: This means that different processes can account for such changes, and it is not easy to distinguish them. To us, this seems to be a general problem of empirical research on in-work poverty that is worth taking into account for all analyses. Furthermore, it is also necessary to consider the panel attrition effect (Rendtel et al., 2004).

   Another interesting methodological problem in working poor research is the choice of the unit of analysis. Since poverty is usually defined at the household level – and because of the relevance of family strategies in this field – it would surely be interesting to perform analyses based on households rather than on individuals.
9. Before developing into panel data models, we tested duration data models (Blossfeld and Rohwer, 2002), but the results were not satisfying because of the few cases due to left-censored spells dropping.
10. In a similar (random-effects logistic regression) but joint (all Italy) model, the interaction between the presence of a person in the household who requires extra care and region was significant; the interaction between household typology and region was not significant.

REFERENCES

Atkinson, T., B. Cantillon, E. Marlier and B. Nolan (2002), *Social Indicators. The EU and Social Inclusion*, Oxford: Oxford University Press.

Banca d'Italia (2006), 'Household income and wealth in 2004', *Supplements to the Statistical Bullettin*, **XVI**, 7.

Becchi Collidà, A. (1979), *Politiche del lavoro e garanzia. del reddito in Italia*, Bologna: il Mulino.

Blossfeld, H.-P. and G. Rohwer (2002), *Techniques of Event History Modeling. New approaches to causal analysis*, 2nd edition, Mahwah, NJ: Lawrence Erlbaum Associates.

Caroleo, F.E. and F. Mazzotta (1998), *Youth Unemployment and Youth Employment Policies in Italy*, Discussion Paper 45, Centro di Economia del Lavoro e di Politica Economica, Università degli Studi di Salerno.

D'Apice, C. and S. Fadda (2003), 'The Italian welfare system in the European context', *Review of Social Economy*, **61** (3), 317–39.

Del Boca, D. and S. Pasqua (2002), *Labour Market Participation of Mothers in Italy: Facts, Studies and Public Policies*, Working Paper 4, Turin: Centre for Household, Income, Labour and Demographic economics (CHILD).

Del Boca, D. and D. Vuri (2005), *Labour Supply and Child Care Costs: The Effect of Rationing*, Discussion Paper 1779, Bonn: Forschungsinstitut zur Zukunft der Arbeit.

Esping-Andersen, G. (1996), 'Welfare states without work: the impasse of labour shedding and familialism in continental European social policy', in G. Esping-Andersen (ed.), *Welfare States in Transition; National Adaptations in Global Economies*, London: Sage.

Esping-Andersen, G. (ed.) (2002), *Why We Need a New Welfare State*, Oxford: Oxford University Press.

Eurostat (2003), *ECHP UDB manual. European Community Household Panel Longitudinal Users' Database. Waves 1 to 8. Survey Years 1994 to 2001*, DOC. PAN 168/2003-12.

Eurostat (various years), *Labour Force Survey*, Luxembourg.

Ferrera, M. (1984), *Il welfare state in Italia. Sviluppo e crisi in prospettiva comparata*, Bologna: il Mulino.

Ferrera, M. (1996), 'The southern model of welfare in social Europe', *Journal of European Social Policy*, **6** (1), 17–37.

Hemerijck, A. (2002), 'The self-transformation of the European social model(s)', in G. Esping-Andersen (ed.), *Why We Need a New Welfare State*, Oxford: Oxford University Press, pp. 173–214.

Iacovou, M. (2003), *Work-Rich and Work-Poor Couples: Polarisation in 14 Countries in Europe*, Working Papers 45, Essex: Institute for Social and Economic Research, University of Essex.

ISTAT (2003), *Rapporto annuale. La situazione del Paese nel 2002*, Rome: ISTAT.

ISTAT (2004), *Rapporto annuale. La situazione del Paese nel 2003*, Rome: ISTAT.

ISTAT (various years), *Rilevazione trimestrale sulle forze di lavoro*, Rome: ISTAT.

Kazepov, Y. (1998), 'Urban poverty and local policies against social exclusion in Italy: the North–South divide', in H.-J. Andreß (ed.), *Empirical Poverty Research in a Comparative Perspective*, Aldershot: Ashgate, pp. 391–422.

Millar, J. and A. Warman (1996), *Family Obligations in Europe*, London: Family Policy Studies Centre.

Negri, N. and C. Saraceno (1996), *Le politiche contro la povertà in Italia*, Bologna: il Mulino.

Ongaro, F. (2001), 'Transition to adulthood in Italy', in M. Corijn and E. Klijzing (eds), *Transitions to Adulthood in Europe*, Dordrecht: Kluwer Academic Publishers, pp. 173–207.

Organisation for Economic Co-operation and Development (OECD) (various years), *Statistical Compendium*, Paris: OECD.

Peña-Casas, R. and M. Latta (2004), *Working Poor in the European Union*, Dublin: European Foundation for the Improvement of Living and Working Conditions.

Powers, D.A. and Y. Xie (2000), *Statistical Methods for Categorical Data Analysis*, San Diego, CA: Academic Press.

Rendtel, U., A. Behr, E. Bellgardt, T. Neukirch, M. Pyy-Martikainen, J. Sisto, R. Lehtonen, T. Harms, E. Basic and I. Marek (2004), *Report on Panel Effects*, Chintex Working Paper # 22, 4 February.

Saraceno, C. (2003), *Mutamenti della famiglia e politiche sociali in Italia*, Bologna: il Mulino.

Schizzerotto, A. and M. Lucchini (2004), 'Transitions to adulthood', in Berthoud, R. and M. Iacovou (eds), *Social Europe. Living Standards and Welfare States*, Cheltenham: Edward Elgar, pp. 46–68.

Sgritta, G.B. (2001), 'Family and welfare systems in the transition to the adulthood', paper presented at the seminar 'Family Forms and the Young Generation in Europe', organized by the European Observatory on the Social Situation,

Demography and Family at the Austrian Institute for Family Studies, Milan, 20–22 September.
Sgritta, G.B. and G. Innocenzi (1993), 'La povertà', in M. Paci (ed.), *Le dimensioni della disuguaglianza, Rapporto della fondazione CESPE sulla disuguaglianza sociale in Italia*, Bologna: il Mulino.
Sorensen, A. and S.S. McLanahan (1987), 'Married women's economic dependence, 1940–1980', *American Journal of Sociology*, **93** (3), 659–87.
Villa, P. (2004), 'La diffusione del modello di famiglia a doppia partecipazione nei paesi europei e in Italia', *Inchiesta*, **XXXIV:146**, 6–20.
Vogel, J. (1997), 'Living conditions and inequality in the European Union', *Statistics in focus. Population and Social Conditions*, **3**, Luxembourg: EUROSTAT.

9. Is work a route out of poverty: what have New Labour's welfare-to-work measures meant for the working poor in Britain?

Sara Connolly

INTRODUCTION

The pioneering studies of poverty in the UK conducted by Rowntree (1901) in the late nineteenth and early twentieth centuries established the points in a life cycle when individuals were most at risk of poverty – childhood, early parenthood and old age – and the associated interactions with the labour market which generated most of these risks – absence of an earned income due to unemployment, ill-health, death of the main income earner or retirement. While much has changed in terms of family structures, the nature of employment and the establishment of the welfare state, Rowntree's insights into the causes of and routes out of poverty remain valid. Most modern-day poverty is associated with the absence of an earned income and the households most at risk remain those with children or those with elderly people.

As a consequence, government intervention in the UK has revolved around finding ways of providing incentives to work for those who can work and supporting those who cannot. This raises the question of whether work does protect households from poverty. Through an examination of trends, incidence and risk factors associated with in-work poverty, the aim of this chapter is to consider the extent to which employment provides an escape route from poverty. We discuss the incidence and composition of the working poor in Britain and consider whether work does indeed pay.

BACKGROUND

The period of Conservative government in the UK (1979–97) was associated with major changes in the style and scope of government policy. The

Thatcher and Major administrations abandoned the post-war consensus on Keynesian-influenced macroeconomic policy and embraced market-led reforms. Labour market policy focused on generating employment and growth through flexible labour markets. This drive towards greater efficiency created a labour market in the UK which is more similar to that in the USA than elsewhere in continental Europe.

Over this period, despite two major recessions, the UK experienced employment growth and there was a change in the composition of employment. Unemployment has fallen from around 12 per cent in the early 1980s to 5 per cent in the early 2000s, the number in employment rose by over 4 million (see National Statistics, 2007). Female employment, particularly part-time employment among women aged 25–40 rose quite markedly, whereas rates of male employment have fallen slightly (see Connolly and Gregory, 2007). The workforce has become better educated, owing to the fall in the numbers leaving full-time education at the earliest age and a growth in participation in higher education (see Department for Children, Schools and Families, 2007). In common with many Organisation for Economic Co-operation and Development (OECD) countries, the UK has experienced a shortening of the typical working life as participation in education delays entry into the labour market and significant numbers of both men and women leave the labour market before the mandatory retirement age (see Connolly and Gregory, 2007). There has also been a significant shift in the industrial composition of employment, with a growth in service sector jobs balancing the contraction in manufacturing.

However, the growth in employment has been accompanied by rising levels of unemployment and labour market inactivity, leading to a growing polarization between households with and without work. Gregg and Wadsworth (2003) show that the number of households without work rose steadily from around 6 per cent in 1975 to 20 per cent in the mid-1990s, falling to around 16 per cent by 2002.

Not only was there growth in the number of households without work, there was also a growth in the variance of income within work.[1] The rising participation in higher education and the high returns to education in the UK[2] led to greater growth in earnings at the upper end of the income distribution. There were also gains at the upper end from returns to investment, particularly in property, and high levels of executive pay. At the same time there were reforms to key labour market institutions which removed protection for those at the lower end of the income distribution. Legislation made it more difficult for unions to organize, influence and take effective action. This combined with the changing industrial composition led to a dramatic decline in trade union membership. Direct government intervention in the setting of pay, either through stipulating minimum levels through the Wages Councils or limiting pay increases through incomes policies, was abolished (see Machin and Gosling, 2004).

These changes in the labour market were accompanied by a variety of tax and welfare reforms which directly influenced the distribution of income.[3] The reforms to the tax system reflected the adoption of supply-side policies as rates of income tax were cut. There were significant gains for those at the upper end of the income distribution when the top rate of income tax was reduced to 40 per cent. Whereas those at the bottom of the income distribution lost out as the shift towards indirect rather than direct taxation meant that those outside the labour market became taxpayers and were paying more in tax as the rate of indirect tax rose from 8 per cent to 15 per cent and is now 17.5 per cent. Finally, the decision to index welfare payments to prices, rather than to incomes, meant that, for those outside the labour market, income levels fell further behind.

The combined effect of these changes was growing inequality primarily driven by gains among those in the upper half of the income distribution. In real terms, the income of the top 10 per cent rose at a much higher rate than that of the median, and the real income of the bottom 10 per cent hardly rose at all (see Figure 9.1).[4]

There were serious implications for the level of poverty which having been stable at around 10–12 per cent for most of the post-war period, suddenly rose to over 20 per cent by the early 1990s. There were particularly worrying rises in the incidence of childhood and pensioner poverty (see Figure 9.2).

When New Labour were elected in 1997, they saw their main challenge as retaining the positive features of the flexible labour market, while at the same time addressing the problems of inequality and poverty. Since 1997 levels of inequality have continued to rise but levels of poverty have fallen. Between 1997 and 2006, the Gini coefficient rose from 0.33 to 0.35 (Institute for Fiscal Studies, 2006). Interestingly, other measures of inequality, such as the 90:10 ratio, have fallen which suggests that the rising inequality is a consequence of changes at the extremes of the distribution of income (see Brewer et al., 2007). Overall levels of poverty have fallen, from 14 million people below the poverty line in 1997 to 12.7 million in 2006, this is the longest sustained fall in poverty recorded in the UK. However, the figures since 2005–06 show the first rise in overall poverty since 1997, an increased incidence of child poverty and a slight rise in pensioner poverty in 2006–07.

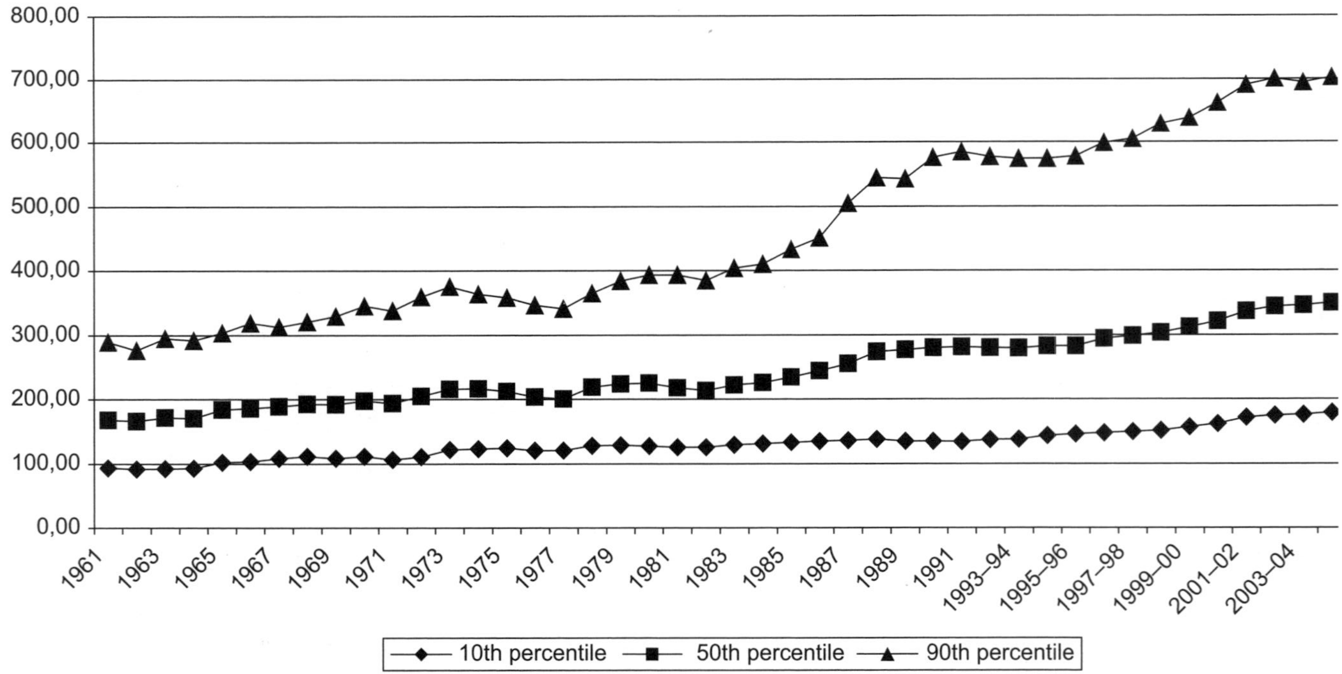

Source: Data taken from the Institute for Fiscal Studies (2006).

Figure 9.1 Growth of income inequality in the UK

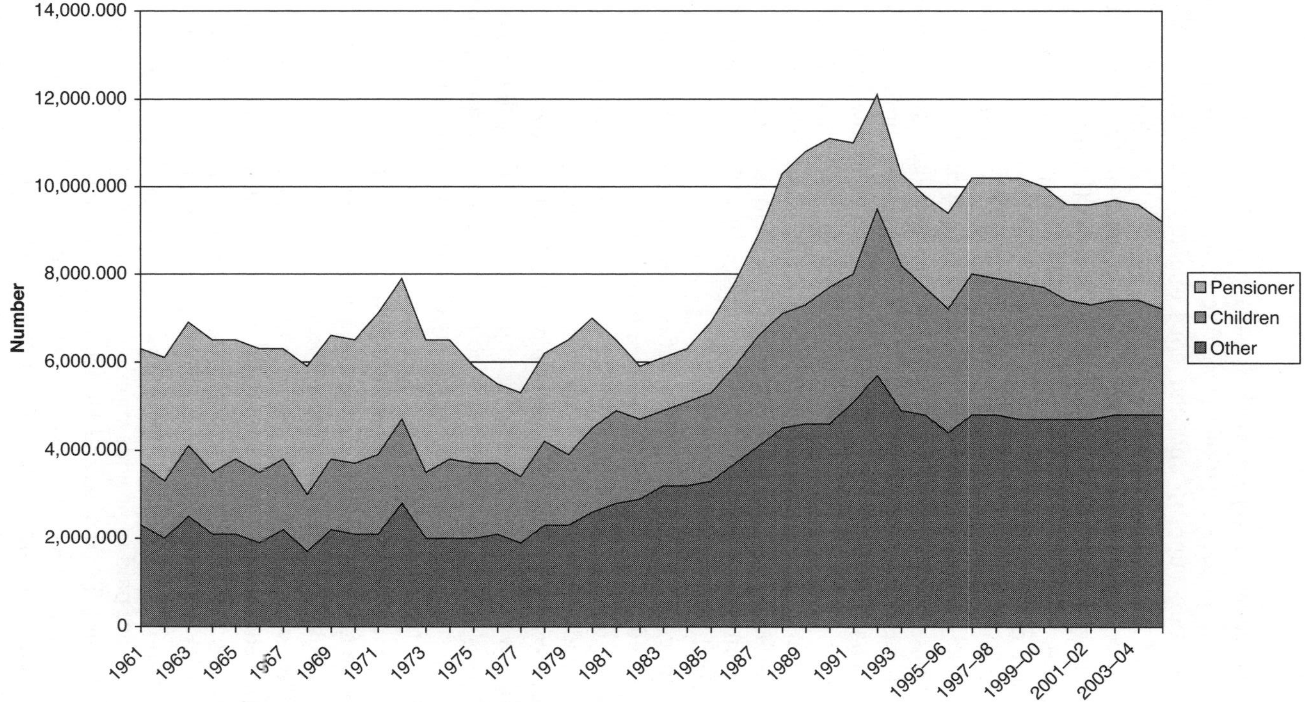

Source: Data taken from the Institute for Fiscal Studies (2006).

Figure 9.2 Growth of poverty in the UK – 60% of contemporary median

WELFARE POLICY IN THE UK

In the UK successive governments have struggled to find an appropriate balance between the safety net of the welfare state, the increasing number reliant on welfare support and the consequences for overall welfare expenditure. Expenditure on benefits has risen steadily from 4.2 per cent of gross domestic product (GDP) in 1948–49 to a peak of 12.6 per cent in 1993–94, falling slightly to 11.3 per cent in 2004–05 (Institute for Fiscal Studies, 2006). Not only is this type of welfare expenditure steadily growing, there is also evidence of greater swings in the cyclical patterns.

Since the 1970s there have been a number of economic and demographic pressures which have led to this steady growth in welfare expenditure: changing economic conditions have led to higher average rates of unemployment; increased life expectancy has led to a rise in the number of pensioners; and changing family structures have resulted in a growing number of lone parent families. These changes have meant that there are more households in receipt of welfare over long periods of time, who may never return to the labour market – this generates a serious challenge to the welfare state which was built upon the assumption of full employment and that relief would be temporary.

The system combines contingent benefits (where a given level of assistance is provided for those falling within a certain category or risk group) with means-tested benefits (where the level of support is related to total household income). There are important trade-offs between the two approaches. Contingent benefits are simple to administer and are less likely to generate poverty or unemployment traps but, unless the risk categories are very closely associated with low income or poverty, are an expensive tool. Means-testing allows greater targeting of assistance and may be more appropriate if the risk factors are more varied, but there are significant administrative costs and they generate disincentives to work. Welfare support in the UK has steadily moved towards a system of income related benefits, although one main contingent benefit – child benefit[5] – remains.

The welfare system in the UK provides five main types of assistance: for the unemployed, for those unable to work due to ill-health or disability, for the retired, for those on low income and, increasingly, for families (see Phillips and Sibieta, 2006, for more details). Rather than giving an extensive discussion of each of these measures, we provide brief details for the benefits which are paid to provide support to those in employment: Income Support, Working Tax Credit and Housing Benefit. Income Support is the main safety net provided for those on low income. This benefit is paid to top up household income which falls below an 'applicable amount'; both the level of payment and the benchmark income is sensitive to age and the household structure.[6] The Working Tax Credit was introduced in 2003, it is means-tested and paid to working households when at least one member of the household is working more than a threshold of hours (discussed below; also see Marx and Verbist in this volume for a more general discussion of tax credit systems in the USA and the UK and their effectiveness as an anti-poverty tool). Finally, Housing Benefit provides households with financial support to cover housing costs – both for rented and owner-occupied accommodation.[7]

WELFARE POLICY UNDER NEW LABOUR

The growing levels of inequality and poverty in the UK have influenced the design and thrust of welfare under New Labour policy. Recent welfare reform combines a focus on sharpening incentives for employment but has been accompanied by measures which directly target the groups most at risk of poverty (for example, families) along with more generous levels of support. Welfare to work is often used as an umbrella term for a range of initiatives introduced by New Labour with the overarching aim of encouraging as many as possible into the labour market and ensuring that work pays. It encompasses the various forms of the New Deal, the system of Tax Credits which aim to smooth the path into employment by reducing/eliminating any welfare traps and preventing low wages through the introduction of a National Minimum Wage. We look at each of these in detail and then assess the likely impact of this range of measures upon overall and in-work poverty.

The New Deal was one of the first major policy initiatives under New Labour. The main aim was to reduce the levels of long-term unemployment that existed in key target groups – the young (18–24-year-olds), older workers (aged over 50) and lone parents. The 'deal' is that each unemployed person (unemployed for more than six months) is allocated a personal adviser who provides help with job search. If, after four months, this is unsuccessful the unemployed person is offered the option of training or employment in the voluntary sector, on the Environmental Task Force or subsidized employment in the private sector. Should the unemployed person reject the option, then benefits are withheld.[8] This mixture of 'carrot and stick' seems to have worked well: the government claims that just under half a million long-term unemployed found work under the New Deal programme (Department for Work and Pensions, 2004).

Historically, most welfare assistance was administered by one department (Social Security) and tax collected by a separate government department (Inland Revenue). This generated administrative costs, and lack of co-ordination between the two systems often led to welfare traps. The recent move towards a system of Tax Credits has meant that many in-work benefits are integrated within the tax system and are the responsibility of a single department – HM Revenue and Customs.[9] The Tax Credit system has been designed to improve incentives to work, particularly for families, through providing more generous welfare assistance (both in terms of value of the benefits and coverage) and subsidizing child care. This was achieved initially by two separate Tax Credits – the Working Family Tax Credit and the Child Care Tax Credit – but these have now been integrated into the Working Tax Credit. Eligibility is dependent upon hours worked and the number of children, for example, in a household with no children, the worker must be over 25 and working more than 30 hours a week, whereas in a household with children, at least one adult must be working for more than 16 hours a week. Further payments are made to support additional costs, associated with childcare, disability or for older workers returning to employment. In line with government policy to provide support for families, eligibility for the tax credits has been extended to include middle-class families who would not previously have been in receipt of in-work welfare assistance.

As part of the policy of making work pay a national minimum wage was introduced in 1999 (see Table 9.1). There are now three rates: an adult rate for all workers aged 22 or older, a development rate for workers aged 18 to 21 and a recently introduced youth rate for workers aged 16 to 17. The National Minimum Wage has had greatest impact upon those working in low-paid sectors of the economy, and has been of particular benefit to women, especially those in part-time employment.[10]

Table 9.1 Rates of the National Minimum Wage

Year	Adult rate workers 22 or older	Development rate workers aged 18 to 21	Youth rate workers aged 16 to 17
1 April 1999	£3.60	£3.00	
1 October 2000	£3.70	£3.20	
1 October 2001	£4.10	£3.50	
1 October 2002	£4.20	£3.60	
1 October 2003	£4.50	£3.80	
1 October 2004	£4.85	£4.10	£3.00
1 October 2005	£5.05	£4.25	£3.00
1 October 2006	£5.35	£4.45	£3.30
1 October 2007	£5.52	£4.60	£3.40

Source: Low Pay Commission (2007).

The main welfare-to-work initiatives – the New Deal, the Working Tax Credits and the National Minimum Wage – have contributed towards the reduction in poverty through increasing employment and by raising the incomes of those in employment. The New Deal has been successful in reducing the levels of long-term unemployment at a rate above that which would have occurred through the general improvement in macroeconomic conditions (Blundell et al., 2003). The combination of the New Deal for lone parents and the Working Tax Credits, seem to have increased employment rates and income levels for lone parents (Gregg and Harkness, 2003).

The National Minimum Wage mainly applies to women and, more recently, young workers – who are typically in households with other workers – and so it was not expected to reduce levels of poverty. However, Dickens (1999) reported a growing link between low pay and poverty, and Dickens and Manning (2003) argue that this has meant that the National Minimum Wage has become a slightly more effective anti-poverty tool. They show that a quarter of those in the bottom two deciles of the income distribution gained from the changes to the National Minimum Wage. There do not appear to have been employment losses generated by either the introduction or upgrading of rates of the National Minimum Wage,[11] so, despite fears voiced by opponents, the minimum wage appears to have slightly reduced the incidence of poverty in the UK.

The various Tax Credit schemes have increased the incomes of those in employment and this, in combination with higher wages due to the growth in the economy and the National Minimum Wage, has meant that there are stronger incentives to enter employment. However, one concern has been that because the Tax Credits, which cover a much larger number of households than under previous systems, are means tested with taper rates of around 40 per cent, more households are now facing higher effective marginal rates of taxation. Therefore, incentives to enter employment may have risen but incentives to work for those within employment may have fallen. Adam et al. (2006) show that for those in employment the average marginal effective rate of taxation has risen, those working longer hours keep 2.5 pence less from each extra pound earned. However, the structure of the Tax Credit system is very sensitive to household composition. Adam et al. (2006) also show that some of those who had traditionally faced the poorest work incentives, for example, lone parents, now have much stronger work incentives.

The welfare-to-work initiatives which were designed to encourage employment and make work pay have reduced levels of poverty but have also created a larger income gap between those in and out of work, which contributes towards the persistence of income inequality. However, not all those in employment benefit equally and the impact on levels of working poverty is likely to be uneven. Tax Credits are mainly paid to families[12] and the eligibility conditions are tougher and rates of benefit lower for the young and single. The National Minimum Wage covers very few men and is set at a lower rate for workers aged 22 or younger leaving the young (and often poorly skilled) with very limited protection against low pay. For example, in 2004–05, someone working a 40-hour week would earn £194 a week if they were covered by the adult rate, £164 if they were covered by the development rate and £120 if they were covered by the youth rate. The poverty line for a single person in that year was £127.73, therefore in the absence of in-work benefits a young single person (aged 16–17) working full-time on the minimum wage would fall below the poverty line.[13] Therefore, while we might expect increased employment among a broad range of workers who benefit from the improved incentives alongside a reduction in poverty for families (especially lone mothers) who are eligible for Tax Credits, there may be a continued exposure to in-work poverty for the young and single – those who are not eligible for Tax Credits or not covered by the Adult National Minimum Wage.

POVERTY AND INEQUALITY IN THE UK

As we have already seen, levels of inequality and poverty in the UK rose quite significantly between the late 1970s and the late 1990s.[14] In the UK, the incidence and degree of poverty is measured at the household level – whether household income falls below a relative poverty line, that is, whether household income (before housing costs) falls below 60 per cent of the contemporary median. As we have already discussed, most welfare support is means-tested, therefore eligibility reflects household demographics and income. As a consequence, the incidence of poverty and the effectiveness of the welfare system is typically measured with reference to the employment status and demographics of the household. Furthermore, recent policy in the UK has sought to tackle these high levels of poverty (the government has set fairly ambitious targets for reductions in child and pensioner poverty), therefore poverty levels are typically calculated across age and family types.

The UK government undertakes an annual analysis of poverty and social exclusion (Households Below Average Income) using data from the Family Resources Survey (FRS). Taking the number of households with income below the poverty line, we find that absence of work is still the main factor leading to poverty in the UK (see Figure 9.3). For example, in 2004–05, the households at greatest risk of poverty are either those

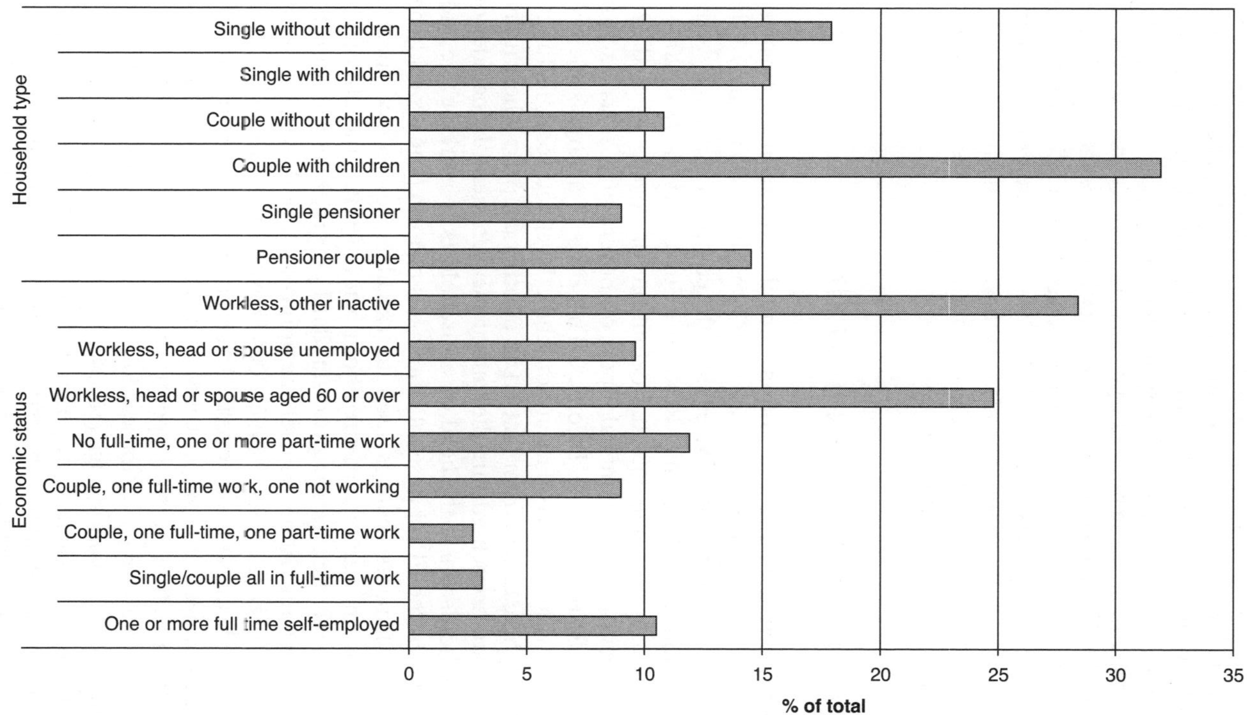

Source: Department of Work and Pensions (1996–2005), data taken from the Family Resources Survey.

Figure 9.3 Composition of poor households, 2004–05 (%)

completely outside the labour market or those with limited attachment to the labour market: workless households account for around 62 per cent, households with only one worker account for around 24 per cent of all poor households, whereas households with two workers in full-time employment account for only 3 per cent of all poor households.

Despite the range of the highly targeted set of policy measures discussed above – for families and pensioners – the households most at risk of poverty remain those with children and pensioners (see Figure 9.3), although, the risks are diminishing (Palmer et al., 2005: 29 – data taken from the Family Resources Survey). However, it seems that these measures have left another group behind, those of working age without children are now more vulnerable to low incomes and poverty.

THE WORKING POOR IN BRITAIN

Despite the strength of the UK economy and the growth in employment, a significant proportion of poor households (35 per cent, see Figure 9.3) have at least one member in work. We explore the composition of the working poor using data from the Family Resources Surveys 1996–97 to 2004–05. Our analysis uses the same data and definitions of poverty as used by the UK government in its own annual report on poverty and social exclusion (Households Below Average Income). The FRS is a large-scale cross-section study which collects data at household level and so, unfortunately, the approach here differs from that taken in other chapters where individuals rather than households are the unit of measurement. It includes over 13 000 households where the head of household is of working age and in employment. In the FRS household income is measured on a weekly basis and the McClements scale is used to calculate equivalized income.[15] Household income can be measured both before (BHC) and after (AHC) housing costs. We start by using two standard poverty lines (60 per cent of median income and 50 per cent of mean income), both before and after housing costs over the period 1996–2005. Beyond this, for simplicity, we focus on a single measure of poverty – whether equivalized income before housing costs falls below 60 per cent of the contemporary median – and contrast the position at three points in time (1996–97, 2000–01 and 2004–05). All figures refer to households where the head of household is in employment and of working age (16–64).

We start by establishing some general trends. First, the incidence of in-work poverty – using all four measures – has risen quite steadily over the 10-year period 1996–2005 (see Figure 9.4). This is in contrast to the fall in overall poverty identified in Figure 9.1.

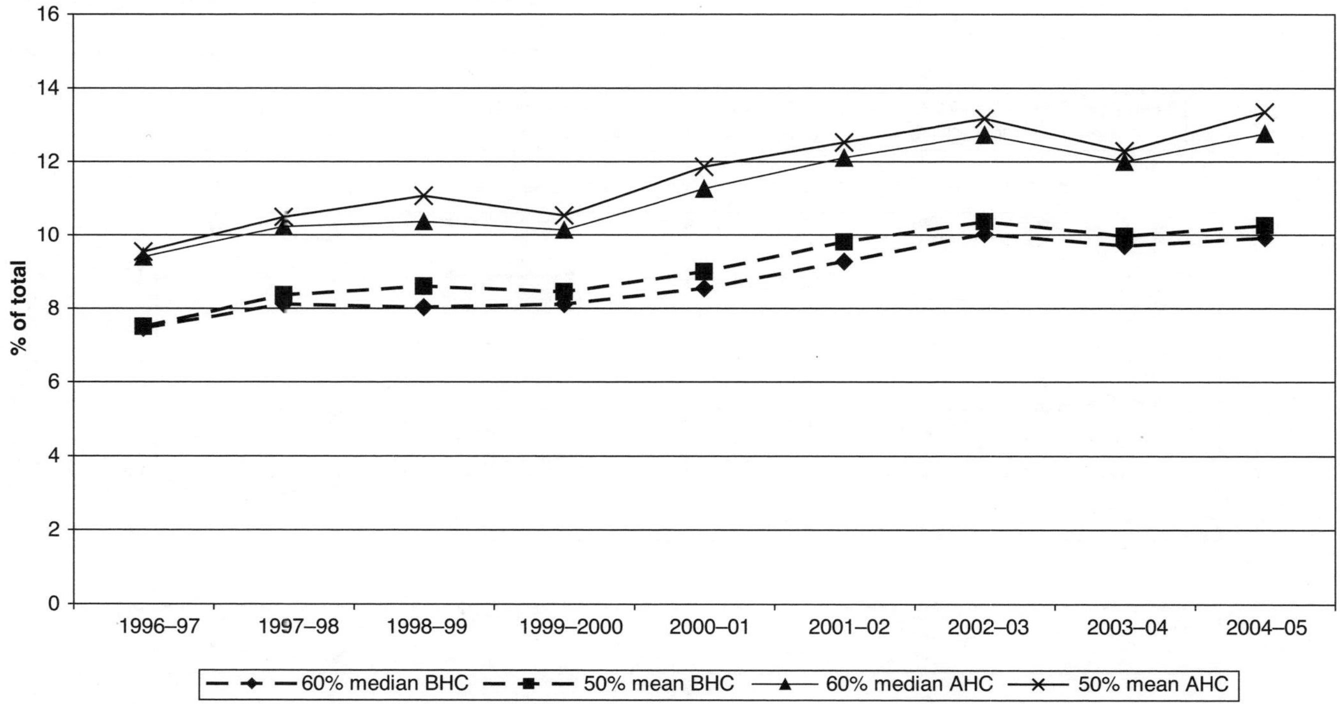

Source: Family Resources Surveys 1996–2005, own calculations.

Figure 9.4 Incidence of in-work poverty, 1996 to 2005 (%)

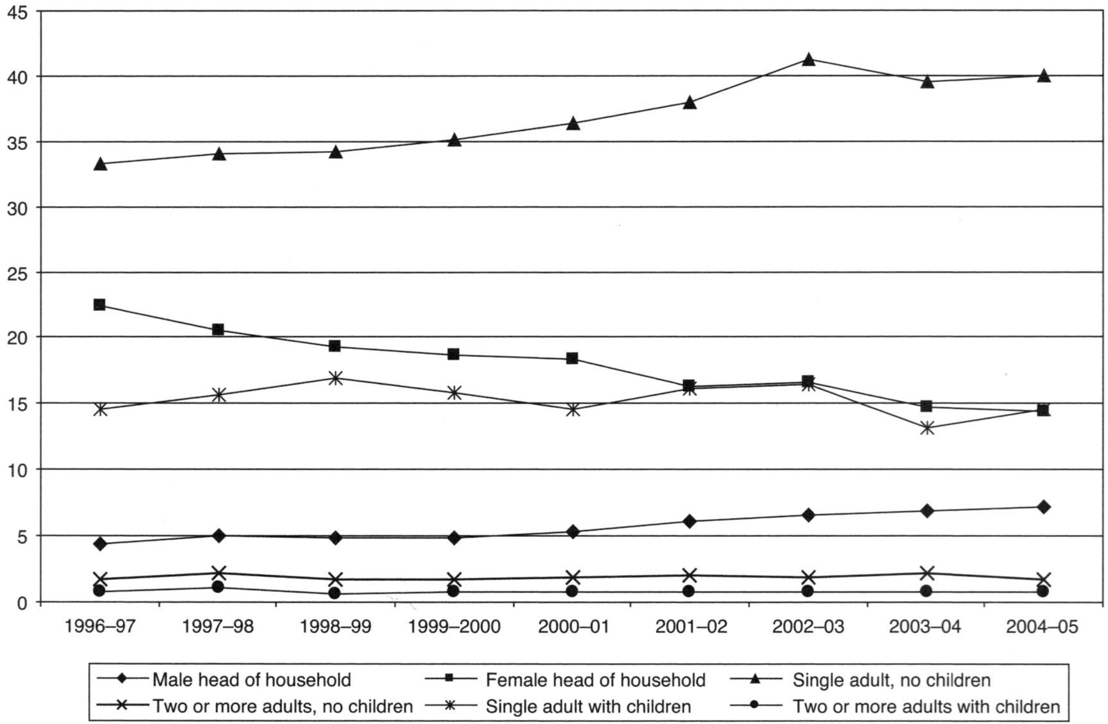

Source: Family Resources Surveys 1996–2005, own calculations.

Figure 9.5 Working poor by gender and household composition (%)

Second, there has been a significant reduction in the proportion of working poor households which are headed by women (see Figure 9.5). Finally, looking at which household types are more at risk of in-work poverty, we see that single adult households with no children are at greatest risk of in-work poverty and that they account for an increasing proportion of the working poor. There is also a high risk of in-work poverty in single-parent households but this risk has remained broadly constant.

We now turn to a more detailed analysis of the composition of the working poor and how this has changed over time (see Table 9.2). The likelihood of being in a single-adult household is related to age. We find that among those in work, the risk of in-work poverty is always highest when the head of household is young – aged 16 to 25. The risk for this group is high but constant over time, the risks are rising for all other age groups and this is most noticeable among those approaching retirement – aged 55 to 64. Most studies of poverty report that education reduces the risk of poverty both in terms of reducing the likelihood of worklessness and of in-work poverty. We find that in-work poverty rates are lower when the head of household left full-time education after the current minimum school leaving age of 16.[16] The risks are greatest – and rising – for those where the head of household left school before age 16 and who are as a consequence without qualifications. There are higher rates of in-work poverty where the head of household is non-white. The risks are highest and rising when the head of household is African or Caribbean (labelled 'Black' in Table 9.2). Interestingly, the risks appear to be falling when the head of household is from the Indian or Pakistani/Bangladeshi population. The likelihood of experiencing in-work poverty is bound to reflect the likelihood of experiencing low pay. Lower rates of pay are associated with certain industries and we find a greater (although slightly declining) incidence of in-work poverty when the head of household works in the hospitality sectors and rising incidence of in-work poverty for those working in agriculture and the retail sectors. Finally, rates of pay are often lower for those whose employment opportunities may be limited by sickness or disability and we find a higher (and rising) risk of in-work poverty associated with poor health status of the head of household.

This analysis has enabled us to identify risk factors but many of the characteristics identified will be interrelated. To disentangle these effects we run a set of logit models and evaluate probabilities controlling for given characteristics. We find that across the period that the same characteristics are associated with the risk of in-work poverty – where the head of household is a single adult, young, poorly educated, non-white – particularly Pakistani/Bangladeshi and working in hotels or restaurants (see Table 9.3).

Table 9.2 In-work poverty rate by characteristics of the household head (%)

Characteristics of the household head	1996–97	2000–01	2004–05
Age group			
16–24 years	22.6	22.1	22.9
25–34 years	6.4	8.6	9.3
35–44 years	4.9	5.7	7.0
45–54 years	7.3	8.2	8.9
55–64 years	11.3	11.7	14.4
Educational background			
Left full-time education before age 16	10.3	11.7	15.7
Left full-time education at age 16	7.4	8.6	10.2
Left full-time education between ages 17 and 18	7.5	8.2	8.8
Left full-time education between ages 19 and 21	4.7	5.7	7.4
Left full-time education aged 22 or older	3.6	6.1	6.4
Ethnicity			
White	7.4	8.3	9.8
Black	13.6	16.2	16.0
Indian	6.3	7.0	3.9
Pakistani/Bangladeshi	8.4	13.3	9.2
Other	8.3	11.3	11.5
Industry of occupation			
Agriculture and fisheries	11.6	14.2	15.7
Mining and mineral extraction	3.6	3.3	2.4
Non-metal manufacturing	7.1	6.8	8.3
Metal manufacturing	4.1	4.5	7.0
Energy and water	1.8	5.8	4.9
Construction	4.6	5.3	7.6
Sales and retail	10.0	12.2	15.5
Hotels and restaurants	22.3	20.8	20.5
Transport and communication	7.0	8.1	8.2
Finance and banking	4.1	4.8	6.1
Other services	5.7	7.5	9.4
Education and welfare	7.9	8.7	8.3
Other	15.9	15.2	15.3
Disability			
No disability	7.1	8.0	9.2
Experiences sickness or disability	11.1	12.8	16.9

Source: Family Resources Surveys 1996–97, 2000–01 and 2004–05; own calculations.

Table 9.3 Risk factors of experiencing in-work poverty (logistic regression coefficients)

Characteristics of the household and the household's head	1996–97	2000–01	2004–05
Female	0.595***	0.536***	0.510***
	(0.099)	(0.092)	(0.083)
Age of head of household			
16–24 years	1.418***	1.374***	1.289***
	(0.171)	(0.174)	(0.156)
25–34 years	0.117	0.315**	0.292**
	(0.118)	(0.112)	(0.104)
35–44 years	–	–	–
45–54 years	0.180	0.332**	0.179
	(0.124)	(0.119)	(0.107)
55–64 years	0.489***	0.596***	0.483***
	(0.142)	(0.139)	(0.118)
Education of head of household			
Left full-time education before age 16	0.548***	0.347**	0.491***
	(0.111)	(0.114)	(0.108)
Left full-time education at age 16	–	–	–
Left full-time education between ages 17 and 18	−0.427***	−0.445***	−0.491***
	(0.117)	(0.114)	(0.103)
Left full-time education between ages 19 and 21	−0.921***	−1.095***	−0.756***
	(0.164)	(0.152)	(0.127)
Left full-time education age 22 or older	−1.187***	−0.874***	−0.987***
	(0.178)	(0.148)	(0.130)
Ethnicity of head of household			
White	–	–	–
Black	0.744**	0.721**	0.646**
	(0.264)	(0.217)	(0.205)
Indian	1.444***	0.851*	0.110
	(0.394)	(0.391)	(0.402)
Pakistani/Bangladeshi	1.538**	2.494***	1.012*
	(0.444)	(0.362)	(0.406)
Other	0.551	0.860**	0.495*
	(0.389)	(0.290)	(0.230)
Industry in which head of household works			
Agriculture and fisheries	0.739**	0.989**	1.080**
	(0.284)	(0.311)	(0.325)
Mining and mineral extraction	−0.169	−1.170	−1.476
	(0.393)	(0.667)	(0.781)
Non-metal manufacturing	−0.140	−0.381	0.001
	(0.198)	(0.208)	(0.203)

Table 9.3 (continued)

Characteristics of the household and the household's head	1996–97	2000–01	2004–05
Metal manufacturing	−0.467*	−0.624**	−0.350
	(0.218)	(0.216)	(0.200)
Energy and water	−1.201	0.098	−0.560
	(0.771)	(0.527)	(0.510)
Construction	–	–	–
Sales and retail	0.465*	0.538**	0.722***
	(0.200)	(0.190)	(0.171)
Hotels and restaurants	1.125***	0.928***	0.971***
	(0.238)	(0.232)	(0.216)
Transport and communication	0.137	−0.064	−0.174
	(0.222)	(0.210)	(0.197)
Finance and banking	−0.800**	−0.772**	−0.651**
	(0.276)	(0.270)	(0.225)
Other services	−0.138	0.033	0.013
	(0.227)	(0.208)	(0.185)
Education and welfare	−0.320	−0.338	−0.409*
	(0.197)	(0.186)	(0.166)
Other	0.802***	0.674**	0.596**
	(0.227)	(0.215)	(0.186)
Disability			
Head of household experiences sickness or disability	0.477***	0.541***	0.797***
	(0.126)	(0.112)	(0.107)
Household composition			
Single adult, no children	3.680***	3.738***	4.075***
	(0.133)	(0.128)	(0.124)
Two or more adults without children	–	–	–
Single adult with children	2.018***	1.976***	2.227***
	(0.190)	(0.173)	(0.162)
Two or more adults with children	−0.393*	−0.824***	−0.388*
	(0.196)	(0.215)	(0.197)
Constant	−5.926***	−5.695***	−5.733***
	(0.275)	(0.260)	(0.249)
Number of obs	13166	12489	13569
LR chi2(39)	2783.74	2944.86	3649.07
Log likelihood	−2101.64	−2172.45	−2560.31
Pseudo R^2	0.3984	0.404	0.4161

Notes: Model also includes controls for regions. Significant at $p < 0.1$ (***), $p < 1$ (**), $p < 5$ (*). Standard errors in parentheses.

Source: Family Resources Surveys 1996–97, 2000–01 and 2004–05; own calculations.

Table 9.4 Estimated probabilities of experiencing in-work poverty (%)

Characteristics of the household's head	1996–97		2004–05	
	Male	Female	Male	Female
Representative	0.19	0.35	0.21	0.36
Left full-time education at age < 16	0.33	0.60	0.35	0.58
Young, age 16–24	0.79	1.43	0.77	1.28
Single adult household	7.17	12.23	11.23	17.41
Young, single adult household, no children	24.09	36.51	31.47	43.34
Young, single adult household, no children, left full-time education before age 16	35.44	49.88	42.87	55.56

Source: Author's own calculations using eimated coefficients from Table 9.3.

To illustrate the results and attempt to identify which might be the greatest risk factors, we evaluate the probability of experiencing in-work poverty for households with average characteristics – where the head of household is in a two or more adult household without children, aged 35–44, left full-time education at age 16, white and working in education and welfare. We then examine the sensitivity of these probabilities to changes in particular characteristics – keeping other characteristics at the mean. Finally, we illustrate some extreme cases by compounding some of the characteristics which we know to be related – age, household composition and educational background (see Table 9.4).

These evaluated probabilities show that for our representative male- or female-headed household the risk of in-work poverty is low but has risen slightly. The risks are higher when the head of household left full-time education before they were 16 and higher still if they are young. We can also see that – controlling for age, education, ethnicity, industry – the greatest risk of in-work poverty is experienced by those in single-adult households and has risen significantly over this period. Finally, when we consider the probability of experiencing in-work poverty for someone who is young and a single adult or a young, poorly qualified single adult, we find that the risks rise quite dramatically reflecting their low earnings potential.

HOW HAVE THE WORKING POOR FARED UNDER NEW LABOUR?

Since 1997, the UK has experienced a period of economic growth – unemployment and inflation have remained low. The combination of favourable macroeconomic conditions, the growth in earnings and the government's welfare-to-work measures have meant that employment has risen, that poverty rates have fallen, but there has been little change in income inequality. However, the incidence of in-work poverty has risen and the UK now has the highest recorded level of poverty among working-age adults without children. Our analysis here has shown that the risks of in-work poverty are particularly acute for those who are young and living on their own.

There are a number of explanations for the rise in in-work poverty. The first is that we are using a relative definition of poverty. Since 1997 average incomes have been rising at a faster rate than those at the bottom (over the period as a whole average incomes rose by 2.3 per cent compared with a 2.2 per cent rise in the bottom quintile). Given this, more households will fall below our poverty line. Second, many of the welfare to work measures which aim to encourage work provide targeted in-work benefits to families, thus exposing those without children to greater risks of poverty. Third, while the National Minimum Wage provides welcome protection against low pay, the full rate only applies to workers aged 22 or older. So not only are younger single workers not entitled to welfare support through Tax Credits, they also experience less protection against low pay. Finally, the National Minimum Wage itself has been set at a cautious rate, balancing protection against low pay against protection of jobs, for example, the adult rate in 2005–06 was £5.35 per hour which was below the two-thirds of the median hourly rate in 2005–06 of £5.60. Therefore, employment at the current adult minimum wage without further welfare assistance does not guarantee an income above the poverty line.

The reductions in poverty, particularly the fall in child poverty have been achieved through a combination of reduced risks of worklessness through the growth in employment and targeted welfare assistance, which have reduced average risks of poverty for families. The Joseph Rowntree Foundation (Palmer et al., 2006) estimate that of the fall of 0.7 million children experiencing poverty – 0.5 million can be attributed to the increased welfare support for families and 0.2 million to the growth in income through employment. In conclusion, in the UK, work on its own does not provide a route out of poverty.

NOTES

1. See Brewer et al. (2007) for a full discussion of trends in inequality and poverty in the UK, earlier studies include Atkinson (1983; 1996), Jenkins (1996), Machin and Gosling (1994) and Jenkins and Van Kerm (2006).

2. The private returns to education, particularly to higher education, are higher than elsewhere in Europe (OECD, 2005).
3. See Institute for Fiscal Studies publications for more details – Adam and Browne (2006) on the UK tax system and Phillips and Sibieta (2006) on the UK benefit system.
4. The Gini coefficient rose from 0.25 to 0.34 between 1979 and the early 1990s (Institute for Fiscal Studies, 2006).
5. This is paid on a weekly basis for all children under the age of 16 (19 if they are in full-time education), there is a higher rate for the eldest or only child (£17.45 in 2006) and a lower rate (£11.70 in 2006) for all other children. In 2006, 7.4 million families were in receipt of child benefit at a cost of £9.77 billion.
6. Income Support is paid to all low income households (within and outside of the labour market). A recent development has been the requirement that new claimants who are unemployed should attend a 'work-focused interview' – the idea, based on some aspects of the New Deal (discussed below), is to encourage claimants to retain some attachment to the labour market.
7. Any household in receipt of Income Support automatically receives the full value of Housing Benefit; it is means-tested for other households.
8. The element of compulsion and penalties have not yet been applied to lone parents. Lone parents have been invited rather than compelled to participate, although recent ministerial statements (spring 2007) suggest that this may change.
9. There have been concerns over the efficiency of this system. Calculations are based on the previous year's income, claimants are then required to inform the department of any changes in circumstances and this has led to overpayments. In addition, the online application process which was intended to facilitate applications has been suspended because it had been targeted by organized gangs of fraudsters. A recent report by the UK National Audit Office (2007) draws attention to the continued high levels of fraud and errors associated with the Working Tax Credit. They estimate these have generated losses of £9.6 billion (14.7 per cent of total payments) since 2003, overpayment accounts for £6.6 billion and fraud £3 billion. These rates of incorrect payment are considerably higher than elsewhere – the 2006 annual report of the Department for Work and Pensions reports an average rate of incorrect payments of just under 6 per cent of total payments for other means-tested benefits (Income Support, Job Seeker's Allowance and Housing Benefit).
10. The proportion of workers aged 22 or over who are paid less than two-thirds of the median hourly wage (£6.50 in 2005) has fallen from 37 per cent of women and 17 per cent of men in 2000 to 29 per cent and 14 per cent respectively in 2005 (see Low Pay Commission, 2007).
11. Although Dickens and Manning (2003) report some small falls in employment in some particularly low-paying sectors (for example, care homes).
12. In 2005–06 5.3 million households received Working Tax Credits, of which 5 million received Child Tax Credits and 1.8 million received Working Tax Credits (see Phillips and Sibieta, 2006; UK National Audit Office, 2007).
13. This was the first year of the youth rate, so the situation would have been more acute in previous years.
14. Townsend (1979) is the classic modern reference for a comprehensive study of the causes and incidence of poverty in the UK. Other more recent studies include Atkinson (1996), Biewen and Jenkins (2005), Cappellari and Jenkins (2002) and Jenkins and Micklewright (2007).
15. The UK government has historically used the McClements scale. The main differences between the McClements and modified OECD scales are the differences in treatment of the additional costs and potential economies of scale associated with different household types. The modified OECD scale is more straightforward, the weights attached to additional adults and children are constant but with the McClements scale they vary according to nature of relationship, number and age.
16. The Minimum School Leaving Age has been 16 since 1973–74.

REFERENCES

Adam, S. and J. Browne (2006), *A Survey of the UK Tax System, Briefing Note No 9*, London: Institute for Fiscal Studies.

Adam, S., M. Brewer and A. Shephard (2006), *Financial Work Incentives in Britain: Comparisons over Time and between Family Types, WP 06/20*, London: Institute for Fiscal Studies.

Atkinson, A.B. (1983), *The Economics of Inequality*, 2nd edition, Oxford: Oxford University Press.

Atkinson, A.B. (1996), 'Seeking to explain the distribution of income', in J. Hills (ed.), *New Inequalities: The Changing Distribution of Income and Wealth in the United Kingdom*, Cambridge: Cambridge University Press.

Biewen, M. and S.P. Jenkins (2005), 'Accounting for differences in poverty between the USA, Britain and Germany', *Empirical Economics*, **30** (2), 331–58.

Blundell, R., H. Reed, J. van Reenen and A. Shephard (2003), 'The impact of the new deal for young people on the labour market: a four year assessment', in R. Dickens, P. Gregg and J. Wadsworth (eds), *The Labour Market under New Labour: The State of Working Britain*, Basingstoke: Palgrave Macmillan, pp. 17–31.

Brewer, M., A. Goodman, A. Muriel and L. Sibieta (2007), *Poverty and Inequality in the UK: 2007*, Briefing Note 73, London: Institute for Fiscal Studies.

Cappellari, L. and S.P. Jenkins (2002), 'Who stays poor? Who becomes poor? Evidence from the British Household Panel Survey', *Economic Journal*, **112** (478), C60–C67.

Connolly, S. and M. Gregory (2007), 'Women and work', in N.F.R. Crafts, I. Gazeley, and A. Newell (eds), *Work and Pay in 20th Century Britain*, Oxford: Oxford University Press, pp. 142–77.

Department for Children, Schools and Families (previously Department of Education and Skills) (2007), *Trends in Education and Skills*, www.dfes.gov.uk/trends/ (accessed 27 November 2007).

Department for Work and Pensions (1996–2005), *Households below Average Income*, www.dwp.gov.uk/asd/hbai.asp (accessed 28 November 2007).

Department for Work and Pensions (2004), *Building on New Deal: Local Solutions Meeting Individual Needs*, London, www.dwp.gov.uk/publications/dwp/2004/buildingonnewdeal/mainreport.pdf (accessed 27 November 2007).

Department for Work and Pensions (2006), *Department for Work and Pensions – Departmental Report*, Cm 6829, www.dwp.gov.uk/publications/dwp/2006/dr 06/ (accessed 28 November 2007).

Dickens, R. (1999), 'Poverty, low pay and the National Minimum Wage', in *The National Minimum Wage, Incomes and the Low Paid*, Low Pay Commission Occasional Paper 2, London: Low Pay Commission, pp. 201–13.

Dickens, R. and A. Manning (2003), 'Minimum wage, minimum impact', in R. Dickens, P. Gregg and J. Wadsworth (eds), *The Labour Market under New Labour: The State of Working Britain*, Basingstoke: Palgrave Macmillan, pp. 98–115.

Gregg, P. and S. Harkness (2003), 'Welfare reform and the employment of lone parents', in R. Dickens, P. Gregg and J. Wadsworth (eds), *The Labour Market under New Labour: The State of Working Britain*, Basingstoke: Palgrave Macmillan, pp. 86–97.

Gregg, P. and J. Wadsworth (2003), 'Labour market prospects of less skilled workers over the recovery', in R. Dickens, P. Gregg and J. Wadsworth (eds), *The Labour*

Market under New Labour: The State of Working Britain, Basingstoke: Palgrave Macmillan.

Institute for Fiscal Studies (2006), *Inequality and Poverty Spreadsheet*, www.ifs.org.uk/projects_research.php?heading_id=8 (accessed 27th November 2007).

Jenkins, S.P. (1996), 'Recent trends in the UK income distribution: what happened and why', *Oxford Review of Economic Policy*, **12** (1), 29–46.

Jenkins, S.P. and P. van Kerm (2006), 'Trends in income inequality, pro-poor income growth and income mobility', *Oxford Economic Papers*, **58** (3), 531–48.

Jenkins, S.P. and J. Micklewright (2007), *Inequality and Poverty Re-examined*, Oxford: Oxford University Press.

Low Pay Commission (2007), *National Minimum Wage*, Cm 7056, Norwich: HMSO.

Machin, S. and A. Gosling (1994), 'What happened to the wages of men since the mid-1960s?', *Fiscal Studies*, **15** (4), 63–87.

National Statistics (2007), www.statistics.gov.uk/statbase/tsdtables1.asp?vlnk=unem (accessed 28 November 2008).

Organisation for Economic Co-operation and Development (OECD) (2005), *Education at a Glance*, Paris: OECD.

Palmer, G., J. Carr and P. Kenway (2005), *Monitoring Poverty and Social Exclusion 2005*, York: Joseph Rowntree Foundation and New Policy Institute.

Palmer, G., T. MacInnes and P. Kenway (2006), *Monitoring Poverty and Social Exclusion 2006*, York: Joseph Rowntree Foundation and New Policy Institute.

Phillips, D. and L. Sibieta (2006), *A Survey of the UK Benefit System*, Briefing Note 13, London: Institute for Fiscal Studies.

Rowntree, B.S. (1901), *Poverty: A Study of Town Life*, London: Macmillan Press.

Townsend, P. (1979), *Poverty in the United Kingdom: A Survey of Household Resources and Living Standards*, London: Allen Lane and Penguin Books.

UK National Audit Office (2007), *HM Revenue & Customs 2006–07 Accounts – The Comptroller and Auditor General's Standard Report*, HC 626 2006–2007, London: National Audit Office.

10. Low pay and household poverty during Ireland's economic boom

Brian Nolan

INTRODUCTION

Ireland has seen a dramatic economic boom over the past decade, with unprecedented levels of growth in employment and living standards. Unemployment has fallen very sharply, substantial numbers of migrants have been attracted to Ireland to work, and a minimum wage has been introduced to protect those in work on low wages. Despite this, the numbers of 'working poor' appear to have grown, certainly if one focuses on the poverty measures incorporated in the European Union's (EU's) Laeken indicators of social inclusion. Here we use data for Ireland from the new EU-SILC, and from the European Community Household Panel it replaced, to assess the extent and nature of 'in-work poverty' after Ireland's economic boom. This is of particular interest for what it reveals about the relationship between economic growth and in-work poverty, and about the importance of how poverty is measured in such circumstances.

MEASURING THE WORKING POOR

As discussed in earlier chapters, the definition of poverty that is widely accepted in industrialized countries refers to exclusion from the ordinary life of the community owing to lack of resources. A household's poverty status is usually measured by looking at whether its disposable income, adjusted for the number and ages of household members, falls below a specified income threshold, often derived as a proportion of mean or median household income in the country.[1] 'In-work poverty' or 'the working poor', then, refers to individuals who live in poor households but are themselves in work. In measuring both income and work status, different periods may be used, depending on the data available.

While much of the analysis in this chapter focuses on income, not all those on low income may be suffering exclusion in terms of ordinary living standards in their country. Various studies using non-monetary indicators of deprivation have found what is often very significant variation among those below such income thresholds in what they have and what they are doing without. This is why the EU's social inclusion indicators (the so-called 'Laeken' indicators) describe those below relative income thresholds as 'at risk of poverty' rather than poor. Non-monetary indicators can be used to hone in on those who are both on low income and experiencing what would be regarded in their own society as serious deprivation, as we will discuss below, and this is particularly relevant in exploring the relationship between economic growth and in-work poverty.

A COMPARATIVE PERSPECTIVE ON IN-WORK POVERTY IN IRELAND

We begin by looking at the extent of in-work poverty in Ireland as conventionally measured, compared to other countries in Western Europe. Table 10.1 shows, for Ireland and other countries in the 'old' EU-15, the percentage of working individuals who are in households falling below 60 per cent of median equivalized income from two EU sources. The first, for 2004, is taken from the 2006 *Joint Report on Social Protection and Social Inclusion* prepared by the EU Commission and Eurostat, mostly using data emerging from the new EU-SILC. The second, for 2001, is taken from analysis by Bardone and Guio (2005) carried out for Eurostat using the last wave of the European Community Household Panel Survey (ECHP). In both cases, an annual income measure is employed, and the employment status of the individual is measured on the basis of their 'most frequent activity status' in the year; to be counted as working, someone must have reported being in work as their status for more than half the months of the year. This is the way in which in-work poverty is now measured in the context of the EU's Social Inclusion Process, providing an obvious point of departure.

We see from Table 10.1 that in the Irish case 7 per cent of adults in work were in households below the 60 per cent of median income threshold, in both the 2004 and 2001 data. Compared with the other countries covered, this is marginally below the average – with Greece, Spain, Italy and Austria having much higher figures, Belgium, Denmark, Finland and Sweden having lower ones, and Luxembourg, the Netherlands, Portugal and the UK having intermediate levels like Ireland.

Comparing the level of in-work poverty to the overall percentage of adults falling below the 60 per cent relative income threshold, Table 10.2 shows that Ireland in fact has a rather lower level of in-work poverty than would be expected from its overall adult at-risk figure. Over one-fifth of

Table 10.1 In-work poverty risk in Ireland and other EU-15 countries, 2004 and 2001 (%)

Country	2004 EU-SILC	2001 ECHP
	% of those in work below 60% median equivalized income	
Belgium	4	4
Denmark	5	3
Germany	9	4
Greece	13	13
Spain	11	10
France	5	8
Ireland	7	7
Italy	10	10
Luxembourg	8	8
Netherlands	6	8
Portugal	7	6
Austria	13	12
Finland	4	6
Sweden	6	3
UK	7	7
EU-15 average	7.7	7.3

Source: 2004: *Joint Report on Social Protection and Social Inclusion 2006*, Annex 1 Methodological Notes and Statistical Tables, Table 5; 2001: *Statistics in Focus, Population and Social Conditions, 5/2005, In-Work Poverty*, Table 1.

Irish adults are below the 60 per cent threshold in 2004, higher than any other country from the EU-15 (actually also highest in the EU-25 according to the figures presented in the Joint Report.) So the in-work at-risk-of-poverty rate in Ireland is only one-third of the corresponding figure for the adult population as a whole, compared with 50 per cent on average for the EU-15 countries. Only in Belgium, France and Finland is the ratio of the in-work risk to the overall risk similarly low. By contrast, countries such as Spain, Portugal and Greece have overall poverty risk levels that are similar to Ireland but much higher figures for in-work poverty risk.

One relevant factor is the size of the self-employed population and of the agricultural sector in particular. In-work poverty for employees versus the self-employed are in many ways distinct phenomena – apart altogether from issues of income measurement for the latter – and therefore it is important to look at the two groups separately. While the figures available from EU-SILC for 2004 at this stage do not allow this, Table 10.3 presents

Table 10.2 In-work poverty risk versus overall poverty risk in Ireland and other EU-15 countries, 2004

Country	In-work poverty risk	Overall adult poverty risk	In-work/total poverty risk ratio
	% below 60% median equivalized income		
Belgium	4	14	0.29
Denmark	5	11	0.45
Germany	9	15	0.60
Greece	13	20	0.65
Spain	11	19	0.58
France	5	13	0.38
Ireland	7	21	0.33
Italy	10	18	0.56
Luxembourg	8	10	0.80
Netherlands	6	11	0.54
Austria	7	12	0.58
Portugal	13	20	0.65
Finland	4	11	0.36
Sweden	6	11	0.54
UK	7	17	0.41
EU-15 average (unweighted)	7.7	14.9	0.49

Source: *Joint Report on Social Protection and Social Inclusion 2006*, Annex 1 Methodological Notes and Statistical Tables, Table 5.

the at-risk rates for the two groups separately taken from the Bardone and Guio (2005) analysis of 2001 ECHP data for Eurostat. We see that in Ireland, as in most of the other countries, the percentage below 60 per cent of median income is very much higher for the self-employed than for employees, and there is also considerably more variation in the latter. For 10 out of the 15 countries, the at-risk rate for employees is in the range 4–8 per cent, and the figure for Ireland, at 6 per cent, is right in the middle of that range. For the self-employed, the Irish figure is much higher at 16 per cent, but this is again in the intermediate range compared with the corresponding figures for the self-employed in the other EU-15 countries. So, while the overall percentage (of adults) in households below 60 per cent of median income is exceptionally high in Ireland in Western European terms, the percentage of employees and the percentage of self-employed in that situation is unremarkable, neither particularly high nor particularly low.

As in other countries, the size of the in-work population means that even with a relatively low at-risk-of-poverty rate that group will represent

Table 10.3 In-work poverty risk for employees versus self-employed in Ireland and other EU-15 countries, 2001

Country	Employees	Self-employed
	% below 60% median equivalized income	
Belgium	3	10
Denmark	1	15
Germany	4	5
Greece	5	25
Spain	7	20
France	6	25
Ireland	6	16
Italy	7	18
Luxembourg	8	2
Netherlands	–	–
Austria	3	24
Portugal	7	28
Finland	4	17
Sweden	2	22
UK	5	14

Source: *Statistics in Focus, Population and Social Conditions, 5/2005, In-Work Poverty*, Table 1.

a substantial proportion of all those below the income threshold. Table 10.4 shows that in the Irish case, 17 per cent of adults below the threshold in 2004 were in work. This is a particularly low figure compared with other EU-15 countries, only Belgium having a lower figure and with one-quarter or even one-third of adults below the income threshold being in work in the other Western European member states. This reflects the fact that a particularly high proportion of adults not in work – notably the retired and the inactive – are below the threshold in Ireland, which is what underlies Ireland's particularly high overall at-risk-of-poverty rate.

A DETAILED PICTURE OF IN-WORK POVERTY IN IRELAND: THE INDIVIDUAL

Having given an overview of the extent of in-work poverty in Ireland in comparative perspective, we now go on to paint a more detailed picture of the nature of that phenomenon. We do so by analysing the micro data from the 2004 EU-SILC, carried out by the Central Statistics Office (2005) (and made available for analysis on a strictly anonymized basis). As we have

Table 10.4 The share of in-work poverty in overall poverty in Ireland and other EU-15 countries, 2001

Country	Adults in work and below 60% of median equivalized income as % of all adults below that income threshold
Belgium	14
Denmark	26
Germany	–
Greece	32
Spain	26
France	21
Ireland	17
Italy	25
Luxembourg	44
Netherlands	33
Austria	34
Portugal	36
Finland	21
Sweden	31
UK	26

Source: *Joint Report on Social Protection and Social Inclusion 2006*, Annex 1 Methodological Notes and Statistical Tables, Table 5.

seen, if the working poor are defined as those at work and living in a household with total (equivalized) income below 60 per cent of median income, then the results from the 2004 EU-SILC survey indicate that 7 per cent of those at work are in that position. This represents about 116 000 persons in the population, out of the working population of about 1.66 million.

We have also seen that the self-employed face a much higher probability of being below the income threshold, in Ireland as in most other countries. However, employees make up over four-fifths of the working population, so despite their low risk almost two-thirds of the working poor are employees. The remainder of the working poor are self-employed, more than half working in agriculture. Farmers face a particularly high probability of being counted as working poor: they comprise less than 7 per cent of those at work in EU-SILC 2004 but almost 20 per cent of the working poor. Self-employed other than farmers comprise about 11 per cent of those at work but 15 per cent of the working poor.

As discussed in the second section, being 'in work' can be measured in different ways, focusing on the person's status at the time of the interview or throughout the year; however, this turns out to make little difference to

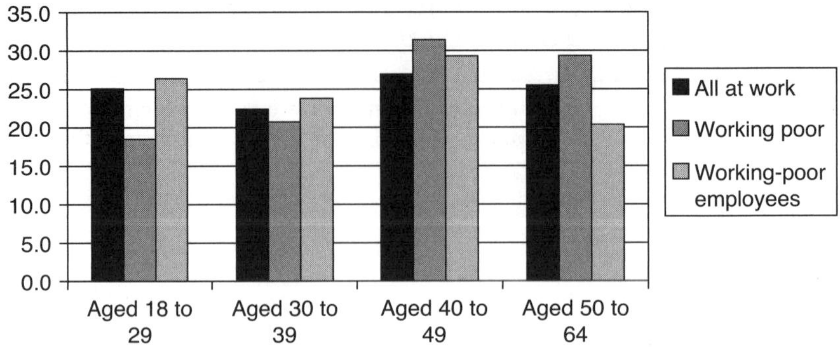

Source: EU-SILC 2004.

Figure 10.1 Age profile of working poor versus all at work, Ireland, 2004 (%)

the pattern of poverty risk or the individuals in the sample identified as the working poor. Concentrating on employees, if we use the 'main activity status' of individuals (based on the activity status in each month recorded in the survey) to identify those who were employees for over half the year, then 6 per cent were below the income threshold (as reported in the previous section). If we look at those who give their current principal economic status in the survey as employee, then 5.3 per cent are in households below the 60 per cent of median relative income poverty threshold. This represents about 71 000 persons in the population, out of a total of 1.34 million employees. Most of those who are currently employed were also in work for most of the previous year, although the at-risk-of-poverty rate is higher for the small minority who were not.

We now examine the profile of those who are measured as 'working poor', focusing first on their own individual characteristics and then on those of their household. Figure 10.1 shows the age composition of all those who are at work and below the 60 per cent threshold. We see that, compared with all those at work, the working poor are more concentrated in the older age ranges – over 60 per cent are aged 40 or more, compared with 52 per cent of the workforce as a whole. This reflects the older age profile of the self-employed (including farmers), though, with working poor employees not very different in age terms from all employees.

The working poor are also slightly more likely to be male: 61 per cent of the working poor are men, compared with 57 per cent of all those at work. However, among employees the opposite is true: 49 per cent of working poor employees are men, compared with 52 per cent of all employees. (Since men make up a clear majority of the workforce, they still face a

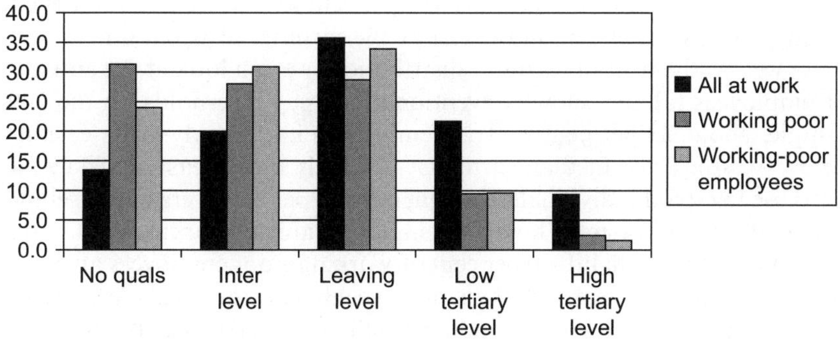

Source: EU-SILC 2004.

Figure 10.2 Educational attainment of working poor versus all at work, Ireland, 2004 (%)

higher probability of in-work poverty.) For both men and women employees, the likelihood of being working poor is lowest in the 25 to 34 age group; for men it is highest in the 45 to 54 group, while for women it is highest in the 55 to 64 range.

As far as educational attainment is concerned, Figure 10.2 shows that the working poor have substantially lower levels of educational attainment than all those at work; almost one-third have no education beyond primary level (compared with 13 per cent of all those at work), and only 41 per cent have attained at least the upper secondary completion qualification, compared with 67 per cent of all those at work. Working-poor employees have slightly higher levels of attainment than self-employed working poor, but still have a significantly disadvantaged profile compared with others at work.

This age, gender and educational profile is reflected in the earnings of the employee, one factor in understanding why they are 'working poor'. The number of hours worked is a significant influence on earnings particularly among employees, and part-time employees face a much higher poverty risk than those who work full-time. (About 4 per cent of full-time male employees, 3 per cent of full-time female employees and 10 per cent of female part-time employees are in households below the 60 per cent threshold; part-time men face an even higher poverty risk than part-time women, with almost one in five below the threshold, but there are far fewer of them.) The risk of poverty is also clearly related to the position of the employee in the weekly earnings distribution. Even when working full-time, the risk of poverty is 12 per cent for employees in the bottom quintile of the earnings distribution; this falls to 8 per cent for the second quintile and is only about 1–2 per cent in the rest of the earnings distribution.

As well as the overall earnings distribution, we can look at the situation of employees falling below conventional low pay thresholds. In the 2004 sample, about 23 per cent of Irish employees had weekly gross earnings below two-thirds of median earnings – a widely used measure of low pay. Of these low-paid individuals, though, only 13 per cent were in households at risk of poverty. So most low-paid employees are not working poor in that sense. On the other hand, 60 per cent of working-poor employees are themselves low paid, in terms of their own weekly earnings. This asymmetric relationship between low pay and household poverty is consistent with earlier Irish studies (for example, Nolan, 1998), and with the pattern found in other Western European countries; for example, Nolan and Marx (2000) note that for full-time employees across the ECHP generally about 60 per cent of the low paid are in the top 60 per cent of the income distribution. This reflects the fact that employees, whether low paid or not, are not mostly to be found in households in poverty or towards the bottom of the income distribution; such households generally do not contain an employee. But where they do contain an employee, most often that employee is low paid. The features that distinguish the minority of the low paid who are in households at risk of poverty then relate to the household context in which it is occurring, as we explore in the next section.

A DETAILED PICTURE OF IN-WORK POVERTY IN IRELAND: THE HOUSEHOLD

We now turn from the individual characteristics of the working poor to the type of households they live in – with those household characteristics likely to be critical in understanding why they are indeed below the relative income threshold. We show in Table 10.5 the composition of the households involved, for all working poor and for working-poor employees. We see that the working poor are predominantly in households with children – only one-third are in households with no children. Only 7 per cent are lone parents with children, so about 60 per cent are in households with two or more adults and children. The largest proportion – 29 per cent – are in households with three or more adults plus children – in many cases these comprise a couple with their offspring, some of whom are still children but others are aged 18 or over. The corresponding profile for working-poor employees shows that these are even more likely to be in households with children. About 9 per cent are in households comprising just one adult with a child or children, but 63 per cent are in households with two or more

Table 10.5 Household composition for the working poor and for working-poor employees, Ireland, 2004

Household composition	Working poor	Working-poor employees
	% below 60% median equivalized income	
1 adult	8.3	2.3
2 adults	16.0	15.5
3+ adults	10.4	11.7
1 adult with children	6.7	9.0
2 adults, 1 child	6.2	3.9
2 adults, 2 children	8.9	9.5
2 adults, 3 children	7.8	6.6
2 adults, 4+ children	6.5	7.3
3 adults+ with children	29.3	34.0
Total	100.0	100.0

Source: EU-SILC 2004.

adults and children. Strikingly, only 2 per cent are living alone. (This profile of course reflects both the distribution of all employees by household composition type and the risk faced by each type of being below the income threshold; single adult employees with children face a much higher probability of being below the income threshold than others, for example, but comprise only a small proportion of all employees.)

As well as household size and composition, the other key feature of the household in this context is the number of people with an income and the source of that income. What is distinctive about the households of the working poor is how few of their working-age adult members are actually in work. This is illustrated in Figure 10.3, which shows that for all those at work, the average number of working-age adults in the household is 2.6. For the working poor, the corresponding figure is only slightly lower, at 2.3. However, for all those at work the average number of persons in the household in work is 2.0, whereas the corresponding figure for the households of the working poor is only 1.3. The gap is even greater when we focus on those in full-time work, where the figures are 1.6 versus 0.8 respectively for the households of those at work versus the working poor.

Focusing on employees, Figure 10.4 shows that for all employees there are 2.7 persons in the household of working age on average, of whom 2.1 are in work and 1.7 are in full-time work. For working poor employees, on the other hand, there are almost as many working-age adults at 2.5 per household on average, but only 1.4 are in work and only 0.8 in full-time work.

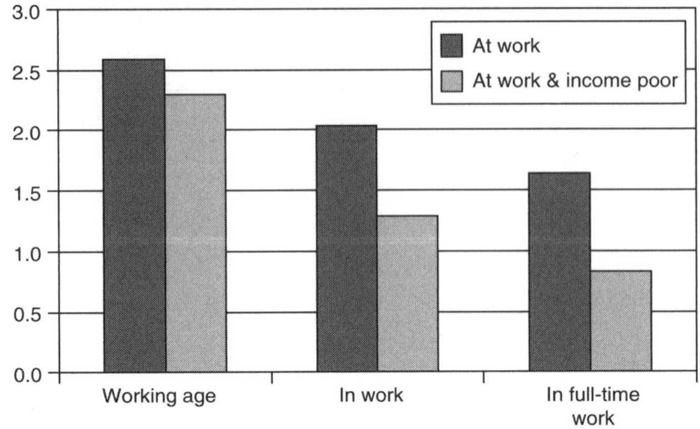

Source: EU-SILC 2004.

Figure 10.3 Numbers in the household in work for the working poor versus all at work, Ireland, 2004 (arithmetic means)

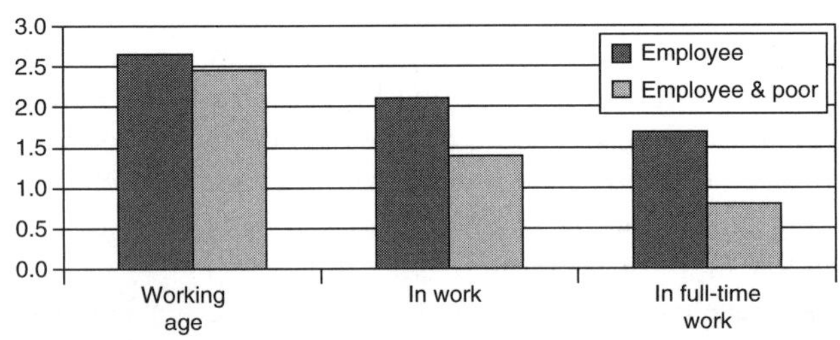

Source: EU-SILC 2004.

Figure 10.4 Numbers in the household in work for working-poor employees versus all employees, Ireland, 2004 (arithmetic means)

The central role played by the number of persons in the household at work is brought out in Table 10.6, which shows for employees in two- and three-adult households how the percentage falling below the 60 per cent threshold varies depending on the presence or absence of children and the number of adults in work. We see that the risk of poverty is relatively high for employees where only one adult is in work, whether there are children or not, but that the risk is very low indeed where two or more are at work except in households of three or more adults with children.

The salience of numbers at work in the household is also reflected in the sources of income received, and Figure 10.5 shows that the households of

Table 10.6 Poverty risk by household composition and number at work, Ireland, 2004

Household composition	% below 60% of median equivalized income
2 adults no children	
1 at work	10.2
2 at work	2.4
2 adults with children	
1 at work	15.1
2 at work	1.4
3 adults no children	
1 at work	11.3
2 at work	2.1
3+ at work	0.0
3 adults with children	
1 at work	32.6
2 at work	5.9
3+ at work	7.9

Source: EU-SILC 2004.

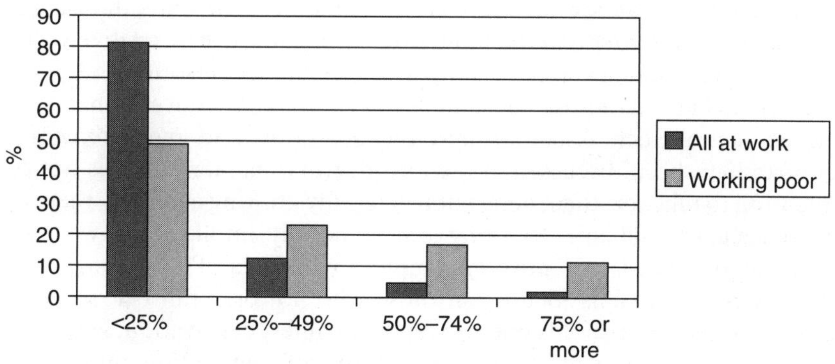

Source: EU-SILC 2004.

Figure 10.5 Social welfare transfers as a percentage of total household income for working poor versus all at work, Ireland, 2004 (%)

the working poor are heavily reliant on social welfare transfers compared with others at work. For 28 per cent of the working poor, at least half of all the income coming into the household was from social welfare (compared with only 7 per cent for all those at work).

ALTERNATIVE PERSPECTIVES ON POVERTY FOR THE WORKING POOR

By construction, the 'working poor' as we have measured them to this point are living in households with total disposable income (after equivalization) below 60 per cent of the median. Median equivalized income for the Irish EU-SILC sample in 2004 was just over €16 000, so the 60 per cent threshold for a single person at that point was €9675. On average, the working poor are well below that threshold: median equivalized income among the working poor was just under €8000, while for working poor employees it was slightly higher at €8200. As we saw earlier, the overall percentage below the 60 per cent threshold is particularly high in Ireland, at just over one-fifth; in terms of position in the overall income distribution, then, the working poor were in the bottom quintile.

While they are 'at-risk-of-poverty' in the sense of falling below the 60 per cent relative income threshold, this is not all we need to know about these individuals and their households to assess whether they can or should be considered 'poor'. As already noted, a wide range of recent studies using non-monetary indicators of deprivation consistently finds that a significant proportion of those below income poverty thresholds do not display (relatively) high deprivation scores, whereas some higher-income households do.[2] This reflects *inter alia* the limitations of income over a relatively short period as a comprehensive measure of command over resources, as well as differences in needs across households not captured by conventional equivalence scales. Such issues around the definition and measurement of poverty have been discussed in the introductory chapter and it is not our intention to rehearse them here, but in a rapidly growing economy they may be particularly salient. To bring out some key implications we use a measure of 'consistent poverty' employed in Ireland's National Anti-Poverty Strategy. This focuses on those who not only fall below relative income poverty thresholds but also report manifest deprivation, in terms of a set of items capturing rather 'basic' forms of deprivation, such as not being able to afford to heat the house, buy new rather than second-hand clothes and have a substantial meal (see also Nolan and Whelan, 1996).

Without going into detail on the specifics of the measure, it suffices for present purposes to say that whereas about one-fifth of the Irish sample were below the 60 per cent income threshold in 2004, only 7 per cent were in 'consistent poverty' in this sense (that is, below 60 per cent of median income *and* reporting basic deprivation). Looking at those in work, we find that whereas 7 per cent were below 60 per cent of the median in 2004, only 2 per cent were 'consistently poor' – that is, also reporting basic deprivation. So only one-quarter of the 'working poor', measured in income terms

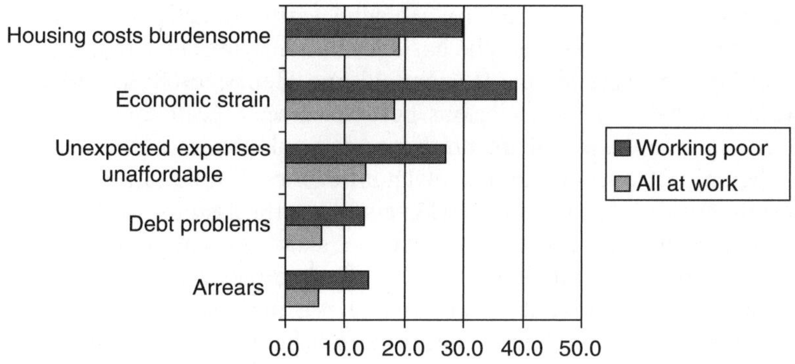

Source: EU-SILC 2004.

Figure 10.6 Subjectively-assessed economic strain for all at work versus working poor, Ireland, 2004 (%)

alone, are in consistent poverty. Similarly, only 1.5 per cent of all employees are in consistent poverty, which means that just over one-quarter of employees below the income threshold are in consistent poverty.

This is not to say that the majority of the 'working poor' defined in income terms are indistinguishable from others at work in terms of their living standards. This is brought out if we construct a deprivation index using a broader range of consumer durables and regular consumption items. This shows 38 per cent of those at work and below the 60 per cent income threshold are deprived of two or more of the items involved, compared with 19 per cent for all those at work. Similarly, as Figure 10.6 illustrates, those working and below the income threshold demonstrate higher levels of subjectively assessed economic strain than others at work. Compared with all those at work, about twice as high a proportion of the working poor said that they had recent experience of arrears on mortgage/rent or utility bills, could not meet unexpected expenses, or experienced debt problems to meet ordinary living expenses.

Finally, we look at another measure recently developed in the Economic and Social Research Institute (ESRI) which relates to 'economic vulnerability'. This is captured by combining information about whether a household is below relative income poverty thresholds, experiencing enforced basic deprivation and reporting difficulty in making ends meet. The statistical methodology latent class analysis is applied to identify an underlying pattern of connection between the variables (see Whelan and Maître, 2005, for details). The approach we adopt in analysing economic vulnerability involves an analysis of manifest indicators in order to identify underlying or latent vulnerability. We achieve this objective by the application of latent class analysis. The basic idea underlying such analysis is long established and very simple (Lazarsfeld and Henry, 1968; Magidson and Vermunt, 2004). The associations between a set of categorical variables, regarded as indicators of an unobserved typology, are accounted for by membership of a small number of latent classes. Implicit in the notion of multidimensional measurement of exclusion is the assumption that there is no one 'true' indicator of the underlying concept. Instead we have a sample of indicators that tap different aspects of a complex phenomenon. Latent class analysis assumes that each individual is a member of one and only one of *n* latent classes and that, conditional on latent class membership, the manifest variables are mutually independent of each other. Conditional independence is a version of the familiar idea that the correlation between two variables may be a result of their common dependence on a third variable. In estimating latent class models the logic is identical but the explanatory variable is unobserved and must be identified statistically. This identifies one-fifth of the total population as economically vulnerable, using data from the 2004 EU-SILC survey. When this approach is applied to the situation of those at work, we find that about 10 per cent would be categorized as 'economically vulnerable'. However, only about half the 'working poor' defined in purely income terms are identified by this approach as 'economically vulnerable'.

These results suggest that many of those who are at work and in households falling below the 60 per cent of median income threshold are indeed disadvantaged, across a wide range of indicators. However, a substantial proportion does not appear to be particularly disadvantaged in these terms. This is more likely to be true of the self-employed than of employees, owing both to the extent to which the incomes of the self-employed fluctuate over time and the difficulties faced in trying to capture their situation in surveys. This merits further in-depth investigation, but here we turn to the implications for interpreting trends over time and policy implications.

ECONOMIC GROWTH AND THE WORKING POOR

We noted in the introduction that Ireland experienced a remarkable economic boom from the mid-1990s. Ireland is now among the richest countries in the Organisation for Economic Co-operation and Development (OECD) in terms of gross domestic product (GDP) per head, whereas in 1995 it was significantly below the OECD average. Foreign direct investment in high value-added businesses has been a key factor, giving rise to substantial outflows of profits and income and making GDP problematic as a measure of trends in domestic income, but alternative measures such as gross national product (GNP) or gross national income (GNI) still show Ireland to have been one of the OECD's fastest growing economies since the mid-1990s. This makes Ireland a particularly interesting setting in which to study the relationship between economic growth and in-work poverty.

Over that decade, based on data from the ECHP and EU-SILC, in-work poverty as it is conventionally measured rose significantly in the Irish case. In the first, 1994, wave of the ECHP, 5 per cent of those in work were also in households below 60 per cent of median income. As we saw earlier, by 2004 the corresponding figure was 7 per cent – so the risk of poverty for those in work had risen. Furthermore, employment rose sharply over the period in Ireland, so this higher risk is being applied to a larger proportion of the working-age population. For employees the percentage in households below the 60 per cent income threshold rose even more sharply, from 2 per cent to over 5 per cent. With very substantial increases in earnings and household incomes being seen over the decade, how is it that in-work poverty appears to have risen?

Answers are to be found in the nature of the changes in household incomes that accompanied the economic boom, and in the way poverty is being measured. The overall impact of rapid economic growth was to increase the proportion in households below relative income poverty lines quite markedly. Figure 10.7 shows the trends in the percentage of persons under relative income thresholds set at 50 per cent and 60 per cent of median equivalized income. It shows that there was a marked increase between 1994 and 2001, the period covered by the ECHP, with the percentage below the 60 per cent line rising from 16 per cent to 22 per cent, and a corresponding increase with the 50 per cent line. Data from EU-SILC is available for 2003 and 2004 and shows a slightly lower percentage below each of the income thresholds: the extent to which this reflects differences between the two surveys rather than real changes is hard to assess. In any case, the overall at-risk-of-poverty rate measured vis-à-vis relative income thresholds is still seen to have risen substantially over the period.

Why did relative income poverty rise so substantially over the period? The answer lies in the pattern of increases in household incomes and in the nature of relative income poverty lines. Falling unemployment contributed directly to improved living standards for those affected, and social welfare support rates for those who remained dependent on transfers increased significantly in real terms. (Means-tested support for the unemployed, for example, rose by over 20 per cent in real terms while state pensions for the elderly rose a good deal more rapidly.) However, in general these social welfare payments lagged behind the even more rapid pace of increase in incomes from work and property, and thus behind average income. As a

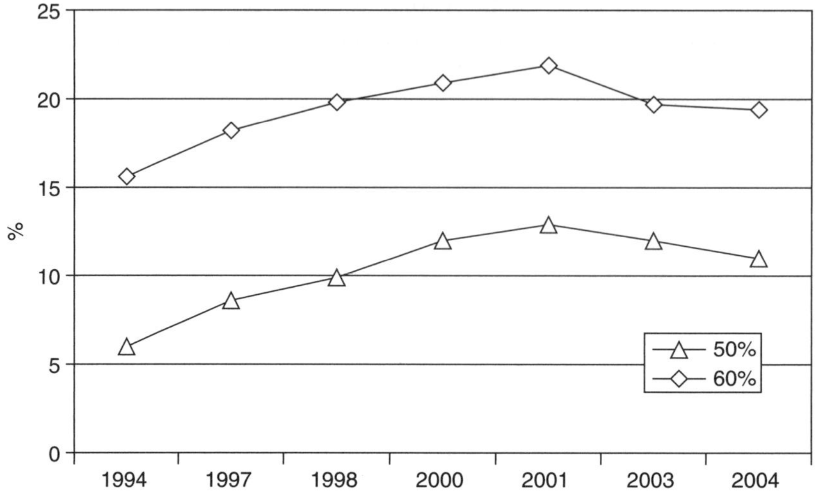

Source: Living in Ireland Surveys 1994, 1997, 1998, 2000 and 2001; EU-SILC 2003, 2004.

Figure 10.7 Percentage of persons below median income poverty lines (%)

result, by the end of the period those relying primarily on social welfare for their income were more likely to fall below poverty lines linked to average income, offsetting the impact of increasing numbers in employment on relative income poverty rates.

This is brought out by the changing make-up of the households below the 60 per cent of median relative income threshold. In 1994, over 40 per cent had an unemployed 'head' (or 'reference person' in Eurostat terms), whereas this was 7 per cent by 2001 and had fallen further by 2004. Conversely, households with a head/reference person who was ill/disabled, working in the home, or retired accounted for far more of those below the threshold in 2004 than they had in 1994, reaching almost two-thirds of those affected. So we see that between 1994 and 2004 there has been a dramatic transformation in the composition of those below the relative income threshold, reflecting the sharp decline in unemployment and the failure of vulnerable groups such as the ill/disabled, the retired and those in home duties to keep pace with the advances made by those in employment. So a key factor in the overall rise in the proportion in the population falling below relative income poverty thresholds has been that pensioners, in particular, rely very heavily on state transfers in Ireland, and those transfers did not keep pace with rapidly rising incomes from work and thus with the median-based poverty thresholds. So one has to be careful in thinking about the relationship between economic growth, overall poverty and in-work poverty. The main channel by which growth is expected to reduce poverty is by raising employment and reducing unemployment: in the Irish case the fall in numbers of poor unemployed was indeed dramatic, but this was not reflected in a decline in the overall poverty rate because it was counterbalanced by an increase in poverty (vis-à-vis relative thresholds) for pensioners in particular.

One also has to be careful in thinking about the relationship between economic growth and in-work poverty. To some extent it might be expected that the numbers of in-work poor would increase as the numbers in employment rise very rapidly and unemployment falls. Many of the formerly unemployed will move into low-paid jobs, and not all will be brought above the income poverty threshold. So, with fewer unemployed, it is likely that there will be some replacement of out-of-work poverty by in-work poverty – even if most of the formerly unemployed do in fact escape above the poverty threshold. This can occur even where a minimum wage and in-work benefits are in place, as the Irish experience illustrates. Ireland actually introduced a national minimum wage for the first time in 2001, at a relatively high level (higher in absolute terms than those operating in any other EU member state except Luxembourg). In-work cash transfers (Family Income Supplement) are also directed at those in work with children but on low household income. Some other countries have welfare regimes that are more effective in keeping those in work above the poverty threshold, as we have seen, but economic growth will not in itself guarantee that this happens if the labour market and social security systems at the outset leave significant numbers of those in work below the income thresholds.

The particular pattern of growth in employment and incomes in the Irish cases also contributed to growing numbers in work and below the relative income thresholds. In some households the numbers at work rose sharply, with the proportion of married women in the labour force rising very rapidly over the decade from the mid-1990s, by 12 percentage points, and the percentage of working-age couples where the wife was in work rose even more sharply. This, in turn, contributed to the very rapid increase in average or median incomes: from 1994 to 2004, median income and thus the median-based income poverty thresholds more than doubled in nominal terms. Households with only one earner, even if that earner saw earnings increase quite considerably over the period, could well fail to keep pace with the poverty threshold, and some thus saw their overall household incomes slip below that threshold. This is a key factor in the growth in in-work poverty measured vis-à-vis relative income thresholds.

The use of such income-based thresholds to measure poverty is also central to the picture we have described where poverty is seen to rise in an economic boom. The picture would be very different indeed if instead of income thresholds linked to average income one used a standard held constant in purchasing power terms. This can be illustrated by taking the 60 per cent of median threshold in 1994 and indexing it to changes in the Consumer Price Index rather than average incomes. Using such a 'constant in real terms' line, the overall percentage falling below that threshold would have fallen from about 16 per cent in 1994 to about 2 per cent in 2001, and even lower by 2004. This reflects the scale of real income growth throughout the distribution seen over this remarkable period in Ireland. On that basis, in-work poverty, like overall poverty for the sample as a whole, would have virtually disappeared by 2004.

The very rapid growth in average incomes since 1994 also means that non-monetary indicators may be particularly valuable in capturing trends in what is generally regarded as exclusion due to lack of resources. The 'consistent poverty' measure combining both low income and manifest deprivation also shows a marked decline over the period for the sample as a whole. In broad terms, the percentage in consistent poverty using a fixed set of deprivation indicators appears to have fallen from 16 per cent to about 7 per cent.[3] One can make a strong case for adjusting the way deprivation is measured over time to take changes in ordinary living standards and views about what constitute 'necessities' into account. This has been investigated in some depth in the Irish case, and a revised set of 'basic' deprivation indicators has been developed based on analysis of the 2004 EU-SILC. (An in-depth discussion of the basic deprivation index and how it might be adapted over time can be found in Maître et al., 2006). For present purposes it suffices to note that even using this expanded and adapted set for 2004, the overall level of consistent poverty, and consistent poverty as it affects those in work, is substantially lower in 2004 than it was 10 years earlier (with the original set of deprivation items). This brings out the way in which the general increase in living standards observed across all groups over the decade in the Irish case has impacted on generalized deprivation.

CONCLUSIONS

As in the EU more generally now, getting more people into work has been the central plank of the Irish government's strategy to combat poverty. This has been an unprecedented success in the Irish case in terms of the scale of employment growth and reduction in unemployment achieved. The strategy has also been a resounding success in terms of improving living standards and reducing deprivation. This has impacted both on those in work throughout, and even more so on those moving from unemployment into work. While those who remain outside the workforce have lagged behind in income terms, even they have seen significant improvements in living standards.

However, the Irish case also illustrates that rapid economic growth does not guarantee declining poverty, at least in terms of numbers falling below relative income poverty thresholds. Since these thresholds rise as incomes from employment rise, certain groups may be left behind – notably pensioners and others who continue to rely on state transfers. Even in-work poverty may be seen to increase, if even a proportion of those who move from employment into work are not lifted above the relative income thresholds. Particularly where the numbers of women in work are rising rapidly, it may become more difficult for households relying on only one earner to stay above these thresholds. To be effective, anti-poverty strategy cannot be focused simply on increasing employment, but has to combine education, labour market and social protection policies to ensure that those in work are kept above the poverty threshold.

NOTES

1. See for example Atkinson (1987), Atkinson et al. (1995; 2002), Förster and Pearson (2002) and Fritzell and Ritakallio (2004).
2. See for example Gordon et al. (2000), Pantazis et al. (2006), Nolan and Whelan (1996), Muffels and Dirven (1998), Halleröd (1995), Kangas and Ritakallio (1998), Böhnke and Delhey (1999), Tsakloglou and Panopoulou (2002), Layte et al. (2000; 2001) and Guio (2005).
3. The precise scale of that decline has to be treated with caution because the switch from ECHP to EU-SILC itself appears to have had an impact on the measured extent of deprivation.

REFERENCES

Atkinson, A.B. (1987), 'On the measurement of poverty', *Econometrica*, **55**, 759–64.

Atkinson, A.B., B. Cantillon, E. Marlier and B. Nolan (2002), *Indicators for Social Inclusion in the European Union*, Oxford: Oxford University Press.

Atkinson, A., L. Rainwater and T. Smeeding (1995), *Income Distribution in OECD Countries*, Paris: OECD.

Bardone, L. and A-C. Guio (2005), *In-Work Poverty*, Statistics in Focus, Population and Social Conditions, 5/2005, Luxembourg: Office for Official Publications of the European Communities.

Böhnke, P. and J. Delhey (1999), 'Poverty in a multidimensional perspective: Great Britain and Germany', mimeo., Wissenschaftszentrum Berlin (WZB).

Central Statistics Office (2005), *EU Survey on Income and Living Conditions (EU-SILC)*, Statistical Release, 12 December, Dublin: CSO.

European Commission (2006), *Joint Report on Social Protection and Social Inclusion 2006*, Luxembourg: Office for Official Publications of the European Communities.

Förster, M. and M. Pearson (2002), 'Income distribution and poverty in the OECD area: trends and driving forces', *OECD Economic Studies*, **34**, 7–39.

Fritzell, J. and V.-M. Ritakallio (2004), *Societal Shifts and Changed Patterns of Poverty*, Luxembourg Income Study Working Paper No. 393, Luxembourg.

Gordon, D., L. Adelman, K. Ashworth, J. Bradshaw, R. Levitas, S. Middleton, C. Pantazis, D. Patsios, S. Payne, P. Townsend and J. Williams (2000), *Poverty and Social Exclusion in Britain*, York: Joseph Rowntree Foundation.

Guio, A.-C. (2005), 'Material deprivation in the EU', *Statistics in Focus*, Luxembourg: Eurostat.

Halleröd, B. (1995), 'The truly poor: direct and indirect measurement of consensual poverty in Sweden', *Journal of European Social Policy*, **5** (2), 111–29.

Kangas, O. and V.-M. Ritakallio (1998), 'Different methods – different results: approaches to multidimensional policy', in H.-J. Andreß (ed.), *Empirical Poverty Research in a Comparative Perspective*, Aldershot, UK: Ashgate Publishing, pp. 167–203.

Layte, R., B. Maître, B. Nolan and C.T. Whelan (2000), 'Targeting poverty: lessons from monitoring Ireland's National Anti Poverty Strategy', *Journal of Social Policy*, **29** (4), 553–75.

Layte R., B. Maître, B. Nolan and C.T. Whelan (2001), 'Explaining deprivation in the European Union', *Acta Sociologica*, **44** (2), 105–22.

Lazarsfeld, P.F. and N.W. Henry (1968), *Latent Structure Analysis*, Boston, MA: Houghton Mifflin.

Magidson, J. and J. Vermunt (2004), 'Latent class models', in D. Kaplan (ed.), *Handbook of Quantitative Methodology*, London: Sage.

Maître, B., B. Nolan and C.T. Whelan (2006), *Reconfiguring the Measurement of Deprivation and Consistent Poverty in Ireland*, Policy Research Series Paper 58, Dublin: Economic and Social Research Institute.

Muffels, R. and H.J. Dirven (1998), 'Long-term income and deprivation-based poverty among the elderly', in H-J. Andreß (ed.), *Empirical Poverty Research in Comparative Perspective*, Aldershot: Ashgate, pp. 229–56.

Nolan, B. (1998), 'Low pay, poverty and policy', in C. Lucifora and W. Salverda (eds), *Policies for Low Wage Employment and Social Exclusion*, Milan: Franco Angelli.

Nolan, B. and I. Marx (2000), 'Low pay and household poverty', in M. Gregory, W. Salverda and S. Bazen (eds), *Labour Market Inequalities: Problems and Policies of Low-Wage Employment in International Perspective*, Oxford: Oxford University Press.

Nolan, B. and C.T. Whelan (1996), *Resources, Deprivation and Poverty*, Oxford: Clarendon Press.

Pantazis, C., D. Gordon and R. Levitas (eds) (2006), *Poverty and Social Exclusion in Britain: The Millennium Survey*, Bristol: Policy Press.

Tsakloglou, P. and F. Papadopoulos (2002), 'Aggregate level and determining factors of social exclusion in twelve European countries', *Journal of European Social Policy*, **12** (3), 211–25.

Whelan, C.T. and B. Maître (2005), 'Vulnerability and multiple deprivation perspectives on economic exclusion in Europe: a latent class analysis', *European Societies*, **7** (3), 423–50.

PART III

Summary and Conclusion

11. Combating in-work poverty in Europe: the policy options assessed

Ive Marx and Gerlinde Verbist

INTRODUCTION

In this chapter, we pose the question: what can policy do to prevent and alleviate in-work poverty? Three initial remarks are in order before we move on to what will inevitably be a concise review of policy alternatives. First, as the chapters in this book make clear, in-work poverty in Europe is a diverse, multifaceted phenomenon that occurs in equally diverse institutional, economic and socio-demographic settings. Any effective set of policy measures to prevent or alleviate in-work poverty will have to reflect this. Consequently, readers should not expect this chapter to present a 'one size fits all' policy prescription. Second, in-work poverty cannot be seen as a separate issue from the wider causes of poverty and low income in any given society. Indeed, the two are essentially inseparable. Policies intended to combat in-work poverty will inevitably be part and parcel of more general anti-poverty policies. Third, a decision as to what policy action – or set of policy actions – is most appropriate cannot be seen as independent from normative notions that underlie the various ways that in-work poverty can be construed. In-work poverty in Europe is concentrated to a considerable extent among dual-adult households with only one working adult – that is, traditional single-breadwinner households. Whether this is construed as a problem of insufficient breadwinner earnings or as a problem of partner non-participation makes a fundamental difference as to what type of policy action is to be favoured.

Broadly speaking, policies can be divided between measures that seek to boost labour earnings, measures that seek to stimulate households to realize their full earnings potential and measures that seek to raise net household income. We begin our review with the policy measure that is arguably most often associated with combating in-work poverty: higher minimum wages, be they legally determined or effectively set through collective bargaining. We then move on to policies intended to boost household labour participation rates and thus multi-earnership. This section discusses both demand- and supply-side measures. Finally, we will discuss policy options that operate at the level of net disposable household income, including tax (credit) policies and social transfers.

HIGHER MINIMUM WAGES

The policy measure most commonly associated with preventing in-work poverty is the minimum wage, be it legally determined or effectively set through collective bargaining. One often-heard argument against raising minimum wages in order to combat in-work poverty is that significant minimum wage hikes would simply be too harmful to employment and would effectively worsen Continental Europe's entrapment in a 'welfare without work' situation.

Whether or not this is actually a valid argument against raising minimum wages as a way of combating in-work poverty remains open for discussion. A great deal of the research now available shows that the overall employment effects of minimum wage increases, where they actually occur, tend to be small (Dolado et al., 1996; 2000; OECD, 1998). Research does suggest that the effects may be stronger for particular subgroups. When significant negative employment effects are found, they tend to be among young people (Bazen and Skourias, 1997; Dolado et al., 2000; Laroque and Salanié, 1999; OECD, 1998).

A more robust and pervasive argument against employing minimum wages as a strategy against in-work poverty is that because of the limited overlap between low pay and poverty, any policy aimed at improving the earnings of the low-paid as a group will directly benefit only a minority of poor households. This is of course true of any policy aimed at helping a particular subset of the population. Policies aimed at that subset must be judged in terms of their effectiveness in benefiting that target group rather than on their overall impact on poverty. This is only true up to a point, however, because the limited (direct) impact which policies aimed at the working poor will have on poverty has to be kept in mind when we consider their role in an overall anti-poverty strategy and the extent to which they can complement other policies – notably those that focus on unemployment and pensions for the elderly. An anti-poverty strategy which has measures targeting the low-paid as its central premises will simply not assist the majority of the poor (Nolan and Marx, 2000).

Policies aimed at the low-paid as a group will also have a very substantial spillover, since a portion of the non-poor will also benefit. This is particularly true in the case of a minimum wage, even one which is highly effective in increasing the gross earnings of the low paid without having an adverse impact on employment levels. Studies suggest that even in those cases where the overlap between low pay and household poverty is the greatest, as is the case in the USA, increases in the minimum wage have a relatively limited impact on poverty or income inequality and a substantial spillover to the non-poor (see, for example, Formby et al., 2005; Horrigan and Mincey, 1993; Neumark and Wascher, 1997). An aspect which tends to be somewhat neglected is the limited direct effect one would expect a minimum wage to have on household poverty on its own. Even in the absence of negative effects on employment, most of the benefits would go to non-poor households, simply because that is where most of the low-paid people are found (Marx and Verbist, 1998; Nolan and Marx, 2000). In most European countries, less than 85 per cent of low-paid workers live in low-income households. Of course, it is also important to consider where any disemployment effects would be felt, but it is far from clear whether the low-paid in poor households are likely to be more or less vulnerable than those in non-poor households.

This limited impact on poverty is not, in itself, an argument against the introduction of a minimum wage or against minimum wage increases. It is also important to note that the pattern in any one country can change substantially over time, as evidenced by the increase in the numbers of the 'working poor' in the UK in recent years. As Gosling (1996) put it in the context of the UK debate at the time, a minimum wage is not a good way to redistribute income from the rich to the poor, but its potential effect in the UK did increase. Yet, as micro-simulation exercises make clear, the isolated poverty-reducing effect of the national minimum wage remains very small even in the UK context (Sutherland, 2001), with the impact being slightly more substantial for single people.

In conclusion, as an isolated measure, higher minimum wages – within realistically feasible ranges – cannot contribute much towards fighting in-work poverty. Which is not to say that minimum wages have no role to play in fighting poverty: they do, but not as an isolated measure. A minimum wage can, for example, help to contain the budgetary cost and possible wage erosion effects of in-work benefits (see below).

BOOSTING MULTI-EARNERSHIP

As this book makes clear, what increasingly matters in advanced economies is the combined labour market position of all the members of a given household. Single earnership has, to a considerable extent, become a poverty risk in an era in which the average living standard – and hence the relative poverty threshold – is increasingly determined by the living standard of double-earner households. Two working adults are the best protection against poverty that a household can have. It does not even matter much whether one or both partners have a low wage or a part-time job – what matters is that there are two incomes. In-work poverty among double earners almost only occurs when they have large families to support.

It is quite evident that throughout Continental Europe in particular, non-employment rates remain particularly high for women with lower levels of education. Non-employment rates for women with less than upper secondary education amount to around 55 per cent in countries like Germany and the Netherlands and around 65 per cent in Italy and Spain (OECD, 2007). Esping-Andersen (1996; 1999) has long argued that Continental welfare states have mistakenly opted to preserve the privileged position of the male breadwinner in the labour market/social security nexus – through, among other things, high (minimum) wages, strong employment protection (for example, limits on temporary and part-time employment), but also through extensive breadwinner-biased social security rights and taxation systems.

Demand-side Measures: Making Less-skilled Work Cheaper

The cost of labour, especially less-skilled labour, is generally perceived to hamper the labour market prospects of the less skilled, especially in European countries where the lowest wages are relatively high compared with average earnings, and where social security contributions are substantial.

Many labour economists (but also organizations like the Organisation for Economic Co-operation and Development [OECD]) have long argued that non-employment rates for the less educated are bound to remain high unless more flexible, relatively low-paid jobs are 'allowed' to emerge in the domestic services sector. Such jobs could then provide many single-earner households with the additional income they need to escape poverty.

But with lower minimum wages not a politically feasible option, many governments have resorted to employment subsidies and cuts in employers' social security contributions to lower the cost of less-skilled labour and to improve the labour market prospects of the less skilled. According to OECD (2003) figures, such programmes account for a significant share of expenditures on active labour market programmes in the OECD area – on average, 24 per cent. Some countries – Belgium and Ireland, for example – devote one-half or more of their active labour market spending to such programmes. Spending on employment subsidies or similar measures is also significantly above the OECD average in countries like the Netherlands, France and Spain.

There are basically two types of subsidies. First, there are subsidies aimed at boosting the employment prospects of very specific groups, such as the long-term unemployed. These tend to be quite substantial, but are provided only for a limited time. Second, there are subsidies (mostly social security reductions) aimed at low-skilled workers in general. These tend to be permanent, but they also tend to be more modest in magnitude compared with highly targeted subsidies.

Theoretical models and simulations generally suggest that reductions in employers' social security contributions have a substantial impact on employment for the less skilled and other vulnerable groups like the unemployed (Jongen, 1998; Malinvaud, 1998; Phelps, 1997; Sneessens and Shadman, 2000; Snower, 1994; 1997). However, the outcomes have been shown to be highly sensitive to the theoretical and parametric assumptions underlying the models (see, for example, Granier and Nyssen, 1995; Hui and Trivedi, 1986; Jongen, 1999; Nickell and Bell, 1997).

More importantly, the empirical evaluation studies that are available to date also provide reason for scepticism. This is particularly the case for employers' social security reductions that aim to boost the demand for less-skilled labour in general.

Kramarz and Philippon (2001), for example, looked at the employment effects of substantial cuts in employers' social security contributions on minimum wages in France. Employers' contributions there were cut from roughly 40 per cent at the beginning of the 1990s to around 22 per cent in 1996. Using time-series analysis, Kramarz and Philippon (2001) found that observed reductions in the cost of minimum-wage labour did not coincide with any net job growth. In the case of the Netherlands, research is available concerning the impact of a similar reduction in employers' social security contributions on low wages, the Specific Social Security Contributions Concession (Specifieke Afdrachtskorting, or SPAK) scheme. One evaluation study (Polanen Petel et al., 1999) estimated the net employment effect to be 7 per cent at the most, which is considerably less than simulation models had predicted (Jongen, 1998). Based on a time-series analysis, Mühlau and Salverda (2000) found that the introduction of the SPAK did not cause any measurable additional employment growth, even in such sectors as the hotel and catering industry or in retailing. This finding stands in stark contrast to the very considerable budgetary cost of the measure, which has now been abolished. Other empirical studies have yielded similar findings (Marx, 2001).

Although more research is clearly needed, it seems legitimate to remain somewhat sceptical about the effectiveness – particularly the cost-effectiveness – of low-wage subsidies as a way of boosting the demand for low-skilled labour and thus multi-earnership.

Supply-side Measures: Facilitating the Combination of Work and Caregiving

In many European countries, second earners face significant adverse work incentives, especially when they take up relatively low-paid work. This is certainly the case in countries which operate joint tax systems. In individualized tax systems, low-wage earners are often taxed at low rates or are exempt altogether from paying taxes. But in joint tax systems, they can face quite formidable effective marginal tax rates.

In countries where the tax system actively supports the breadwinner model, the situation can be even worse. Belgium, for example, makes use of a so-called marital quotient, which allows a single earner to transfer part of his or her income to the non-working partner, where it is then taxed at a lower rate. This is financially advantageous for single-earner households, but at the same time it dampens the pay-off of becoming a secondary earner.

In countries like Belgium or Germany, low-paid (defined as below 67 per cent of the average wage of a production worker) second earners face effective marginal tax rates of 50 per cent; in France, this figure is upwards of 60 per cent (Immervoll and Barber, 2006). In contrast, the financial pay-off to becoming a second earner is quite substantial in countries like Spain and Portugal – although this has more to do with the overall low tax burden in those countries than with the design of the tax system. The Anglo-Saxon countries also do relatively well, as do the Nordic countries – Denmark being a notable outlier at 69 per cent.

Another very important impediment to dual earnership can be the cost of childcare. In some countries, the gross cost of having one child in full-time care can amount to one-third of an average production worker's (APW's) wage – the OECD average being 16 per cent (Immervoll and Barber, 2006). Even after deducting all relevant subsidies, tax deductions and other forms of government support, the net costs can remain prohibitive.

The ways and extent to which governments intervene to alleviate the cost of childcare differ greatly across Europe. Childcare expenses often are (partially) tax deductible. The problem here is that low-income earners often do not pay any taxes at all, or they pay only very low rates. Tax deductions, therefore, tend to be most advantageous for moderate to high earners. An equally important problem is the temporal mismatch between the timing of the actual expenses and that of the tax benefits, which tend to come after tax returns have been filed and approved (often more than a year later).

A better alternative, therefore, may be to subsidize the suppliers rather than the parents. This makes sense in so far as providing childcare at a good quality level tends to be expensive (with considerable fixed start-up and investment costs), and in many countries, a shortage of adequate childcare is as much if not more of a problem than its cost. The problem with subsidizing suppliers may, again, be that the benefits flow disproportionately to middle and higher-income households. However, this problem could be alleviated by making fees in some way directly related to income, as is the case in a number of countries (see, for example, the chapter on Belgium in this volume).

Immervoll and Barber (2006) also calculated effective tax rates for secondary earners who take up low-paid jobs (67 per cent of APW), taking into account net childcare costs – that is, taking government subsidies into account. These turn out to be strikingly high all across the OECD (69 per cent on average). The results show that countries like the Netherlands (78 per cent), the UK (82 per cent), France (89 per cent) and Ireland (101 per cent) impose the highest effective tax rates on low-paid second earners with children to care for. In all these cases, childcare fees are the main culprit. The Nordic countries do much better in this respect, with Sweden and Norway at 41 and 53 per cent, respectively. Denmark (85 per cent) is the Nordic outlier, owing to the effect of taxation. Perhaps more surprising is the relatively good performance of 'conservative' welfare states such as Germany (60 per cent) and Austria (63 per cent). Portugal, which does relatively well when it comes to the taxation of second earners, does worse once childcare costs are accounted for (73 per cent).

However, it is important to stress that these measures of effective taxation are not linked in any straightforward way to female or maternal employment outcomes. The Nordic countries, including Denmark, score predictably high. But France, for example, has a higher maternal employment rate than Germany, as does the Netherlands. Portugal also does much better than Germany. The lack of any straightforward relationship between the extent of policy support for maternal employment and the effective labour market participation of mothers is demonstrated in many studies (see, for example, Del Boca and Viuri, 2005; Gornick and Meyers, 2003; Steiber, 2007). This is perhaps because factors other than net cost are likely to play a role. The effective availability of childcare places is likely to be a major factor, especially when it comes to the availability of childcare at non-regular hours – which may be of particular importance to less-skilled women seeking employment in the personal services sector. The (perceived) quality of childcare is probably another factor. However, less is known about the impact of such factors. It has also been argued that the extent of cultural support for maternal employment is a key driving factor in cross-country differences (Steiber, 2007).

The Limits to Boosting Double Earnership

While boosting labour participation, particularly among single-earner households, could have a substantial impact on poverty, it would clearly not offer a full solution. On the basis of a simple shift-share exercise, Fritzell and Ritakalio (2004) found that some countries would have considerably lower poverty rates if they had a *household* labour participation (and socio-demographic) structure similar to Sweden's – the best-performing country. Interestingly, however, the impact of boosting labour participation – especially double earnership – levels to those of Sweden would vary widely, with some countries like Germany or Canada ending up with higher hypothetical poverty rates. A similar exercise by Whiteford and Adema (2006) relating to child poverty yielded similar results: the poverty reduction pay-off of increased double earnership would be generally favourable, but the effects would range from very strong in some countries to negligible elsewhere.

It is the differential impact of taxes – and, even more crucially, social transfers – that accounts for much of the cross-country variation in reduced poverty 'returns' from higher employment. The intuition behind this should be clear enough: single-adult households, who would have to make ends meet on relatively low earnings even if they were to work full-time, would often find themselves in poverty, especially if they had dependent children. In some cases, even double-earner couples would not generate sufficient earnings to support large households, especially if they included other dependent persons besides children. In the next section, we turn to the impact of taxes and transfers.

TAX REFORM AND SOCIAL TRANSFERS

Taxation of Low Earnings

Given the fact that tax burdens are already high even at low wage levels, tax reform can considerably influence the net incomes of low-wage workers. Tax calculations from the OECD (see Immervoll, 2007) show that in 2005, the average tax rate on full-time minimum wages was still considerable, despite serious reductions over the previous five years. Personal income taxes and employees' social contributions amounted, for example, to 18.8 per cent in Belgium, 17.6 per cent in France and as much as 23.8 per cent in the Netherlands. For low wages (wages below 67 per cent of the average full-time wage), the tax burden is above 25 per cent in the Continental and Nordic European welfare states (with peaks in Belgium (34.8 per cent),

Denmark (38.7 per cent) and Germany (36.4 per cent)). As we have seen in the Belgian chapter, this burden can tax households into poverty – especially single-earner households with children.

These high levels indicate that there is still scope for improving the income position of low-wage households through cuts in employee social contributions and personal income taxes. Many countries have introduced reductions of employees' social contributions on low wages, thus increasing the progressivity of social contributions. Such a shift from proportional to progressive contributions enhances the solidarity principle of social security and weakens the insurance nature of the system. This implies that the approach of reducing employees' contributions has its limits, as most Continental social security systems are mainly insurance-based.

In search of an alternative, governments all across Europe have introduced or contemplated the introduction of Anglo-Saxon style tax credits for low-paid workers or households. Countries which have already introduced a low income tax credit include Belgium (although it has already been abolished there), Finland, France (Prime pour l'emploi) and the Netherlands. Both in the academic and in the policy world, reference is often made to schemes like the American Earned Income Tax Credit (EITC) or the British Working Tax Credit (WTC) – and understandably so, as we show below. But this does not mean that similar measures would prove equally successful in Continental Europe. After a review of the (in many ways encouraging) evidence which we can glean from the American EITC and the UK's WTC, we consider the appropriateness of emulating Anglo-Saxon low-wage tax credits in Continental Europe.

Tax Credits in the Anglo-Saxon Countries

The Earned Income Tax Credit (EITC) was first introduced in the USA in 1975 as an exemption from employees' social security payments for poor working households with children. The system was subsequently expanded in 1986, 1990 and 1993. The 1993 reform, in particular, turned the scheme into the country's pre-eminent anti-poverty programme for families of active working age, as the amounts have been increased systematically. Eligibility for the EITC is tied to the level of earnings and the number of children. For each dollar earned up to a maximum amount, the parent receives a refundable tax credit. For one parent with two or more children, the credit is 40 per cent of his or her earnings up to a maximum credit of roughly $4700 (in 2007). For a minimum wage worker, this amounts to a 40 per cent pay increase. As a family's earned income rises above $15 400, the credit is gradually reduced at a rate of 21 cents per additional dollar earned, and the credit is fully phased out for families with incomes over $37 750. The effect of the EITC on the living standard of low-income households has been reinforced by several increases in the minimum wage.

Introduced in 1988, the UK's Family Credit (FC) was a social security allowance for working families with dependent children. The Working Families Tax Credit (WFTC) was an extension of the FC and offered a tax credit to families with children where at least one adult worked a minimum of 16 hours per week. The Working Tax Credit (WTC), introduced in 2003, is mainly an extension of WFTC. However, as was not the case with the WFTC, families and individuals without children as well as handicapped persons now also qualify for the credit (Brewer, 2003). The amount of the tax credit can be changed throughout the year if the beneficiary's circumstances change (for example, changes in earned income or in number of hours worked). The thresholds for granting a tax credit are determined on the basis of gross joint taxable income (that is, before deduction of work expenses and social security contributions) instead of on net taxable earned income. This change was introduced in order to improve incentives for dual-earner households (Inland Revenue, 2002). The WTC consists of a basic element (a maximum of £1730 in 2007–08) to which may be added a couple or solo parent element (£1700). This amount may be increased if the claimant works 30 hours or more per week (£705), is a disabled worker (£2310 plus £980 when severely disabled) or is 50 years of age or older and returns to work (£1185 or £1770). Moreover, up to 80 per cent of childcare costs can be reclaimed from the state.

The Effects of Tax Credits in the Anglo-Saxon Countries

The EITC in the USA has had striking results, especially following the expansion of the programme in 1993. Several studies point to a notable decline in poverty among children, especially children living in single-parent households. This decline was due to a combination of significantly increased levels of labour market participation on the part of single mothers and an increase in their income. In addition, female-headed households with children at the bottom end of the income distribution – those most affected by the policy changes – gained in terms of their average income. There appears, however, to have been a slightly negative effect on the labour supply from families in the phase-out zone, and especially on the labour supply from the second earner (Blank and Robins, 1999; Eissa and Hoynes, 2004; Eissa and Liebman, 1996; Hotz and Scholz, 2003; Marx, 2007; Scholz, 1996).

As for the UK programme, Brewer et al. (2006) concluded that the British tax credit has been successful in encouraging labour supply, especially among single parents. Moreover, the measure has also helped considerably in reducing poverty in the UK (see, for example, Sutherland, 2006; Sutherland and Piachaud, 2001).

Are Anglo-Saxon Tax Credits an Appropriate Model for Europe?

Inspired by the EITC and similar tax credits in the Anglo-Saxon countries, several Continental European countries have studied this type of policy measure (see, for example, the report by the advisory board of the German Ministry of Economics and Technology (Bundesministerium für Wirtschaft und Technologie, 2002)). Some countries have actually introduced tax credits for low wages: in 2001 the Prime Pour l'Emploi (PPE) was introduced in France, and the Employed Person's Tax Credit in the Netherlands. Belgium has also experimented with this approach, introducing a Low Wage Tax Credit in 2002 with the 2001 personal income tax reform (Cantillon et al., 2003a).

Tax credits for low wages serve a double purpose, namely, (1) to make work more attractive and (2) to reduce poverty among low-income families. In the Anglo-Saxon welfare states, the tax credit is most important for reducing poverty because of the high incidence of low-paying jobs and large income differences. In Continental Europe, low-wage tax credits are primarily aimed at reducing unemployment traps. In-work benefits have a major effect on the living standards of poor households in the Anglo-Saxon world because they are substantial, and they are aimed at households with low earnings rather than at low-paid individuals. However, it is not evident that these measures will or would be equally successful in Continental Europe. As an assessment of the tax credits introduced in the UK makes clear, the specific design of the tax credit and the institutional environment in which they are embedded can be very important (Brewer et al., 2001).

Since Continental European tax credits primarily aim to make work more attractive, tax credits are granted mainly on the basis of individual earnings, and not on household earnings (as is the case for both the EITC and the WTC), which can limit the anti-poverty impact of the measure (see below). Another major difference is that the level of Continental European tax credits is considerably lower than that of their Anglo-Saxon counterparts. Many of the benefits/tax credits that have recently been introduced in Europe provide only small financial gains (for an overview see OECD, 2005). In France, the maximum amount of the PPE is around 1 000 euros per year. The maximum amount of the Belgian low wage tax credit was only 520 euros per year, whereas the amounts can be about six times higher with the WTC and the EITC (for a more detailed comparison between the Belgian tax credit and the EITC/WTC, see Verbist et al., 2007). These amounts are so small that it is difficult to imagine that they could generate a significant work incentive effect or have a large impact on poverty.

Most evaluation studies focus on the employment effects of in-work benefits, whereas the effect on poverty is often neglected. Given the differences in design and in institutional and socio-economic setting, we can expect that a tax credit for low wages will have a considerably smaller effect on poverty in Continental Europe than it does in the USA and the UK. Analysis indicated that the introduction of the Belgian LWTC was most beneficial to middle- to high-income households, mainly because of its individualized structure, whereas its effect on poverty turned out to be negligible, mainly due to the low amount of the credit (Cantillon et al., 2003a). An ex-ante analysis of the French scheme – which is similar to the Belgian scheme (that is, the benefit amounts are small and aimed at individuals) – comes to an equally pessimistic conclusion as far as the likely poverty effects are concerned (Cahuc, 2002).

Bargain and Orsini (2007) have investigated the effects on poverty of the hypothetical introduction of the British 2001 WFTC in Germany, France and Finland using the microsimulation model EUROMOD (see Table 11.1). One of the questions posed in their study is what could happen if these three countries were to invest the same budgetary amount into a low-wage tax credit as the UK has done. The effects presented here are only first-round effects – that is, they do not take potential behavioural effects into account.

Such a policy shift would have the strongest poverty-reducing effects in France (according to both the 60 per cent of median equivalent income poverty line, as well as the more severe 50 per cent line; for more details on the definition of income poverty see the introduction to this volume). Poverty reduction would be very limited in Germany and Finland. Comparing the more generous 60 per cent poverty line with the stricter 50 per cent poverty line, we see that the introduction of the WFTC would redistribute relatively more income to the better-off households, and far less to the poorest. Bargain and Orsini (2007) have also calculated the efficiency cost of this policy – that is, the cost per year per household taken out of poverty. This cost turns out to be very high, ranging from 14 600 euros per household in France to about 33 800 euros in Germany and 54 600 euros in Finland.[1] A significantly higher poverty reduction could probably be reached at a much lower efficiency cost through efficient activation measures. Apparently, both from the perspective of effectiveness and efficiency, introducing an Anglo-Saxon tax credit for low wages would lead to disappointing results.

The conclusion that these policies are apparently less suitable for Continental European countries is illustrated by the Belgian experience.

Table 11.1 *Poverty indicators before and after the hypothetical introduction of the WFTC in France, Germany and Finland*

Poverty rate	France	Germany	Finland
60% of median equivalent income			
Pre-reform	14.0	11.2	12.0
Post-reform	12.3	10.7	11.6
50% of median equivalent income			
Pre-reform	7.0	5.7	3.8
Post-reform	6.4	5.5	3.7

Note: Poverty rates in post-reform scenarios are computed on the basis of the pre-reform poverty line.

Source: Bargain and Orsini (2007).

Effective on 1 January 2005, the low-wage tax credit was abolished and replaced by the 'work bonus'. This 'work bonus' is, in fact, an elaboration of the reduction of employees' social security contributions on low wages, which was introduced in January 2000. Hence, we again observe a shift from tax policies towards social security policies. Bargain and Orsini (2007) conclude that interest in in-work tax credits will probably fade away, despite the attractiveness of both the US and the UK experiences. They argue that 'at least in Continental and Nordic Europe the attention should be shifted towards demand side policies (given the level of structural involuntary unemployment) and active labour market policies that aim at permanently increasing the productivity of less skilled workers' (Bargain and Orsini, 2007: 193).

Direct Cash Transfers

At the country level, there is a remarkably strong and consistent relationship between the level of cash spending on social transfers and the incidence of poverty among the non-retired population. Not a single advanced economy is able to achieve low poverty rates with a low level of social spending, regardless of how well it does at maximizing self-sufficiency through high employment and low unemployment. This is arguably one of the most striking and robust findings of the past decades of comparative poverty research (Cantillon et al., 2003b; Förster and d'Ercole, 2006).

This association between social spending and low poverty rates is not only driven by the direct impact of transfers. High-spending countries have other institutional features that contribute to low poverty rates – most notably, strong collective bargaining that compresses wages (hence limiting overall inequality), more extensive public and subsidized employment as well as active labour market programmes, higher levels of public spending on education and so on. Disentangling the effects of these various factors is inherently fraught with difficulties (Alvarez, 2001; Cantillon et al., 2003b).

Still, a significant number of studies have sought to gauge the direct impact of social transfers and taxes (including social contributions) on poverty. A crucial general finding here is that, paradoxically, systems that target transfers primarily towards the poor have less of an impact on poverty than universal systems. As Oxley et al. (2001) showed, some countries achieve better 'efficiency' (that is, poverty is reduced to a greater degree for each euro spent) through focusing more on low-income groups. For every additional euro spent, means-tested systems are more efficient when it comes to reducing poverty. However, 'effort' and 'targeting' are negatively related; thus, countries that achieve higher 'efficiency' due to targeting have traded a good part of this away by reducing 'effort' (see also Nelson, 2004). As a consequence, targeted systems tend to have a weaker overall effect than universal systems.

Studies that have looked at the broader redistributive impact of transfers have come to a similar conclusion. In a seminal contribution, Korpi and Palme (1998) demonstrated that, paradoxically, systems that target proportionally more resources towards the needy have less of a redistributive impact than universal systems. They find that this relationship is mediated by the relative size of the available means for redistribution. It appears that some degree of redistributive inefficiency (what has been called the Matthew effect) helps to foster robust and broad-based political support for redistribution (Goodin and LeGrand, 1987).

Following the heightened attention to this issue, a number of recent studies have focused on child poverty (Corak et al., 2005; Whiteford and Adema, 2007). These studies are especially important because dependent children are the dominant reason why fully employed households – be they single- or double-adult households – sometimes fall below the poverty line.

Again, a fairly strong relationship emerges between the sheer level of child-contingent cash spending and the child poverty rate. Corak et al. (2005) showed that the countries which performed best tend to have systems of universal child benefits and tax concessions that are not particularly strongly targeted towards low-income children. Indeed, in the best-performing countries, more tends to be spent on non-poor children than on the poor. Strikingly, countries like the UK and Ireland – which rank as above-average spenders on child-contingent benefits, but target most by income – are among the least well-performing countries in terms of child poverty outcomes.

CONCLUSION

As we have stressed throughout this chapter, in-work poverty should not be seen as a separate issue from the broader poverty problem among the working-age population. In-work poverty as observed through the working individual living as part of a single-earner couple with children and unable to make ends meet is the same phenomenon as when it is observed through the non-working partner in that household, only in that case it is associated with unemployment or non-employment. It is also the same phenomenon as when it is observed through the child or children in that household; in that case it happens to be categorized as child poverty. Asking what helps when it comes to combating in-work poverty is, to a very large extent, akin to asking what helps when it comes to combating poverty among the working-age population in general.

In-work poverty in Europe is concentrated to a large extent among households with only one working adult – that is, traditional single-breadwinner households. Substantially higher levels of minimum wage protection would – even in the unlikely absence of negative employment effects – have a marginal direct impact on poverty at an immense spillover cost. It is more useful to look at poverty among single earners as a consequence of the persistent low levels of labour participation among women with lower levels of educational attainment which exist throughout much of Europe. A wide range of policy options are available to stimulate higher levels of multi-earnership. Countries can try to boost the employment prospects of those for whom labour demand appears to be weak. Higher levels of wage dispersion and lower minimum wages are a theoretical option, but not a particularly politically realistic one. For these reasons, governments have focused on trying to reduce the cost of less-skilled labour, mostly through employers' social security reductions. Although theoretical models suggest that such measures might have a substantial impact on the employment chances of the less skilled, the empirical evaluation literature provides reason for scepticism as to the cost-effectiveness of such measures. The empirical evidence is clearly more encouraging when it comes to measures that operate on the supply side – particularly measures that reduce the effective taxation of second earners and those that facilitate the combination of work and caregiving.

Stimulating and facilitating double earnership would go a long way towards reducing in-work poverty. But as simulation exercises show, generalized double earnership would not be enough. There would still be single-adult households who are unable to make ends meet, especially when there are children involved. There would even be double-earner couples who are unable to support large households. In other words, there would still be a need for household income supplements. This approach is now often associated with Anglo-Saxon-type 'tax credits' such as the EITC in the USA and the WTC in the UK. We have documented the substantial positive impact of programmes like the EITC in the USA on in-work poverty. But success in a setting as unique as the American one does not constitute sufficient reason for straightforward policy emulation elsewhere. The socio-demographic, economic and institutional context is vastly different in Europe. It is particularly important to keep in mind that in much of Europe, considerable scope remains for alleviating in-work poverty through tax reforms aimed at reducing effective marginal tax rates for households with low earnings. It seems premature to contemplate Anglo-Saxon-type negative tax credits before the scope for targeted tax alleviation has been well and truly depleted.

That said, targeted tax cuts – or Anglo-Saxon-type tax credits for that matter – have their limits. In order to be effective as an anti-poverty device, such tax measures need to be strongly targeted, which almost inevitably implies a high cost in terms of disincentive effects. Tax and other measures strongly targeted at households with low earnings are bound to create mobility traps. From the perspective of horizontal equity and public support for the system, there are also limits to targeting. By contrast, universal measures such as universal child benefits have an immediate impact on poverty – both among those who depend on earnings and those on replacement benefits – without adversely affecting work incentives. As the empirical evidence before us today shows, universal, comprehensive social protection systems consistently perform better in preventing poverty – including in-work poverty – than strongly targeted systems do.

NOTE

1. These figures refer to the 60 per cent poverty line; with the 50 per cent line, the amounts are much higher, namely 38 000 euros, 113 000 euros and over 840 000 euros for France, Germany and Finland, respectively.

REFERENCES

Alvarez, P.B. (2001), 'The politics of income inequality in the OECD: the role of second order effects', LIS-working paper, No. 284.

Bargain, O. and K. Orsini (2007), 'Beans for breakfast? How exportable is the British Workfare Model?', in O. Bargain (ed.), *Microsimulation in Action. Policy Analysis in Europe Using EUROMOD*. Research in Labour Economics, vol. 25, Oxford: Elsevier, pp. 165–98.

Bazen, S. and N. Skourias (1997), 'Is there a negative effect of minimum wages in France?', *European Economic Review*, **41**, 723–32.

Blank, R., R. Card and P. Robins (1999), *Financial Incentives for Increasing Work and Incomes among Low-Income Families*, NBER Working Paper 6998, Cambridge: National Bureau of Economic Research.

Brewer, M. (2003), *The New Tax Credits*, Briefing Note no. 35, London: Institute for Fiscal Studies.

Brewer, M., T. Clark and M. Myck (2001), *Credit Where It's Due? An Assessment of the New Tax Credits*, Commentary 86, London: Institute for Fiscal Studies.

Brewer, M., A. Duncan, A. Shephard and M.J. Suarez (2006), 'Did working families' tax credit work? The impact of in-work support on labour supply in Great Britain', *Labour Economics*, **13**, 699–720.

Bundesministerium für Wirtschaft und Technologie (2002), *Reform des Sozialstaats für mehr Beschäftigung im Berich gering qualifizierter Arbeit*, Report Bundesministerium für Wirtschaft und Technologie.

Cahuc, P. (2002), 'A quoi sert la prime pour l'emploi?', *Revue Française d'Economie*, **16** (3), 3–61.

Cantillon, B., B. Kerstens and G. Verbist (2003a), 'Les effets rédistributifs de la réforme de l'impôt des personnes physiques', *Cahiers Economiques de Bruxelles*, **46** (1), 71–98.

Cantillon B., I. Marx and K. van den Bosch (2003b), 'The puzzle of egalitarianism: relationship between employment, wage inequality, social expenditure and poverty', *European Journal of Social Security*, **5** (2), 108–27.

Corak, M., C. Lietz and H. Sutherland (2005), *The Impact of Tax and Transfer Systems on Children in the European Union*, IZA Discussion Paper 1589, Bonn: IZA.

Del Boca, D. and D. Vuri (2005), *Labour Supply and Child Care Costs: The Effect of Rationing*, DP #1779, Bonn: IZA.

Dolado, J., F. Felgueroso and J. Jimeno (2000), *The Role of the Minimum Wage in the Welfare State: An Appraisal*, Discussion Paper 152, Bonn: IZA.

Dolado, J., F. Kramarz, S. Machin, A. Manning, D. Margolis and K. Teulings (1996), 'The economic impact of minimum wages in Europe', *Economic Policy*, **23**, 319–72.

Eissa, N. and H. Hoynes (2004), 'Taxes and the labor market participation of married couples: the Earned Income Tax Credit', *Journal of Public Economics*, **88**, 1931–58.

Eissa, N. and J. Liebman (1996), 'Labor supply response to the Earned Income Tax Credit', *Quarterly Journal of Economics*, **112** (2), 605–37.

Esping-Andersen, G. (1996), 'Welfare states without work: the impasse of labour shedding and familialism in continental European social policy', in G. Esping-Andersen (ed.), *Welfare States in Transition; National Adaptations in Global Economies*, London: Sage.

Esping-Andersen, G. (1999), *Social Foundations of Post-Industrial Economies*, Oxford: Oxford University Press.

Formby, J., J. Bishop and H. Kim (2005), *Minimum Wages and Poverty: An Evaluation of Alternatives*, Amsterdam: Elsevier.

Förster, M and M. Mira d'Ercole (2005), *Income Distribution and Poverty in OECD Countries in the Second Half of the 1990s*, OECD Social Employment and Migration Working Papers No. 22, Paris: OECD.
Fritzell, J. and V.-M. Ritakallio (2004), *Societal Shifts and Changed Patterns of Poverty*, Luxembourg Income Study Working Paper No. 393, Luxembourg: LIS.
Goodin, R. and J. LeGrand (1987), *Not Only the Poor; The Middle Classes and the Welfare State*, London: Unwin Hyman.
Gornick, J. and M. Meyers (2003), *Families that Work: Policies for Reconciling Parenthood and Employment*, New York: Russell Sage Foundation.
Gosling, A. (1996), 'Minimum wages: possible effects on the income distribution', *Fiscal Studies*, **17** (4), 31–48.
Granier, P. and J. Nyssen (1995), *Réduction des charges sociales sur les emplois non-qualifiés, chomage et croissance*, GREQAN Document de Travail 95A05, Marseille: GREQAM.
Horrigan, M. and R. Mincey (1993), 'The minimum wage and earnings and income inequality', in S. Danziger and P. Gottschalk (eds), *Uneven Tides: Rising Inequality in America*, New York: Russell Sage Foundation, pp. 251–75.
Hotz, V.J. and J.K. Scholz (2003), 'The Earned Income Tax Credit', in R. Moffit (ed.), *Means-Tested Transfer Programs in the U.S.*, Chicago, IL: University of Chicago Press, pp. 141–98.
Hui, W. and P. Trivedi (1986), 'Duration dependence, targeted employment subsidies and unemployment benefits', *Journal of Public Economics*, **31**, 105–29.
Immervoll, H. (2007), *Minimum Wages, Minimum Labour Costs and the Tax Treatment of Low-Wage Employment*, OECD Social, Employment and Migration Working Papers No. 46, Paris: OECD.
Immervoll, H. and D. Barber (2006), *Can Parents Afford to Work? Childcare Costs, Tax-Benefit Policies and Work Incentives*, IZA Discussion Paper 1932, Bonn: IZA.
Inland Revenue (2002), *The Child and Working Tax Credits*, London: HM Treasury.
Jongen, E.L.W. (1998), *Vouchers for the Long-Term Unemployed: A Simulation with MIMIC*, Research Memorandum No. 139, Den Haag: Centraal Planbureau.
Jongen, E.L.W. (1999), 'What can we expect from subsidies for the long-term unemployed?', *De Economist*, **147** (2), 205–28.
Korpi, W. and J. Palme (1998), 'The paradox of redistribution and strategies of equality: welfare state institutions, inequality and poverty in the Western countries', *American Sociological Review*, **63**, 661–87.
Kramarz, F. and T. Philippon (2001), 'The impact of differential payroll tax subsidies on minimum wage employment', *Journal of Public Economics*, **82** (1), 115–46.
Laroque, G. and B. Salanié (1999), *Breaking Down Married Female Non-Employment in France*, CEPR Discussion Paper 2239, London: Centre for Economic Policy Research.
Malinvaud, E. (1998), *Les cotisations sociales à la charge des employeurs: analyse économique*, Rapport au Premier Ministre, Paris: Conseil d'Analyse Economique.
Marx, I. (2001), 'Job subsidies and cuts in employers' social security contributions: the verdict of empirical evaluation studies', *International Labour Review*, **140** (1), 69–85.
Marx, I. (2007), *A New Social Question? On Minimum Income Protection in the Postindustrial Era*, Amsterdam: Amsterdam University Press.

Marx, I. and G. Verbist (1998), 'Low-paid work and poverty: a cross-country perspective', in S. Bazen, M. Gregory and W. Salverda (eds), *Low-wage employment in Europe*, Cheltenham, UK and Lyme, USA: Edward Elgar, pp. 63–86.
Mühlau, P. and W. Salverda (2000), 'Employment effects of low-wage subsidies: the case of "SPAK" in the Netherlands', in W. Salverda, B. Nolan and C. Lucifora (eds), *Policy Measures for Low-Wage Employment in Europe*, Cheltenham, UK and Northampton, MA, USA: Edward Elgar, pp. 67–92.
Nelson, K. (2004), 'Mechanisms of poverty alleviation: anti-poverty effects of non-means tested and means-tested benefits in five welfare states', *Journal of European Social Policy*, **14** (4), 371–90.
Neumark, D. and W. Wascher (1997), *Do Minimum Wages Fight Poverty?* Working Paper 6127, Cambridge: National Bureau of Economic Research.
Nickell, S. and B. Bell (1997), 'Would cutting payroll taxes on the unskilled have a significant impact on unemployment?', in D.J. Snower and G. de la Dehesa (eds), *Unemployment Policy: Government Options for the Labour Market*, Cambridge: Cambridge University Press, pp. 296–328.
Nolan, B. and I. Marx (2000), 'Low pay and household poverty', in M. Gregory, W. Salverda and S. Bazen (eds), *Labour Market Inequalities: Problems and Policies of Low-wage Employment in International Perspective*, Oxford: Oxford University Press, pp. 100–119.
Organisation for Economic Co-operation and Development (OECD) (1998), *Employment Outlook*, Paris: OECD.
Organisation for Economic Co-operation and Development (OECD) (2003), *Employment Outlook*, Paris: OECD.
Organisation for Economic Co-operation and Development (OECD) (2005), *Employment Outlook*, Paris: OECD.
Organisation for Economic Co-operation and Development (OECD) (2007), *Employment Outlook*, Paris: OECD.
Oxley, H., Th.-Th. Dang, M. Förster and M. Pellizari (2001), 'Income inequalities and poverty among children and households with children in selected OECD countries', in K. Vleminckx and T. Smeeding (eds), *Child Well-being, Child Poverty and Child Policy in Modern Nations: What Do We Know*, Bristol: Policy Press, pp. 371–405.
Phelps, E. (1997), *Rewarding Work*, Cambridge, MA: Harvard University Press.
Polanen Petel, V.C.A. van, T.W. Hu, J. de Koning and C. van der Veen (1999), *Werkgelegenheidseffecten van de SPAK en VLW*, Rotterdam: NEI.
Scholtz, J.K. (1996), 'In-work benefits in the United States: the Earned Income Tax Credit', *The Economic Journal*, January, 156–69.
Sneessens, H. and F. Shadman (2000), 'Analyse macro-économique des effets de réductions ciblées des charges sociales', *Revue Belge de Securité Sociale*, **3**, 613–30.
Snower, D.J. (1994), 'Converting unemployment benefits into employment subsidies', *AEA Papers and Proceedings*, **84**, 65–70.
Snower, D.J. (1997), 'The simple economics of benefit transfers', in D.J. Snower and G. de la Dehesa (eds), *Unemployment Policy: Government Options for the Labour Market*, Cambridge: Cambridge University Press, pp. 163–98.
Steiber, N. (2007), *The Linkages between Work and Family: State of Knowledge and Policy Implications*, Equalsoc Policy Paper #2.
Sutherland, H. (2001), *The National Minimum Wage and In-Work Poverty*, DAE Working Papers 0111, Department of Applied Economics, University of Cambridge.

Sutherland, H. (2006), 'Can child poverty be abolished? Promises and policies in the UK', *The Economic and Labour Relations Review*, **17** (1), 7–32.
Sutherland, H. and D. Piachand (2001), 'Reducing child poverty in Britain: an assessment of government policy 1997–2001', *Economic Journal*, **111** (469), F85–F101.
Verbist, G., L. De Lathouwer and A. Roggeman (2007), 'Labour market activation policies: a comparison of the use of tax credits in Belgium, the UK and the US', in J. De Koning (ed.), *The Evaluation of Active Labour Market Policies*, Cheltenham, UK and Northampton, MA, USA: Edward Elgar, pp. 57–92.
Whiteford, P. and W. Adema (2007), *What Works Best in Reducing Child Poverty: A Benefit or Work Strategy?* OECD Social Employment and Migration Working Papers, No. 51, Paris: OECD.

12. Explaining in-work poverty within and across countries

Henning Lohmann and Hans-Jürgen Andreß

We started our research with the assumption that the incidence and socio-demographic profile of the working poor in Western Europe cannot be analysed without a thorough understanding of each country's institutional context. In this final chapter, we discuss the most important empirical findings with respect to this institutional explanation. Starting with a summary of the main institutional features of the countries represented in this study, we attempt to draw some general conclusions about the level and structure of in-work poverty as it is typically found in different institutional settings. Finally, we discuss the development of in-work poverty over time and its implications for employment growth.

The methodological design of this study consisted of a series of in-depth case studies focusing on single countries, which were then complemented by two comparative analyses focusing on many European countries. Each case study presented information on the country's institutional context and used nationally representative micro data to describe patterns of in-work poverty within that country. The comparative analyses, on the other hand, focused on overall determinants of in-work poverty and used cross-nationally equivalent micro data to describe different institutional contexts in statistical terms and to test the effects of individual and societal characteristics on in-work poverty. In conducting these analyses, we tried to combine the advantages of in-depth qualitative information on the institutional context in each country with the comparative quantitative information from a large cross-nationally equivalent database. The following discussion starts with the evidence from the eight case studies and then generalizes this information using the evidence from the comparative analyses.

For the purpose of presenting our results, we use a welfare regime typology. For us, this typology mainly serves as a heuristic tool which allows us to bring out more clearly the commonalities and differences between the countries in our study. As we see shortly, the explanatory power of the concept of welfare regimes is rather limited. Instead, specific policies or the current state of the national economy very often seem to do a better job of explaining why in-work poverty is high in one country and low in another. The third section attempts to generalize from these seemingly national idiosyncrasies by looking at the underlying dimensions of the welfare regimes that have been discussed in the previous chapters. Instead of using the concept of welfare regimes, we ask whether the level of decommodification and defamilization itself – or the respective systems of wage-setting – explain why some countries do a better job than others in protecting their workforce from poverty.

We then look at trends in in-work poverty over time (in the fourth section). Almost all the country chapters contain analyses conducted in a longitudinal perspective. Referring to the discussion of welfare state retrenchment and labour market deregulation, many authors expect to see an increase in in-work poverty over time. In a time period of increased global competition between national economies, the idea behind this policy change has been to increase work incentives and job opportunities. While these new policies may be effective with respect to economic growth and employment, they are not without risk with respect to in-work poverty, because increased work incentives and new job opportunities may push vulnerable groups into the labour market, who will have problems making ends meet. The same section discusses the corresponding evidence from the single country studies and then tries to draw some overall conclusions. We are especially interested in the question of whether there is a trade-off between economic growth and employment, on the one hand, and in-work poverty, on the other.

THE INSTITUTIONAL BACKGROUND

This book contains case studies of eight European countries. Before discussing patterns of in-work poverty in these countries, it is useful to summarize their institutional backgrounds. At the beginning of our research, these 'cases' were deliberately selected to represent different regions and, thus, possible variations in in-work poverty across Europe. Finland and Sweden stand for the Northern European countries; Ireland and Britain for the Anglo-Saxon countries; Belgium, Germany, and the Netherlands for the Continental European countries; and, finally, Italy for the Southern European countries. Each of the previous country chapters includes a detailed account of national labour market institutions and welfare state regulations, and we first focus our discussion on these eight countries. Occasionally, however, we also refer to the other European countries represented in the two comparative analyses by Lohmann and Marx and

Lohmann, although the background information – other than the statistical data – for these other countries is rather limited.

Finland and Sweden, our Northern European representatives, are usually classified as typical examples of the social democratic welfare regime, which is characterized by a comprehensive welfare state with benefits based on universal social rights. Individual independence of market forces and family traditions is the overall policy orientation. Indeed, according to the statistical data in Lohmann and Marx (in this volume), both countries are characterized by (comparatively) high degrees of decommodification, generous replacement rates in case of unemployment, high spending on family services (in addition to munificent family cash benefits), centralized wage bargaining and high union density.[1] But as we have learned from the case studies by Halleröd and Larsson and Airio, Kuivalainen and Niemelä, both countries had to cope with a severe economic crisis at the beginning of the 1990s, accompanied by unprecedented unemployment figures. As a consequence of this economic downturn, both countries have cut back their systems of social transfers and flexibilized their labour markets. Both case studies, however, interpret these reforms as gradual adjustments and not as a general change of welfare policies. Nevertheless, both the economic crisis and the policy adjustments have left their mark on the Swedish and Finnish societies. Women's employment decreased by more than 10 percentage points in the first half of the 1990s, and has only partially recovered since then (OECD Labour Force Survey database); the degree of bargaining centralization is much lower in Sweden at the turn of the twenty-first century than it was at the beginning of the 1990s (Visser, 2004: 43); and there have been gradual cutbacks in the social security systems of both countries. Furthermore, we should not forget the within-regime variation that is typical for any kind of country classification. Hence, when we study both countries in more detail, significant differences begin to emerge behind the overall commonalities. For instance, a closer look at family policies suggests that Finland is a little bit more familialistic, while Sweden is committed to strengthening the egalitarian model (Hiilamo, forthcoming). Accordingly, the employment rate is lower for Finnish women, and one finds fewer toddlers in public childcare than in Sweden.

The Anglo-Saxon representatives, Britain and Ireland, are often classified as examples of the liberal welfare regime, although the Irish case is contested in the literature. The liberal welfare regime is characterized by a residual welfare state and a strong market orientation. The market functions as the main provider of individual welfare. Welfare provisions by the state are minimal and restricted to those who have proven need (means-tested programmes), while the extent of social insurance programmes and universal transfers is only modest. A typical representative is the USA. Compared to this prototype, British and Irish social transfers are not as meagre as one might expect. Of course, the degree of decommodification is lower than in the Continental European countries (see below) and certainly below the level in the Northern European countries. But it is not as low as it is in the USA or in some of the Southern European countries. Both countries spend significant amounts of money on family cash benefits, and it appears that targeted welfare assistance within work activation programmes has improved the economic position of families in Britain (Connolly, in this volume). Nevertheless, the British labour market – with its decentralized wage-setting and its low level of dismissal protection – very much resembles the US prototype. Union density is low in Britain and Ireland compared with the situation in the Northern European countries, but not very much different from the experience in the other countries in our study. Statistical data also reveal why Ireland does not fit well into the liberal cluster. The Irish wage-setting system is much more centralized (even more centralized than in Sweden and Finland), and the welfare state has a much more familialistic orientation, investing more into family cash benefits than into family services (Gallie and Paugam, 2000; see also the figures in Lohmann and Marx in this volume). Accordingly, the female labour participation rate is much lower than it is in Britain. Overall, Britain and Ireland may be used as examples of the liberal welfare regime, but they are not as liberal as one might expect – and Ireland in particular has a slightly different policy orientation with respect to families. However, what definitely distinguishes these two countries (particularly Ireland) from most of the other countries in our study – and especially from our two Northern European representatives – is the absence of any economic crisis. On the contrary, both Britain and Ireland experienced an economic boom within the observation period, accompanied by rapid growth in employment (Connolly, in this volume; Nolan, in this volume).

The conservative welfare regime is characterized by a rather comprehensive welfare state based on subsidiarity and status preservation. Social benefits depend on work performance (that is, previous earnings) and preserve status with negligible redistributive impact. Therefore, protection against market forces depends primarily on one's labour market position, with (male) employees and their families being decommodified to a high degree, while other social groups (for example, single parents) are only insufficiently supported. The conservative welfare regime describes the institutional setting in the Continental European countries quite well. Germany is definitely a prototype of this model. It has an extensive welfare state in terms of cash transfers, both for the unemployed and for families. Decommodification and replacement rates are nearly as high as in the

Northern European countries. However, it lacks the Northern orientation towards gender equality and invests less money into family services (childcare, and so on) which allow women to combine work and caregiving. Correspondingly, female labour market participation is lower in Germany than it is in Sweden, and fewer toddlers attend public childcare facilities. Although policies to increase female employment are becoming more popular in Germany, the traditional orientation towards a modernized version of the male-breadwinner model (full-time working husband, part-time working wife) is still dominant in German social security and taxation (Gießelmann and Lohmann, in this volume). The same is true for the German labour market: although measures of flexibilization and deregulation are increasing – at least since the turn of the twenty-first century – job protection is still quite extensive for (the mostly male) insiders in the labour market (ibid.).[2]

But the conservative welfare regime is also well known for its internal heterogeneity. Belgium, the Netherlands and, even, Germany are good examples of this within-regime variation. As shown by Gießelmann and Lohmann (in this volume), Eastern Germany (the 'new' federal states after reunification) deviates in several aspects from the aforementioned picture. The public system of childcare is much more developed, and the male-breadwinner model is less dominant – although it has been difficult for Eastern German women to realize their employment wishes owing to the economic problems in Eastern Germany after reunification. Hence, for Germany, it has always been necessary – at least during our observation period – to tell a second story for the Eastern parts, and it is an open question as to whether the experiences of the working population in Eastern Germany (less job protection, more decentralized wage bargaining, less powerful unions, lower wages) will gradually disseminate into the Western German labour market.

Belgium and the Netherlands are deviant cases for other reasons. At first glance, Belgium bears many of the 'hallmarks' of the conservative welfare state model. At the same time, however, childcare provisions for working parents are extensive, as Marx and Verbist (in this volume) argue, giving families the option of being unburdened from childcare responsibilities if they so wish ('optional familialism'). In Germany, this option does not exist – at least in the Western parts – owing to the insufficient system of childcare. The Netherlands has been a borderline case from the very beginning of welfare state research. Esping-Andersen (1990) classified the Netherlands into the social democratic welfare regime type because of the extensive Dutch welfare system. Decommodification and replacement rates are as high as they are in Sweden and Finland. Employment protection and centralized wage bargaining are also similar to the Northern European countries (but union density is much lower). Other welfare researchers (for example, Visser and Hemerijck, 1997), however, put the Netherlands into the conservative cluster due to the corporatist set-up of the welfare state. Esping-Andersen (1999) also saw reasons to regard the Netherlands as a hybrid case: namely, its focus on the modernized version of the male-breadwinner model and its low degree of support for dual-earner families in terms of public childcare, both of which result in female participation rates that are mainly based on part-time employment. Furthermore, recent labour market reforms and retrenchment policies in the social security system, as described by Snel, de Boom and Engbersen (in this volume), do not really fit into the social democratic welfare regime model. All in all, Germany, Belgium and the Netherlands may be treated as examples of the same (conservative) welfare model, but the institutional heterogeneity of this group of countries is possibly much higher than in the other welfare regimes.

Finally, with Italy, we have one representative of the Southern European countries which Esping-Andersen (1990; 1999) treats as a variant of the conservative welfare regime. Its social security system is oriented towards status preservation for the (mostly male) insiders of the labour market, and it is generous to these groups, at least if they retire. Employment protection is at least as high as it is in Germany, Belgium and the Netherlands. The same is true for union density. However, Italy (and similarly, the other Southern European countries) is characterized by the absence of any significant support for families, either in terms of cash benefits or in terms of family services. Furthermore, social benefits for other social risks besides old age or for other social groups besides the (male) insiders of the labour market are scarce. Accordingly, overall indices of decommodification place Italy in the lower ranks of our country sample (together with Ireland and Britain). In all these cases, the Italian family is the last safety net, and this is especially true in the Southern parts of Italy (the 'Mezzogiorno'), as Biolcati-Rinaldi and Podestà (in this volume) plainly demonstrate with micro data from a large household panel. Overall, because of its rudimentary welfare state and its reliance on the family as the main provider of individual welfare, Italy can be treated as a typical example of what has become known as the familialistic welfare regime (for example, Bonoli, 1997; Ferrera, 1996; Leibfried, 1992).

CROSS-SECTIONAL PERSPECTIVE: EXPECTED OUTCOMES AND SURPRISES

With the aforementioned regime typology in mind, Lohmann and Marx (in this volume) postulated several expectations about the incidence and structure of in-work poverty, which they tested against the statistical evidence from a large cross-national data set (the European Community Household Panel – ECHP). In principle, the institutional explanation proved to be useful, but some cross-cluster and cross-country differences remained unexplained. Naturally, the ECHP lacks the detailed information that is available to us from the eight case studies. In the following section, we will attempt to use this in-depth information to clarify some of the complexities of in-work poverty, at least for the eight European countries that were studied.

Differences in Levels of In-work Poverty

Concerning the level of in-work poverty, Lohmann and Marx (in this volume) expect to find a rather low level in the social democratic welfare regime, a medium level in the conservative regime and a rather high level in the liberal and the familialistic regimes. Table 12.1 summarizes their main expectations. In-work poverty is expected to be low in the social democratic regime because of the decommodifying effects of its universal social benefits, its comprehensive system of childcare that gives all parents the option to work, and its compressed wage distribution that decreases the risk of low pay. At the other end of the continuum, in-work poverty is expected to be high in the liberal welfare regime, where the market is the main provider of individual welfare and wage inequalities are high, increasing the risk of low pay, while state support in case of income loss (due to unemployment, sickness, retirement), low pay and restricted earnings capacity (for example, because of parenting) is scarce. The same expectation applies for the familialistic regime, but for slightly different reasons: the family is the main provider of individual welfare, and meagre social benefits are almost exclusively focused on the male breadwinner, who is also protected by a well-regulated insider–outsider labour market. Here, in-work poverty is high because this system of protection is insufficient for some male-breadwinner families (for example, for those with many economically dependent family members) or because it ignores groups outside the core of the labour market, where the risk of low pay is high. A similar insider–outsider constellation – both on the labour market and in the system of social security – can also be found in the conservative welfare regime, but the level of in-work poverty is expected to be lower because social benefits are extensive, female employment – at least on a part-time basis – is supported and low pay is less frequent. Therefore, the conservative welfare regime is, in many respects, a hybrid model combining elements of the old stratified Bismarckian system of social security with elements of the egalitarian Northern European welfare model.

Table 12.1 Welfare regimes and levels of in-work poverty

Welfare regime	In-work poverty	
	Expected	Percentage (2001)
Social democratic	Low	6.5 (SWE) 7.1 (FIN)
Conservative	Medium	5.7 (B) 6.8 (D) 10.5 (NL)
Liberal	High	6.6 (GB) 7 (IRL)
Familialistic	High	9.7 (I)

Note: See Chapter 1 by Lohmann and Marx in this volume.

Table 12.1 also shows the percentage of working poor individuals in each country in 2001.[3] Disappointingly, most of the hypotheses are falsified – except in the case of Italy, which as a member of the familialistic welfare regime shows the expected high incidence of in-work poverty. Surprisingly, in-work poverty in the Netherlands is even higher than it is in Italy, and the remaining six countries show medium levels of in-work poverty ranging between 5.7 per cent in Belgium and 6.8 per cent in Germany, although they represent different institutional contexts. These surprising results raise several questions: why do Sweden and Finland – which, according to the discussion in the previous section, fit well into the social democratic welfare regime – hardly differ from most of the Continental European countries? Or to put it differently: why do Germany and especially Belgium perform as well as Sweden and Finland, although the institutional context in Belgium (and even more so in Germany) bears many traits of the conservative welfare regime? Finally, what is the explanation for the extremely high percentage of in-work poverty in the Netherlands, and why do we not observe similar negative results for Britain and Ireland, which are often classified as examples of the liberal welfare regime?

Let us start our discussion with the latter two cases. In the previous section, our review of both countries' institutional contexts ended with the conclusion that Britain and Ireland are not as liberal as one might expect. According to Connolly (in this volume), recent welfare reforms in Britain have been successful in improving the economic position of families. Furthermore, the government's welfare-to-work measures significantly decreased unemployment, and favourable macroeconomic conditions led to growth in earnings without much change in income inequality. As a consequence, 'risks of in-work poverty are particularly acute for those who are young and living on their own', as Connolly says. If this group is not particularly large, and if vulnerable groups (like single parents) are kept out of the labour market, this may explain why Britain scores relatively well with respect to in-work poverty.

As far as economic growth and increasing employment are concerned, the story is pretty much the same for Ireland as the chapter by Nolan demonstrates. But, as already mentioned in the previous section, Ireland has a slightly different policy orientation with respect to families. It invests more into family cash benefits than into family services. Accordingly, female labour market participation is much lower than it is in Britain, and the percentage of dual-earner couples is the second lowest among our eight countries. Furthermore, Ireland's economic growth has been accompanied by a significant rise in income inequality, so that with a relative concept of income poverty, certain groups fall below the rising poverty threshold. In this situation, households which rely on only one earner have particular difficulties in staying above these rising thresholds (Nolan, in this volume). Given the more 'traditional' division of labour in Irish households, this is quite a frequent setting and may explain why Ireland is not as successful as Britain in coping with in-work poverty. In other words, while Britain is able to integrate high-risk groups into the economic upturn through well-designed in-work benefits, Ireland's economic boom leaves behind some of the more traditional groups of the Irish working population.

Now let us turn to the question of why in-work poverty in Sweden and Finland is at about the same level as it is in Belgium and Germany, although ideally, the social democratic welfare regime intends – as Halleröd and Larsson (in this volume) put it – 'that most people are working, wages are sufficiently high to keep those who are working out of poverty, and income losses during temporary periods of unemployment, sickness, and so on, are replaced via income maintenance programmes'. At first sight, it is tempting to answer the question the other way round: Belgium and Germany perform as well as the two Nordic countries do because the negative features of the conservative welfare regime discussed in the previous section are not as pronounced as we expected. Belgium, for example, with its well developed system of public childcare, gives parents the opportunity to combine work and caregiving, and thus improves their economic position. Germany, on the other hand, with its encompassing system of unemployment and welfare benefits, is able to keep high-risk groups out of the labour market and hence the in-work poverty rate low – however, at increased costs in public spending.

Unfortunately, the optional familialism of Belgian family services can only partially explain the country's extremely low level of in-work poverty, because contrary to what we might expect, female labour market participation is among the lowest in the conservative cluster (Lohmann and Marx, in this volume). Even if Marx and Verbist (in this volume) are correct in stating that Belgium's maternal employment rate is at the level of the Nordic countries, overall labour market participation among women is still heavily influenced by the traditional focus of the Belgian welfare state on the male breadwinner model. Thus, publicly available childcare can only be part of the explanation of low in-work poverty in the Belgian case. Another point is, perhaps, the compressed wage distribution due to strong labour unions and extended job protection in Belgium. As a consequence, low-wage work is less frequent than it is in other countries in the conservative cluster (Lohmann and Marx, in this volume) – which also translates into lower levels of in-work poverty, even if the link between low-wage work and poverty is less direct, as emphasized at various places in this volume.

A more general explanation, however, may be found in the former contention about the German case, which directs our attention to the more general question of who is at risk of poverty in the countries we compared. Indeed, if we look at overall employment in Sweden, but also in the UK, we realize that the former comparison is quite 'unfair'. While in-work poverty rates are about the same size in all four countries, Sweden and the UK reach this level with more than 75 per cent of their working-age population in gainful employment, while the employment rates in Germany and Belgium are much lower (around 67 to 70 per cent).[4] The differences are even more pronounced in the group of workers with the lowest qualifications (ISCED 0-2). In other words, if more Germans and Belgians were gainfully employed, more individuals with high poverty risks – who are now living on unemployment and welfare benefits – would be active on the labour market. Naturally, this would increase the overall in-work poverty rate significantly above the values presented in Table 12.1 – which are only seemingly low if this contention is true. Its validity, however, is easily justified with the following thought experiment: it starts off from the qualification-specific poverty and employment rates in a given country. If we assume in a counterfactual manner that Belgium were to have the same level of employment in all qualificational groups as Britain does, we can estimate the effect of policies which put more stress on inclusion into gainful employment among the less qualified. If we do this thought experiment and apply the British employment figures to the Belgian case, Belgian in-work poverty increases slightly, from 5.7 per cent (the original rate) to 6.1 per cent (the counterfactual poverty rate). One could argue, however, that the poverty rate among the less qualified would also increase because increased employment also entails more high-risk groups among the less qualified. Correspondingly, if we assume that the poverty rate of workers with low qualifications would increase by 2 percentage points as well, the overall Belgian poverty rate would increase by another 0.5 percentage points. In total, we would end up with an in-work poverty rate of 6.6 per cent, which is exactly the level which can be found in Britain, and slightly above the rate in Sweden.

Finally, we will have a look at the Netherlands, whose poverty rate is remarkably high. How can this high rate be explained? First, we have to acknowledge that the Netherlands – together with Germany, Ireland and the UK – belongs to the group of countries with high part-time and low-wage rates. But even compared with these three countries, the Netherlands is an extreme case. Almost one-third of the workforce is working part-time. Given the higher poverty risk of part-time work, the share among the working poor is even higher. More than half of the Dutch working poor are part-time workers. Obviously, the mechanism described for Germany by Gießelmann and Lohmann (in this volume) – namely, that the poverty risk of lower-paid part-time workers is moderated within the household context – does not work equally well in the Dutch case. Second, this result can be read against the background of the shift in welfare and labour market policy described by Snel, de Boom and Engbersen in this volume. In the past 10 to 15 years, the Netherlands was one of the countries with the fastest growing activity rates. To a relevant extent, this employment growth is based on the proliferation of low-wage and part-time work. If we take Belgium as a country of comparison, which consequently keeps some of the risk groups out of the labour market, the Netherlands, in contrast, has fundamentally altered its policies and opted for a strategy of labour market inclusion. As a consequence, the Netherlands not only stands out with its high in-work poverty rate, but also because of the fact that more than half of the poor are working poor (see Lohmann and Marx in this volume). This could be read as a positive result with reference to the non-working poor, but certainly not with reference to the working poor.

Who are the Working Poor? Does the Group Differ by Country?

Now let us turn to the question of who is at risk for in-work poverty. Again, the assumption is that the institutional context provides specific safeguards and risks against poverty which put certain groups of the working population in a favourable position, while other groups have problems making ends meet. According to Lohmann and Marx (in this volume), each welfare regime has its own profile of the working poor. For example, in a context of almost generalized double earnership and no preferential tax/benefit treatment for single-earner households – as is typical for the social democratic welfare regime – in-work poverty affects mostly single-earner households. Another risk group are young adults, who tend to become economically self-reliant earlier in the social democratic regime than in the others. In the conservative welfare regime, the structure of the working poor is supposed to be dominated by the insider–outsider problem typical of most Continental European labour markets. Hence, Lohmann and Marx (in this volume) expect to see significant in-work poverty among young people and other non-core workers. The institutional focus on the male-breadwinner model may also be a handicap, if the assumptions of this model – that is, adequate wages earned by the breadwinner and sufficient state support for economically dependent family members – do not hold for certain groups of the working population. Both assumptions may be wrong in the case of less-skilled workers and large households, but the negative consequences may be offset by additional incomes from secondary earners within the household. Similar arguments apply to the familialistic welfare regime, which is also characterized by a strong focus on the male-breadwinner model and a highly segmented labour market. In case of the familialistic welfare regime, however, state support for families is meagre, especially when it comes to measures that support female employment. Thus, in the familialistic welfare regime, single earnership and large households are the prime causes of in-work poverty. The expectations for the liberal regime are based on the notion of an unregulated labour market (which we find in a most pronounced manner only in Britain). While in other countries, older workers are protected by seniority rights, this is not the case in Britain. Hence, we expect that the risk of being poor is not located mainly in the group of young workers, but spread more evenly over the total age distribution. We can also expect a higher risk of in-work poverty among women. In the liberal regime, female employment rates are high, but women lack the support of policies to promote gender equality in the labour market, which often puts them in precarious positions.

Each of the case studies presents a socio-demographic profile of the working poor in the corresponding country. Additional evidence can be found in the comparative analyses in the first part of this volume. In many aspects, these studies draw a similar picture of potential poverty risks. The risk of in-work poverty is associated with young and old age, low education, partnership dissolution, household size (positively), number of earners (negatively), low pay, self-employment, and occupational status (negatively). Most of these effects are perfectly in line with current poverty research postulating that poverty increases with the needs and decreases with the resources of individuals and households. However, we also find differences between countries. These are mostly related to the influence of age and gender. The age profile of the working poor differs strongly between the countries of the social democratic, liberal and familialistic clusters. While in social democratic welfare states in particular, younger workers face a high risk of in-work poverty, age is a much less important predictor in the liberal countries and has the opposite influence in the familialistic countries (the evidence for the countries of the conservative regime type is, again, mixed). Here we see the effect of early self-reliance on the part of young adults in the social democratic countries, the influence of an unregulated labour market in the liberal ones (which puts workers of all age groups at risk), and the result of the redistribution of labour market risks within the family in the familialistic welfare regime. At first glance, the result that older workers in particular face higher in-work poverty risks in countries like Italy seems to be counter-intuitive, since the welfare state mainly protects older, core workers. However, what happens to the younger ones? Owing to the lack of own social security rights, and without proper access to the labour market, they are more likely to live with their parents than are their Northern European counterparts. While living with the family provides protection for young adults, it puts older workers at risk because they are expected to provide an income for a larger family. We find a similar paradox if we look at the poverty risk of women compared to men. A lower degree of labour market integration is related to lower in-work poverty risks. Similar to the case of young workers, in countries of the familialistic regime type in particular, women are protected within the family context.

How Can We Explain the Differences?

Explaining the incidence and structure of in-work poverty by means of simple welfare typologies provides some insights, but it also has obvious shortcomings, as the discussion in the two preceding sections showed. Instead of bundling all the different dimensions of the institutional context into one categorical variable, Andreß and Lohmann suggested in the introductory chapter that it may be more promising to analyse each of the dimensions separately. This idea has been pursued in Lohmann's analysis (in this volume), which tested the effects of decommodification (one indicator), defamilization (three indicators), labour market centralization (one indicator) and union power (one indicator). Unfortunately, with only 15 countries available in the ECHP data, it has been difficult to prove the statistical significance of these macro indicators in one (multivariate) statistical model. But the effects from simpler bivariate models showed the expected signs. In-work poverty decreases with the replacement rate of unemployment benefits (as an indicator of decommodification), with expenditures for family cash benefits and family services (as indicators of defamilization), and with wage bargaining centralization and union density

Notes:
Income data refers to the month of the interview (Sweden: annual income data).
Poverty line = 60 per cent of the median of equivalized net household income.

Source: ECHP 2001 (weighted); OECD Labour Force Survey Database.

Figure 12.1 In-work poverty and union density (2001)

(as indicators of labour market institutions). On the other hand, in-work poverty increases with the number of adult household members (as an indicator of inter-generational dependencies).

How do these results extend to our eight case studies? As an example, let us look at the degree of union density. Figure 12.1 shows the bivariate relationship between in-work poverty and union density. Overall, we can see a clear tendency for poverty rates to be lower if the degree of union density is higher (with a Pearson correlation of −0.53). Comparing the eight countries which are covered in the case studies in this volume, we see that union density in the Netherlands is the lowest and its in-work poverty rate is the highest. At the other end of the figure we find Denmark, which combines the second-highest union density with the lowest in-work poverty rate. Likewise, the results for Italy, Ireland and Belgium unambiguously support the negative association between in-work poverty and union density: the higher the share of organized workers, the lower the share of working poor. However, Finland in particular does not fit into the picture. Despite the fact that its union density is the highest, the in-work poverty rate is not lower than it is in countries such as Ireland, Germany and the UK, where union density is less than half as high.

It is certainly important to stress the fact that we cannot explain variation in in-work poverty based on a single factor such as union density. Similar graphs can be drawn for the influence of family cash benefits and the unemployment replacement rate, which prove – together with union density – to be the most important factors according to Lohmann's analysis (in this volume). Hence, if someone asks 'Does the institutional context matter for the incidence and structure of in-work poverty?' we would answer by presenting three results of our analysis. First, as discussed in this section, we find quantitative evidence for institutional influences (as measured by our macro indicators) on the overall level of in-work poverty. Second, as discussed in the country chapters and previously in this chapter, the structure of in-work poverty differs according to the national context. Third, these group-specific poverty risks can be verified with significant cross-level interaction effects in multilevel regression models (see Lohmann's analysis in this volume).

TRENDS OVER TIME: MIXED EVIDENCE

So far we have only looked at country differences in a cross-sectional perspective. However, almost all of the country studies in this volume contain analyses in a longitudinal perspective. Some of the analyses extend back to the 1980s (Sweden, Netherlands), but most start in the early or mid-1990s. In many cases, the analyses cover recent years up to 2005. Although the period covered by the analyses differs, there is a core period which is observed in all the studies.

For most countries, the discussion on welfare state retrenchment and labour market liberalization (Gilbert, 2002; van Kersbergen, 2000; Visser, 2005; Western, 1995) provides the background for expectations concerning the development of in-work poverty during the given period. The process of retrenchment is partly seen as a consequence of economic globalization, although this position is contested (see, for example, Korpi, 2003; Pierson, 2001). If we regard the process of welfare state retrenchment as a process of declining decommodification, we can expect that market forces will have a stronger impact on the welfare of working households. In addition, processes of labour market deregulation and decentralization of wage bargaining work in the same direction. Consequently, many of the authors in this volume expect to find that employees in the labour market are in a weakened position, with the consequence of increasing in-work poverty rates.

In addition to the changing degree of decommodification, deregulation and centralization, a more fundamental development is the changing position of welfare states towards employment. The latter is often discussed with reference to the concept of activation. In broad terms, activation can be understood as the strengthening of the relationship between social protection and labour market integration. The idea of activation is prominent in a number of countries (see, for example, Barbier, 2004). We acknowledge that activation strategies differ, ranging from qualification-enhancing programmes in some countries to pure workfare programmes in others. Nevertheless, the basic idea of activation as a way to produce welfare via inclusion into the labour market rather than by social transfers has become relevant all over Europe. We can find examples of this development in many of the countries covered in this volume. Snel, de Boom and Engbersen describe the radical change in activity rates in the Netherlands. Connolly stresses the impact of the so-called New Deal programmes in Britain. Airio, Kuivalainen and Niemelä write of reforms in the benefit system in Finland since the mid-1990s which are directed at reducing negative economic work incentives and promoting employment. Although not all these policy shifts are directly inspired by some common agenda, it is certainly not wrong to see connections to developments in a more general perspective (see also the chapter by Marx and Verbist on policy options for fighting in-work poverty). At the European level, an increase in labour market participation is regarded as a core element that is necessary in order to enhance the competitiveness of the EU member states in a globalized economy. We can find this aim in the European Employment Strategy as early as the 1990s, and it was reinforced at the Lisbon summit in 2000. We also find clearly specified targets: by 2010, 70 per cent of the working-age population should be employed. This target is particularly hard to reach in countries which have implicitly or explicitly excluded less-qualified workers and other groups with poor chances on the labour market from gainful employment. We discussed previously in this chapter the effect of such strategies on the incidence of in-work poverty. Assuming that qualification-specific poverty risks are not altered, an inclusion of disadvantaged groups into the labour market will result in a shift from non-working poor to working poor and an increase in the working poor rate.

While the results previously in this chapter were based on a thought experiment, the empirical evidence from the country studies gives us the opportunity to see whether an increase in in-work poverty has in fact taken place over time. Seven out of eight chapters provide results in a longitudinal perspective. In four countries, we find an increase in in-work poverty (Ireland, the Netherlands, Germany and Britain).[5] In two countries, the development has no clear direction (Finland, Sweden). Italy is an example of a country where in-work poverty has declined. How do these results fit into the picture of welfare state retrenchment, labour market liberalization and the shift towards activation? On the basis of the evidence provided in the country chapters, this question is hard to answer. If we look at the four countries with rising poverty rates, we will find different explanations. The increase in in-work poverty in Ireland must be seen within a context of growing incomes all over the income distribution, where certain groups do not profit as much as others from this general upswing. The Netherlands is described as a Continental forerunner of the so-called 'enabling state', with a growing number of people who are pushed into the labour market without being fit to secure a proper income. Germany has experienced an increase in low-paid employment. This translates into in-work poverty if the moderating effect of the household context (with low-paid workers being secondary earners) loses its traditional importance – as we can observe particularly in Eastern Germany. In Britain, the conditions for families have improved, owing to new measures to combat child poverty, while the situation of young workers and workers without children has deteriorated.

Such explanations from a country-specific perspective are certainly important. They help us to understand that there is a multitude of factors which affect the poverty risk of the working population. However, it would be even better if we could also provide some more general evidence. As we argued above, the trend towards increased labour market inclusion can be observed to a differing degree all over Europe. If we are right to assume that the (forced) inclusion of certain groups of workers into the labour market is connected with a higher level of in-work poverty, we should be able to see a positive relationship between the level of employment growth and the growth of in-work poverty. Figure 12.2 shows this relationship for a number of European countries during the period from 1994 to 2001. The results support our expectation of a positive relationship between employment growth and the change in in-work poverty. Unfortunately, during the observation period, all the countries were characterized by increased labour market inclusion. Hence, our independent variable lacks the necessary variation in the negative direction. However, even in the majority of countries with modest increases in employment (less than 10 per cent), we can find decreasing poverty rates. On the other hand, we can find a group of three or four countries with strong increases in employment which are accompanied by a growth in in-work poverty (Spain is a notable counterexample).

Unfortunately, the data do not provide enough information to allow us to dig deeper for the explanation of the relationship between in-work poverty and employment growth. For such an analysis, we would need comparative data which cover a period longer than seven or eight years in order to be able to cover periods of economic upswing as well as downturn.

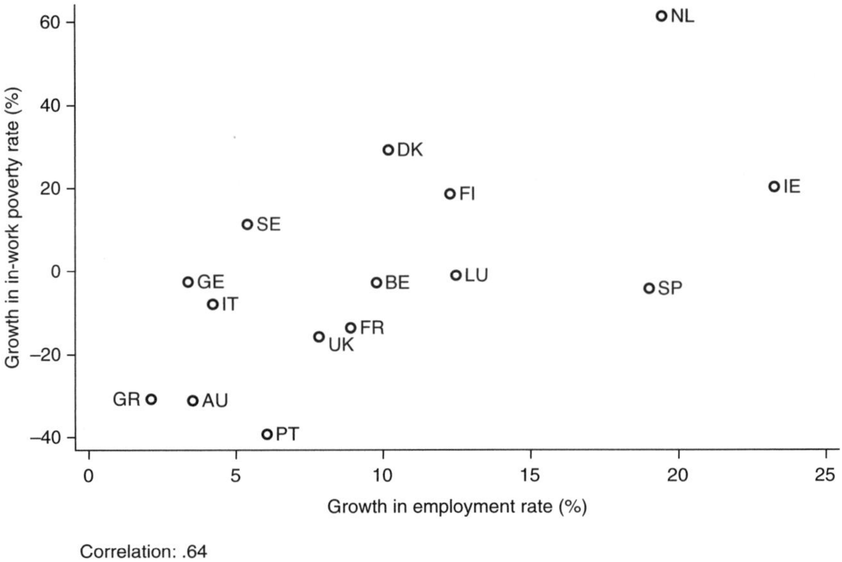

Notes:
* Austria=1995, Finland=1996, Sweden=1997.
Data refers to the month of the interview in a given year (Sweden: annual income data).
Poverty line = 60 per cent of the median of equivalized net household income.
Growth is defined as relative growth, e.g. ((rate 2001 – rate 1994)/rate 1994) × 100.

Source: ECHP 1994–2001 (weighted).

Figure 12.2 Development of in-work poverty and employment growth (1994–2001)*

However, time-series data on in-work poverty are not available; nor can they be generated on the basis of microdata for a larger number of countries. On the basis of the available data sources, we have found clear evidence for institutional causes in a cross-sectional perspective. It is apparently much harder to gather such evidence in a longitudinal perspective. We would need more information on changes in the institutional framework and on changes in in-work poverty over a larger number of years than the available data allow.

CONCLUSION

As the chapters in this book make clear, in-work poverty in Europe is a diverse, multifaceted phenomenon that occurs in equally diverse institutional, economic and socio-demographic settings. Nevertheless, we were able to demonstrate some overall regularities. Much of the evidence from traditional poverty research can be used to describe the working poor. It is the combination of having few resources on the one hand and high economic needs on the other that creates problems in making ends meet for working people. Large families headed by only one breadwinner, single parents, employees at the margin of the labour market, and young adults (in some countries) are the prototypical members of the working-poor population in Europe. At the same time, however, both the level and the structure of in-work poverty depend on societal factors. Individual risk factors are moderated and filtered by the institutional context. Important aspects of this institutional context include the labour market and its system of industrial relations, the welfare state and its system of social transfers and public infrastructure, or the overall model of family relations that is typical for a given country. Depending on the mechanisms of wage-setting, working people are more or less protected against the risk of low pay. Strong labour unions have a similar effect. A well-developed public infrastructure for children and the elderly relieves (mostly female) caregivers from their family obligations, and hence provides more opportunities for working people to pool several incomes through the gainful employment of all family members. Social transfers for non-active household members or family cash benefits for breadwinners can constitute additional sources of income equally well. And, finally, the pattern of family relations determines where in-work poverty shows up – in the households of male breadwinners who provide shelter for their grown-up children or in the households of young adults who prefer to live on their own. Since these societal factors are developed differently among different European countries, the proportion of working people in poverty and the socio-demographic profile of the working poor appears to be diverse. But, hopefully, the analyses presented in this volume have shed some light on the driving forces behind these differences.

NOTES

1. Here and at various places in the rest of this section, we refer to the statistical data presented in Tables 1.1 and 1.3 of Lohmann and Marx (in this volume). From now on, we will not explicitly note these sources at each text passage in order to keep the text readable.
2. Table 1.1 in Lohmann and Marx (in this volume) reports a very high degree of employment protection, but comparatively low degrees of bargaining centralization and union density. This result is due to the East–West divide. While the index of employment protection measures the legal framework, which – for evident reasons – is the same all over Germany, the other two indicators measure the actual number of union members and

collective labour agreements, which are affected by much lower union density and more frequent decentralized wage settings in Eastern Germany.

3. The percentages are based on the ECHP data (Lohmann and Marx, in this volume) because some of the case studies use national data sources that are hard to compare between the countries. However, the overall ranking is more or less the same when we include these national data. The most notable exception concerns the British case. This is probably due to the fact that Connolly's analyses (in this volume) are based on a different definition of in-work poverty (households with a working *reference* person instead of households containing working persons). There are also larger differences for the Netherlands: the in-work poverty rate based on the ECHP is very high. This is probably due to the broad definition of employment which includes all workers working at least one hour in the month of the interview. In contrast, the latest figures in Snel, de Boom and Engbersen (in this volume) are based on annual income and employment data. It is not unlikely that marginal workers are not covered in their analysis, which would explain the lower poverty rates compared to Lohmann and Marx's analysis (in this volume).
4. The basis for all figures in this paragraph is the European Community Household Panel (own computations).
5. The development in the analysis of Britain (Connolly, in this volume) differs from results based on the European Community Household Panel (Figure 12.2). See note 3 for an explanation for such differences.

REFERENCES

Barbier, J.-C. (2004), 'Systems of social protection in Europe. Two contrasted paths of activation and maybe a third', in J. Lind, H. Knudsen and H. Jørgensen (eds), *Labour and Employment Regulation in Europe*, Brussels: Peter Lang, pp. 233–53.

Bonoli, G. (1997), 'Classifying welfare states: a two-dimensional approach', *Journal of Social Policy*, **26** (3), 351–72.

Esping-Andersen, G. (1990), *The Three Worlds of Welfare Capitalism*, Cambridge: Polity Press.

Esping-Andersen, G. (1999), *Social Foundations of Postindustrial Economies*, Oxford: Oxford University Press.

Ferrera, M. (1996), '"The Southern Model" of welfare in social Europe', *Journal of European Social Policy*, **6** (1), 17–37.

Gallie, D. and S. Paugam (2000), 'The experience of unemployment in Europe: the debate', in D. Gallie and S. Paugam (eds), *Welfare Regimes and the Experience of Unemployment in Europe*, Oxford: Oxford University Press, pp. 1–22.

Gilbert, N. (2002), *Transformation of the Welfare State. The Silent Surrender of Public Responsibility*, Oxford: Oxford University Press.

Hiilamo, H. (forthcoming), 'Divergences in the Nordic model: economic consequences of partnership dissolution in Sweden and Finland', in H.-J. Andreß and D. Hummelsheim (eds), *Economic and Social Consequences of Partnership Dissolution: European Countries in Comparison*, Cheltenham: Edward Elgar.

Korpi, W. (2003), 'Welfare-state regress in Western Europe. Politics, institutions, globalization and Europeanization', *Annual Review of Sociology*, **29**, 589–609.

Leibfried, S. (1992), 'Towards a European welfare state? On integrating poverty regimes into the European Community', in Z. Ferge and J.E. Kolberg (eds), *Social Policy in a Changing Europe*, Frankfurt and Boulder, CO: Campus/Westview, pp. 245–79.

Pierson, P. (2001), 'Coping with permanent austerity: welfare state restructuring in affluent democracies', in P. Pierson (ed.), *The New Politics of the Welfare State*, Oxford: Oxford University Press, pp. 410–56.
Van Kersbergen, K. (2000), 'The declining resistance of welfare states to change?', in S. Kuhnle (ed.), *Survival of the European Welfare State*, London: Routledge, pp. 19–36.
Visser, J. (2004), 'Patterns and variations in European industrial relations, in European Commission', *Industrial Relations in Europe 2004*, Luxembourg: Office for Official Publications of the EC, pp. 11–57.
Visser, J. (2005), 'Wage bargaining institutions in Europe: a happy marriage or preparing for a divorce?', AIAS Working Paper 05-42, Amsterdam: Amsterdam Institute for Advanced Labour Studies.
Visser, J. and A. Hemerijck (1997), *A Dutch miracle? Job growth, welfare reform and corporatism in the Netherlands*, Amsterdam: Amsterdam University Press.
Western, B. (1995), 'A comparative study of working-class disorganization: union decline in eighteen advanced capitalist countries', *American Sociological Review*, **60** (2), 179–201.

Index